D1538969

Coaching the Child Behind the Athlete

A Developmental Approach to Youth Sport

i

Warde Publishers, Inc.
Box 452/90 Resaca Ave.
Forest Knolls, CA 94933
info@wardepub.com

Copyright © 2018 by Warde Publishers, Inc.

Reproduction or translation of any part of this work beyond that permitted by Section 107 or 108 of the 1976 United States Copyright Act without permission of the copyright owner is unlawful. Requests for permission or further information should be addressed to the Permissions Department at Warde Publishers, Inc.

Library of Congress Cataloging-in-Publication Data

Feigley, David A.

Coaching the child behind the athlete : a developmental approach to youth sport / David A. Feigley.

Forest Knolls, CA : Warde Publishers, 2018.

ISBN 978-1-886346-10-9 (pbk.)

LCSH: Coaching (Athletics) | Sports for children--Coaching. | Child athletes--Training of. | Sports--Psychological aspects. | Conduct of life. | BISAC: SPORTS & RECREATION / Coaching / General.

LCC GV709.2 .F45 2018 (print) | LCC GV709.2 (ebook) | DDC 796.077--dc23.

Manufactured in the United States of America

10   9   8   7   6   5   4   3   2   1

Publisher, Jake Warde; proofreader, Eliza Pande; text designers, Detta Penna and Jeanne Schreiber; cover designer, Jeanne Schreiber; illustrator, Robin Mouat. The text was set in 10/14 ITC Stone Serif by Sky View Creative and printed by Versa Press, Inc.

Photo and Figure Credits

Figure 2.4: Editorial credit: Joseph Sohm / Shutterstock.com

Figure 4.2: Editorial credit: Joseph Sohm / Shutterstock.com

Figures 14.6 and 14.7: Figures 14.6 and 14.7: Reprinted with permission from SHAPE America-Society of Health and Physical Educators, 1900 Association Drive, Reston, VA 20191, www.shapeamerica.org

Figure 14.10: Courtesy Dr. Terence Kavanagh. Originally appeared in Take Heart (Key Porter Books, 1998) by Dr. Terence Kavangh.

Brief Contents

Contents

About the Author

 David A. Feigley, Ph.D. is a developmental sport psychologist at Rutgers – The State University of NJ, New Brunswick in the Department of Kinesiology and Health, a department of which he chaired for 17 years. He is the founder and current director of the Rutgers Youth Sports Research Council which, since 1988, has trained more than 300,000 volunteer youth sports coaches in New Jersey. He has coached national and international competitors in springboard diving, platform diving and gymnastics. He was owner of Feigley's School of Gymnastics for more than 35 years, a program that was nationally ranked for 7 of the 12 years that he was the head coach. He was the Elite Development Director for Region VII of USA Gymnastics and served on NASPE's Task Force on Sport whose primary purpose was to establish and promote coaching education standards for all sports at all levels throughout the United States. He has served on a number of national boards related to sport including the United States Association of Independent Gymnastics Clubs where he served as the Association's Education Director.

Preface

The goal of this book is to provide the reader with information on healthy child development within the context of organized youth sports. The lives of children and adolescents who participate in youth sport can be profoundly influenced by these experiences – both positively and negatively. The aim is not to tell coaches how to coach but to provide them with the type of information that they can incorporate into their coaching to help them coach children and adolescents more effectively from a perspective where the development of the individual is the highest priority. Few youth sport participants go on to the highest level of competitive sports but virtually all – from the most to the least athletic – have experiences which influence their personal growth and development. Self-esteem and self-confidence can be enhanced or undermined. Strong moral behavior can be developed through the promotion of good sportsmanship or self-centeredness can run rampant because of deferential treatment of those with exceptional physical prowess. Healthy physical growth and a positive attitude to being physically active can be offset by overtraining and early specialization leading to overuse and often chronic injuries.

Young athletes come in contact with well-meaning adults who range from those who believe that sport is a competitive "dog-eat-dog" world to those who believe sport is the ultimate opportunity to cooperate with teammates and – surprisingly to some – with opponents. Caring about children is a necessary but not sufficient attribute to become an effective youth sport coach. Coaches must also have the energy, information and opportunity to display that caring. This book is an attempt to help them with as much information about positive child development as can be packed into a single volume.

The chapters have been strongly influenced by my academic background including but not limited to my role as founder and director of the Youth Sports Research Council at Rutgers University. My personal experiences in sport are incorporated in virtually every aspect of the book, ranging from my involvement as an athlete at the youth, high school and collegiate levels, to my roles as a coach of multiple sports at multiple levels of competition. Finally, my professional and volunteer experiences as a youth sport administrator have ranged from being a coordinator of summer swim leagues and private club gymnastics programs to serving as a founding member of the initial version of the gymnastics safety association. I had the opportunity to sit on NASPE's original Task Force on Sport in its cooperative efforts with the United States Olympic Committee to establish and promote coaching education standards for all sports at all levels throughout the United States.

This is a book that, had I written it 20 years ago, would not have had the same perspective as it now does. The technical side of sport, as important as it is for success in competition, pales in comparison with the impact sport has on the personal development of the millions of children and youth who participate at all levels of sport from the casual recreational programs to international forums in such sports as swimming and gymnastics, where the presence of teenaged athletes is not uncommon.

A number of the topics, such as the chapters on self-confidence, mental toughness, sportsmanship and working with parents may appear to go far beyond recreational youth sports. That is true by design. For such topics, it matters not whether I coach youth at the recreational or elite level. What matters is that I coach the development of the child at the highest level of which I am capable. Self-confidence, mental toughness, and sportsmanship, are attributes that will influence an individual's life long after the sport-specific skills have faded. This book was written with the goal of helping coaches coach, not specific sports, but rather the development of the parents' most precious treasure, their child. Hopefully after absorbing the material in this book, when asked "What is the most important thing that you coach?", more coaches will answer, not with "conditioning, sports skill techniques or football, soccer and gymnastics" but rather with "The most important thing that I coach is children!"

SPECIAL FEATURES

Three features are interspersed throughout most of the chapters to encourage coaches to get involved and to think about how the concepts presented might best be integrated into their coaching.

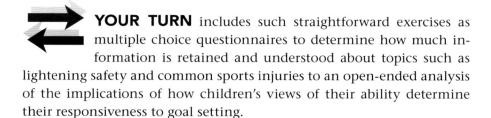

YOUR TURN includes such straightforward exercises as multiple choice questionnaires to determine how much information is retained and understood about topics such as lightening safety and common sports injuries to an open-ended analysis of the implications of how children's views of their ability determine their responsiveness to goal setting.

SPOTLIGHT ON YOUTH SPORTS

Spotlight on Sport highlights specific areas that have both obvious and non-obvious implications for effective coaching. These include how civil immunity legislation protects volunteer coaches to how to use a teaching model of skill progressions that fits both basic and complex skills.

From Chalkboard to Playing Field

From Chalkboard to the Playing Field attempts to apply principles based upon sound scientific evidence to specific applications in practical coaching situations.

ACKNOWLEDGEMENTS

Special tribute to Jake Warde who helped me resurrect a project stalled for 10 years and guided me through the myriad of details required to go from an inspirational idea to a full-fledged, professionally done book. Jeanne Schreiber whose patience made possible my requested changes in the manuscript after she had typeset word-for-word my original submissions, only to have me make addition after addition in the quest for clarity and readability.

Thanks to Alejandro (Hondo) Diaz, Senior Programmer in the Department of Kinesiology & Health as well as the members of the Advisory Board of the Youth Sports Research Council, all of whom contributed in meaningful ways to the development of this book and the Coaching Educational Program in New Jersey, of which this book a supporting factor: Gloria Bachman, MD, William Foelsch, Alan Goldberger, JD, David Johnson, Jeanne Montemarano, Jack Roberts and Dina Trunzo. Thanks also to Javier Robles, JD, and Robb Rehberg, Ph.D. for their contributions to the chapters on disabilities and conditioning respectively.

Special thanks to Diane Bonanno and Neil Dougherty, the two people whose counsel and contributions have been instrumental in my professional life almost from start to finish. Even in their retirements, their influence continues to guide my efforts to make meaningful professional contributions to the world of sport and recreation that has been such an important part of my life.

Finally, I must acknowledge my wife, Ellen Kennedy, who provided me with the time away from family to actually write and re-write manuscript after manuscript and served as a patient, careful proofreader of literally every page in the book to critique the manuscript's readability and professional preparation.

RUTGERS YOUTH SPORTS RESEARCH COUNCIL

This book is part of the mission of the Youth Sports Research Council in the Department of Kinesiology and Health at Rutgers University, New Brunswick, NJ. The Sports Council, founded in 1983, has trained more than 300,000 volunteer youth sport coaches in New Jersey alone and helped provide them with civil immunity under the state liability laws as a result of the willingness to partake in youth sport safety training.

Developing a Philosophy for Coaching Youth Sports

CHAPTER OUTLINE

- Importance of a Coaching Philosophy
  YOUR TURN: Conflicting Goals
- Coaching Philosophy and Child Development
  SPOTLIGHT ON YOUTH SPORTS: The Role of Winning
- What is the Right Age for Children to Begin Sports?
- Defining Excellence
- Benefits of the Youth Sports Experience
- Philosophy: From Concept to Practical Applications
  YOUR TURN: Your Philosophy—In One Line

Why do you coach? What benefits do you want your child and the children of others to get from their youth sports experience? Is helping the development of children into healthy, confident, well-adjusted adults part of your role as a youth sports coach?

While many specific answers are likely, when asked, 80% of youth sport coaches say "Development" is the primary reason why they coach. Another 15 to 20% say to allow the kids to have "Fun." Less than 1% typically say "Winning." The low percentage of coaches choosing winning is very likely influenced by social acceptability. A large proportion of those saying "fun" are coaches who work with the youngest age groups, say 8 years and younger.

Development, fun, and winning are not mutually exclusive goals. They can all be important parts of a coach's motive for coaching young athletes. But occasionally, even these positive goals come in conflict. Removing your star player for disrespectful behavior toward an official may help develop the young athlete's long-term self-control and sportsmanship but in the short term might undermine the chance to win today's game, something the other players on the team have worked hard for. Which choice is your highest priority?

Your answers to these questions form the foundation of your coaching philosophy. Every coach has a philosophy of coaching whether it has been carefully thought out or developed only informally while making day-to-day coaching decisions and behavioral choices.

The Importance of a Coaching Philosophy

Although a philosophy may be conceived by some as an abstract, idealistic, somewhat vague set of guidelines shaping one's approach to the "very meaning of life," a philosophy is more often quite concrete. Specifically, a coaching philosophy is a set of personal guidelines by which you can determine whether **your** behavior, **your** decisions and **your** coaching style are consistent with your reasons for coaching and **your** agency's reasons for providing the program. Many different philosophies legitimately exist. There is no right or wrong, only appropriate or inappropriate relative to the athletes you serve.

FIGURE 1.1. Question: Should you be deciding which kids should benefit or how to benefit them all?

Determining and clarifying your philosophy of coaching is a crucial first step once you have decided to coach children and adolescents. A well thought out philosophy provides **practical guidelines to compare your day-to-day coaching decisions with your self-chosen, overall purpose for working with young athletes.** A philosophy of coaching affects your decisions throughout your coaching career whether it lasts a single season or a lifetime. This set of concrete priorities c*an help you choose between legitimate, but sometimes, conflicting goals.*

Organizations have philosophies too, so that goals are clear and conflicts can be resolved within a framework. Ideally, your organization has already developed a statement of purpose, but if not, consider recommending that such a program philosophy be prepared. When you represent an organization or agency, you should be prepared to work within that agency in ways consistent with that group's expressed purpose. Is it "all get to play regardless of skill level;" or is it focused on "the most highly skilled earn the right to play?" Conflicts often result when coaches are unaware of differences between their personal goals and the goals of their sponsoring organization (Figure 1.1).

YOUR TURN
Conflicting Goals

What would you do in this situation? Last year, a coach had 30 qualified kids try out for the traveling youth soccer program* in the 12 and under age group. As a result, "A" and "B" teams were formed based upon skill level and both teams had successful seasons. This year, only 22 kids returned for tryouts. The rules permit only 18 kids per team, and the conventional wisdom within the organization is that 15 kids per squad is ideal for fielding a strong squad where all kids on the team get sufficient playing time. The tryouts are held in late July with the season beginning the second week in September. However, the deadline for submitting all rosters is August 5th. Any team withdrawn after that date is fined a significant amount of money and, just as importantly, a withdrawal would be an embarrassment to the entire organization. What would you do?

Below are two potential "solutions."

1. Decide there are not enough kids for two teams. Select the 15 best kids and cut the remaining seven. Suggest that those kids who are cut return to play in the in-town league.

2. Establish two teams of 11 children each, knowing that additional kids would have to be recruited by the start of the season since illness and other factors would make it very difficult to field the necessary number of players for every game throughout the season. The skill level, availability, and commitment of new recruits would be in doubt.

Is your choice consistent with your answer to "why do you coach?" If you chose #1, selecting the most highly skilled players and cutting the rest, how does that fit with your philosophy of helping kids to develop? What influence would you have on the kids who were cut? Chances are,

---

*You can modify this scenario to fit different sports by substituting appropriate numbers (e.g. Youth Football: You have 32 positions and 36 qualified kids try out).

those kids who were cut might be the ones who would benefit most from a sporting experience. Telling them to "suck it up" and "try out again next year" is likely to fall on deaf ears. While they can return to play in-town soccer or attend skill development clinics, many kids who are "cut" or demoted refuse to play at lower levels unless they have supportive parents and/or understanding, sensitive coaches who encourage them to play despite the public "demotion." Trying out again next year against the kids who made the team this year and thus who will receive an entire year of coaching has some obvious drawbacks. However, choosing #1 is likely to provide you with a group of young athletes whose skills are higher and more similar, permitting you to teach higher level skills more efficiently because of the higher level talent. How important is it to you and your organization that you field the highest possible skill-level team to represent your community?

If you chose #2, fielding two teams with minimal rosters so that all can play may well produce teams that are too weak to be competitive against teams from other communities that have a different philosophy. Further, experienced coaches know that birthdays, homework, illnesses and family vacations produce absences at practice and competitions so that carrying a bare minimum of athletes on the roster can result in a shortage of players on game days.

Fielding weak, non-competitive teams can be discouraging for adults with a traditional sports perspective; however, cutting less talented kids at an early age when talent is difficult to identify simply because adults want a highly skilled team to represent their community would seem to place the desire to develop sports excellence ahead of the desire to develop all youngsters within the community. How can youngsters be helped if they are eliminated from the program? A philosophy of coaching helps you make difficult choices consistent with your primary purpose when you have conflicting goals or are pressured to field winning teams. Your philosophy—and that of your program—should be consistent with each other and, hopefully with healthy child development.

Coaching Philosophy and Child Development

Since 80% of youth sport coaches say their primary purpose is to foster the development of their young athletes, a logical question is, "What

TABLE 1.1 Models of Sport

The Professional Model emphasizes:	The Educational Model emphasizes:	The Developmental Model emphasizes:
• Maximal performance • Winning as the major outcome • Entertainment of others • Economic gain	• Sport as a vehicle for developing positive societal values and good citizenship	• Personal development of the athlete • Fun and self-satisfaction • Placing the child-athlete's needs ahead of the organization's needs

does sports participation actually help to develop in young athletes?" Typical responses from coaches include the following possible answers.

Health and Physical Fitness	Self-Confidence/Self-Esteem
Cooperative Skills	Sports Skills
Leadership Skills	Self-Discipline
Sportsmanship	Emotional Self-Control

While sport can develop each of these traits in a positive direction, the quality of the adult leadership from coaches and parents and programs purposely structured to teach such positive social skills are likely to be the prime determinants of whether positive traits such as these are focused and strengthened or weakened and distorted.[1]

Even the best of intentions are likely to be ineffective if coaches are unaware of the needs of children at different ages. Your effectiveness at implementing a philosophy of positive development will depend, to a great extent, upon your understanding of children's developmental stages, not just "good intentions."

A range of philosophical models exist. At the extreme ends of the spectrum, compare the **Professional Sports Model** to the **Developmental Sport Model** in Table 1.1.

The Professional Model is consistent with playing the maximum number of strongest players for the strongest possible single team for the longest possible portion of the game. Other than concern for a possible disruption of efficient team play, the coach has little interest in whether players and parents become disgruntled when substitute players receive only the minimal playing time required by youth sport rules.

There are a variety of Children's Sport Models. They range from the purely recreational model to the high school model to the elite sport model. While the selection of which model is best is rightfully the judgment of the agency and the coach, the Rutgers Youth Sports Research Council believes that the Developmental Model is the most appropriate for the majority of youth sport programs. The key characteristics of the Developmental Model[2] are:

1. Sports are primarily for the benefit of the child, not the adult nor the organization.
2. Children's needs differ at different ages and maturity levels.
3. Successful experiences are reflected by personal growth and development.

Is winning important to kids? Contrary to conventional wisdom and from a developmental perspective, the answer is "Yes" because:

1. Winning and losing are clear, concrete events easily recognized by children as young as 5 and 6 years old.
2. Many children use winning and losing to assess how competent they are, especially if adults pay particular attention to winning and losing.
3. Winning means the child is doing well – as opposed to exerting power and domination over others.
4. Winning means excellence as opposed to status and prestige.

Very young children (typically under 7 years of age) lack the ability to understand competition from a third-party perspective.[3] They know that winning is "good" and losing is "bad" but they usually fail to understand that fairness is essential for competition and that there is a difference between trying hard and being talented. If you give a 5-year-old a 10-yard head start in a race against an adult who purposely runs slowly, the 5-year-old will still be excited at winning the 40-yard race. They can physically run the race but do not understand what constitutes competition – only that they have "won." Their ability to take the necessary third-party perspective begins to develop about age 7 and continues to develop in sophistication until it reaches adult-like levels at about age 12.

SPOTLIGHT ON YOUTH SPORTS
The Role of Winning

Part of your coaching philosophy should deal with the role of winning. This important topic traditionally has been filled with clichés. One extreme is the belief that winning is unimportant in youth sports, and the other is the belief that winning is the only thing. A healthy perspective is somewhere in between.

Clearly, there can be an overemphasis on winning; however, those who believe that winning is not important in youth sports often miss the point that *without an attempt to win the contest, the activity is no longer sport.* The essence of sport is striving to win; without that attempt, the activity is of a different nature. Consider two athletes of dramatically different skill levels playing tennis. Often the superior athlete will begin to teach the less skilled player by hitting the ball where it may more easily be returned over the net. While admirable, teaching is not sport. Two individuals jogging on a running track who are more interested in each other's company change the situation from a competitive sport race to a friendly social interaction.

Athletes can have a strong desire to win and still be involved with healthy, appropriate competition if they are more concerned with *what they win* and *how they win.* If basketball coaches teach their athletes to fake a foul, even if such a sham is successful and deceives the official, the game is no longer basketball. It is "fool the official." Winning the game that day based on an incorrectly awarded foul shot, is not basketball. The team has violated the basic spirit of the game and has won at a different activity-- called cheating. The best basketball team can no longer be determined.

Winning within the context of the rules and within the spirit of the game is important and should be valued and taught. That is, *how you strive to win* becomes a critical aspect of winning. Winning by way of distorting the essential rules of the game devalues success. Striving to win is not the cause of poor sportsmanship. Poor sportsmanship results from the lack of emphasis on how you win within the context of the rules and the spirit of the game.

The following citation made many years ago by Rainer Martens, a noted sports psychologist, illustrates this point. "Competing to win, however, is not necessarily a negative goal; striving to achieve can foster personal growth. In fact, it may be that moral development is nurtured more when moral decisions come into conflict with winning."[4] The significance of Martens' statement is that if winning is not a highly prized goal in its own right, playing fairly is not a noteworthy achievement in the individual's moral development. The conflict between the desire to win and the need to do so ethically is necessary for sportsmanship to exist. Appendix 1.1[5] contains a discussion of the role of winning in youth sports that can be copied and shared with your assistant coaches and parents of your youth sport athletes.

MODIFYING SPORT FOR CHILDREN

In accordance with the Developmental Model, sports should be modified to meet the needs of children. Young children need appropriately sized fields, equipment and time spans. Very young children have difficulty understanding such abstract concepts as offense and defense. For example, children under the age of 7 have difficulty understanding offside in soccer. Thus, in soccer, playing on small fields with 3 to 5 players on each team without enforcing the offside rules is a very appropriate modification for 5-, 6- and 7-year-old children. Another example of a developmentally appropriate modification related to a child's developing cognitive ability is the use of praise for effort. "Trying hard" is equivalent to "being talented" to very young athletes.[6] Praise for effort (i.e., trying hard) enhances self-esteem in kids 8 and under, but praise for effort has little effect on the self-perception of 14-year-olds **unless** that effort is linked to the perception of success at the task.[7] (See Chapter 9 for a more detailed coverage of this important topic.) Appendix 1.2 lists a number of developmentally appropriate modifications for a variety of sport programs for children under the age of 7 years.

Modifications must be developmentally appropriate. Not keeping score might be appropriate with 5- and 6-year-olds but would be totally inappropriate with 10-year-olds. The 10-year-olds would keep score in their heads even if the adult coaches did not. Using developmental modifications designed for very young children with older children is just as inappropriate as expecting very young children to benefit from adult-like competitions.

FIGURE 1.2 Play. How can your philosophy keep it an essential part of youth sports?

As children get older, they should be prepared for the rigors of adult sport. They must learn to handle the pressures of competition and of success and failure. The key is to avoid the adult model at too early an age.

IMPORTANCE OF PLAY

All children play. The forms of play may differ substantially around the world from culture to culture but the purpose is similar. Play serves important functions such as helping children socialize with their peers. For example, the playful "tussling" in mock fights is a major factor in developing a "pecking order" of dominance that minimizes actual fights later on at older ages when significant injuries could be inflicted (Figure 1.2).

There are marked differences between the play and games led by children and the play and games led by adults. These differences are evident both in the way the games are played and in what is learned by the children as a result of their play. In games led by children:

1. **Action is the predominant measure of fair play and fun.**
   Stopping the game to argue over rules rapidly leads to the isolation of children who continually do so. They are less likely to be picked

as teammates or invited to play on the playground regardless of their skill level.

2. **Scoring is higher in games led by children.** "Do overs" are common.

3. **Organizational rules are not as important.** The teams need not have equal numbers of players as long as the teams are evenly matched to produce excitement. Placing more outfielders in the "pick up" baseball game on the weaker rather than stronger team is not uncommon.

4. **Decisions about what is fair are made by the players.** When the ball rolls foul and lands underneath the car parked nearby, is it in play or not?

In adult-led games, however, children learn that preset rules are the dominant measure of fair play, that teams must be of equal size, including limits on the total number of players on the roster, that safety equipment must be worn even if the look is not cool, and that players must come from the correct geographical area or else it isn't fair. In adult-led games, leaders (usually picked by coaches as the captain) pick from a few limited decisions: e.g., heads or tails at the coin flip to see who gets to kick off. Which end of the field will we defend? Even these minimal choices are often decided ahead of time by the adult coaches.

Both adult-led and child-led games are important. One is not necessarily better than the other but they teach different things. Free play teaches decision making and leadership skills. Organized sport teaches obedience to legitimate authority and following the rules.

What Is the Right Age for Children to Begin Sports?

The answer: "It depends!" Children can become involved with physical activity literally while they are still in the crib batting away at a mobile suspended over the crib. Three to 5-year-olds regularly are invited to play t-ball. However, children typically do not begin to understand competition until approximately the age of 7 when they begin to develop the cognitive ability to make **social comparisons.** The ability to make such social comparisons develops gradually over a period of years with most children being able to understand such comparisons by 10 years and

FIGURE 1.3 By 7 years, children are capable of making self-judgements based upon social comparisons. By 12, they recognize that "trying hard" and "being talented" are not equivalent.

virtually all normally developing children being able to do so quite well by age 12.

WHAT ARE SOCIAL COMPARISONS?

At about the age of 7, children begin to develop the ability to make self-assessments by comparing themselves to others. If they can perform a skill that others of the same age cannot, they make the inference that they are competent and that the skill they are performing is relatively difficult. Prior to this age, assessments of their skill level and the task difficulty were judged, not by how others were doing, but by how complex the skill was and how hard they tried at the skill. Puzzles with more pieces are more difficult than puzzles with fewer pieces. Performing a cartwheel on a high, narrow balance beam in gymnastics is more difficult than performing that same skill on a low, wider, padded beam. Perception of effort (i.e., the player tried hard) was assumed if the skill was successfully completed. Not until the age of 7 do children develop the ability to differentiate between having talent and trying hard. They compare themselves with their peers and begin to realize that they can perform skills successfully with less effort than some of their teammates, or that no matter how hard they try, they may never be as good as some of their other, more talented friends (Figure 1.3).

By 12, children have become skilled at making social comparisons and realize that expending effort no longer guarantees success. They understand that their efforts may be of no avail if the others are of higher ability or if the task does not depend upon their effort. That is, no matter how intensely they flap their elbows, they cannot fly. This is the age at which young athletes are the most vulnerable to dropping out, a topic we will return to in much more detail in Chapter 9.

SPORTS COMPLEXITY

Another major factor determining sport readiness is the complexity of the sport both in terms of physical and cognitive demands. Gymnastics, for example, requires that multiple skills be chained together to form a choreographed routine, a task much more complex than a springboard diver performing a single basic skill on a one-at-a-time basis. Remembering multiple plays in youth football is more cognitively demanding than a hundred-yard dash in track and field. Thus, some sports lend themselves more easily to younger participation.

Defining Excellence

While few youth sport coaches will publicly say "Winning is everything!" many focus on high sports performance as an acceptable alternative. However, when excellence is defined *solely* as winning or high-level sports performance, the following negative outcomes regularly occur.[8]

1. **Participation is discouraged.** Children drop out of sport if they cannot play well enough. They learn that poor play is not tolerated. Weaker players are given less time and are often resented by their teammates..

2. **Fewer entry level programs are offered for older beginners.** Coaches are reluctant to accept older beginners and older children are less likely to try new physical activities at which they are not skilled.

3. **Early specialization is encouraged.** Children play only one position in order to play better, but this early specialization often retards an overall understanding of the game.

4. **Promotes Standardization.** There are only a few ways to play the game the right way. Standardization stifles creativity.

5. **Overtraining is commonplace.** If practice improves skills, then more practice will improve them even more. Psychological staleness, burnout, dropout and overuse injuries become

predictable outcomes of training intensities that rival the intensities of adult sports.

If traditional definitions of excellence based upon winning and/or high level sport performance lead to such potentially negative outcomes, what other definitions of excellence might be more appropriate for youth sports? Alternative definitions fall into two broad categories: personal definitions of excellence and organizational definitions of excellence.

PERSONAL DEFINITIONS OF EXCELLENCE

A high quality sporting experience can be defined as developing competency in a variety of sports rather than simply excelling at one. For the vast majority of youth sport participants, being competent and comfortable in playing multiple sports is probably desirable. Even for those athletes who ultimately specialize in order to play at a high level, sampling a variety of sports before deciding upon which one to specialize in allows for more informed choices as the pressure to specialize increases. Choosing a specialization when you have had only a limited number of experiences can be self-limiting. There is also a growing body of evidence suggesting that there is at least a modest relationship between early specialization in sport leading to a higher incidence of injuries, especially overuse injuries.[9][10]

Excellence can also be related to the quality of the experience. For example, being part of a team that hangs together and supports one another may be just as important in determining one's love of sport as is the level of competition attained. Talented young athletes who are "moved up" into older age groups because of their exceptional ability may feel less a part of an important group of friends because of the age differential.

Developing health and fitness attributes through sports is a desirable goal. However, in the quest for excellence, health is often jeopardized as athletes overstrain and fitness is often undermined if athletes are encouraged to work through injuries to be mentally tough. A highly regimented conditioning workout controlled almost exclusively by the adult coach might actually undermine a love of physical activity. When the athlete's control over the activity is limited and little instruction is provided to help athletes learn to develop their own fitness workouts, intrinsic motivation to stay fit is much less likely to grow. While guidance about effective fitness training must come initially from the coach, as athletes become more knowledgeable, providing them with more control over their fitness workouts increases the likelihood that their involvement with fitness will continue after their competitive sport career is over.

Providing opportunities for young athletes to practice social decision-making skills such as "what is fair play?" "who shall bat first?" and "how can I help my teammate when he or she is disappointed?" are all skills that transfer to real life. High-quality sport programs provide young athletes with the opportunity to practice these skills over and over again, learning from mistakes and improving their ability to relate to other members of their teams.

ORGANIZATIONAL DEFINITIONS OF EXCELLENCE

What constitutes an outstanding youth sport organization? Excellence has traditionally been defined as an organization that produces winning teams and high-level athletes. That definition is limited. Excellence can also be defined as "how many athletes are served?" An organization that serves larger numbers of athletes and provides playing time for all excels in those important dimensions. Programs that provide high-quality instruction for all participants, as opposed to only a few, is also a form of excellence. Programs that provide additional programs such as parent education, sportsmanship training for players, coaches and parents, as well as programs in sport psychology, healthy nutrition and preventive and rehabilitative sport medicine are programs that rise above the norm.

These alternative definitions of excellence—both personal and organizational—are not incompatible with winning and/or high-level performance. In fact, they can enhance and broaden those more traditional definitions of excellence.

Benefits of the Youth Sports Experience

Can children learn positive character traits and enhanced self-esteem through sports participation? The answer is clearly yes. Can they learn selfish behavior and unsportsmanlike behavior? Again, the answer is yes. What determines which type of behavior will ultimately be the result of their sport involvement? While many factors are involved, the primary determinant in organized youth sport is the **quality of the adult leadership.** That many of these adults are volunteers does not lessen the importance or the impact of their roles in teaching and modeling positive behaviors.

WHAT DOES SPORT DEVELOP?

If appropriate adult leadership in organized youth sports contributes to the development of the young athlete, what attributes can be developed through that participation? What do you think sport helps develop in young athletes? Compare your thoughts with those of professionals in the field of child development.

    A. Good Citizenship

    B. Sportsmanship/Morality

    C. Work Ethics

    D. Psychological Hardiness (Mental Toughness)

    E. Social-Decision Making

    F. Health & Fitness

    G. Self-Esteem & Self-Confidence

    H. Sense of Teamwork

    I. Self-Control

These characteristics can all be developed through sport; however, they do not develop spontaneously. They develop through the same process that children learn other attributes – through practice, modeling others, reinforcement and direct instruction. Just as these positive traits can be learned through sport, their polar opposites can be learned as well.

    A. Poor Citizenship

    B. Poor Sportsmanship/Lack of Morality

    C. Working just enough to get by

    D. Collapsing under pressure

    E. Poor Social-Decision Making

    F. Injury and Overuse Syndromes; Poor Health & Substance Abuse

    G. Low Self-Esteem & a Lack of Self-Confidence

    H. Egocentric/Selfish Behavior

    I. Lack of Self-Control

Philosophy: From Concept to Practical Applications

A practical approach to developing the positive outcomes above is to use your philosophy as a guide by: (1) identifing your belief system, (2) then specifying an overall policy that flows from that philosophical belief, and finally (3) determining specific behaviors (i.e., bottom lines) that are consistent with the policy. Table 1.1 provides examples of this "philosophy, policy, bottom line" approach in six different traditional domains.

TABLE 1.2 Examples of Philosophy, Policy and Bottom Lines

Philosophy	Policy	Bottom line
Safety is a priority, then fun and learning in that order	All safety standards must be met in both practices and games	a. The wearing of mandated protective gear (e.g., shin guards, helmets, and athletic supporters) is required for participation. b. All coaches are safety certified with first aid/CPR training. c. A fully stocked first aid kit is always available and regularly replenished after disposable items are used.
A primary reason for children participating is sport is to enhance self-esteem	Self-esteem is developed via positive coaching and successful accomplishments	a. Skills progressions are individualized for athletes of different skill levels. b. Positive reinforcement is the primary teaching tool. c. Coaches are strict and demanding but not harsh and punitive.
Coaching the Whole Child	Coaches should know their athletes on and off the field	a. Coaches should regularly ask about school work. b. Parents are regularly asked how the child is doing outside of the gym or field. c. Conversations should include non-sport topics of interest to the child.

continued

TABLE 1.2 *continued*

Philosophy	Policy	Bottom line
Professionalism is expected in the coaching staff, volunteers or not	Coaches should be seen as responsible, competent people	a. Dress should be appropriate for the activity. b. Sarcasm and profanity language are forbidden. c. Coaches should regularly attend coaching clinics.
Sports should be enjoyable for all participants	Positive atmosphere must be maintained during practices	a. Avoid having the athletes stand in line except when specifically to rest. b. Instructions should be brief and to the point. c. Drills to develop the same skills should be varied sufficiently to avoid boredom.
Successful programs are fiscally sound	Reasonable costs of participation must be met	a. Parents should be informed of all costs during registration. b. Fund raising should be organized and efforts fairly distributed across the entire group. c. Entry fees must be paid in full before participating in tournaments or clinics.

YOUR TURN
Your Philosophy—in One Line

One aspect of formulating a clear philosophy of coaching is to develop a "tagline," a brief phrase that captures the essence of your sports program or your sports involvement. Here are some examples:

1. The American Sport Education Program: "Athletes First, Winning Second."[11]

2. The Rutgers Youth Sports Research Council: "Coaching the Child Behind the Athlete."[12]

3. A private gymnastics school: "We teach lessons that last a lifetime."[13]

Do these phrases suggest the underlying philosophy of those organizations? If so, they are successful and, in a brief phrase, capture what is important in their program's philosophy. Normally such taglines are developed formally by organizations. However, they can be just as useful to you as an individual coach. Developing an effective tagline aids you in identifying the overarching priority of why you coach and allows you to share that priority with others. What would be your tagline? (Figure 1.4).

FIGURE 1.4 Can you capture in a phrase your purpose for coaching kids?

In sum, when youth sport coaches are asked, "What is the most important thing that you coach in order to achieve success?" an answer that says in some way or another, "the child" is most likely to produce a healthy, beneficial experience for young children regardless of their athletic skill levels.

CHAPTER REFERENCES

1. Bean, C., & Forneris, T. (2016). Examining the importance of intentionally structuring the youth sport context to facilitate positive youth development. *Journal of Applied Sport Psychology, 28,* 410-425. doi:10.10 80/10413200.2016.1164764.

2. Smoll, F. L. & Smith, R. E. (2004). *Sports and Your Child.* Palo Alto, CA: Warde Publishers, (p. 13).

3. McCarthy, P. J., & Barker, J. B. (2009). Stress in young athletes: Time for a developmental analysis? In: C. H. Chang (Ed.), *Handbook of Sports Psychology* (pp. 171-193). Hauppauge, NY: Nova Science Publishers, Inc.

4. Martens, R. (1982). Kids sports: A den of iniquity or land of promise. In R. A. Magill, M. J. Ash & F. L. Smoll (Eds.), *Children in Sport,* Champaign, IL: Human Kinetics Publishers (p. 215).

5. Feigley, D. A. (2014). Role of winning in youth sports. *Coaches Reference Manual, Rutgers SAFETY Clinic* (4th ed.), 67-68.

6. McCarthy, P. J., & Barker, J. B. (2009). Stress in young athletes: Time for a developmental analysis? In: C. H. Chang (Ed.), *Handbook of Sports Psychology* (pp. 171-193). Hauppauge, NY: Nova Science Publishers, Inc.

7. Henderlong, J., & Lepper, M. R. (2002). The effects of praise on children's intrinsic motivation: A review and synthesis. Psychological Bulletin, 128(5), 774-795.

8. Coakley, J. J. (2016). *Sport in Society: Issues & Controversies* (12th ed.). McGraw Hill: New York, NY.

9. Myer, G. D., Javanthi, N., Difiori, J. P., Faigenbaum, A. D., Kiefer, A. W., Logerstedt, D., & Micheli, L. J. (2015). Sport specialization, Part I: Does early sports specialization increase negative outcomes and reduce opportunity for success in young athletes? *Sport health,* 7(5), 437-432.

10. Fabricant, P. D., Lakomkin, N., Sugimoto, D., Tepolt, F. A., Stacciolini, A., & Kocher, M. S. (2016). Youth sport specialization and musculoskeletal injury: A systematic review of the literature. *Physician and sportsmedicine,* 44(3), 257-262.

11. American Sport Education Program, (2018). Human Kinetics Publishers, Champaign, IL.

12. Rutgers SAFETY Clinic (5th ed.), Rutgers – The State University of New Jersey, New Brunswick, NJ (2018).

13. Feigley's School of Gymnastics, South Plainfield, NJ (1995).

2

Teaching Strategies for Effective Coaching

CHAPTER OUTLINE

- Selecting What to Coach
- Teach the Skills of "Learning to Learn"
  YOUR TURN: Open Skills, Closed Skills
- Positive Coaching vs. Negative Coaching
- Positive Coaching
  FROM CHALKBOARD TO PLAYING FIELD: What is the Best Coaching Style?
- Strict and Demanding vs. Harsh and Punitive Coaching
- Elements of Effective Practices
- Coaching Fundamental Sports Skills
  SPOTLIGHT ON YOUTH SPORTS: Coaching "Tidbits"

There's never enough time! Virtually all teachers and coaches, regardless of their sport or activities, are faced with the dilemma of too much to teach and not enough time to get everything done. Techniques that speed the learning process not only help coaches and athletes deal with large amounts of information but also significantly enhance motivation. It is more fun when both the coach and the athlete see real progress. Some coaches regularly help their athletes to achieve competence in their sport faster than other coaches. This chapter focuses on some of their methods for helping athletes to learn the skills and strategies of their sports more quickly and efficiently.

In this chapter, we will examine how coaches can learn to select "what is most important to coach" and how to help young athletes "learn to learn." You will learn positive coaching strategies that nurture motivation and aid in the mastery and development of skills in your athletes. Techniques are presented that will help you create efficient practice sessions and understand how to vary your coaching styles effectively based upon both the situation and the age of your athletes.

Selecting What to Coach

A truism in teaching and coaching is the KISS method. KISS is an acronym for "Keep It Simple, Stupid!" The implication of this less-than-complimentary recommendation is that athletes have difficulty learning when they are bombarded with complex instructions about multiple things all at the same time. A more positive phrasing of this recommendation is "Teach one thing at a time," which immediately raises the essential question: "What should be that one particular thing?" Expert coaches seem to be better at analyzing this question than less experienced coaches. While identifying those characteristics that differentiate expert from non-expert coaches is a matter of substantial controversy,[1] experts use at least two interrelated strategies for deciding the priority aspects of a skill, technique, or strategy: (1) **coach the first error first**; (2) **coach causes, not symptoms.**

COACH THE FIRST ERROR FIRST

Typically, a young, developing athlete will make a number of errors in a sequence of physical skills. A springboard diver who dives too far away

FIGURE 2.1 Without a proper toss, a good serve is very unlikely. Correcting the first error often eliminates subsequent errors and permits the successful execution of the skill.

from the diving board to complete the dive may simultaneously show poor form, not be aware of where he is in space, and over- or under-rotate the dive. A tennis player who tosses the ball in an awkward, ineffective manner while serving has difficulty with her overhead stroke, creating a less-than-efficient follow-through and finishes the serve in an ineffective position to prepare for her opponent's return shot (Figure 2.1). In both of these examples, the coach should select a single error for correction from the many errors being made by the athlete. But which one?

The coach should note the sequence of errors and select an error early in the sequence. Correcting an error early in the sequence often eliminates or permits the self-correction of errors occurring later in that sequence.

In the tennis player example, the awkward toss on the serve leads to adjusting her overhead stroke which leads to a poor follow-through which leads to finishing in a difficult position for playing the return shot. Correcting the first part of the serve, the toss, may allow her to correct the later portions of the entire serve with little or no instruction on the part of the coach.

COACH CAUSES, NOT SYMPTOMS

Closely linked to this concept of selecting earlier rather than later occurring errors is the recommendation to coach the causes of errors, not just the errors themselves. Errors are often just the symptoms of an earlier cause. In the diving example above, cautioning the diver to walk slowly instead of running during the forward approach may eliminate many of the subsequent errors. Even if those errors are not totally eliminated, the greater control gained during the earlier portion of the skill may now permit the young athlete to self-correct later errors.

Determining what are "causes" and what are "symptoms" is not always as simple as it first appears. The coach must be able to discriminate what are performance factors (causes) and what are outcomes (symptoms). Part of such an analysis is biomechanical. Failure to align her body properly may prevent a gymnast from pirouetting without a wobble. A second part of the analysis is recognizing what aspect of the skill is under that particular athlete's control. A baseball batter who lacks the necessary power may not be able to swing the bat quickly enough to be a successful hitter. Coaching the batter's swing technique is likely to be less helpful than providing that player with a set of strength exercises designed to increase strength and power. Once sufficient power is obtained, coaching the techniques of the swing now becomes the "cause." Once the hitting techniques have been mastered, knowing the pitcher strategy or sequence of pitch selections may become a "cause" of further improvements in hitting. However, focusing on "knowing the pitcher" is unlikely to be valuable until the prerequisites of power and hitting technique are mastered.

COACH SKILL DEVELOPMENT, NOT LAPSES

Many athletes know how to perform a skill or a technique, but for a variety of reasons, they simply make a mistake in a practice or game. An athlete who has just dropped an easy fly ball or slipped while trying to guard a basketball opponent fully realizes that he or she has made a mistake. Effective coaches often ignore such lapses or respond by showing empathy and support. Instead of scolding the athlete or coaching how to better field a ground ball after an easy rolling ball is missed, the coach might respond: "Oops! You could have made that one! Try it again. I know you can do it!"

This is not to say that coaches should ignore aspects of the mistake from which an athlete can learn additional skills. For example, if the ground ball was missed because the fielder was not sufficiently ready when the pitcher pitched, then coaching better alertness or being in the proper physical position to readily move left or right is an essential part of good coaching. If, on the other hand, the player was alert, in the proper position, and had regularly handled the skill aspect of fielding, then simply accept the lapse and do little, if any, coaching. Telling a player what he or she already knows is not only irrelevant from an informational point of view, but also can be irritating, embarrassing, and demotivating.

Teach the Skills of "Learning to Learn"

Many athletes learn slowly because they lack the skills related to how to learn. They may have short attention spans, be easily distracted, focus more on the coach's mood than his instructions, or fail to ask questions when confused about instructions. Effective coaches try to develop progressions that teach young athletes the required skills for efficient learning. This strategy is called *"learning to learn."*

TAKING INSTRUCTION

Teach young athletes how to take instructions. Ask questions to see if they understand what you just taught. If they fail to understand, encourage them to ask questions rather than scolding them for remaining silent or not listening. Encourage them to show that they are paying attention by coaching them to maintain eye contact with you while you are providing both group and individual instruction. Eye contact provides you with feedback concerning whether your instruction is understood or accepted. A frown, a quizzical look, a nod of understanding can all help you be aware of the effectiveness – or the lack of effectiveness – of your instruction.

WORKING INDEPENDENTLY

Demand that beginners work independently* for brief periods of time and then gradually increase the time during which they must continue to focus and concentrate independently. Give simple work assignments that require short periods of independence; then gradually increase the length and complexity of those assignments while complimenting the athletes for "staying focused."

---

* This technique does not mean the young athletes work unsupervised!

THINKING AND MAKING JUDGMENTS

Perhaps the most important skill of learning to learn is to think and make decisions. All sports require decision making but some (open skills) require more decision making in competition than others (fixed skills). Encourage athletes to make decisions about what will help them improve. For example, set aside one practice a week for athletes to work on "what they think they need most to improve their game" – not their favorite skills or their worst techniques, but rather what skill that they judge to be the one they could improve the fastest in the shortest period of time or what would make the biggest improvement in their competitive performance. If their judgments do not initially match yours as the coach, encourage them to think more critically but do not become critical of their judgments. Your job is to improve their judgment so they become actively involved in their own improvement.

YOUR TURN
Open Skills, Closed Skills

FIGURE 2.2
Pitching (a closed skill) vs. Hitting (an open skill). The pitcher determines the type of pitch while the batter must react to what is thrown.

Open skills are variable; closed skills are fixed. A wrestler performs open skills. He must respond to the ever changing and often unpredictable moves of his opponent. A diver performs a closed skill. She is attempting to perform a skill that is virtually identical each time it is performed. Most actual sports skills have both components, some elements fixed, some open. The diver performs on different diving boards with different degrees of spring in different pools with different lighting. The wrestler's lunge for his opponent's leg for a take-down has to attain the same biomechanical leverage in order to drive the opponent to the mat.

Which skills in your sport are open and require more individual decision making? Which are closed? (Figure 2.2) How would you encourage your athletes to develop their judgment in those skills?

A powerful technique for teaching young athletes to think is called **Facilitative Questioning.**[2] One form of facilitative questioning is: "Ask, Suggest, Tell." You pose an open-ended question followed by increasingly directive prompts to athletes who initially may be too young, too immature, or too inexperienced to respond appropriately.

Example: Teaching decision making for defending in soccer

Ask – "Where's the best position to guard your man?"
    If no answer or weak answers, shift to provide a simple choice between two or three options.

Suggest – "Should you mark him goal side or away from the goal?"
    If the athlete still shows a lack of understanding and judgment or is too shy to respond, shift to the traditional command style of coaching using explicit directions.

Tell – "Mark your man goal side."

This simple technique provides athletes with real opportunities to think and make decisions, yet still provides the coach with control over the teaching situation. Asking a question promotes thinking, but when inappropriate or ineffective answers are given, the coach can shift from "ask" to "suggest" to "tell."

PAYING ATTENTION

A truism when working with young athletes is that they are often very distractible and have difficulty, at least initially, paying attention. Effective coaches give instruction that is light on verbal instruction and heavy with demonstrations and participation. If an athlete rarely looks at you and often gives the impression that he doesn't care, avoid ineffective statements such as "Can't you ever pay attention?" or "Don't you care?" The first is an overstatement, while the second questions motives, often difficult to correctly identify. Instead, be direct and say:

"When you don't look at me, I don't know if you're listening."

"When you make eye contact with me, I know you're listening and I'll continue to coach you."

Positive Coaching vs. Negative Coaching

What factors distinguish positive from negative coaching? The distinctions are far more complex than simply being nice or nasty (Figure 2.3).

Positive coaching increases motivation and inspires athletes to improve their skills and their teamwork—and by doing so, to develop self-control and mastery. Positive coaching includes effective communication, an understanding of the proper use of rewards and punishments, setting clear, realistic, yet demanding standards, and efficient strategies for error corrections. Some very "nice" coaches who lack these skills can be quite negative.

Negative coaching decreases motivation and erodes the coach-athlete relationship. At first glance, the phrase "negative coaching" may elicit the image of a coach yelling at athletes and making them run laps. Negative coaching is far more than that. Raising one's voice and requiring demanding conditioning drills are not, by themselves, negative. In fact, they may very well be essential to positive coaching. Coaching a soccer player 80 yards away across the field to "Mark

FIGURE 2.3
Positive coaching is more than smiling vs. scowling. Positive coaching is closely tied to teaching what to do and providing opportunities for success.

your man!" requires more than a whisper to be heard. It can be positive if it provides instruction about what to do and if marking the opponent is within the young athlete's ability level. Instruction in a soft voice that sarcastically asks athletes to perform skills beyond their current ability levels is far more negative than yelling. Negative coaching literally expends the athletes' energy and motivation ineffectively as it steals the joy of participation.

HOW TO AVOID NEGATIVE COACHING

So what can you do to avoid negative coaching and coach positively?

- **Avoid Teaching "Learned Helplessness"**

Asking athletes to perform skills beyond their ability or outside their ability to control is negative because such instruction leads to **learned helplessness.** Learned helplessness refers to situations in which athletes have learned that their efforts to improve a skill make no difference. They have tried over and over again without success. Eventually they come to believe that they cannot, in fact, succeed. As a result, they exert less effort and less perseverance. Their reduced effort lowers the probability of success, and the lack of success further reduces their effort. This negative cycle produces an athlete who believes he or she cannot succeed. Such a negative, self-fulfilling prophecy may develop when an athlete with great potential is progressing too rapidly and is actually attempting a skill for which he or she is not yet ready. The athlete may be quite capable of learning that skill when older, more mature, or more experienced, but the attempts to master the skill before having the pre-requisite skills leads to the perception that additional efforts are futile.

A young quarterback on a youth sport football team is asked to select the sequence of plays during a competition. Such a task is beyond his current ability level. Later in high school or college, when he has mastered the basic football skills, has the cognitive maturity to remember multiple plays, and can recognize the many variables that determine the best options, that young quarterback might easily become an excellent play caller. However, because of his early failure and frustration, he comes to believe that he is just not very good at calling plays. A tentative approach to calling the plays results in poor play selection and self-doubt, which, in turn, may interfere with his actual performance in carrying out a given play.

FIGURE 2.4
One definition of patience is the willingness to prepare your lesson plan sufficiently to enable every athlete, regardless of skill level, the opportunity to improve!

Coaches who work with special populations, such as Special Olympians, may find that the typical breakdown of skills is not sufficient to allow a slower learner to progress at a noticeable rate. Continued practice of skills that are not being mastered leads to learned helplessness and reduced effort. The belief that the coach should simply "be patient" does little to promote a feeling of success on behalf of either the athlete or the coach. Re-analyzing the skill and the capacity of the athlete may develop skill progressions in which significant daily progress can be achieved, thus, combating the learned helplessness syndrome. It is also a sign of "patience" that the coach spends the necessary time analyzing skills and designing the workout to allow recognizable progress rather than simply accepting the belief that skill progressions with Special Olympians "take a long, long time."** (Figure 2.4)

- **Avoid Blaming Slow Learning on a Lack of Motivation**

**Many thanks to Marc Edenzon, Chief of Global Programs, Special Olympics Inc., for pointing out to me that "patience" is not simply accepting no change or slow progress, but rather it is a willingness to take the time to plan sufficiently so that every athlete can experience significant success.

Motivation is a convenient fiction. You can't see it, hear it, touch it, or directly manipulate it. This extremely important concept is actually an abstraction that represents the many factors that energize, direct, sustain, and influence the quality of an athlete's behavior. Because of its abstractness, motivation may be an easy scapegoat to blame when both the coach and the athlete are frustrated by a lack of progress or by disciplinary problems.

Very few athletes, if any, lack motivation. They may be motivated to do things other than what the coach wishes but they are rarely unmotivated. Often the very behavior that appears unmotivated is a highly motivated attempt to protect their self-esteem. A youngster who lacks the confidence that he or she can succeed may very well respond by clowning around, by avoiding adequate preparation, or by derogating teammates who are working toward success.

The learned helplessness discussed in the previous section appears to be low motivation when, in fact, the athlete is highly motivated. The desire to learn is overwhelmed by the realization that "no progress has been made over a long period of time" implying that the task is beyond the ability of the athlete. The reduced effort, often accompanied by depressed moods, gives the appearance that the athlete is not trying. Equating this lack of overt effort with a lack of motivation ignores the fact that the depression and lack of effort develop directly from the athlete's strong desire to learn the "impossible" skill.

Motivation is the result of a large number of factors – factors that are often in conflict with each other. "I want to learn, but I'm afraid." "I want to be attentive, but I don't want to be made fun of as the 'coach's favorite' by my teammates." "I want to get better, but I don't understand how this drill makes any difference -- and it hurts!" Instead of assuming the absence of motivation, coaches may be more effective at energizing their athletes by looking for **demotivators** and helping their young athlete with solutions to combat those demotivating factors. For example, an athlete who fears falling and being hurt can be taught specific falling techniques to minimize risk and to enhance safety should a fall occur. The coach who has an athlete who is concerned about "fitting in" with his or her buddies might avoid singling that athlete out for public praise or demonstrations.

Finally, a lack of progress can be due to many non-motivational factors: a lack of flexibility, strength, conditioning; a lack of prerequisite skills; biomechanical errors; failure to understand instructions; ignorance of the importance of drills to competitive success. Motivational concerns are often assumed to be the problem long before these others factors have been considered and ruled out. It is easy to blame simply because it is so abstract. In fact, **motivation should be the last** of the potential factors to which a lack of progress is attributed.

- **Avoid the Misuse of Praise**

Excessive praise for non-accomplishments can actually undermine self-confidence. As children reach the maturity level necessary to begin thinking like adults (between 7 and 12 years of age), they begin to recognize that teachers and coaches often "are nice" to the less talented children both in school and on the playing field. After working with the klutzy kid who has had trouble mastering a skill, the coach may finish with a gratuitous compliment such as, "Good enough. Now let's move on." With a child who is more talented, the coach may very well say something about the non-progress: "Focus and pay attention. You can do better." The expectation is that the klutz can do no better while the more talented athlete is chastised for not making sufficient progress. Young athletes see this differential application of praise and recognize how the less talented athlete is treated differently with praise for non-accomplishments. They recognize that praise for non-accomplishments often indicates that the teacher/coach believes that the athlete can do no better. Therefore, they often judge the recipients of undeserved praise (both themselves and others) as less competent, especially if that undeserved praise is meted out to individuals on a regular basis.

This example is not to say that positive encouragement of less talented athletes is unwarranted. Just the opposite. However, the encouragement should be for accomplishments, no matter how basic. A good effort, even if unsuccessful, can be praised specifically for the effort itself while still acknowledging the lack of success. "Good effort. We need to work on that skill more to improve, but that was a strong effort. Let's move on." The athlete knows from the comment that the coach recognizes the athlete's lack of success but was still impressed with the athlete's effort. Effort might be the only aspect of the task under a low-skilled athlete's ability to control. Further efforts by the athlete might be better directed by the coach to prerequisites of the task – e.g., getting stronger, more flexibility, earlier preparation.

- **Avoid Rigid Authoritarianism**

  The legitimate use of authority is not the same as being an authoritarian. There is an important distinction being an authority who is in charge and who effectively uses an autocratic decision making style as opposed to being an authoritarian who uses an inflexible, rigid approach to coaching. Athletes often look to coaches to be decisive and to provide clear, unambiguous directions. They want decisiveness and predictability but not rigidity in their coach.

- **Avoid Sarcasm**

  Sarcasm is a lazy way of making corrections. Its embedded humor is lost on the very young and for those athletes old enough and mature enough to sense its meaning, sarcasm is more likely to foster resentment than a redoubling of effort to succeed. It serves as a put-down to athletes who are struggling to master the skills that they legitimately expect the coach to teach. Avoid asking unanswerable questions such as "Why did you make that mistake?" or "How many times have I told you to . . .?"

Positive Coaching

So what are the skills and attributes of positive coaches? Positive coaches display empathy. They use rewards and punishments effectively and fairly. They are strict and demanding without being harsh and punitive. They are consistent but not unyielding with their rules and discipline. These coaching strategies are discussed in detail as part of the positive discipline techniques covered in Chapter 4. They are just as important for positive coaching as the following concepts which deal with the use of reinforcements and praise.

UNDERSTANDING REWARDS AND REINFORCEMENT

Positive coaches understand that rewards can be made contingent upon different types of behaviors. Specifically, rewards can be categorized in a progression:[3]

- **participation rewards:** rewards for simply getting involved; for being there; for taking part.
- **effort rewards:** rewards for trying hard, for hustling, for doing one's best.

- **mastery rewards:** rewards for learning the skills, for improving one's performance, for an accomplishment.
- **competition rewards:** rewards for being the best, for performing better than others, for winning.

Rewards for **participation** are appropriate for very young, very shy, or very uncertain children who have had little or no expertise in the sport. Rewards that are symbolic of special group membership are very effective when the group or sport carries a substantial amount of prestige or value to the young athlete. Belonging to a sports team, for example, can provide a strong sense of identity to many youngsters. Rewards that signify that "I belong" or "I'm part of a special group" can be quite satisfying.

Rewards can also be given for **effort.** Such rewards are very appropriate for children below the age of 10 for whom "trying hard" is equivalent to "being good." Rewards for effort have less effect upon older children unless that effort is coupled with success. Rewards for effort when the outcome is failure can be quite demotivating for older children.

With older children, rewards for performing well are quite motivating because they reflect **mastery** such as the learning of new skills or accomplishing a meaningful task. Such awards are particularly valuable because they can be earned regardless of how well others do. Furthermore, the coach can set the criteria for mastery based upon the ability, age, and experience of the young athlete.

Finally, rewards can be given based upon **competition.** Making the All Star Team or being selected as the most valuable player tends to be motivating for highly successful athletes who believe that such rewards are within their capacity to achieve. Such rewards, by their very nature, are available only to a select few and as a result tend to have motivational value only to those athletes who believe they have a realistic chance for such awards.

As a general rule, coaches should gradually shift their emphasis from (1) participation to (2) effort to (3) mastery to (4) competition as the athlete becomes more skilled, more mature, more self-confident, more aware, and more experienced. These categories are not mutually exclusive nor should the emphasis be all-or-none. Even a mature, skilled, experienced athlete should be rewarded for effort and participating, but some praise can also be withheld until performance reflects mastery (successful completion of a skill) or a competitive achievement (ranking in a competition).

Coaches who confuse positive reinforcement with the indiscriminate use of praise are often frustrated that little progress is made in skill learning. An athlete who can earn sufficient praise simply by being there (participatory rewards) may not exert the energy necessary (effort rewards) to learn the skill (mastery rewards) to rank high among his opponents (competitive rewards). His behavior may very well be arrested at a point far below his capabilities simply because the coach, in an effort to be positive, is giving rewards for behaviors that require little or no effort on the part of the athlete.

Often athletes must work on a difficult skill or technique without seeing immediate improvement. As a coach, avoid saying "Good," or "O.K." for progress when you have not seen an improvement. Praising learning when none has occurred is not positive reinforcement. Phrases that reflect an understanding of the athlete's efforts despite a lack of progress might be: "Way to hustle! That still needs work. We'll come back to that tomorrow. Let's go on for now."

Positive motivational programs do not eliminate the use of all punishments. In fact, rewards and punishments are intimately related and are merely different sides to the same coin. See the section in Chapter 4 (Positive Discipline), under the topic of Reward-Punishment Connection.

What Gets Rewarded Gets Done

The behaviors that you acknowledge and praise are likely to be those behaviors that the athletes focus on. For example, after a new skill has been learned, if you want the athlete to perform it consistently, then you praise consistency, even when the skill is not always performed at a maximal performance levels. If you wish to teach young batters in baseball to avoid taking called third strikes, then praise the athlete's swing even if a strikeout is recorded or she hits into a double play. If you want your young soccer players to increase the number of shots on goal, then praise the shots whether a goal is scored or not or whether the shot is near the goal post (desirable) or straight at the goalie's chest (undesirable).

UNDERSTANDING THE EFFECTIVE USE OF PRAISE

Praise is an important tool for good coaching and the backbone of any successful motivational program. By itself, however, praise is not positive coaching and can, under certain circumstances, actually undermine learning and enjoyment of the activity.

Specific vs. General Praise

Praise is a form of feedback. Generalized praise such as "good job" is a common style of feedback from low-skilled coaches. Such praise lacks a reference to specific behaviors that you want the athlete to learn. Expert teachers are more likely to provide specific, credible and directive feedback "geared to the students' motivation and ability level."[4] Such specific praise tells the athlete what he or she did to earn the praise. Therefore, the athlete can duplicate those behaviors that earned the praise. Here are some examples of general vs. specific praise:

- "Nice job" vs. "Excellent, that's the way to get your glove down with the thumb out and hand over the glove to protect yourself from the ball."

- "Wonderful" vs. "Super, you anticipated well and were in the right position to field the ball."

- "You're doing great" vs. "Good. That's the way to follow through as you shoot the basketball."

Praise in Public; Criticize in Private

While public shame can quickly change behavior, it also has numerous negative side effects such as resentment, fear of taking chances, and teammates rallying against the coach to defend a teammate. Public praise that is deserved helps establish a positive team climate where athletes work for acknowledgment rather than shy away from potentially negative recognition from the coach (Figure 2.5).

FIGURE 2.5 Important information contained in a criticism by the coach given privately compared to publicly is less likely to be undermined by the athlete's concern for "How'd I look to others?"

Developing Respect and Rapport with Your Athletes

Predictability is an essential step in the development of a trusting atmosphere. When the athlete perceives that good things (rewards) consistently happen as a result of their efforts, trust develops. The rapport and respect a coach develops with his or her athletes is a direct result of the consistency the coach uses with the athlete. Coaches often believe mistakenly that they must first develop a rapport with the athlete and then begin teaching. In fact, those coaches who begin with consistent teaching and predictable reinforcement contingencies quickly develop the rapport that makes their teaching even more effective.

Coaching Abstract Behaviors

The behavior you wish to teach or modify (the target behavior) must be defined in observable, measurable terms. Performing a fixed number of skill attempts or regular attendance patterns are easily defined types of behaviors. Measuring them is clear-cut. Defining concepts such as "trying your best," "intensity," or "sticking to it" is much more difficult. Ambiguous, but important, concepts must be clarified to athletes and coaches by listing specific types of behaviors that illustrate the concept.

Give very explicit and specific instructions: Do not assume that your athletes have the same perceptions initially as you do. A coach who continually asks athletes to "hustle" or "work harder" may sound specific, but many athletes may already feel as if they working intensely. On the other hand, saying "Do 5 sets of these exercises in the next 15 minutes," gives both the athlete and the coach a very clear idea of what is to be done in what time period and a very clear idea of whether the task was completed. Rather than saying, "You must try harder," the coach should state minimal acceptable standards, for instance, "You must complete two routines before you can rest," or "You must complete all the specified warm-up exercises before the game begins."

Relevance of Practice Requirements

Coaches should regularly point out the purpose of a specific exercise or drill. Drills, especially, in the early stages of skill development, are often only a small portion of the skill ultimately being taught. The more removed a drill is from a competitive use, the more important it is for athletes to learn the drill's relevance. What may seem obvious to the coach, may appear quite irrelevant for a young, inexperienced athlete.

From Chalkboard to Playing Field

WHAT IS THE BEST COACHING STYLE?

Coaching styles range from the classic authoritarian "drill sergeant" style to a hands-off approach described as laissez-faire. Which style is best depends upon a number of factors including the coach's personality, why the athletes have chosen to participate, the maturity of the athletes, and the specific task to be taught. Let's examine three of the most commonly recognized styles – but clearly not all possible styles.

AUTHORITARIAN STYLE

The classic "drill sergeant" style is often referred to as command style. The coach dictates and the athletes respond. Athletes normally look to their coaches for direction and decision making. Athletes in interactive team sports such as volleyball, basketball and soccer actually prefer coaches who use an autocratic style where most decisions are made independently by the coach.[7]

Strengths. This style is most useful when information must be transmitted to the athletes in a short amount of time; for example, when calling a play in basketball in the last few seconds of a close game. It is also preferred when dealing with safety issues or when an athlete is disrupting the lesson plan. When a young athlete is doing something dangerous to himself or others, a command to stop is required as opposed to a discussion of why safety is important! If the lesson is disrupted by unruly behavior or clowning around, the coach has a responsibility to demand that such behavior stop immediately for the benefit of the other athletes who are paying attention and wish to learn. It also is necessary when the coach must decide who plays a particular role on the team (say, starting pitcher in baseball) when multiple players aspire to the same role or position. Coaches often use this style with very young or immature athletes, at least initially, until the athletes have been taught sufficient skills and strategies to begin participating in the decision making process.

Weaknesses. The authoritarian style takes control away from the players and provides little opportunity for decision making. In the long run and particularly with older, more mature athletes, a controlling attitude on the part of the coach can undermine long-term motivation resulting in athletes leaving the sport, particularly in recreational sport programs where participation is optional.

LAISSEZ-FAIRE STYLE

This style basically permits the athletes to do whatever they wish and has been labeled "baby sitting." Volunteer coaches lacking technical knowledge often resort to this technique as do beginner coaches who wish to avoid the drill-sergeant reputation in youth sports.

Strengths. This style permits the athletes to feel as if they have control over their involvement and is used by experienced coaches when they want their athletes to experience the consequences of specific decisions – sometimes positive consequences, sometimes negative. Used correctly, it can help coaches teach the athletes to be decision makers.

Weaknesses. With immature and/or inexperienced athletes, this style can lead to chaos and may be unsafe. Athletes who do not know or appreciate the consequences of certain behaviors may make choices that increase the risk of injury.

COOPERATIVE STYLE

With this style, both athletes and coaches participate in the decision making process.

Strengths. Participants tend to have a greater understanding of the reasoning behind certain decisions (why we work on our weaker skills in practice rather than practice our favorite moves), and they tend to be more committed to achieving the mutually determined goals.

Weaknesses. This style takes time to arrive at decisions when all participants' concerns are taken into consideration. It can also lead to conflict if conflicting goals are held by teammates (for example, "Who gets to start?").

Effective coaches select different styles to accomplish different goals. As you can see from the brief outline above, there does not appear to a "best" style. Choose the style that is most appropriate for your objectives. In effect, the different coaching styles are like a tool kit. Effective coaches choose the tool that is best for the task at hand.

Showing a young gymnast the relevance of a split for staying on the beam during a side aerial or showing a shortstop in baseball the importance of an agility drill for pivoting and throwing during a double play takes only a few seconds but may dramatically increase the athlete's commitment to improvement.

STRATEGIES FOR ERROR CORRECTION

Recognizing errors is an essential first step in correcting errors but it is not the same as coaching young athletes to improve. Teaching young athletes how they should correct errors and providing them with age-appropriate opportunities to improve are both essential parts of positive coaching.

Coach "What to Do" vs. "What Not to Do"

An occupational hazard of coaching is the emphasis on recognizing errors and mistakes. Good coaches learn quickly that simply telling an athlete how to perform the idealized correct technique is not sufficient to improve the athlete's skills. They must be able to identify what specific errors are preventing the athlete from performing successfully and give the athlete a strategy for making corrections. Saying "Don't bend your knees," to a diver or "Don't overthrow your receivers," to a quarterback tells the athlete what they have done wrong but does not provide them with information on how to correct their errors. On the other hand, saying "Tighten your thigh muscles," or "Throw the ball chest high while leading the receiver," tells the athlete what to do.

Age-Appropriate Communication About Errors

Correcting errors can be intertwined with praise and support in different ways for athletes at different stages of maturity. With the very young, success can be defined so broadly that no child fails. With elementary and middle school age children, criticism can be sandwiched between statements of praise and encouragement. With teens and adults, criticisms can be quite direct but be followed by statements of support.

For very young children from pre-school to 2nd grade: Use a Movement Education Approach.[5] Tasks or instructions are designed so that virtually all the youngsters can accomplish the assignment successfully (e.g., "How many sides of your foot can you use to dribble the soccer ball?"). Whether the child gives only one answer or many, the task can be successfully performed and thus becomes praiseworthy. With this method, no one fails. This approach is rarely appropriate in older children who would quickly note the differences in performance between children of differing abilities.

For late elementary school and middle school: Use a Sandwich Approach.[6] Criticism and/or technical instruction is sandwiched between two positive statements. For example, note a praiseworthy behavior, such as effort. "Good effort!" Then inject the technical criticism, coaching "what to do" as opposed to "what not to do." "Next time, follow the ball all the way into your hands to make the catch." Follow the technical correction immediately with a future oriented statement of support. "Try again. I know you can do it." Thus, the technique is a "+, –, +" sequence. While this technique can be used with any age, skill, or maturity level,*** with more sophisticated athletes a steady diet of sandwiches results in the initial positive statement becoming a cue for the ensuing technical instruction and/or a criticism. Older athletes then begin to discount the initial praise as they anticipate the correction.

For older athletes (late middle school and high school): Use Supportive Truths. Athletes who are capable of adult-like judgments prefer coaches who get right to the point. Point out the error and then provide a future oriented statement of support. "You are reacting late to the batted ball. Stay on the balls of your feet and anticipate a hit when the batter swings the bat." This technique is most appropriate with athletes who already know they've made a mistake but may not be aware of how to correct it.

Strict and Demanding vs. Harsh and Punitive Coaching

There is a dramatic difference between a coaching style which is strict and demanding and a style which is harsh and punitive. One critical skill which permits coaches to be strict without being harsh is called a contingency, or more informally, an "if …, then …" relationship. Coaches who say to the athletes, "**If** you hustle and finish the drills, **then** we can scrimmage" are using a contingency. The behavior desired by the athletes (scrimmaging) is made contingent upon first exhibiting a less

---

***John Wooden, who won an unprecedented ten NCAA Division I basketball championships in a row, used this technique regularly with collegiate athletes.

frequent behavior desired by the coach (hustling on the drills). A second skill is setting appropriate standards as part of the contingency. Standards are the criteria set forth in the contingency statement. Standards can be set as either the quality or quantity of a skill. An example of quantity might be to attempt 5 foul shots in basketball regardless of whether or not each shot is successful before we can move to the next drill. Quality might be setting the standard at 5 "makes" in a row before moving on.

SETTING POSITIVE CONTINGENCIES

What do contingencies and standards have to do with strict vs. harsh coaching? Strictness is adhering to the standards and contingencies while harshness is determined by whether the contingency is presented as an opportunity or a punishment. For example, the coach can say in a supportive fashion, "If you make five in a row, we can scrimmage!" (the opportunity). Conversely he can say in a negative tone, "If you don't make five in a row, we won't scrimmage." (the punishment). In both statements, the contingency is the same. The first is set as a challenge; the second threatens a sanction. Which coach would you prefer to play for? The coach who continually offers opportunities – or the coach who is continually threatening a punishment? It is more than a word game. It is how the coach sets the attitudes within the practice. Adhering to the contingencies is strictness ("Your 4 of 5 makes just missed! Com'on. Let's try again! You can do it!"). Saying "You missed, therefore, you can't scrimmage" is punitive.

SET POSITIVE STANDARDS

Do not lower standards to reward "near misses." If your standards have been set appropriately based upon the skill level and maturity of the athlete, the athletes are not helped by being rewarded for less than what the standard demands. Inconsistent applications of a standard will confuse athletes about what specific behaviors earn the rewards.

This is not to say that standards which are not working because they were set too high should not be reexamined. When a contingency's standard is not working, it must be modified; but once modified, the standard should be applied consistently and fairly to all athletes in the program. Flexibility can be built into a standard. For example, the basketball player can be told the standard is either make 5 free throws in a row or make 4 of 5 two times in a row.

BE CONSISTENT

Consistency not only increases the likelihood that a contingency standard will appear fair in the eyes of the athletes, but also consistency develops the appearance of "inevitability." When athletes perceive a contingency standard as inevitable, they are more likely to focus their efforts on meeting that contingency rather than circumventing it. Athletes who believe they must successfully complete a skill or coaching directive in order to obtain a reward are more likely to concentrate on completing that task rather than imploring the coach for the reward merely because they have "tried hard." The strict adherence to a high but realistic standard is likely to be seen as demanding but not harsh or punitive. Harshness is related to the perception of being punished if the contingency is not met. Strictness is related to perceiving that the contingencies must and can be met.

One important point should be made about consistency. Consistency is not an unyielding application of the same contingency or style to every athlete in every situation. Consistency is applying the same standards and coaching style to similar situations regardless of whether that application is convenient or not. If athletes are at different maturity levels, different types of rewards may be necessary. Younger athletes may need more reinforcement for participation and effort as opposed to older athletes who might benefit more from praise for mastery and competitive accomplishments. As an individual athlete matures, the contingencies the coach provides him should shift from participation and effort to mastery and competitive success.

Elements of Effective Practices

Good planning and good execution are fundamental to running an effective practice. Even a plan written on the back of an envelope as you commute home from work is better than walking into practice cold, telling your young charges to take a few laps for warm-ups, and then trying to figure out what you will do in practice that evening.

SHARP STARTS

Warm-ups can serve not only to warm up the athletes' bodies but also to serve as the clear and unambiguous start of the practice. As your athletes rotate from one phase of the practice to another, the first minute of each phase is by far the most important time period. Sharp starts with brief, clear instructions outlining what you want your athletes to do during this phase of the practice dramatically increase the efficiency of your workouts. Do not use this first minute to speak with an individual athlete, discuss issues with an assistant coach, or simply take a deep breath and relax. Any task that intrudes in the first few moments of each successive phase of the workout will result in many, if not most, of your athletes waiting to begin or beginning haphazardly without your leadership. This is especially true with young, inexperienced athletes.

OLD SKILLS, NEW SKILLS

A regular cycle of reviewing previously taught skills followed by the introduction of new skills permits the necessary repetition to master the previously taught skills while providing athletes with new skills, a procedure that promotes both enhanced motivation and systematic progress.

MODIFIED GAMES

Modified games are more complex than basic drills, providing the athletes with more variation and more opportunities to make game-like choices (e.g., passing the ball to the open man rather than the guarded teammate). They also often allow you to use scoring criteria, which teach athletes to focus on important parts of the skills (e.g., bonus points for scoring a goal in soccer within a yard of the goal post instead of shooting directly toward the center of the goal where the goalie could easily block the goal).

SCRIMMAGES

Scrimmages simulate "real games" but permit you to stop the action periodically to reinforce a learning point. For example, after a fast break has occurred, you can stop the game, have players rethink the choices they made and explore alternative choices, and reinforce good choices. The players can then run through the situation again applying some of the alternatives. Scrimmages allow coaches to capitalize on "teachable moments" that arise during the flow of a game but normally would fade into the next phase of the game.

CONDITIONING

As young athletes reach the ages where conditioning is appropriate, you can integrate skill learning and conditioning. Teaching dribbling tech-

FIGURE 2.6 What did we accomplish? What was incomplete? What should we do next? All are important post-practice questions.

niques with the ball can be combined with having your athletes run laps for endurance in sports such as basketball or soccer. Use age-appropriate training. (See Chapter 13 on training and conditioning techniques.)

POST-PRACTICE EVALUATION

A brief assessment of the effectiveness of each practice can help determine what should be done in the next practice, what was unsuccessful and perhaps should be eliminated, and what should be adjusted for the next practice. Even a brief assessment can prevent a succession of ineffective practices and coordinate systematic progressions from practice to practice (Figure 2.6).

Coaching Fundamental Sports Skills

While specific coaching techniques usually depend upon the specific sport and the competitive level of your athletes, a number of general principles can guide your approach to coaching basic sport skills.

- **Progress from the Simple to the Complex.** Plan your practices to move from single skill drills to drills involving a sequence of skills, to modified games to controlled scrimmages to full game play.

- **Effective Demonstrations.** Orient your athletes away from potential distractions to keep them focused on the demonstration. For example, if other teams are practicing on a nearby field, hold

FIGURE 2.7
Without the focused
attention of these
young athletes, the
instructions from
this coach would
be less effective.
Focused attention
is a skill that can be
taught.

the interesting scrimmage on the next field. Make certain every
athlete is in a position to see clearly. Combine verbal descriptions
with visual demonstrations and ultimately physical participation
to maximize learning (Figure 2.7).

- **Name the "Critical Elements."** Identify and teach the "critical
  elements" of each skill. Critical elements direct athletes to what
  aspect of the skill should receive most of their attention (Figure
  2.8). These critical elements can also serve as reminders or cues to
  athletes when they get ready to perform. ("Remember to stay on
  the balls of your feet," or "Watch his mid-section on defense, not
  his eyes").

- **Be Brief.** Brevity that is effective usually requires prior
  preparation. Brief presentations help ensure that you do not
  cover too much information, nor overload athletes with detailed
  instructions. Multiple brief presentations are usually more
  effective with young athletes than long, drawn out descriptions,
  explanations and justifications.

- **Check for Understanding BEFORE Starting.** Verify that your
  athletes understand your instructions before athletes move to
  their different drill stations to save time, avoid confusion, and
  minimize the possibility of injury resulting from misunderstood
  instructions. Asking your athletes to identify the critical elements

FIGURE 2.8
Can this young player identify precisely what the coach is teaching? Ask the young athlete to identify that critical element before beginning the drill!

you just taught is an excellent way to check for understanding. Asking "Does everyone understand?" is likely to get a "Yes" answer from young athletes regardless of their level of understanding.

• **Maximize Participation.** Young athletes learn by doing. Too much verbal instruction is confusing, de-motivating and ineffective at improving performance. Standing in line awaiting a turn should occur only when athletes need a rest between vigorous bouts of activity, not because there is only one ball for 15 players.

SPOTLIGHT ON YOUTH SPORTS
Coaching "Tidbits"

When You, as the Coach, Make a Mistake. Acknowledge your error briefly and then move on. Athletes respect and admire coaches not because the coaches are perfect but because they are problem solvers.

Coaching During Practice vs. Coaching During Games. Practice is the place to introduce new concepts, strategies, and techniques. During the actual competition expert coaches rarely try new strategies regardless of the score of the game. Introducing new concepts during competition is likely to create confusion. Coaches who effectively change strategy during half-times are able to do so because they have had their athletes rehearse those changes in practice. Switching from man-to-man defense to a zone because the opponents are effectively beating the man-to-man defense is possible when both defenses have been practiced and are well within the skill levels of the athletes on the team.

Be Aware of What Is Really Happening. The athletes' behavior and the coaching environment must be monitored consistently. The coach must know what is happening! While the coach does not need to watch every movement of every athlete in practice, there must be a systematic plan by which the coach maintains awareness of how the athletes are doing. Expert coaches are typically more aware than less experienced coaches. They see details or information that others miss. This awareness permits them to better anticipate likely outcomes and, thus, to develop better contingency plans.[8,9]

CHAPTER REFERENCES

1. Nash, C., Martindale, R., Collins, D., & Martindale, A. (2012). Parameterising expertise in coaching: Past present and future. *Journal of Sports Sciences, 30*(10), 985-994.

2. Elias, M. J. & Clabby, J. F. (1992). *Building social problem solving skills: Guidelines from a school-based program.* San Francisco: Jossey-Bass

3. Feigley, D. A. (1990). Influence of rewards on motivation. *U.S. Gymnastics TECHNIQUE: The Official Technical Publication of the United States Gymnastics Federation, 10* (1), 4-5.

4. Manross, D., & Templeton, C. L. (1997). Expertise in teaching physical education. *Journal of Health, Physical Education, Recreation and Dance, 68*(3), 29-35 (page 32).

5. Abels, K. W., & Bridges, J. M. (2010). *Teaching movement education: Foundations for active lifestyles.* Champaign, IL: Human Kinetics.

6. Weinberg, R. S., & Gould, D. (2015). *Foundations of Sport and Exercise Psychology,* 6th ed. Champaign, IL: Human Kinetics. (p. 240-241).

7. Weinberg, R. S., & Gould, D. (2007). *Foundations of Sport and Exercise Psychology,* 4th ed. Champaign, IL: Human Kinetics. (p. 218).

8. De Marco, Jr., G. M., & McCullick, B. A. (1997). Developing expertise in coaching: Learning from the Legends. *Journal of Health, Physical Education, Recreation and Dance, 68*(3), 37-41.

9. Tan, S. K. S. (1997). The elements of expertise. *Journal of Health, Physical Education, Recreation and Dance, 68*(2), 30-33.

3

Developing Mental Toughness
STRATEGIES FOR PEAK PERFORMANCE

CHAPTER OUTLINE

- Mental Toughness and Self-Confidence
- Definitions and Prerequisites
- Praise and Self-Confidence
  FOCUS ON YOUTH SPORTS: Excessive Praise
- Coaching Strategies Before the Competition
  YOUR TURN: Enhancing A Sense of Control
  FROM CHALKBOARD TO PLAYING FIELD: Visual Imagery For Baseball, Swimming, Football, Soccer
- Coaching Strategies During the Competition
- Coaching Strategies After the Competition

Some athletes compete well; others do not. Some teams consistently perform well under pressure; others have difficulty. What distinguishes those who do well under pressure from those who do not? A descriptive answer is mental toughness. The coach's questions are: "Can mental toughness be developed?" and if so, "How?" Mental toughness can be developed using sound training principles and proper progressions. Just as all athletes benefit from strength training even though some athletes are initially stronger and though strength differences still exist after training, all athletes can also benefit from programs to develop tough-mindedness.

In this chapter, we will examine how coaches can enhance mental toughness and self-confidence, with specific strategies for fostering peak performance before, during, and after competitions.

Mental Toughness and Self-Confidence

Mental toughness is not simply winning, nor is it a disregard for one's safety and the safety of others. It is not talent nor is it an unthinking commitment to pleasing the coach or others. **Mental toughness is playing your best regardless of the circumstances:** Whether you are ahead or behind, whether you feel well or not, whether the refs' calls are in your favor or not, whether your opponents are better, equal, or worse, whether you are at home or away, whether the fans are rooting for you or against you, whether you just previously made a great play or an error. Under all these circumstances, if you play your best with appropriate effort, you are tough-minded. Playing your best is not merely trying hard. It is staying focused, playing smart, rising to the occasion, and making good choices. Winning is a by-product of, not a measure of, mental toughness. Winning happens when your performance is better than your opponents on the day of the competition.

Definitions and Prerequisites

The most obvious characteristic of self-confident competitors is their strong belief that they can be successful. This belief is based upon more than a history of past successes. While one's level of self-confidence is strongly influenced by past successes and failures, it becomes more independent of the past to the extent that it is based upon the belief that **"I control the factors that permit me to improve. Yes, I lost today, but wait until next week. I will be better!"** Coaches cannot control an athlete's self-confidence directly, but they can influence their athletes' experiences with improving skills, especially in practice. The coach's choice of progressions, the matching of athletes against comparably skilled opponents, and defining success as "making the changes the coach has been teaching" are all examples of how coaches can arrange for situations in which the athlete's efforts lead to improvement. In competition, the coach has less control but can still enhance the athlete's likelihood of progressing by ensuring that the athlete is prepared with the necessary skills and by setting performance goals that are independent of winning and losing (e.g., reducing the number of fouls a player makes in a basketball game or decreasing called third strikes in softball).

Two types of self-confidence[1] are related to mental toughness:

Trait self-confidence is my general perception of how much I control my life. Trait self-confidence is relatively stable and cuts across most areas of a person's life. Athletes high in trait self-confidence consistently distinguish between their performance vs. the outcome of the competition; for example, "I played well even though I lost"; or "I mis-hit the ball even though I scored." An athlete low in trait self-confidence might perceive that "I am doing well because I am beating the others." This athlete's self-confidence is likely to be shaken if his ranking falls because he graduates to an older age group or moves from the Jr. Varsity to the Varsity. Those high in trait self-confidence typically see errors as a form of information rather than a negative evaluation (i.e., "I'm over swinging" vs. "I'm a bad player").

Situational self-confidence relates to the perception of how much control I have in a particular situation. While I may be quite confident on the ski slope where I have grown up, I am quite nervous about deep water since I have never learned to swim. This type of confidence is often directly related to the amount of preparation for a specific task rather than a judgment about one's general ability. Coaches can enhance their athletes' situational self-confidence and, thus, the likelihood of competing well (Figure 3.1).

FIGURE 3.1
Situational self-confidence is one aspect of mental toughness that coaches can have considerable influence over.

Before examining the factors that can contribute to peak performance under pressure, let's look at the **prerequisites** for mental toughness and athlete self-confidence.

PREREQUISITES FOR MENTAL TOUGHNESS

Mentally tough athletes are skilled and in shape. Mental training is not a replacement for physical preparation. While mental skills can help beginners to learn faster and to have confidence in their ability to improve, mental toughness in a specific competitive situation requires that the athletes know they are capable of doing the skills required. As obvious as it may sound, to feel confident, athletes must be both physically conditioned **and** competent at the sports skills before anything else. The classic statement of football coach Vince Lombardi that "Fatigue makes cowards of us all" speaks to this first prerequisite. Athletes must have the strength, flexibility, and cardiovascular conditioning to meet the demands of their sport. Second, they must know not only how to perform the sports skills but also have rehearsed them to the point where such skills are an automatic response to a given sports situation. No amount of psychological preparation can make up for a lack of physical preparedness or a lack of competency with the required sports skills.

Veteran coaches who point out that "success is 90% mental" are referring to prepared athletes who have the skills and physical conditioning necessary to compete. Any remaining differences in the performance between equally physically well prepared athletes under competitive pressure are then most likely to be the result of mental skills and strategies.

Praise and Self-Confidence

Coaches have long advocated the use of praise as a primary means of enhancing an athlete's self-confidence. Praise enhances motivation and a sense of personal control when it is: (1) seen as non-controlling; (2) based upon performance; and (3) specific.

However, if athletes sense that praise is designed to manipulate them, the praise is rejected and its influence on self-confidence development is substantially reduced. When praise is specific and based upon the actual behavior of the athlete, the athlete learns that he has controlled the behavior that earned that praise and develops a sense of confidence about his ability to influence the world about him. Therefore, an effective teacher should distinguish between generalized praise and specific encouragements. **Generalized praise** may make one feel better temporarily but provides little information about what earned the praise and what can be done to improve. **Specific encouragement** gives precise information about what warranted the praise and how the athlete can continue to earn it.

SPOTLIGHT ON YOUTH SPORTS
Excessive Praise

Praise is not a panacea for enhancing confidence and mental toughness. Indeed, it can undermine self-confidence in certain circumstances. If, for example, adults regularly give excessive praise to children who perform no better or worse than other children, those children receiving the excessive praise are seen by the others and by themselves as less competent. Thus, too much praise may lower rather than raise confidence levels. This paradoxical effect depends upon the age of the child. **Children older than 10 years** see the excessive praise as indicating lesser ability. **Children younger than 10** see excessive praise as indicating higher ability.* Excessive praise

---

*The age of 10 is used as a general stage of development, not as a hard and fast line of change. Some 11- and 12-year-olds are less mature than some 10 years and some 8- and 9-year-olds are more mature than some 10-year-olds.

for mediocre performance and/or for success at a very easy task implies to relatively mature children that the rewarded performance is the maximum expected from that child. **This perception is also likely to be used to assess their own abilities relative to others.** That is, too much praise for a mediocre performance tends to be seen as a sign of lesser personal ability by children who have attained near adult levels of cognitive maturity. Apparently, children learn that adults are more generous with lower-ability children and more demanding and critical of more talented children.

Competitively-Based Praise. Coaches who consistently praise an athlete by saying "You're the best!" "That's the best on the team!" "No one else has done that well!" are basically teaching athletes to assess their self-worth based on external standards – the competition. These phrases sound positive and are often used in a genuine attempt to bolster a youngster's self-esteem. Unfortunately, a steady diet of such praise consistently ranks a youngster relative to his peers and promotes an external perspective based upon rank. "I'm good because I rank high," or "I'm good because I'm better than the others." While performing well relative to others can enhance self-confidence, **such comparisons are externally based and can change independently of the athlete's performance.** An athlete can actually improve, yet fall behind his comparison group if the members of that group are improving at a faster rate. Second, **externally-based comparisons are difficult to apply positively to all members of a group or team.** Fifty percent of every group is in the bottom half of the class. If coaches perceive their role as assisting all members of their teams, externally-based comparisons are unlikely to affect all team members in the same fashion.

General, Internally-Based Praise. Coaches sometimes attempt to direct a youngster's perception inward to develop the perception that the youngster is responsible for her own performance: "You could have done better!" "You ought to do better!" Sometimes adults make such statements in a more socially acceptable way: "You could have concentrated more!" "You should have paid attention!" "You have to focus more!" Such comments promote an inward focus by the athlete but provide little detailed information concerning **how** the athlete should improve her performance. Holding a child responsible for her performance is desirable if that performance is within her ability to control. Athletes who internal-ize such generalized internally oriented coaching statements are likely to take the blame for poor performances but feel helpless to improve.

Specific, Competency-Based Praise. Directing young athletes to per-formance-based goals within the athlete's ability to control represents the best of both worlds. First, athletes develop feelings of responsibility for their own actions in settings in which the coach directs the athlete's attention to performances that are clearly within the athlete's abilities to control or that can, with reasonable effort, be brought under that ath-lete's control. "Just make contact with the ball" is a performance goal for a baseball batter who is of similar ability to the pitcher but not for a batter whose bat speed is far below that of the pitcher. When athletes perceive that they can successfully control those factors that lead to improved sports performance, self-confidence develops rapidly and becomes more independent of winning and losing.

Coaching Strategies Before the Competition

Most mental training takes place before you and your athletes leave the practice field for actual competition. Teaching mental toughness skills should be ongoing and integrated into your normal practice routines.

The concept of a sense of **control** will be used in numerous ways throughout this chapter. Basically it refers to an athlete's understanding of **what factors are within his control and what factors are not.** Ath-letes who understand the difference and are able to direct their focus to factors within their ability to control are said to have "focus and concen-tration." Without this understanding, athletes spend their time and ef-fort thinking about factors outside their ability to control, often referred to as "worry and distraction."

A third category of factors are prerequisites to control, i.e., factors the athlete "**could control if. . .**" For instance, controlling the time and energy put into the strength and conditioning training program will likely provide the athlete the strength to throw the ball further or hit with more power or to run further and longer. Having practiced a backup plan for defense allows the team to switch defense at half time if the original defensive strategy is not working. During the actual competition attempting to switch to a new defensive alignment that has been rarely practiced is likely to have disastrous consequences. Thus, high level per-formers and their coaches understand and act upon the following factors:

- What you do control (effort makes a difference)
- What you don't control (effort makes no difference)
- What you could control if. . . (prerequisites for control)

Table 3.1 provides a number of examples that illustrate these three important categories.

YOUR TURN
Enhancing A Sense of Control

Add your own examples in the blanks in Table 3.1. First, identify an aspect of sport important to you and your athletes. Second, identify a performance factor that is clearly within the athlete's ability to control. Third, identify a different factor beyond the athlete's ability to control. Finally, identify a factor that, if mastered, would lead to more control over the previously uncontrollable factor.

TABLE 3.1 Controllability

	The Issue	I Control	I Do Not Control	I Could Control If . . .
1	Work Intensity	How hard I work	How much fatigue I feel at the end of the workout	My post-workout fatigue if I train harder during the conditioning sessions
2	Officials' Judgment	Whether I complain after a "bad break"	Whether others complain after a "bad break"	Whether I look for advantages of a "bad break;" e.g., an injury restricts me but now I have time to study the rules of the sport in detail
3	Focus	My concentration	How many distractions exist in competing before an audience	I were more familiar with performing before an audience because I regularly use mental imagery to simulate performing in front of an audience
4	Performance	My sport performance	An unfair score or official's call	My emotional reaction where I choose to "show composure and class"

continued

TABLE 3.1 Controllability continued

	The Issue	I Control	I Do Not Control	I Could Control If . . .
5	Rest			
6	Equipment			
7	Rules			
8	Starter v. Reserve			
9				
10				

HELP YOUR ATHLETES BECOME FAMILIAR WITH COMPETITIVE SITUATIONS

Familiarity reduces the likelihood that new or strange circumstances will distract athletes. Coaches can enhance familiarity and experience with competitive situations in a number of ways.

Simulate Competitive Situations in Practice

Good competitors practice not only their sports skills but also their competing strategies. If a situation is likely to occur in a game, practice it. While certain experiences can only be attained through actual competition, most can be practiced. For example, basketball players can practice 20-second drills in basketball; gymnasts and figure skaters can have judges score a practice routine; softball players can scrimmage under game conditions; swimmers and runners can practice false start procedures; and soccer players can defend or attack in 1 v. 1, 2 v. 1, 3 v. 2, 4 v. 3, etc. The more important the circumstances and the more likely they will occur in competitions, the more a coach should design simulations for the athletes (Figure 3.2).

Help Your Athletes Plan Their Warm-ups

Warm-ups are not the place to correct problems that have not been corrected in practice. Rather, use the warm-up period to become familiarized with the equipment and field/facilities.

FIGURE 3.2
Simulations of competitive situations enhance the likelihood that the skills learned in practice can be successfully executed in actual competitions even when the actual competitive circumstances are difficult to reproduce precisely.

Look for Naturally Occurring Situations in Which the Athlete Can Experience Competitive Pressure

For example, a practice assignment in gymnastics could be for the gymnast to "stick" five routines in a row on the balance beam. When the athlete has stuck the first four and is about to attempt the fifth, have her visualize a meet situation with the judges sitting by the beam and formally present to them before mounting the beam. Have her imagine the crowd watching her. She can even pretend that if she sticks this particular routine, she will make the finals, or that her team will win the team championship. She has the "real" pressure of having to stick this fifth routine. If she misses, she will have to start the five routines again. Even if she misses, she has an excellent chance to practice a meet pressure situation. How did she handle the situation when she fell? Did she lose her composure, become angry, or quit before finishing? Or did she take a deep breath, regain her composure, and finish as best she could? When something occurs in practice that has the potential to be upsetting to the athlete, both the athlete and the coach have an excellent opportunity to practice keeping calm, focused, and mentally tough. Not only will they increase their chances of keeping their composure* in competitive situations, but their practices will be more effective also.

*An often overlooked dimension of teaching sportsmanship is that good sportsmanship is a crucial ingredient of mental toughness. Keeping your composure after a "bad" call by an official or not retaliating after being harshly fouled in the heat of the moment is the essence of good sportsmanship. Keeping your composure in difficult situations is an essential aspect of mental toughness. (See Chapter 6 Sportsmanship for a more detailed discussion.)

Practice Predictable Ceremonial Situations

Young athletes often feel self-conscious during the march-in or while presenting to judges or officials. Have the athletes practice such presentations until they can do them comfortably.

Familiarize the Athletes with the Competitive Surroundings

Experienced athletes tend to be familiar with the exact situations in which the competition occurs. Coaches can help less-experienced competitors by describing what to expect, by visiting the competitive site for a practice session, by arriving early the day of the competition, by identifying the competitive equipment to be used and practicing on identical or similar equipment in training sessions, or by having the athletes visualize the competitive settings with crowds, noise, officials, etc. Prior to the hustle and bustle of the competition, especially in tournaments, playoffs or championship settings, the coach should familiarize the athletes with such things as where the restrooms are, whom to ask for assistance, where the check-in area is, what the order of competition will be, etc.

Familiarize Your Athletes with Their Opponents

Whenever appropriate, describe the opponents to your athletes along with realistic ways of competing against them; for example, "They're bigger, but we're quicker!" "Her forehand is strong, so hit to her backhand." If opponents are clearly superior or inferior, give your athletes performance goals. "We can't keep them from scoring baskets, but we can force them to take more outside shots."

Teach the Athletes what is Expected of Them – in Precise Detail

Many coaches and athletes expect to compete well without a complete knowledge of what is expected of them. Such knowledge is essential for competing well. Perhaps most obvious is the rules of their sport. A wrestler should know that "clasping" both hands around the opponent's waist while both are down on the mat means one point for his opponent; a basketball player should understand what constitutes the 3-second rule; runners and swimmers should understand the rules about false starts. In some sports, the athlete should know equipment settings. For example, how far from the vaulting horse should the springboard be set in gymnastics? Exactly how many feet down the runway should a broad jumper or high jumper start his run? How many strokes should be taken

FIGURE 3.3
Encourage young
athletes to watch
what the more ex-
perienced athletes
are doing BEFORE
the success – run-
ning without the
ball, recovering
from a lapse, main-
taining composure
in warm ups.

to reach the wall after a backstroke swimmer passes under the flags in a
swim race?

WATCH AND LEARN FROM THE BEST

Coaches can arrange for their novice athletes to observe more experienced athletes in competitive conditions. Coaches can take their athletes
to high school, college or professional contests just to watch. Novice competitors can observe more experienced teammates in game situations.
Often young athletes can learn about successful competing by watching
what top athletes do just before and just after they compete. Guide your
athletes' attention to those behaviors that lead to success. What does the
experienced, successful athlete do without the ball, before the action,
before the score? For example, how do the more experienced athletes
warm-up? How do they react if they have difficulties during a warm-up?
How do they work with their coaches during the pre-meet times? How
early do they arrive at the competition site? How do they prepare just
before they step out onto the field? How do they behave immediately after a missed or disappointing play? Observing how the best competitors
behave in such situations can teach young athletes tremendous amounts
about competing effectively (Figure 3.3).

HAVE SPECIFIC, REALISTIC GOALS FOR EACH COMPETITION

The word *specific* means that the goal should be very concrete. For example, the athlete's goals might be to "stick" her beam dismount; to successfully execute a bunt; to eliminate fouling during a broad jump, to raise the team's score by two points; or to eliminate turnovers in basketball or soccer. Specific goals contrast with generalized goals such as "to be the best that I can be," or "to improve," which are too vague to be measured. If the athlete has a variety of specific goals, even if one or two goals are missed, the athlete can be successful with others.

The word *realistic* means that the goal is determined by factors within the athlete's control. True self-confidence – and thus, mental toughness – is based upon distinguishing between what can and what cannot be controlled and believing that you can control the controllable. Realistic performance goals within the athlete's control are likely to enhance self-confidence and lead to higher performance. Goals that are established outside the realm of what the athlete can control are likely to produce frustration, lower self-confidence, and superstitious behavior.

EXPLAIN THE ADRENALINE RESPONSE TO YOUR ATHLETES

During competitive events, almost every athlete will experience the excitement and nervousness of competition. The increased heartbeat, the jittery feelings in the stomach, the need to go to the restroom, and/or the increased muscular tension are all normal, predictable responses to an exciting situation. Athletes who have never experienced such feelings may worry about what is happening to them and may interpret such feelings as a negative event: "I'm uptight and nervous," or "I'm upset." They focus on their feelings which can often be a distraction, lowering performance.

High level performers have similar adrenalin responses but as the time to compete draws nearer, they focus on what to do and the skills they have practiced in preparation for the competition. Coaches can set the stage for such an adrenaline response by describing it to their athletes and by providing a positive interpretation for such a feeling: "Butterflies in your stomach mean you are ready to go! Focus on what to do!" or "The muscular tension will make you stronger and quicker! Use that strength and quickness!" Athletes who expect the adrenaline response and believe it will help them to compete better are likely to interpret its sensations as "I'm pumped!" or "I'm ready to go!"

DEVELOP THE ATTITUDES OF CHAMPIONS

Competing well and winning mean more than simply beating the other competitors. First of all, champions believe that their efforts are worthy regardless of whether they win or lose. Second, if you win when your opponents perform well, your accomplishment is worth more than if you win when your opponents perform poorly. An important side effect of this attitude is that athletes can focus all their attention on their own performance rather than on their opponents'. Such a focus increases the likelihood of performing well. Tough-minded athletes try to succeed rather than try to avoid mistakes. Coaches should continually teach their athletes not to be afraid of making mistakes. If mistakes are made, learn from them rather than holding back to avoid errors. John Wooden, the famous basketball coach of UCLA, once said that "mistakes are the building blocks of success!"[2] Athletes learn whether to believe this attitude or not based on how their coach reacts to their mistakes in practices and competitions.

PLAN FOR THE UNEXPECTED

Many athletes and coaches feel that if something unexpected happens at a competition, nothing could have been done to prevent it. Nothing could be further from the truth! Since the unexpected can be expected to happen no matter how much planning has occurred, athletes and coaches might as well prepare for the unexpected. For example, being late for a meet can occur as a result of unexpected traffic, a flat tire, or getting lost because of poor directions. Given such possibilities, those who leave a few minutes earlier for an important meet are planning for the unexpected. If the unexpected does not happen, the athletes simply arrive early and have extra time to prepare. To prepare for the unexpected, many athletes carry an "emergency kit" to competitions. It contains an extra of everything that is absolutely essential for them to compete. For example, a young, female gymnast may have a backup copy of her music, an extra pair of already broken-in hand grips, and an extra leotard in case any of these items are lost, broken or stolen.

TEACH FOCUS AND CONCENTRATION

Many coaches ask athletes to focus and concentrate without teaching it. Concentration has many teachable aspects. It is not a single dimension. First, it is **degree of alertness.** Alertness has to do both with degree of arousal and attention to the specific task the athlete is preparing to do. Second, concentration is **attending to cues.** As athletes concentrate, they focus on cues that allow them to perform. Inexperienced athletes frequently pay attention to too many cues, too few cues, irrelevant cues, or cues occurring too late in a sequence of sport moves to allow the athlete to make any significant adjustments. To the extent that coaches can teach their athletes **to focus on fewer, earlier, and more relevant cues,** the athletes are more likely to successfully complete the task. Coaches should assess whether the athlete is attending to the crucial cues. An inability to attend to crucial cues may signal arousal levels that are too high for optimal performance. A simple illustration of this process might occur in high jumping where a beginner focuses almost predominately on the raised crossbar while the more experienced performer focuses on the ideal takeoff point where the foot is planted. A strong push-off with the leg in the correct position is more important for success than watching the crossbar.

Concentration often involves **shifting one's focus to the appropriate cues or task.** Athletes who have difficulty concentrating often focus too long on errors and/or the emotional feelings that result from such errors (frustration, anger, embarrassment, disappointment). Athletes who have been taught that mistakes are part of learning and are necessary for success are less likely to react as emotionally to errors as do athletes who have constantly been criticized for making mistakes. Athletes should practice shifting their focus from errors back to the task at hand in preparation for competition. Shifting focus can also be an important part of a sports skill. A soccer player can focus on the kinesthetic feel of kicking a pass and almost simultaneously shift his focus externally to see the accuracy of that pass.

A characteristic of intense concentration is an **athlete's ability to block out distractions.** Athletes who have practiced under noisy conditions, in front of a large crowd, or with the same or similar equipment as used in the competition are less likely to be distracted. Finally, concentration can also be viewed as **paying attention to what to do** rather than worrying about what not to do. The focus is on succeeding rather than avoiding failure.

TEACH VISUAL IMAGERY

Imagery skills are essential tools for mental toughness. Imagery can be used to picture success, eliminate errors and plan for contingencies. Effective imagery is more than a picture. It involves using all the senses (sight, hearing, kinesthesis, touch, and smell) to increase the **vividness** of an image. Effective imagery also involves **controllability**. For instance, speeding up or slowing down the image of a pitched ball while swinging the bat.

There are two major types of imagery. **External imagery:** The athletes picture themselves as if they were watching themselves on a DVD or video. **Internal imagery:** The athletes see only what they normally would see if they were actually performing a skill or playing a game. To date, there is no clear evidence showing that one form of imagery is superior to the other although external imagery may be more useful with experienced athletes with open skills such as karate and rock climbing[3]. External imagery may also be more useful for learning new skills regardless of the type of sport. Internal imagery seems to be more useful for developing strategies regardless of the type of sport. However, more research is necessary before a clear picture can emerge of when and how one technique is superior over the other. On purely logical terms, coaches tend to use external imagery to correct errors of form and technique while they favor internal imagery when rehearsing skills or preparing immediately before competition.

For mental toughness training, teach both **"idealized performance" and "what if . . ." imagery.** Some athletes prefer to visualize a perfect performance. Others athletes prefer to visualize using an "if . . ., then . . . " approach. "If my opponent goes right, then I go right also." "If the pitch is to the outside, then I'll drive the ball to the opposite field." Responding quickly and effectively to contingencies is a major component of mental toughness. Self-confidence produces quick, unhesitating choices in rapidly changing sport settings.

The Functions of Imagery

Traditionally, imagery has been used for a variety of purposes:

- **Visualize idealized performances.** This type of imaging is used to enhance self-confidence and as a preparation immediately before the actual physical execution of sport skills to increase the likelihood of an optimal performance.

- **"What if ..." imagery.** Athletes often have to make split-second decisions. Should I pass the soccer ball to the forward making the breaking run or pass across the field to spread the defensive players? Should I throw for the easy out at first base or should I throw to second in an attempt to make a more difficult, but more desirable double play?

- **Rehearsal of physical skills.** When athletes are tired or injured, mental imagery can be used to literally practice their physical routines in their heads to improve their motor skills without risking further injury or fatigue.

- **Error correction.** External imagery is used to examine the athletes' performances to identify and correct errors. Furthermore, some athletes actually visualize mistakes. Visualizing success takes practice. If errors are pictured, have the athlete visually erase the picture and start again. Another strategy, when errors are pictured, is to instruct the athlete to identify exactly where the error started. Stop the mental image at that point, correct the error, and then continue the visualization.

- **Emotional imagery.** Imagery is used to experience and learn to cope with strong emotions that can help or hinder performance. Learning to feel, yet keep anger or exhilaration under control, helps avoid performance deterioration. Athletes who believe they are stronger when feeling angry have actually been shown to lose strength unless they keep the intensity of their emotions at a moderate rather than an extreme intensity.[4]

- **Gain the feel of skill execution.** Internal imagery is used to emphasize the kinesthetic feel and feedback of high-level skill performance.

- **To learn new skills.** Visualize the performance of a new, yet to be performed skill. Such imagery requires that the athletes draw on similar but different experiences – e.g., performing a simple backward roll on the tumbling floor may be used to transfer the upside down rolling sensation with a new but similar sensation of somersaulting in the air as a back salto is performed by a novice gymnast. The image of performing a right-handed layup in basketball can provide the information for imaging a left-handed layup.

General Guidelines for Teaching Imagery

Beginning imagery exercises should emphasize activities that are quite familiar to the athletes (e.g., image the furniture in their bedrooms). Team exercises can start with a scene that is common to all players and then progress to scenes that are more individual to a player's position. Start by assuming a comfortable position in a quiet place free from distractions. Imaging can be done with eyes closed or open at the discretion of the athletes. Imagery is quite straightforward. Many of your young athletes may already image as they practice their favorite moves "in their heads." Your instructions merely guide them to incorporate **all the senses** into their image, creating as realistic a perception as possible. Also, suggest they practice **controlling the image** (e.g., See the ball moving faster, slower or in real time).

As your athletes become comfortable with visualizing familiar skills, encourage them to individualize the images around the specific playing positions (e.g., offensive lineman vs. wide receiver in football; backstroke start in the water vs. butterfly stroke in swimming). Encourage your athletes to image those skills they wish to improve or perform under competitive pressure. With interactive sports such as wrestling, basketball, and soccer, suggest they image "what if ..." situations where they must mentally react to varying moves of their opponents.

In self-paced activities, such as a foul shot in basketball or a pitched ball in baseball, have them focus on the internal sensations so that they can replicate those feelings during their actual physical performances. Suggest they image executing their skills while in those competitive situations that they are likely to experience; e.g., hearing the fans in the background, hearing your teammates calling for the ball when they are open for a shot in soccer or basketball, hearing the referee's whistle. Suggest that your athletes practice imaging in their "down time" just before going to bed or when they are relaxing in the car as their parents drive them to or from practice.

Do not be surprised if some of your athletes describe negative imagery; they see themselves repeating errors or performing poorly. This is not uncommon during the initial stages of learning to image. Have them "freeze frame" the error as if it were on a tape. Then have them back up the image until they reach the point at which the error occurs mentally, then visually correct the error and move on through the performance sequence.

From the Chalkboard to the Playing Field

VISUAL IMAGERY FOR BASEBALL

Internal Imagery

Ask your athletes to image catching a thrown ball. Direct their attention first to the picture of the ball itself. Can they **see** the seams on the ball as it spins toward them? Can they **hear** the smack of the ball in their glove as they catch the ball? Can they **feel** (sense) the impact of the ball through the glove as it is caught either in the webbing of the glove (their wrists are pulled back) or in the pocket of the glove (the mild sting in the palm of their hand)? Can they **smell** the leather and/or the dust that puffs up from the leather glove after the impact of the ball? Can they sense their fingertips **touching** the seams on the ball as they retrieve the ball from the glove as they prepare to throw the ball to the first baseman?

Ask them to repeat the image, but this time have them imagine a slower, change-up pitch. Repeat this process asking them to image a fast ball straight down the middle. Again, ask if they can see the seams rotating as the ball travels toward their glove. Can they speed up or slow down the ball's rotation as it flies toward them? You are asking them to practice their **controllability** of the image.

After they have practiced such imagery to the point that they report a realistic image, have them individualize the image. An outfielder can image a fly ball or a bouncing single that he retrieves and throws to the cut-off man. The first baseman can image the third baseman's throw and his trapping the ball on one hop from the dirt just in front of first base, then the ball catching in the webbing of his glove. The second baseman can image running to second, stepping on the bag as he receives a ball flipped from the shortstop, and then pivoting and throwing to first after the force play at second.

External Imagery

Suggest that your athletes picture a batter at the plate swinging the bat as part of the warm-up in preparation for stepping into the batter's box. Ask them to picture the pitcher pitching a fast ball. Encourage them to see the swing of the bat as the batter makes contact with the ball, driving it on a line drive to the shortstop who snags it chest high, plants his feet quickly and makes a long, low throw to first where it is caught by the first baseman who stretches out in a long stride toward the ball to catch the ball just an instant before the runner crosses the bag. Encourage them to see the action moving in real time emphasizing their **control** of the image.

VISUAL IMAGERY FOR SWIMMING

Internal Imagery

Ask your swimmers to image themselves standing on the starting blocks just before the start of the race. Can they *see* the calm water settling in the pool between the lane guides just below and in front of them? Can they *smell* the scent of chlorine as they lean forward into their starting position? As they bend over to grip the starting blocks for the take-off, can they feel their fingertips *touching* the undersurface of the starting block and the nonskid texture of the surface of the starting block on the soles of their bare feet? Can they *hear* the crack of the starter's gun (or the horn)? Can they feel the pressure on their feet against the starting block as they explode into the jump start? Can they feel the shock of the cold water as they hit the water? Can they *sense* the kinesthetic contractions of their back and abdomen muscles as they use the dolphin kick under water before rising to the surface to take their first stroke? (Figure 3.4)

FIGURE 3.4. Effective visualization is more than a picture. It involves feeling the nonskid surface of the starting blocks under your feet; feeling the muscular tension in your fingers and arms as you grip the block; hearing the starter's gun; smelling the chlorine as well as picturing the water in front of you and anticipating the shock when you hit the cold water.

External Imagery

Ask your swimmers to mentally image a flip turn. Encourage them to visualize the swimmer approaching the wall. Have them note just how far away from the wall she begins her flip turn, pivoting her body underwater so she can thrust off the wall with both legs into an undulating dolphin kick that brings her to the surface so she can begin her first stroke off the wall. Hear the "slap" of the water as her legs finish the flip turn. See if you can control her velocity by speeding her up as she nears the wall and executes the flip turn faster and faster on each imaging attempt.

VISUAL IMAGERY FOR FOOTBALL

Internal Imagery

Ask your players to image a clean hit as they block an opponent. **See** the opponent moving toward you and then stepping into him to initiate the contact. **Feel** the impact on your shoulder pads as you drive the opposing player backward. **Sense** the kinesthetic sensations of driving your legs against the ground as you come up under his ribs with your shoulder. **Hear** the smack of the pads and hear him grunt as your shoulder impacts his chest. **Smell** the grass as your body drops to the ground after the block and your face mask slides along the ground. **Taste** the plastic mouth guard as you bite down on it at impact.

External Imagery

Watch the receiver line up at the line of scrimmage. Listen to the count from the quarterback and hear the linemen lunge forward at the snap count. Watch the receiver sprint toward the defensive back, feint to the inside, and then quickly move to the sideline, turning to see the ball as the quarterback leads the receiver slightly with the throw that hits the receiver in his hands while he is tackled by the defensive back followed by both players falling to the ground. Hear the crowd in the background cheer as the receiver holds onto the ball after literally bouncing off the ground with the defensive back on top of him. Can you repeat this image **controlling** the image with greater speed and force?

VISUAL IMAGERY FOR SOCCER

Internal Imagery

Ask your players to image a running shot on goal with the ball on the ground rolling a few steps in front of you. **See** the seams of the ball as it rotates on the ground. **Feel** yourself planting your support leg beside the ball so you can shoot a strong, low shot. **Sense** the kinesthetic extension of your thigh muscles in your support leg as you swing the shooting leg toward the ball. **Hear** the impact of your leather shoe against the ball. **Smell** the air as you inhale while you watch the line of flight as the ball flies to the side of the far goal post. Encourage the player to **control** the image of the ball circling away from the goalie as it flies toward the inside of the goal post.

External Imagery

Suggest that your players watch a defensive player marking an offensive player who is dribbling the ball. See the defensive player mark the offensive player on the inside, forcing the attacker toward the sideline away from the goal. Watch the defensive player as he feints multiple attempts to tackle the ball. Just as the attacker touches the ball on the last dribble, the defender makes his move, stepping in and blocking the ball. Watch it ricochet off the defender's foot and fly back past the attacking player. The defender steps around the attacker and controls the ball quickly passing it to one of two fellow defenders who have come up from behind to provide support to the original defender. Encourage your athletes to repeat this image but increase the speed at which the action takes place, thus **controlling** the pace of the image.

Coaching Strategies During the Competition

On the day of competition, athletes should be expected to perform only those skills that are already well learned. Competition is not the time for improving partially learned skills or learning new skills. Very little, if any, coaching of technique should occur. Reminders of previously well-rehearsed techniques should be offered basically as a method of calming an athlete by giving them a familiar focus.

The coach's goal should be to make the athletes as comfortable as possible in the competitive setting so that they can perform well-learned sports skills as well as possible. Coaches who attempt to further refine skills on the day of competition are likely to disrupt the performance of their athletes during the warm-ups and the competition. Learn the art of "under coaching" during competition. Your focus is on the mental factors: goals, optimal level of arousal, flow, error recovery, and grit.

COACH "WHAT TO DO" AS OPPOSED TO "WHAT NOT TO DO."

Goals provide a clear direction for success strategies. Rather than saying "Don't chase the ball," say "Guard your man." Rather than saying "Don't lose control of the puck," say "push the puck slowly." Rather than saying "Don't foul your opponent," say "Guard him loosely by staying at least 3 feet away from him if he drives to the basket."

HELP ATHLETES ATTAIN THEIR OPTIMAL LEVEL OF AROUSAL

Each athlete has an optimal level of arousal for maximizing sports performance. Arousal above or below this optimal point causes poorer performance. Merely "psyching up" an athlete may actually cause poorer performance if the athlete is already excited or nervous about the upcoming competition. Young, inexperienced athletes are typically quite excited as they enter their first competitions and rarely need to be "psyched up." Coaches can often help their athletes by providing a calming atmosphere just prior to competition. A reassuring word, a reminder of an already well-learned technique, or just the presence of the coach can help bolster an inexperienced athlete's confidence.

On the other hand, athletes who have competed frequently or who are playing a decidedly inferior opponent may be candidates for increased arousal. Also athletes who need explosive power in relatively simple sports (short sprints, shot put) may benefit from being aroused. Arousal is a very individual matter. Three major factors determine optimal level of arousal: task difficulty, degree of learning, and ability of the athlete.

- **Task difficulty.** Complex tasks have a narrower range of optimal arousal. Complexity is often determined by the amount of information the athlete must process or by the margin of error possible. For example, the goalie in a soccer or ice hockey game should not become too aroused because he must be constantly aware of the oncoming ball or puck as well as the position of other offensive players. A gymnast has a more complex task on the balance beam than on the floor exercise because her margin of error on the narrow beam is smaller than on the floor exercise mat. Simpler tasks, especially those requiring explosive efforts (e.g., short sprints, throwing the shot put or a softball), have a broader range, often at higher levels of arousal.

- **Degree of learning.** Under pressure, well-learned tasks are performed better while partially learned tasks are often performed more poorly. The "clutch performer" is typically an athlete who has a high level of proficiency under conditions of low arousal and who has had many experiences performing under the same or similar conditions as that in which the clutch performance occurred. It is poor coaching strategy to expect an athlete to "come through under pressure" when attempting skills that are only partially learned. Furthermore, athletes under the pressure of competition will quite often choose skills, techniques or strategies that are well-learned and familiar. Thus, in competition, athletes frequently revert to "bad habits" that had been recently eliminated in practice because the athlete is still more familiar with them than with the newer, more correct skills. Unfortunately, the coach may think that the athlete has "choked" or that such regression is inevitable. Such is not the case. Regression is common in the learning of physical skills. The problem should be attacked by increasing the athlete's degree of learning and familiarity with the skill. Do not fall prey to the common coaching error which labels such predictable regression by novices as "choking." (See Appendix 3.1 for an in depth analysis on choking and strategies for combatting choking.)

- **Ability of the athlete.** A difficult task becomes even more difficult in relative terms for an athlete of lesser ability. Thus, other things being equal, higher levels of arousal will be more disruptive to athletes of lesser ability. Nonetheless, performance of lesser skilled athletes can be quite high if arousal levels are lowered, if degree of learning is high, and if the athlete feels comfortable in the competitive situation.

FLOW

Telling athletes to concentrate on concentrating is almost certain to disrupt their performance. With well-learned skills, the athlete would be better advised simply to "do it!" Flow describes total involvement in performance in which there is very little conscious thinking yet there is an awareness of simply doing what the athlete is prepared to do. Clearly, prior preparation has much to do with this sensation, but so does simply telling the athlete to just go and do what he or she has trained for, with little emphasis on thinking. Such concentration with well-learned skills is clearly different from the concentration necessary for learning new skills.

RECOVERING FROM AND ACCEPTING ERRORS

Mentally tough competitors see errors as a natural, even necessary, part of performing. Accepting errors is neither lowering one's standards nor accepting sloppiness but rather a realization that errors are part of "going for it." A .300 hitter in baseball is out 70% of the time. Mentally tough competitors disguise errors whenever possible. Some errors are obvious and cannot be disguised. However, in some sports, errors only become obvious because of the actions of the athlete. Falling off a balance beam cannot be hidden, but going beyond the intended full pirouette certainly can. The gymnast who grimaces, hesitates, and then abruptly returns to the ending position of the full pirouette tells the judge in no uncertain terms that a mistake was made. The gymnast who follows through to the one and one-quarter turn position with a flowing motion of her arms hides the fact that only a full turn was originally planned.

ACT "AS IF . . . "

"Never let 'em see ya sweat!" "Fake it 'til you make!" As simple and as long-standing as these phrases are, they are the backbone of mental toughness. People live up to and down to expectations. That statement is true both for the athlete and the opponents. Head up, shoulders high, and "look 'em in the eyes" regardless of your internal feelings. Competition is fun! That's what we worked for all season.

Coaching Strategies After the Competition

You can often make a substantial impact on the mental style of your athletes immediately after a competition. A perceptive coach can use the post-competitive period to teach the athletes about mental toughness and competing well.

USE SPECIFIC EXAMPLES FROM THE COMPETITION TO TEACH ABOUT COMPETING OR TRAINING

Immediately after a competition, events – both good and bad – are still fresh in the young athlete's mind. While coaches should avoid an "I told you so" approach, often mistakes made in competition can be related to poor practice behaviors, and corrections can be pointed out for the next practice session. Athletes who have done particularly well can be praised and told that such performance will be expected in practice.

GUIDE THE ATHLETES' ATTRIBUTIONS TOWARD BELIEFS THAT SUSTAIN OR INCREASE EFFORT

Athletes make judgments about what has caused their successes or failures in practices and competitions. These judgments are called **attributions.** Regardless of whether or not attributions are factually correct, they have a powerful effect on an athlete's subsequent behavior. Attributions that my success was caused by my high ability and/or my stable effort typically produce sustained or increased effort in subsequent similar situations. Attributions that my success was due to poor performance by an inferior opponent or by a lucky bounce of the ball typically produce little change and may even reduce effort. Attributions that my failure was due to my low, unchangeable ability or by a task that is simply too difficult for me also may lead to reduced effort. On the other hand, if my failure is attributed to bad luck or my own lack of effort, subsequent attempts may show sustained, higher levels of effort.

Attributions are influenced greatly by an athlete's goal orientation.[*] Goal orientations are learned attitudes that represents one's perception of what constitutes success. What an athlete defines as success may differ substantially depending upon their type of goal orientation.[5] A Performance Oriented Athlete (PO) sees success as evidence of self-improvement (I have become competent; therefore, I am successful). PO athletes see defeats in competitive sport as resulting from not yet having learned the necessary skills, not as a lack of ability. Athletes with a Success Orientation (SO) define success as ranking high. Such an orientation appears positive at first but rank can often be affected by factors outside the athlete's control, for example, the skill of the opponents or graduating to an older age group. SO athletes typically have had substantial competitive successes relative to their age-group peers and, therefore, expect

---

[*]The implications of these three different goal orientations on goal setting are examined in greater detail in Chapter 5 (Goal Setting).

themselves to be successful. That expectation is relative stable but often results in them selecting only opponents or tasks in which they have a reasonable expectation of succeeding. They may be reluctant to seek out higher, more challenging competition, an important trait for mental toughness. A Failure Orientation (FO) is also based upon rank; but, because of a past history of poor performances and little success, the FO athlete is likely to be more concerned with avoiding failure than with attempting to succeed.

Each of these styles just described can be substantially influenced by the athlete's prior history of success, whether they are in competition or practice and their expectancy of success. Thus with both SO and FO athletes, coaches should attempt to guide their focus to self-improvement and task mastery rather than rank. With SO athletes, the emphasis can be on the fact that skill improvement, while not the sole determinant of competitive placements, often leads to higher rank. On the other hand, with FO athletes who tend to avoid challenges, the coach can attempt to help the athlete recognize that ability is changeable. That is, ability is a skill that can be improved with sustained effort rather than an innate talent that is relatively unchangeable. Guiding the direction of such attributions can have substantial and positive effects on persistent, intensity and direction of the athlete's efforts, i.e., mental toughness.

Mentally tough athletes believe that their efforts make a difference. They believe their decisions, their planning and their behavior have a strong impact on the competitive outcomes. Further, they also understand that "bad" things can happen despite their best effort but they realize the "bad" will eventually pass if they keep on working hard. They don't make excuses as in "It wasn't my fault," but understand that losses can happen despite one's best effort. What separates the mentally tough from the less resilient athlete is the acceptance that the losses are likely to be temporary if they keep on striving for success. Athletes who lack mental toughness tend to interpret negative outcomes as a lack of ability resulting in subsequent lowered effort.

While the athletes' orientations are not directly under the coach's control, especially in the short run, over time, coaches can encourage a performance orientation by reinforcing the idea that ability is changeable and efforts leads to changes in skill. Table 3.2 describes attributions that athletes are likely to make naturally after wins and losses.

Coaches can help guide the attributions of those young athletes to "causes" that increase the probability of effort rather than "causes" that typically reduce effort (Figure 3.5). The following examples illustrate what a coach might say to young athletes to guide them toward making effective attributions.

TABLE 3.2 Predicted Personal Attributions Following Success or Failure

Athlete's Style	Following Success	Following Failure
Performance Oriented	High Effort (Ability Assumed)	No Perception of Failure (Just haven't learned it yet)
Success Oriented	Internal, Stable (Confirms belief in high ability)	Internal, Unstable (Low effort, poor preparation)
Failure Oriented	External, Uncontrollable (Got lucky; easy opponent)	Internal, Stable (Confirms belief in low ability)

FOLLOWING LOSSES

Focus on: Personal Control of Unstable Effort

"Had we hustled more, we could have won." "They outhustled us today. Let's learn from that!"

Focus on: Skill as Changeable

"They were better than we were today, but we're getting better; wait until the rematch!"

Shift the focus away from: Ability, Negative Personal Traits

"Don't let anyone tell you that you can't!"
"What we lack in size, we more than make up for in . . . " (hustle, savvy, grit, etc.)."

FOLLOWING WINS

Focus on: Positive Personal Traits

"I'm proud of you. You never quit!"
"You hustled just like you're capable of! With effort like that we can play with the best!"

FIGURE 3.5 What you discuss with your athletes after a competition can guide their attributions and be as important or even more important than what is discussed before a competition.

Shift the focus away from: Luck

"We got all the breaks today! But we can't depend on such good luck in the future. Athletes who hustle make their own breaks!"

Shift the focus away from: Easy Tasks

"Those guys weren't very good today, but don't be misled. The next time they'll have nothing to lose and everything to gain. They could be our most dangerous opponent if we take them for granted."

TEACHING RESPONSIBILITY AS OPPOSED TO BLAME

Finally, mentally tough coaches and athletes **assume responsibility but not blame for their performances.** Assuming responsibility means you take steps beforehand to compete better. Assuming blame involves remorse about not performing well after the competition has ended when there is nothing you can do about it. Changing the past is impossible! Taking responsibility means preparing ahead of time by controlling those factors that are controllable and are likely to influence performance on the day of competition. Developing mental toughness is determined, in large part, by what you do prior to the competition. Even "coming through in the clutch" is influenced by prior preparation.

CHAPTER REFERENCES

1. Vealey, R. (2007). Mental skills training in sport. In Tenenbaum, G, & Eklund, R.C. (Eds.), Handbook of sport psychology 3rd ed. pp. 287-309). Hoboken, NJ: Wiley

2. Wooden, J. (2009). *Coach Wooden's pyramid of success playbook.* (Baker Publishing Group: Ada, MI

3. Yu, Q., Fu, A. S. N., Kho, A., Li, J., Sun, X., & Chan, C. C. H. (2016). Imagery perspective among young athletes: Differentiation between external and internal visual imagery. *Journal of Sport and Health Science, 5*(2), 211-218.

4. Murphy, S. M. (1985). Emotional imagery and its effects on strength and fine motor skill performance. Doctoral dissertation. Rutgers University. New Brunswick, NJ.

5. Burton, D., Gillham, A., Weinberg, R., Yukelson, D., & Weigand, D. (2013). Goal setting styles: Examining the impact of personality factors on the goal setting practices of prospective Olympic athletes. *Journal of Sport Behavior, 36,* 23-44.

Positive Discipline and Young Athletes[1]

CHAPTER OUTLINE

- Preventing Discipline Problems
- Coach's Personal Style and Attitude
- An Ounce of Prevention . . . Doesn't Always Work
- Analyzing the Problem
- Empathetic Strictness
- The Reward-Punishment Connection
- Positive Discipline Techniques
- Is There a Best Way?
  YOUR TURN: What Positive Discipline Techniques Do You Use?
- The Ripple Effect

The word discipline often elicits images of punishment, raised voices and the use of power to control the misbehavior of subordinates. But the "drill sergeant" image of demanding "good behavior" is only a very small part of a well-disciplined program.

You can have a huge impact on molding the character of young athletes by cultivating within each athlete a personal sense of responsibility for their own actions – in other words, self-discipline. The overriding theme should be to encourage in each athlete the development of a sense of self-discipline that ultimately places the responsibility for self-control and discipline on the shoulders of the athlete. Coaching provides many such opportunities for teaching self-discipline, and many of the techniques discussed in this chapter can help to instill it. Athletes who understand the consequences of their actions are more likely to behave responsibly. Responsibility is not blame or guilt. Rather, responsibility is an important character trait that helps athletes to understand that their ability to make good choices permits them to exert some degree of control over the consequences – both positive and negative – of those choices.

This chapter looks at a variety of positive discipline techniques realizing that there is no single best method of cultivating discipline. However, a number of principles, when properly applied, can have a positive influence on the effectiveness of your coaching. Your choice of techniques should vary depending upon the circumstances. Misbehaviors are rarely directed at the coach personally. Coaches who see their role as one of developing athletes and facilitating their growth and maturity will see the techniques of positive discipline as important strategies for assisting their athletes rather than as a tool for keeping those athletes "in line".

Preventing Discipline Problems

Pre-empting discipline problems is preferable to solving such problems after they have disrupted practice, agitated the coach, or undermined team morale.

WELL PLANNED PRACTICES

The most effective way to deal with disciplinary problems is to prevent their occurrence.

A well-planned practice is a major factor in providing a disruption-free learning environment. The more interesting and productive the workout, the less likely you are to experience disciplinary problems. Practice sessions should be geared to the athletes' needs and interests, and the assignments should match their ability levels. Tasks that are either too easy or too difficult result in boredom or frustration which, in turn, lead to behavioral problems. Stimulating, meaningful, learning tasks maintain involvement, often making disciplinary actions unnecessary. For example, mini-scrimmages in soccer using two to three players per team can be just as effective for cardiovascular conditioning as running wind sprints or laps and are much more likely to be fun and involving for young athletes.

Structure is important. With consistently structured practices, athletes learn to anticipate "What's next?" For example, after warm-ups will come individual drills, followed by one-on-one drills, followed by group drills, etc. Thus, they are much more likely to be in the right place at the right time than athletes whose practice rotations have been sporadic and unpredictable. Effective coaches try to find a balance between predictable, consistent practices vs. monotonous, boring repetitions.

SHARP STARTS

Perhaps the most important times during a workout are the first few minutes at the start of practice or the start of the next rotation or station. These few moments set the tone for the workout. Sharp starts, clear directions, and challenging, yet realistic assignments clearly stated during these initial moments decrease discipline problems simply by eliminating opportunities for horseplay, distractions, and boredom. Athletes standing in line reflect poor planning, with one major exception: standing in line after vigorous exercise when the coach has explicitly planned a rest period. Standing in line should not be the result of weak excuses such as, "There wasn't enough equipment." If you wish to teach your young baseball players to effectively steal second base by watching the pitcher from first base and learning to "take off" the instant the pitcher releases the ball, then place several carpet squares along the first base

FIGURE 4.1 When kids are aware that the coach is present and attentive, many discipline problems are pre-empted, especially when they know the coach expects them to live up to the standards of the team.

path to simulate bases and have several runners practice the takeoff simultaneously while watching the pitcher's motion. Eliminating inactivity can substantially reduce discipline problems.

PROPER SUPERVISION

A public display of supervision also affects discipline and control. When athletes are aware the coach is watching, their behavior is more disciplined, especially if behavioral expectations have previously been clearly established by the coach. (Figure 4.1) Supervision also permits a greater awareness of potential discipline problems before they actually occur. Pre-emptive interventions can occur before minor disruptions become major and require disciplinary action. Recognizing that athletes have started clowning around, identifying inactivity and boredom, or observing that a drill is not working as planned, all allow early interventions if the coach maintains continual alert general supervision. Coaches who become distracted with conversations with other coaches or with spectators fail to maintain proper supervision and often fail to detect the early warning signs leading to disruptive behavior by their athletes.

PROMPTING

"Practice is over! Let's gather up the equipment." Such prompts avoids having to scold athletes for walking away from practice without cleaning

FIGURE 4.2
Minimizing distractions avoids having to discipline young athletes for "not paying attention.

up. "Dressing time, five minutes," prompts the beginning of the physical workout without having to reprimand athletes for arriving late.

MINIMIZE DISTRACTIONS

Another potential obstacle is the presence of distractions within the environment. Practice sessions often occur in less than perfect situations. Several teams may share the same field or gymnasium. Even under the best of circumstances, the noise levels created by the presence of others and young athletes' natural inclination to "see what the other kids are doing" can present serious obstacles to the smooth functioning of a workout. While these obstacles cannot be completely removed, many of their effects can be minimized. For example, provide instruction by standing in such a position that the athletes have to turn their backs to the distraction to face you as the coach. (Figure 4.2.) If young basketball players are holding basketballs while you are providing instruction, have them sit on the balls or hold them in their laps, to prevent their natural response of bouncing the balls instead of focusing on your instructions.

COACH PROXIMITY

Another factor with a major effect on athlete behavior is the coach's proximity to the athletes. Many problems can be corrected or entirely avoided by simply adjusting one's physical location. Moving closer to athletes whose attention has wandered often helps them refocus their attention to the desired learning task. Coaches should always try to position themselves in such a manner that the entire group is within their field of vision. Maintaining an atmosphere of control and careful supervision is one of the most effective methods of avoiding misbehavior.

RULES

Rules are necessary in all learning situations because they define the boundaries of acceptable behavior. The exact number and type of rules will vary with the team and the sport. Two points, however, are crucial: First, rules should be clear and concise. Regardless of whether the rules are arrived at democratically or autocratically, they should be simple and clearly understood by everyone involved. Second, the list of rules should be limited. There should be no more rules than absolutely necessary for the maintenance of a productive learning environment. Fewer rules are more likely to be fairly and consistently enforced. Use rules as standards to be lived up to rather than regulations to be enforced.

Involving your athletes in the development and enforcement of rules is desirable for two reasons: First, when young athletes have a part in developing rules, they are more likely to develop a sense of responsibility and self-direction, and second, athletes respond better to rules they have helped formulate.

The manner in which the rules are explained to the athletes is as important as the manner in which they were developed. While all rules should be explained verbally, recollection of such explanations tends to dim with time, especially with younger athletes. Thus, the provision of regular verbal reinforcement and posted written reminders is important. Safety rules and rules of conduct should be prominently and permanently posted.

Rules should, whenever possible, be expressed in positive terms. A soccer team's rule that simply states "Shin guards must be worn at all times," is more clear and concise than one that states "No one may participate in practice or games unless they are wearing shin guards." Lists of all the *don'ts* tend to create a feeling of oppression and restrictiveness. Lists of the *dos* provide the security of knowing what is expected. Posting what athletes are expected to do gives more guidance than listing those things they may *not do.*

Negotiable vs. Non-Negotiable Rules. Rules pertaining to safety and team values are often considered to be absolute – i.e., non-negotiable. A catcher's mask is to be worn when a player is catching behind the plate with a batter in the batting box – no exceptions! Treating team-mates with respect regardless of a player's skill level is expected at all times. Bullying and hazing are absolutely forbidden. These are examples of non-negotiable rules. There are certain circumstances where rules can and should be occasionally modified. During exam periods at school, attendance requirements at practice might be relaxed somewhat or the length of the training sessions might be reduced.

Coach's Personal Style and Attitude

What distinguishes successful from unsuccessful disciplinary approach-es often lies in the style of interaction between the coach and the ath-letes. This interaction is determined by both the coach's attitude toward himself and his attitude toward his athletes.

CONFIDENCE

The best coaches tend to feel comfortable and confident while coaching. While confidence is clearly a product of successful prior experiences, it is also related to the way that a coach perceives the athletes. Insecure coaches often perceive athletes as threats, problems, or intrusions. Con-fident coaches view their athletes as being basically good and capable of productive learning so long as their energies and interests are properly channeled. Such coaches select and develop coaching styles that meet the needs of the athletes yet still fit comfortably within the constraints imposed by the coaches' personalities and preferences.

The key to building self-confidence is not a belief that I, as a coach "need to know everything," but rather a belief that I am capable of improv-ing. "I may not know exactly what to do and how to behave on my first day of coaching – even after having read this book – but I can learn some-thing every day and tomorrow will be even more successful than today!"

Coaches should develop a variety of techniques for controlling and modifying athlete behaviors. Coaches who have multiple tools for deal-ing with discipline are likely to feel more confident. Such confidence in-creases the likelihood that a coach can relax and evaluate options in the midst of disruptions and, thus, be more likely to make effective choices.

FIGURE 4.3
Effective communication is more of an attitude than a specific skill or technique.

COMMUNICATION SKILLS

Effective communication is more of an attitude than it is specific communication techniques. (Figure 4.3.) Coaches whose attitudes reflect a desire to understand, an acceptance of others, and an expectation of mutual respect are likely to be perceived as effective communicators. Nonetheless, specific communication techniques such as active listening, assertiveness skills, body language, and knowing how to send unambiguous messages are extremely useful tools for enhancing communication effectiveness.

Effective communication is important not only because it permits the sending of accurate information but also because it tends to enhance the coach's credibility among the athletes. Coaches whose credibility is high tend to be sought out by athletes. Their approval and attention is seen as valuable. Thus, effective communicators have an effective disciplinary tool of withdrawing their attention and/or approval from those young athletes who misbehave. Such a withdrawal has little effect on athletes who do not see the coach's attention as valuable. Poor communicators often resort to yelling and harassment as a means of dealing with their athletes.

MODELING

Coaches are clearly primary role models for young athletes. Displaying self-control and composure when things go wrong (such as a controversial close call by an official that goes against you) serves as a powerful example of proper behavior. Athletes who exhibit such self-control and composure tend to have fewer errors and fewer penalties in high-pressure situations where becoming flustered undermines performance and hinders decision making.

An Ounce Of Prevention...Doesn't Always Work

Despite concerted efforts to prevent discipline problems, some athletes will, on occasion, misbehave. When this occurs, the coach is usually faced with two distinct challenges. First, order must be restored, and second, the cause of the problem must be eliminated or dealt with to prevent a recurrence of the same or similar misbehavior. Some actions that curtail misbehavior in the short run may, in the long run, actually encourage offenders to repeat those inappropriate behaviors. A sarcastic comment may immediately stop an athlete's clowning behavior, but the embarrassment and resentment from such a public humiliation may well produce additional misbehavior by athletes who hold a resentment or who attempt to regain status in the eyes of teammates. Before selecting and implementing disciplinary actions, effective coaches analyze the problem – that is, think before you act!

Analyzing the Problem

There are two major categories of misbehavior. An individual either does something that has been prohibited or fails to do something that has been required. In either case, the alternative solutions must be based upon the probable cause(s) of the problem.

IS THE APPROPRIATE BEHAVIOR POSSIBLE?

The first question should be, "Is the desired behavior within the capacity of the child?" When the answer to this question is no, then disciplining your young athletes will not solve the problem and should not even be considered. Expecting 6-year-olds to work independently on drills and skills for any extended length of time is unrealistic. However, 8-year-olds can be taught independence skills using progressions just as would be done when teaching physical sport skills. Having 8-year-olds stretch for 20 minutes by themselves with only general supervision is normally thought to be unrealistic. However, by using progressions, such behavior can be successfully taught. Have them stretch for 2 minutes by them-selves using drills that they are familiar with, followed the next week with 5 minutes, followed ultimately by 20 minutes of such independent work. While general supervision is always required for liability and safe-ty reasons, the use of such progressions can develop behavior that would normally not be expected until the athletes were significantly older and more mature.

IS THE MISBEHAVIOR REWARDING?

Strange as it may sound at first, some young athletes may find the atten-tion they receive for misbehaving so satisfying that they are willing to tolerate whatever punishment may be imposed. In such cases, again the strategy is conceptually quite simple: Remove the rewards. Unfortunate-ly, simple does not always translate as easy. For example, other members of the team may be rewarding the negative behavior. Moreover, when inappropriate behavior results in an increased social status within the team, the punishment from the coach is often ineffective and may actu-ally increase the status of the offender. Solutions lie in modifying the attitude of the team members so that team members, as a group, tend to discourage rather than reward behavioral problems. A team talk about the problem can help to develop desirable attitudes toward team disci-pline. A final possibility is that the coach's own reaction to the misbe-havior is rewarding. If a coach gets flustered, becomes involved in bick-ering, or exchanges sarcastic remarks, there is a strong likelihood that the coach can be unwittingly fostering misbehavior because some team members like the drama.

Perhaps the worst approach for dealing with misbehavior is to at-tempt to correct that misbehavior and fail. Coaches who set out to cor-rect a situation should not stop until they have succeeded. Coaches who say "Stop!" but fail to follow through until the behavior ceases are, in ef-fect, telling athletes that the directive is not going to be enforced. Young athletes will search for the *enforceable* behavioral limits, which may be quite different from the desired limits expressed by the coach.

WHAT CONDITIONS MAINTAIN THE MISBEHAVIOR?

In some situations, events preceding or following the behavior may actu-ally be fostering it. If two athletes who regularly sit together continually disrupt practice with horseplay, then separating them or selecting one of them to be coached one-on-one may substantially reduce the misbehavior displayed by both.

HAS SOMETHING BEEN OMITTED?

When a young athlete's behavior fails to meet the coach's expectations, the coach should investigate the possibility that some factor or factors beyond the athlete's control might be causing or contributing to the problem. For instance, the problem might be created because the athletes do not know what is expected of them. Have the rules of conduct been clearly defined? Have the rules been explained to the entire team? When was the last time the coach followed up the punishment of misbehavior with a statement outlining the behaviors that are expected? Are the rules posted to serve as a reminder? The answers to these and other similar questions could very well provide simple discipline solutions to many behavior problems.

Empathetic Strictness

Probably the single most important characteristic of successful youth sport coaches is empathy – an understanding and awareness of the situations experienced by young, developing athletes. Effective coaches help their athletes set high standards, that require strict self-discipline to achieve those high standards yet do so without becoming harsh, punitive taskmasters who appear insensitive to the needs and feelings of those young athletes. You can achieve the proper balance by incorporating the following three concepts into your coaching.

First, **present demands as opportunities.** Such an approach can dramatically affect whether athletes perceive these standards as positive or negative. The athletes' perceptions and feelings can greatly influence their acceptance of the coach's standards. Their reactions are likely to be more positive to a demand that states, "As soon as everyone is in position, we'll start the game;" as opposed to, "No one gets to play until everyone is in position!" The actual demand is identical in both cases but is presented as an opportunity in the first case and as a punishment in the second.

Second, **strictness does not preempt empathy.** Strictness involves clearly defined demands and then rewarding athletes only when those demands have been met. A coach can actively support and encourage an athlete to meet a demanding standard without lowering those standards. Having high and clear-cut standards is not incompatible with showing empathy or understanding the difficulties faced by the athlete. **Empathy, however, is not sympathy.** A coach can express concern for the athlete without expressing pity or condescension and without feeling badly that the athlete had a difficult challenge to meet. For example, an athlete who must make a fixed number of successful attempts before ending a daily practice may encounter difficulty with completing the assignment. An empathetic but demanding coach may express concern for the athlete's feelings but still require the successful completion of the assignment before permitting the practice to end, often providing extra assistance to the struggling athlete.

Third, **effective coaches distinguish between authority and authoritarianism.** The coach is the ultimate source of authority within the team and must retain the balance of power for maintaining a safe, effective learning environment. In fact, athletes often seek out such firm authority, particularly in situations where they are uncertain as to how to behave[2]. The selective use of power as a technique to help athletes overcome difficulties such as fatigue, fear, or uncertainty is often perceived as desirable by the athletes. The unilateral use of power and authority by the coach is sometimes necessary and desirable – for example, when safety is involved.

Nonetheless, effective coaches permit as much self-direction and sharing of authority as their athletes can effectively handle. The inflexible use of power without consideration for the athletes' needs for some personal control over their roles as athletes is a major cause of athlete resentment and rebellion. Strictness and high expectations are not the defining characteristics of authoritarianism; **inflexibility** is what sets authoritarianism apart from legitimate authority and discipline.

Consistency is not the automatic application of the same rule to every athlete regardless of the circumstances. Consistency is the similar application of a standard to similar athletes in similar situations regardless of whether that application is convenient or not or whether that application requires special efforts. For example, a coach who disciplines an athlete differently depending upon whether that athlete's parents are present is most likely inconsistent. On the other hand, a coach who gives an athlete who is unaware of a policy a second chance can be very consistent if that "second chance" policy is applied uniformly to all athletes who were originally unaware of a policy or team rule.

The Reward-Punishment Connection

Rewards and punishments are intricately related. If you can give something positive (a reward), you can also choose not to give it (a punishment when it is expected). If you can impose a sanction (a punishment), you can also remove that sanction (a reward). *Rewards and punishments are simply two different sides to the same coin.* (Figure 4.4.)

FIGURE 4.4
Rewards and punishments are simply two different sides of the same coin.

This point is important because positive reinforcement is sometimes mistakenly thought to be the essential aspect of a positive coaching program while punishment is thought to be part of a harsh or negative program. In actuality, **both reward and punishment are essential parts of positive instruction and both can be misused and, thus, be ineffective and negative.** Unearned praise and rewards can be just as disruptive in the long run to the development of a positive coaching climate as can harsh, inappropriate punishment.

Many parents and coaches believe that rewards are good and should be used while punishment is bad and should be avoided. However, punishment is a naturally occurring phenomenon that should not be ignored. Stubbing your toe tends to encourage you to look carefully where you walk. Not playing defense allows your opponent to score the winning goal.

From a coaching perspective, punishment involves the application of something unpleasant or the removal of something pleasant. As a general rule, punishment tends to bring about an immediate cessation of the unwanted behavior, but it may fail to eliminate or reduce the factors that prompted those behaviors. While punishment tends to stop unacceptable behaviors, it does not, in and of itself, give guidance concerning what type of behavior should replace the bad behavior. To be most effective, punishment should initially be accompanied by an explanation of why it is being imposed and what type of behavior is expected in the future. However, once the athletes fully comprehend the rationale, continued explanations of "why" are no longer useful.

Too much punishment tends to produce a general restriction of behavior, increased anxiety levels, and a hostile team climate. Coaches can avoid much unpleasantness by clearly distinguishing between punishable offenses and those that can be handled effectively in other ways. Also, effective coaches indicate clearly that the athlete's misbehavior is the focus of the displeasure, not the athlete himself.

Paradoxically, removing rewards that generated misbehaviors often increase that behavior temporarily. The absence of the expected reward produces rigorous attempts to regain the reward. Only when it becomes obvious the reward is "gone forever," does the undesired behavior subside. For example, a coach recognizes that his youngsters have been clowning around to gain his attention. To eliminate the inappropriate behavior, the coach withholds his attention; but rather than decreasing their horseplay, the athletes redouble their efforts in vain attempts to regain his attention before finally stopping the behavior.

THE EFFECTIVE USE OF PUNISHMENT

Punishment can be effective if the following guidelines are kept in mind:

1. It is most effective when it interrupts or immediately follows the undesirable behavior.
2. It should be applied with firmness and consistency.
3. Threats that cannot or will not be carried out are ineffective and should be avoided.
4. Vague references to some unspecified punishment are also ineffective.
5. Unless you can be sure that the entire team is responsible, mass punishment should be avoided. It tends to be unfair to non-offenders, offers no real educational advantage, and, despite the social pressure from teammates to conform, it often forces the coach and the team into adversary roles.
6. Exercise or extra work should rarely be used as punishment. Avoidance responses brought on by such punishment are frequently generalized to an entire activity, thereby undermining the enjoyment of the sport.
7. Avoid public censure. Vince Lombardi, the famous Green Bay Packers football coach, has been credited with saying: "Praise in public, punish in private." Embarrassment is the worst form of punishment and virtually guarantees resentment and/or rebellion.
8. Punishment for inappropriate behavior is most effective when rewards are simultaneously available for appropriate alternative behaviors that the athlete sees as producing the same results. For example, punishing the clowning behavior that had gained

recognition from teammates works better if the punishment is coupled with public praise from the coach for working hard at team-related drills.

Positive Discipline Techniques

Effective coaches have a variety of positive discipline techniques that they can draw on when the behavior of their athletes is disruptive.

"IF..., THEN..." CONTINGENCIES

These are simple but powerful conditions under which athletes can earn rewards or privileges. **If** we complete the drills, **then** we can scrimmage. **If** you sit quietly and maintain eye contact with me, **then** the instruction will start. **If** the assignment is completed within the allotted time, **then** you'll have free time to rest or work on something you'd like to improve. Effective contingencies involve more than merely dispensing rewards and punishments. The coach must have a clear idea of:

a. **What is the specific target behavior to be developed or eliminated.** Rather than telling your players if you hustle more, then we'll scrimmage, the target behavior should be expressed in more concrete terms such as, "If you finish 10 of these drills within the next 5 minutes, we'll scrimmage for the final 20 minutes of practice."

b. **What is the specific contingency; i.e., the "if..., then..." relationship.** "If you are dressed and ready to start at the designated time, then when you ask for help on a specific skill, I'll spend coaching time with you."

c. **What are the least intrusive rewards that are effective for that particular athlete or group of athletes.** A smile, a verbal acknowledgment, or a pat on the back are often more effective than an ice cream break that disrupts the continuity of the practice session.

"SEE ME AFTER"

If an athlete is misbehaving or clowning around during a team talk, rather than stop the meeting to discipline a single youngster, simply say to the offender, "Jimmy, see me after practice." First, you have acknowledged there is a problem so that Jimmy's teammates realize he is "not getting away with anything." Second, you are not forced to disrupt what you are doing with the athletes who are already behaving well. Third, Jimmy has just been placed on notice that his misbehavior is going to be dealt with at some point in the near future. He literally has to "sweat it out" until after practice before finding out what the consequences of his misbehavior will be.

TIME-OUTS

A time-out simply holds a youngster out of a desired activity for a short period of time. If, after a warning, a youngster is still disobeying or fooling around, he or she can be told to sit out for a brief period of time. Time-outs work only when the youngster wants to be involved with the activity. They don't work if the youngster is avoiding an activity because of fear, embarrassment, or shyness. In such cases, the time-outs can actually become a reward rather than a punishment. Likewise, for youngsters who are daydreaming, time-outs allow more of the same behavior. To be effective, time-outs should be brief with the athlete sitting off by herself in a relatively sterile environment where she can still be supervised by the coach but is no longer the center of attention. Time-outs are particularly effective for misbehavior that is reinforced by the presence of others. They are relatively ineffective for behaviors that are self-stimulating such as daydreaming or for negative behavior that serve as an escape from a boring task or a frustrating task beyond a young athlete's skill level.

TIME AND PLACE

Sometimes athletes display behaviors that are not permitted on the field but often occur in other settings such as the locker room where the coach's immediate supervision is not always possible or at home where the coach's supervision is not appropriate. If an athlete swears at practice or a game and if that behavior is unacceptable to you, that athlete can be brought to the sideline and told, "Perhaps swearing is permissible elsewhere, but in our practices, it is unacceptable." Often that approach is sufficient in and of itself to teach an athlete that such behavior is not tolerated in the team's practices. A reference to "our practices" can draw the athletes into the team's standards rather than simply having the coach's standards imposed upon him or her.

CONTINGENT PUNISHMENT

Contingent punishment, as the name implies, involves dispensing punishment contingent on the occurrence of the problem behavior. Just as with positive reinforcers, a number of factors influence the effectiveness of the punishment contingency. Punishment that is consistent, immediate, and clearly linked to the behavior is more effective than punishment that is inconsistent, delayed, or ambiguously related to the behavior. Punishment can appear in various forms: material (loss of candy), social (disapproval), activity (loss of the opportunity to participate in a favored activity), symbolic (demerits), and covert (shame or guilt). Just as with positive rewards, the nonmaterial punishments are usually more appropriate in most coaching settings.

WITHDRAWN ATTENTION

This technique focuses on the removal of a desired reinforcement whenever the athlete misbehaves. A coach who explicitly does not coach an athlete for a set period of time because the athlete was not prompt or failed to pay attention to instruction is teaching the athlete that misbehavior costs that athlete instructional time with the coach.

DIFFERENTIAL REINFORCEMENT

This technique refers to simultaneously giving positive reinforcement for the desired behavior while withdrawing reinforcement or applying punishment for the negative behavior. Frequently, undesired behavior has sources of reinforcement over which the coach has little or no control. Thus, differential reinforcement also exists when the coach attempts to counter the rewards for the misbehavior with more potent rewards for the desired behaviors. The application of differential reinforcement is one of the most powerful reinforcement tools at the coach's disposal. Differential reinforcement not only provides information about "what to do" and "what not to do" but also provides a contingent payoff for selecting the desired behavior and eliminating the misbehavior. Verbal praise for paying attention to detailed instructions coupled with the admonition that failure to focus will result in our doing that same drill again until it has been mastered illustrates differential reinforcement.

WHISPER AND WAIT

Surprise the athletes by speaking in a whisper, then pause briefly to gain their attention rather than constantly exhorting them to "Listen up!"

The change in volume and uncomfortable silence usually draws immediate attention to your instructions and athletes who cannot hear often "shush" teammates into paying attention.

PROMPT INCOMPATIBLE CHOICES

Give the athlete a choice of one or more activities that are incompatible with the misbehavior. If athletes are running around, not paying attention, ask "would you like to start with batting practice or fielding?" Offering two choices decreases the likelihood of their simply saying "No, we don't want to do that," and offers behaviors that preclude the misbehavior. As the coach, you can also prompt the decision making by saying, "You choose, or I'll choose for you."

Is There a Best Way?

Hopefully, this chapter's discussion of discipline makes clear that there is no single best way to approach behavioral problems and behavioral control. Because disciplinary approaches are subject to a wide range of variables, any given course of action or combination of approaches may work beautifully at some times for some coaches and fail miserably at other times when attempted by a different coach. Therefore, coaches should work consistently to develop multiple tools for controlling and modifying athlete behaviors. Having back-up plans provides you with multiple solutions, increasing your confidence that you can evaluate options and handle disruptions effectively.

When first meeting a new group of athletes, it is best to begin with a more authoritative approach and gradually increase the involvement of athletes as they demonstrate responsibility and self-control. The old maxim is quite true. Controls are easier to loosen than to tighten. Further, increased responsibility tends to be interpreted as a privilege to be enjoyed within definable limits. This is a comfortable experience for most athletes and one to which they usually respond favorably. Many new coaches fear that if they are strict in their approach to control they will not be liked. This is simply not true. Athletes will, in fact, often interpret the absence of sufficient control as failure of the coach to be in charge of the situation. The athletes then seek to establish their own limits of behavioral freedom, resulting in a very trying experience for both coaches and athletes alike.

YOUR TURN
What Positive Discipline Techniques Do You Use?

While lists concerning complex subjects rarely can be considered complete, lists can help simplify and organize what might otherwise be an overwhelming amount of material. Here are 20 simple guidelines that can influence discipline:

1. Establish your authority early. In other words, be prepared; know what you want done; confront discipline problems early before they get worse.

2. Relate in a warm, natural way, but **never** as a peer.

3. Get to know all of the athletes by name and develop an understanding of their individual and collective personalities as quickly as possible. The best coaching behaviors are those that are clearly directed at specific individuals.

4. Talk less. Keep in mind that while you are speaking, your athletes are less likely to be involved and participating. Furthermore, effective communication is based as much on effective listening skills as on verbal skills. Talk **with** your athletes not **at** them.

5. Avoid screaming. A firm, confident request or statement is usually far more effective than violent, threatening demands.

6. Avoid sarcasm. Show the same respect that you wish to receive.

7. Use corrective behaviors that are different from the ordinary. The greatest impact is usually achieved by such behaviors. Silence, a sharp command, a scowl, or a simple clap of the hands are all effective means of correcting misbehavior in the proper circumstance as long as they are not used repeatedly.

8. Try to view the problem from the athlete's frame of reference and always keep in mind the possibility that something you are doing may be the cause. Assume initially that there had to be a justifiable reason.

9. Avoid public criticism. Although public praise can be very effective, scolding an athlete in public is usually a poor choice of action.

10.   Develop a direct and sincere approach to praise. If an athlete is told what they did well and why, there is a greater likelihood that the approved behavior will be repeated. Do not give praise when it is undeserved. Praise must be an earned reward.

11.   Have a sense of humor but do not make learning a joke or use humor that is insulting to either yourself or the athletes.

12.   Be enthusiastic and encourage enthusiasm.

13.   Be fair with attention, praise, and opportunities. Fairness does not necessarily mean equal but rather that every athlete has an equal opportunity to earn such attention or praise within his or her skill or maturity level.

14.   Give your athletes your complete attention when you are speaking to them. Such attention is a sign of respect for both the athlete and what that athlete has to say. Those who wish to receive respect must be willing to give it.

15.   Say no without feeling guilty; say yes without feeling resentment. If you are uncertain what you wish to decide, say "I'll think about it and get back to you by..." Then follow through by the deadline.

16.   Do not be afraid to say "I don't know"; or "I made a mistake" when it is appropriate to do so. Acknowledging errors without being apologetic will usually enhance your credibility, not detract from it.

17.   Delegate responsibility in doses that your athletes can handle and from which they can learn. Most athletes will live up to your expectations if your expectations are based on a realistic assessment of their skills and maturity.

18.   Be predictable. Predictability does not mean that your behavior is always the same. It means that your reactions to your athletes' behavior is consistent.

19.   Be a model when it counts -- when there is pressure.

20. Discipline quickly and briefly without holding a grudge. Welcome the athlete back as an equal member of the team once the punishment has been administered.

Which of these 20 guidelines are already part of your coaching style? Which do you want to work on?

The Ripple Effect

The effects of a disciplinary action often go far beyond the particular athlete or athletes being disciplined and may affect the overall motivational climate of the entire team. The coach's style can have a profound influence on both the disciplined athletes and other team members. Good coaches set limits and recognize that positive control and positive discipline enhance rather than detract from the learning environment. Effective disciplinarians **act** rather than **react.** Positive discipline tends to increase the stature and respect of the coach in the eyes of the athletes. On the other hand, if the coach becomes visibly flustered and angry with a misbehaving athlete, the entire team is likely to become upset. Team members may perceive the coach as having lost some measure of control and the positive learning environment may, at least temporarily, be lost. If athletes feel publicly embarrassed, they may respond with face saving devices such as sarcasm or defiance even if done so out of sight of the coach. In such circumstances a ripple effect is set in motion affecting the entire team. Effective coaches maintain their dignity and poise while simultaneously allowing athletes to maintain their self respect. Team members who perceive the coach as fair minded and interested in their welfare will submit more readily to the coach's judgment and control and the ripple effect will tend to work in the coach's favor. (Figure 4.5.)

Respect cannot be demanded. It must be earned and continually nurtured. Without it, coaching can degenerate into a constant battle for situational control. If a public conflict appears unavoidable, assign the rest of the team another activity while dealing with the situation quietly, off to the side. On occasion, a coach may overreact or be unduly abrupt or unfair. If that has occurred, the coach should admit to the error. Attempting to hide the obvious or covering an error with a show of

FIGURE 4.5. Your
response to an
incident with one
athlete often has
repercussions for
the entire team.

FIGURE 4.5. Your response to an incident with one athlete often has repercussions for the entire team.

power diminishes the respect for the coach in the eyes of the athletes. Honesty and sincerity tend to increase it and, more importantly, prevent the ripple of bad feelings that sweeps through a team when one member is perceived as having been treated unjustly or too harshly.

Finally, the goal of good teachers and coaches is to help the athlete understand the natural, logical negative consequences of misbehavior. This development is an essential aspect of learning both self-discipline and an appreciation of rewards for appropriate behavior. Do the athletes recognize that benefits are likely to occur if rules and standards of behavior are upheld? Conversely, do they anticipate any negative consequences associated with noncompliance? In short, how will the athlete benefit? Is there a consistent system of reward and punishment? Effective coaches use a complementary blend of reward and punishment to guide athletes' behaviors toward productive and responsible behaviors.

CHAPTER REFERENCES

1. Much of the chapter is based on: Feigley, D. A. & Dougherty, N. J. (1986). "Discipline and class control." In N. J. Dougherty & D. Bonanno, *Contemporary Approaches to the Teaching of Physical Education.* Scottsdale, AZ: Gorsuch Scarisbrick Publishers, pp. 190-206.

2. Research has indicated that older athletes and athletes on interactive teams such as basketball, soccer, and football actually prefer autocratic coaches. Weinberg, R. S., & Gould, D. (2015). *Foundations of Sport and Exercise Psychology.* (6th ed.), Champaign, IL: Human Kinetics. p. 212

5

Guidelines for Effective Goal Setting

CHAPTER OUTLINE

- Goal Setting
- Basic Goal Setting Techniques
  YOUR TURN: Evaluating Goals for Effectiveness
- Goal Setting Styles
- Matching Goal Setting Techniques to Personal Styles
  YOUR TURN: Goal Setting Orientations

Goal setting is one of the most effective techniques for enhancing motivation. Goals set direction. Goals tell us what to do. They increase effort, persistence, and the quality of performance. Goals require athletes and coaches to develop specific techniques for how to achieve those goals once they have been set.

On the other hand, sport psychologists have recently found that under certain circumstances and for certain personal styles (called goal orientations), goal setting can actually undermine motivation. This chapter will cover specific goal setting techniques, describe the various types of goal orientations your athletes are likely to have, and outline goal setting strategies for coaches that are effective with the different goal orientations.

Goal Setting

Virtually every athlete and coach, at times during their athletic experience, have set goals. What attributes distinguish effective goals? How are goals set? What types of goals have the greatest impact on success in sports?

A major role of coaches is to help young athletes recognize the many possible goal-setting domains -- that is, to broaden the athletes' perception of those areas in which goal setting can be an effective tool. To name only a few of the possible goal setting domains, goals can be set to:

enhance fitness

improve attendance

increase intensity

promote sportsmanship

develop team spirit

find more free time

to establish consistency

PERFORMANCE, PROCESS AND OUTCOME GOALS

Sport psychologists have identified three important types of goals: Performance, Process and Outcome.[1]

Performance goals focus on goals that can be achieved primarily by the individual or team. That is, they are primarily influenced by the skill, effort and decisions of the athletes themselves. Achieving such goals is essentially independent of what competitors or officials do or do not do. They are relatively independent of the influence of others. Throwing a baseball to second base is primarily a performance goal regardless of how fast the runner sprints or how effectively the first baseman fields the ball.

Outcome goals are influenced to a great extent by factors outside of the athlete's direct control. Whether I win the game is determined to a great extent by the skill of the opponents, the skill of one's teammates and the lucky or unlucky bounce of the ball. In other words, factors outside of the individual's direct control. Successfully throwing the runner out at first base is controlled substantially by the first baseman's ability to catch the thrown baseball, not to mention the speed of the runner. Athletes may have outstanding performances but not win because others have performed even better. Conversely, they may perform poorly yet still win if all others perform even more poorly.

Process goals are essentially performance goals used as stepping stones to achieve a more sport-related performance goal. Process goals are similar to mastery goals in that they are performances which the athlete can control. However, they are a means to an end. Working to improve my strength (general, process goal) so that I can throw the ball faster to first base (sport-related, process goal) is a stepping stone to successfully throwing the runner out (sport-related performance goal) and ultimately winning the game (sport-related outcome goal). Similarly, increasing one's leg strength (process goal) allows a football linesman more success in driving back an opponent. Once the leg strength has been mastered, effectively driving the opposing linesman backward now becomes a process goal that permits the running back to gain more yardage, the mastery goal. Gaining more yardage can then become a process goal that is likely to lead to more scoring (now a mastery goal) that, in turn, leads to more wins. Thus, what is a process goal or a mastery goal often depends upon the stage of learning of the athletes.

The three goal characteristics are clearly related. I do strength drills to get stronger (general, process goal) so that I can swim the length of the pool in fewer strokes (sport-related process goal) so that I can swim faster (sport-related performance goal) so that I can win the race (sport related outcome goal). Be careful not to think of these characteristics as separate categories of goals because virtually all goals have all three elements. In the example of a baseball performance goal used earlier, throwing a baseball to second base is primarily a performance goal BUT successfully throwing the runner out is highly dependent upon the runner's speed and the first baseman's fielding skills.

Effective goal setting takes into consideration what the athlete can actually control. This judgment requires an understanding that the distinction between performance and outcome is a sliding scale based upon the athlete's ability, skill and experience. Coaches and athletes must make realistic judgments how much of a specific goal is within the athlete's ability to control. For example, if a baseball player's skill is similar to the skill level of a pitcher, the goal of making a hit is reasonably within his control but even this goal is partially controlled by the skills of the other defensive players. If the pitcher is much more skilled than the batter, the goal of getting a hit shifts to more of an outcome goal. If the batter's goal shifted to simply making solid contact with a pitched ball, his control over his performance is further increased, but even here part of the performance is controlled by the skills of the pitcher. Finally, if his goal is focused on maintaining a correct stance or swinging at only strikes, the control of the performance is almost entirely his, unless a physical disability prevents even that basic control! (Figure 5.1)

Since goals can be set that have varying degrees of personal control, coaches and athletes must make practical judgments concerning how much control is necessary for the athlete to feel in command of his success rate. For example, the ability of a pitcher to throw a strike is jointly determined by the pitcher's ability to throw the ball within the strike zone and the umpire's ability to make a split second decision whether the pitch was in that strike zone. That umpire's judgment is outside the pitcher's control. On the other hand, the young pitcher's ability to maintain his composure after a "bad" call by the umpire can be almost entirely within the athlete's ability to control, especially if such composure has been previously taught by the adult coach and now valued by the young player!

To effectively set performance goals, the coach and athlete must recognize what are the causal factors which determine an outcome.

FIGURE 5.1
Effective throwing requires proper foot placement (the cause) before making the successful throw (the outcome).

Coaching only the outcome is analogous to a doctor treating a symptom without dealing with the underlying causes of that symptom. If a doctor treats the symptom such as a fever without treating the underlying infection, improvement, if any, is likely to be superficial and temporary because the underlying cause still persists. Coaches should look beyond the outcomes (the symptoms) to the causes of success that lie within the ability of the athlete to control. A baseball outfielder who throws weakly and off direction, may not be planting her feet properly before the throw. Coaching the athlete to "hit the cut off man" illustrates coaching the symptom of the error. Little improvement is likely to occur since the causal factor is the improper positioning of the player's feet. Giving her a goal to plant her feet firmly ("step and throw") is much more likely to result in improved performance than telling her that her throw is weak or off-line, something that she probably already realizes.

The following portion of this chapter briefly outlines "tried and true," well-established techniques that successful coaches have used for decades for setting effective goals.

Basic Goal Setting Techniques[2]

SET SPECIFIC, MEASURABLE GOALS

Effective goals are specific and measurable. Goals stated in the form of "I want to be the best that I can be!" or "I want to improve my performance," are positive sounding but vague and difficult to achieve. Another important aspect of measurable goals is that athletes must establish a baseline from which to measure improvement. Improvement is more difficult if athletes do not have a clear idea of their starting points.

Set Demanding but Realistic Goals

Effective goals are perceived as challenging not threatening. A challenging goal is difficult but attainable within a reasonable amount of time, effort, or ability. A threat is perceived when the goal is seen as beyond one's ability. Athletes may set unrealistic goals for at least four reasons. First, they may not have a clear understanding of their ability or the requirements of the task because of their inexperience or lack of maturity. Second, they may be setting goals based upon the expectations of others (parents or coaches). Third, they may be basing their judgments on being in peak condition, not considering limiting factors such as illnesses or injuries. Fourth, they may have experienced an exceptional performance that is virtually impossible to duplicate. Goals based upon a current baseline of actual performance recorded during the past two weeks are likely to be realistic.

When in doubt about your athlete's ability to achieve a specific goal, set the goal lower rather than higher. Why such a contra-intuitive recommendation? Because it is easier to set a higher goal upon successful completion of a goal than it is to lower a goal that turns out to be unachievable. Lowering goals can demotivate the athlete and undermine the credibility of the coach. Successful completion of a goal that subsequently leads to a higher goal can be quite motivating because "success breeds success!"

Set Both Long- and Short-Term Goals

Both long- and short-term goals provide direction but short-term goals appear to have the greatest motivational effects. Long-term goals are still very important in providing an overall blueprint for the short-term goals, but the more distant a goal seems, the less energizing effect it is likely to have. Athletes perceive short-term goals as more readily attainable and should view them as stepping-stones to achieve the more distant long-term goals. The accomplishment of a short-term goal becomes the baseline for the next short-term goal. Just as importantly, unrealistic short-term goals, because of their immediacy, are easier to recognize than unrealistic long-term goals. Once recognized, unrealistic goals can be modified before substantial, valuable practice time has been lost. If the long-term goal is to bat .300, the short-term goals might be to reduce the number of called third strikes or to practice hitting the ball toward the gap between the third baseman and the shortstop.

Set Positive Goals

Positive is linked with good while negative connotes bad. However, positive goals go far beyond these connotations. First, positive goals tell us what to do rather than what not to do. Negative goals direct our attention to the errors we wish to avoid. Try telling someone not to think of pink elephants! Second, there are typically far more factors to be avoided than need to be done to successfully perform a skill. Knowing what to do allows an athlete to focus on fewer concerns rather than on all the variety of things that might go wrong. Third, positive goals also require coaches and athletes to decide **how** they will reach those specific goals; in other words, they must problem solve to determine what are the specific strategies and techniques necessary to accomplish what they are trying to do. Fourth, negative goals often involve holding back. For example, "Don't rush," or "Don't make that mistake." Effective sports performance often requires an intense effort. Goals that tell the athlete "what to do" allow improvement by substituting a correct movement for an incorrect one, rather than holding back on an incorrect aspect.

Set Priorities

Setting a limited number of high-priority goals requires athletes and coaches to decide what is important and fundamental for continued development. Effective goals have a high priority and are few in number. While an athlete may have many different aspects of his sport to master, setting too many goals diffuses their focus. As the athlete's skill at goal setting improves, more goals can be set simultaneously, but even

FIGURE 5.2
Prioritizing your goals tends to avoid the problem of becoming overwhelmed by too many goals.

advanced athletes should avoid establishing so many goals that the practice sessions are confusing. (Figure 5.2) Fewer goals also allow athletes and coaches to keep more accurate records without becoming overwhelmed with record keeping. Athletes are more aware of their progress when they focus on a few, high-priority goals. Not only is seeing progress quite motivating; but also goals can quickly be modified whenever a lack of progress is observed.

Set Mutually Determined Goals

Goal setting becomes an effective motivational tool when athletes become committed to those goals because they have had significant input in establishing the goals. When goals are imposed or established without significant input from the athletes, motivation can be undermined rather than enhanced. An exception to this principle is that athletes with an external locus of control may actually prefer coach-set goals[3]. Coaches can use various strategies to involve their athletes and, thus, improve commitment. (Figure 5.3)

First, athletes must feel that the goals are **their** goals, not just the coach's. This is not to say that the coach's knowledge, experience and preferences should not be involved but rather that the goals are **owned**

FIGURE 5.3 Mutually determining goals tends to be most effective when such decisions involve the coach's guidance coupled with the athletes' involvement with the decisions made.

by the athletes. Athletes should be involved in goal setting at a level compatible with their sports experience and emotional maturity. Very young or inexperienced athletes might be given a number of goals to choose from, while older and more advanced athletes might develop their goals more independently.

Second, coaches should be highly supportive of both the goal setting process and the day-to-day training done to achieve those goals. When the value of goals is not obvious, the coach should explain those benefits in a language the athletes can understand. If the athlete sets goals that are too high, the coach can point out the steps to be done first and encourage those steps to be the athlete's initial goals. If the goals are too low, the athlete's goals can become the first step to attaining a higher goal. Athletes tend to set higher goals when they trust their coach and are not afraid of failure or of punitive actions from the coach.

Coaches can be supportive by providing athletes with regular feedback about their progress toward attaining goals. Feedback not only enhances motivation, it is a major determinant of how quickly an athlete achieves a specific goal. Feedback can be praise, recognition, and rewards or it can be self-paced progress along a tangible series of steps that provides the young athlete with concrete evidence of improvement.

Set Specific Time Lines

Deadlines provide an urgency to the athletes' efforts. Target dates help to establish realistic steps (short-term goals) to the overall practice objective (long-term goals). Specific target dates tend to eliminate wishful thinking and clarify which goals are realistic and which are not. Time lines are especially valuable in high-risk sports, such as gymnastics or diving where fear often promotes procrastination in learning of new skills.

Set Both Formal and Informal Goals

While the initial establishment of goals can be quite formal, as the athletes and coaches become comfortable with the techniques of goal setting, goals can be established even as the athlete is in the midst of a workout. Particularly with short-term goals, the accomplishment of a prior goal can lead to setting a new goal within the context of a single practice session. Often, goals can be chosen in sequence. They are literally progressions that coaches have been using for years but are now expressed in measurable, performance terms rather than as vague, generalized outcomes.

Set Both Team and Individual Goals

Since effective goals are those for which the athlete has maximal control, individual goals are likely to be more effective than team goals. Of course, team goals and individual goals are often closely related. For example, a soccer team's goalie can give the defensive players correct field instructions even though the defensive players fail to respond to the verbal instruction. The team defense might falter but the goalie did his or her part. Conversely, the defensive players might respond to the goalie's words but the goalie might have called the wrong strategy. If both are working toward their individual goals, the team goal of a cohesive, interactive defense can be met, yet the individual elements are still under the control of the individual athletes. (Figure 5.4)

FIGURE 5.4
The team goal of coordinating the defense can still be broken down to individual assignments – the goalie directs the positioning of the defensive line but her teammates must respond.

YOUR TURN
Evaluating Goals for Effectiveness

Which is a good and which is a poor example of the goal setting principles? Evaluate these goals for their effectiveness.

SITUATION 1:

A swimmer discusses with her coach her ability to swim one length of the pool using freestyle with 13 arm strokes per length compared to her previous best of 15 arm strokes per length within one week of setting the goal.

SITUATION 2:

Despite a 2-10 Team Won/Loss record by late July, a 12-year-old with a .250 batting average wants to set the goal of earning a berth on the all-star baseball at the end of the summer.

Answers to Your Turn: Evaluating Goals for Effectiveness on page 117.

Goal Setting Styles

Three different **goal setting styles**, or **orientations**, have been identified:[4][5] Performance Oriented (PO), Success Oriented (SO), and Failure Oriented (FO). These goal setting styles reflect how different athletes attempt to answer the question "What is success?" "Success" occurs when a person infers personally desirable characteristics or attains personally meaningful objectives as a result of his or her efforts. These three styles interact with the person's perceived ability (Am I competent?), the type of situation (e.g., practice vs. competition), and performance expectancies (Do I think I can do it?) to guide the setting of specific goals. These styles are basically learned attitudes and reflect the experiences the young athlete has had within the family, at school and in their initial exposures to sports. These orientations are often formed during their early years and brought to the athletic field. Let's identify the characteristics of each personal style.

PERFORMANCE ORIENTED (PO)

These athletes focus on learning. They assume they have the ability to succeed, and success and failure are related to degree of learning. If they fail, it is because they just have not learned yet. But they believe they can and will learn. Failure at a task is considered a lack of having learned a skill, not an inability to learn or a personal weakness. PO athletes are typically concerned about skill improvement, mastery of the task, and competency. They sustain effort on difficult tasks and look upon self-improvement as success. Said differently, their goals are self-referenced.

SUCCESS ORIENTED (SO)

These athletes judge success and failure by social comparisons ("How well do I compare to others?" "How high do I rank?"). SO athletes actively seek competition because they expect positive social comparisons to others. They typically have been better than others and expect similar high rankings to continue in the future.

FAILURE ORIENTED (FO)

These athletes also judge success and failure by social comparisons. However, FO athletes have consistently ranked low in the past and now avoid competitive situations because they continue to expect negative social comparisons. They may participate in competitive sports because of factors beyond the enjoyment of competition (parental encouragement, their desire to affiliate with friends, concrete rewards for participating).

For both SO and FO athletes, improvement and task mastery are important primarily as a means of achieving positive social comparisons such as winning or ranking high compared to opponents. Thus, their judgments of success are often based upon factors outside their personal ability to control. For example, SO and FO athletes might find that promotion from the Junior Varsity to the Varsity is threatening because now their chances of winning or ranking high are diminished because the other athletes are better.

Matching Goal Setting Techniques to Personal Styles[6]

Athletes with different goal setting styles prefer different types of goals. Performance oriented athletes prefer specific, objectively measured, challenging goals. While success oriented athletes have similar preferences, they prefer goals that are based upon how they rank compared to others while failure oriented athletes prefer vague, long-term, generalized, group goals where objective measurement – and therefore their relative rank – is often difficult to measure. The coach should focus on causal, performance factors, even though SO athletes tend to prefer ranking goals and FO athletes tend toward preferring non-threatening generalized goals. Table 5.1 summarizes the preferred goal attributes for athletes with these three different goal setting styles.

IMPROVING ONE'S SELF VS. PROVING ONE'S SELF

These three different orientation styles predict three different approaches to learning. Learning involves risk-taking. The more demanding a skill is, the greater the risk of failure. Failure in a public setting such as sport can, for some, be quite threatening. PO athletes assume they have ability; they see failing at a task as simply not having yet learned the skill. Their competency is not threatened. Both SO and FO athletes interpret failure as a lack of competency. The PO athlete has the objective of *improving* oneself – self-referenced, while the SO and FO athletes have the objective of *proving* oneself to others – social comparison[7].

SO athletes believe they are capable but will reduce risk, especially in highly competitive situations, by choosing tasks they believe they can

TABLE 5.1 Preferred Types of Goals As a Function of Goal Setting Style

Goal Attribute	Style		
	Performance Oriented	Success Oriented	Failure Oriented
Frame of Reference:	Self-Referenced (Self-Improvement)	Social Comparison (Ranking)	Social Comparison (Ranking)
Specificity:	Specific	Specific	General
Task Difficulty:	Difficult	Moderately Difficult	Very Easy or Very Difficult
Positive vs. Negative Approach:	Positive	Positive & Negative	Positive
Group vs. Individual Responsibility:	Individual	Individual	Group
Immediacy:	Long & Short Term	Long & Short Term	Long Term

learn relatively quickly. FO athletes sacrifice learning by regularly choosing moderately easy or extremely difficult tasks. Failure at an extremely difficult task (say, swimming the English Channel) has less risk because few could be expected to succeed. On the other hand, after selecting a very easy goal, FO athletes are likely to work very hard to succeed at the easy goal because they do not wish to be seen as failing at something that others would consider "easy." If they have difficulty with moderately easy goals at which they believe others can succeed, they will often quickly discontinue their efforts or turn their attempts into jokes. They often avoid preparation for achieving these moderately difficult goals because they can then always say that "they could have" if only they had more time to prepare. "I wasn't ready" is often used to justify failure and/or lack of effort.

PO athletes are able to work hard at achieving difficult goals even after failure. The persistence of SO athletes deteriorates only after extensive failure because they typically believe they are capable. However, the persistence of FO athletes deteriorates sharply after even minimal failure. Thus, PO athletes are the most likely to approach their learning potential. They tolerate failure well and persist because they do not perceive failure as a threat to their competency. SO athletes perform well enough to win but they are likely to approach their potential only if external factors require the full development of their skills. This translates into the common finding that the most physically talented athletes on your team are often the most difficult to motivate to work hard at improving their skills because they already are the best in the group. FO athletes commonly show poor or erratic skill learning and frequently display avoidance behavior. They don't like setting goals because goals become a standard against which they can be judged. Their lack of confidence in their ability makes such evaluation stressful as opposed to the PO athletes who most often finds evaluations challenging.

SPECIFIC COACHING RECOMMENDATIONS

Based upon the patterns just described, the following specific recommendations can be made:

For All Athletes

- Teach your athletes to "learn to shift" their orientations back and forth between performance orientations (Did we play well?) and outcome orientations (Did we win?). Very high-level athletes typically report that they have both orientations and use them differently depending upon the circumstances. Competitive settings, by their very nature, tend to promote outcome orientations. But it is performance orientations that tend to promote higher performance, more skill development, more risk taking, and greater self-improvement. Performance orientations are more likely in practices than competition.

- Emphasize performance orientations in practice. Encourage the development of performance orientations by directing your coaching to performance goals. Performance orientations produce consistently high effort and intensity by athletes. Outcome goals will follow.
- Use a combination of performance and outcome goals in competition.
- Use short-term goals to motivate and energize behavior. Use long-term goals to provide direction. Short-term goals can be long-term goals broken down into the performance steps required to achieve the long-term goal.

For SO Athletes

- Highly skilled SO athletes on **well-learned tasks** are motivated effectively by both positive ("Make your foul shot!") and negative ("Don't miss your foul shot!").
- Success orientations promote effort and intensity only sufficient enough to rank high. Thus, SO athletes often display low motivation when competing against very weak opponents or very strong opponents against whom the odds of winning are very low.

For FO Athletes

- Left on their own, FO athletes tend to choose very easy or very difficult goals. Direct them to moderately difficult goals that promote learning but do not generate excessively high levels of anxiety because they typically expect to fail at attaining difficult goals.
- With athletes who focus primarily on avoiding failure, allow generalized, group and long-term goals to minimize stress and de-motivating their efforts. Gently encourage setting more measurable, specific performance goals.

YOUR TURN
Goal Setting Orientations

Think about the members of your team and evaluate their goal setting orientations. Which are PO athletes? SO? FO? (Figure 5.5)

FIGURE 5.5 Can you identify which kids on your team are performance, success or failure oriented?

THESE ARE THE ANSWERS TO YOUR TURN ON PAGE 111.

Situation 1:

Primarily a process goal – interested in swimming faster by using less strokes. Performance goal if she is strong enough to propel herself for 15 strokes/length – she can then attempt to reduce the number of strokes by 13.3% (2/15). Reasonable time – one week. Easily measured; mutually agreed upon using experience of the coach and the athlete's belief that she can do it. Reasonably difficult.

Situation 2:

Primarily an outcome goal – placement on the all-star team is decided by the coaches. That far into the season, the batting average is unlikely to change sufficiently to warrant consideration; not enough time for personal improvement on a team where fewer at bats are likely.

CHAPTER REFERENCES

1. Sanderson, C. A. (2017). *Sport Psychology.* Oxford University Press: Oxford, UK. p. 123.

2. Feigley, D. A. (1987). "Motivation Through Goal Setting." *THE REPORTER: The Journal of the New Jersey Association for Health, Physical Education, Recreation and Dance.* 61, 3-6.

3. Lamber., Moore, D. W., & Dixon, R. S. (1999). Gymnasts in training: The differential effects of self- and coach-set goals as a function of locus of control. *Journal of Applied Psychology, 11(1),* 72-82. doi: 10.1080/0413209908402951

4. Burton, D., Naylor , S., & Holliday, B. (2001). "Goal Setting in Sport: Investigating the Goal Effectiveness Paradox." In R. N. Singer, H. A. Hausenblas, & C. M. Janelle (Eds.), *Handbook of Research on Sport Psychology* (2nd ed.) (pp. 497-528). New York: John Wiley & Sons.

5. Harwood, C., Hardy, L. & Swain, A. (2000). "Achievement goals in sport: A Critique of Conceptual and Measurement Issues." *Journal of Sport & Exercise Psychology, 22,* 235-255.

6. Feigley, D.A. (2002). Matching goal setting techniques to your athletes' personal styles. *THE REPORTER: The Journal of the New Jersey Association for Health, Physical Education, Recreation and Dance, 76 (2),* 10 20.

7. Hodge, K. & Petlichkoff, L. (2000). "Goal Profiles in Sport Motivation: A Cluster Analysis." *Journal of Sport & Exercise Psychology, 22,* 256-272.

6

Developing Sportsmanship

CHAPTER OUTLINE

- What Is Sportsmanship?
- Sport Participation and Sportsmanship
- The Value of Sportsmanship to the Community
- The Value of Sportsmanship to the Individual
- Issues Confused with Sportsmanship
  SPOTLIGHT ON YOUTH SPORTS: Rules and Codes of Conduct
- Levels of Sportsmanship
- Strategies for Developing Sportsmanship
  FROM CHALKBOARD TO PLAYING FIELD: Sportsmanship Awards
- Factors That Undermine Sportsmanship
- Summary
  YOUR TURN: Teaching Sportsmanship

Teaching sportsmanship is one of the overriding issues in youth sports today. While many other issues may appear to be more urgent (the use of performance-enhancing drugs, the professionalization of youth sport, the overemphasis on winning), most of these issues could be dealt with more effectively if the moral reasoning skills underlying sportsmanship behaviors were used by coaches in guiding their young athletes and if that moral reasoning were taught more effectively to the young athletes themselves.

This chapter will discuss the benefits good sportsmanship offers to the community and to the individual, even when other individuals or teams do not display such behaviors. It also provides you with specific strategies and instructional techniques for developing sportsmanship in your young athletes.

What is Sportsmanship?

Sportsmanship is more than "good behavior." It is a complex form of moral reasoning by which we judge what is right and wrong. While definitions of sportsmanship vary, they consistently involve "doing the right thing for the right reasons."[1]

Sport Participation and Sportsmanship

Young athletes might do the right thing for the wrong reason or the wrong thing for the right reason. While coaches should demand positive sportsmanship **behaviors** from their athletes, they should also be concerned with teaching their young athletes the **reasoning** behind good sporting behaviors so that those behaviors become internalized by the athletes and occur regularly whether the coach is present or not. Demanding the "right" behavior teaches young athletes what to do. Encouraging the development of moral reasoning skills teaches young athletes "why" such behavior is "right" which ultimately permits them to make better and better decisions in more and more complicated life situations.

For example, shaking hands, by itself, is not sportsmanship. (Figure 6.1) An athlete might shake hands with opponents after a game

FIGURE 6.1
Shaking hands, by itself, is not necessarily an act of sportsmanship. When the ritual of shaking hands after the competition becomes internalized as a sign of respect for one's opponents and their efforts, it becomes true sportsmanship.

not so much to show respect for the opponents but because he fears losing playing time if he does not follow his coach's instructions. Similarly, he may believe that he has to get involved in an argument on the field with opposing players to "protect" his teammates from perceived unfair practices by those opponents. While sticking up for your teammates is normally viewed as a positive trait, public altercations with opponents usually show poor sportsmanship.

Participation in sport does not automatically teach sportsmanship. If values such as honesty, cooperation, fair play, and respect for one's self and others are desired outcomes of a sporting experience, then those values, as well as the behaviors associated with them, must be explicitly taught using instructional progressions just as coaches teach other sports skills.[2] Sport can be an excellent **vehicle** for teaching moral behavior to children; but sport can teach children poor sportsmanship as well as fair play.

Because winning and losing are so clear-cut, sport provides many great opportunities for teaching meaningful positive character traits (maintaining composure, emotional resiliency, mental toughness, good sportsmanship). Not only does it provide repeated situations where fair play can be displayed by players who are striving to win; but just as importantly it provides children with many clear-cut opportunities **to decide** between right and wrong. To ultimately demonstrate true sportsmanship, athletes must have the opportunity to choose for themselves between fair and unfair behaviors. Without free choice, the resulting behaviors, no matter how civil they might be, cannot be considered true sportsmanship. They may be obedience to authority or conformity but without voluntary choices, they are not moral behaviors.

The Value of Sportsmanship to the Community

SPORTSMANSHIP DECREASES THE NEED FOR MONITORING ATHLETES' BEHAVIORS

While officials will always be necessary to officiate sports (say, calling balls and strikes and deciding the outcomes of close plays), the need to enforce rules of fairness, to stop cheating, and to enforce rules of conduct decreases dramatically as athletes play fairly and live up to codes of conduct defining good sportsmanship. The development of an idealized set of values and the desire to live by those values is the essence of good sportsmanship. Such positive values eliminate the need for constant surveillance and threats of punishment of the individual by officials.

SPORTSMANSHIP HELPS YOUNG ATHLETES WITH REAL-LIFE MORAL DILEMMAS

Moral dilemmas[3] occur when logical but selfish choices result in a substantial gain for the individual but if every individual in the group makes that same logical, selfish decision, all the members of that group suffer a loss. Conversely, if the individual makes an altruistic response, the result for that individual is a loss or smaller gain; but, assuming everyone makes the altruistic response, the net result is a gain for everyone. Moral dilemmas occur in many important areas of our lives. For example, it is cheaper for individuals to discard their waste products into local streams than to pay to have it carted off; however, if every member of the community discarded their waste into those streams, no one could escape the polluted water supply. If each member of the community pays to have the garbage carted away (greater cost to the individual), the entire community benefits with a clean water supply (gain for the entire group). In a similar vein, a soldier who chooses to fight to defend his/her country often places his/her life at risk. Choosing to avoid the fight clearly has advantages to the individual; but if every soldier refused to fight, the society which he/she defended could no longer exist. Likewise, an individual who violates the concepts of fair play may have a better chance of winning, but if everyone cheats, the sporting competition degenerates into a farce. If each athlete plays fairly, all the participants can enjoy the true sporting competition.

"WHO IS THE BEST?"

Sportsmanship helps answers this question. To determine the best at any sport, one must play within the context of sportsmanship. Every sport has an essential, often implicit, agreement about the nature of the game. In soccer, the nature of the game is to advance the ball down the field and into the net more often than the other team. Part of that essential agreement is the intent to do so without using the hands to advance the ball or without physically harming an opponent. Without sportsmanship, the nature of the contest changes dramatically. The question moves quickly from **"Who won the game?"** to **"Who won the event?"** The **event** is an activity with the same outward appearance as the game but lacks the essential internal agreement about how the contest *should* be played. For example, the original intent of American football is to advance the ball down the field and across the goal line more often than the other team. A team can win today's event, as opposed to the game, by ignoring or violating the original agreement. The football game can be changed to who can injure the quarterback or who can intimidate the offensive receivers with late hits. A basketball game changes from who can put the ball through the hoop more often to who can fool the referee by feigning fouls or by using less talented players to goad talented, opposing players into fouling out of the contest. Only when the game is played in a fashion consistent with the original agreement can the true winner of the game be determined.

The Value of Sportsmanship to the Individual

SPORTSMANSHIP SKILLS TRANSFER TO LIFE

Many physical skills are not life skills. However, the temperament needed to learn such skills and to perform them in an athletic contest can transfer directly to other areas of life. Self-control, awareness, empathy for others, and conflict resolution skills are quite likely to be important skills in both sport and non-sport settings at many stages of one's life.

SPORTSMANSHIP HELPS YOU PLAY BETTER

Striving for excellence is a primary reason why young teens enjoy sport. Coaches can emphasize that playing "in control" regularly permits higher levels of performance than is likely to occur when "playing angry" or "out of control." The "red hot" athletes often feel as if they are playing with more intensity and strength -- and, therefore, with higher levels of performance; but objective measures indicate that this is often not the case.[4] Sportsmanship contributes directly to emotional stability and self-control, which permit significant and enduring athletic success. Peak performance, flow, and "being in the zone" are virtually incompatible with emotional outbursts, distortions of the rules and mistreatment of opponents. Maintaining one's composure in the face of adversity is a crucial dimension of mental toughness.

GOOD SPORTSMANSHIP INCREASES SELF-RESPECT AND RESPECT FROM OTHERS

Being in control of many sports situations first requires being in control of oneself. As that personal control develops, both self-respect and the respect earned from others tend to increase. Respect is a primary determinant of friendship and self-esteem.

SPORTSMANSHIP STRENGTHENS AND MAINTAINS FRIENDSHIPS

Being with friends is a major reason why young children initially become involved in organized sports. (Figure 6.2) Cooperation and fair play – characteristics of good sportsmanship – are essential ingredients to being accepted by others and making and enhancing friendships.

Issues Confused with Sportsmanship

A number of issues are frequently confused with good or poor sportsmanship. Differentiating these issues from sportsmanship is crucial before strategies for teaching sportsmanship are considered.

EMPHASIS ON WINNING

Poor sportsmanship is not the direct result of a strong desire to win **Striving to win is an essential part of sport.** If the participants are not striving to win, the activity is not sport and true sportsmanship cannot

FIGURE 6.2 Sportsmanship strengthens and maintains friendships – Affiliation with their friends is a major reason why children and youth enter and stay in organized sports.

exist. If, during a scrimmage, a basketball defender is far superior to his offensive opponent and begins to defend less intensely allowing his less experienced opponent to successfully drive to the basket for a layup, the activity has changed from the sport of basketball to an instructional activity or a social interaction. As physical as the activity may be, it no longer contains one of the essential, defining ingredients of sports -- striving to win. Winning within the context of the rules and within the spirit of the game is important and should not be devalued. If winning is not a highly prized goal in its own right, playing fairly is not a noteworthy achievement in the individual's moral development. **How you strive to win** is the critical aspect. The conflict between the desire to win and the need to do so within the context and spirit of the rules is essential for sportsmanship to exist in the first place.[5] Unfortunately, the awards for winning can become more important than the win itself. Acquiring money, fame, status, and privilege may well become the dominant theme. When the value of these external rewards outweighs the value of winning, the concept of "how one wins" often becomes less important.

ROUGH AND AGGRESSIVE PLAY

Rough and aggressive play becomes poor sportsmanship only if it violates the original spirit of the sport. Intense physical contact in rugby or American football is expected. Hard tackling and clean blocks are a necessary and desired part of the game. However, even in contact sports, there are limits to the nature of the aggressiveness expected and permitted. When a rugby player's intent during a tackle changes from a desire to wrestle the ball loose from an opponent's grasp to a desire to injure that opponent, the original spirit of the game has been violated and the rough behavior becomes unsportsmanlike conduct. A late hit in football or a tackle made out of bounds when the opponent expects the play to have ended crosses over from expected and desired aggressive football plays and becomes a reprehensible "cheap shot."

OBEDIENCE TO AUTHORITY

Behaving in a civil manner and following the rules merely because one fears the possible sanctions from a referee or coach cannot be considered sportsmanship in the truest sense of the word. While behaving well may be a necessary step toward developing sportsmanship, it does not yet reflect moral and ethical reasoning.

Nonetheless, there are circumstances when such distinctions are of little value. A high school principal placed in charge of the safety of all participants must demand that all spectators at a high school basketball game behave in a civil manner as they cheer for their team. As a safety administrator, he or she is probably not overly concerned that different students behave properly for different reasons: e.g., fear of punishment, pride in their school, or a personal code of conduct. Sportsmanlike conduct in such a situation focuses on the behavior rather than the reasoning behind the behavior. Nonetheless, the principal (and the other coaches and adults involved in the program) probably realize that the "good behavior" may not sustain itself unless the students believe that such behavior is "right". To the extent that school educators wish to teach moral behavior, they should continue to focus on developing the internal reasoning that is essential for sportsmanship behavior to become independent of external controls such as an authority figure or fear of punishment.

COMPETITIVENESS

The distinction between competitiveness and poor sportsmanship is closely linked to the issues previously discussed concerning the emphasis on winning. However, one additional point should be made. True competition is the ultimate in cooperation. The participants must agree to the same rules, the same basic equipment, and the same initial starting points in order to allow such dimensions as effort, ability, skill, perseverance, and strategy to be the determining factors in the outcome of a contest. Without such a cooperative foundation, competition cannot be considered sport. In effect, true sports competition requires the highest form of cooperation, which is why the often-cited comparison of "sport as war" is nonsense.

JUSTIFIED AGGRESSION

Paradoxically, poor sportsmanship is often displayed by those who profess strong beliefs in sportsmanship and fair play.[6] For example, their loud complaints about officiating frequently occur because they believe that they or their team have been treated unjustly. Often those people who behave in the poorest manner are those who feel that they are the wounded party. They often express quite elaborate rationales for justifying their unjustified behavior. (Figure 6.3) For example, coaches who interpret the behavior of others as attacks on relatively defenseless members of their team often justify a counterattack as a protective measure. Comments such as "You can mess with me, but you can't mess with my kids!" illustrates such self-justifying techniques. Recognizing and understanding this tendency to "justify the unjustifiable" is not grounds for tolerating such inappropriate behavior. However, such recognition can help immunize participants from such illogical logic!

FIGURE 6.3
Paradoxically, poor sportsmanship is often displayed by those who justify their behavior with such misguided beliefs such as, "I was just protecting my kids!"

SPOTLIGHT ON YOUTH SPORTS

Rules and Codes of Conduct

Moral behavior directs the individual toward what *should* be done as opposed to what *should not* be done. Even a cursory examination of the formal rules of most sports illustrates that sport rules tend to be written in the negative rather than the positive. That is, rules focus predominantly on what you cannot do and provide sanctions for violations of those prohibitions. Knowing what cannot be done does not necessarily guide people toward what should be done. Sportsmanship on the other hand provides direction by focusing on "shoulds" and "oughts."

Codes of Conduct can provide both *shoulds* and *should nots*. Appendices 6.1 and 6.2 present two dramatically different ones. The first (6.1) represents a code of conduct developed by the Attorney General's office in response to legislation passed in 2002 that required an enforceable code of conduct for all participants in organized youth sport programs in New Jersey. It basically states what is unacceptable behavior. The second (6.2) is an educational code of conduct developed in that same year by the Youth Sports Research Council of Rutgers University. The education code specifies the type of behavior desired by all participants within organized youth sports. It is unenforceable by the standards required for law enforcement yet it spells out higher levels of behavior than does the Attorney General's code. They serve different purposes. The Attorney General's code spells out what is grounds for dismissal from youth sport events while the Rutgers code establishes educational guides not only for sportsmanship but for different levels of sportsmanship. At the first level, **Basic Civility,** the Rutgers code differs little from the Attorney General's code. At the second level, **Good Sportsmanship,** the Rutgers code tells participants what is expected. Finally, the third level, **Conduct of Distinction,** identifies idealized, somewhat abstracted behaviors that participants should aspire to in order to respect opponents, officials, teammates, themselves, and the spirit of the game.

Levels of Sportsmanship

Not swearing at an official's call. Not exhibiting mild dissent at the same call. Expressing thanks to the referee at the conclusion of the game. Expressing thanks for the official's effort even after the game was decided against you based on a controversial call late in the game. Each of these successive behaviors requires a greater commitment to and understanding of living up to one's code of sportsmanship.

HOW SPORTSMANSHIP DEVELOPS

Sportsmanship is essentially moral reasoning in the context of sport. It develops in much the same fashion as morality in any other sphere of an individual's life. Current understanding of moral development – and thus sportsmanship development – focuses on social learning and structural developmental approaches, two quite different, but not incompatible approaches. The social learning approach believes that morality (and thus sportsmanship) is learned just as other skills are learned – through modeling and reinforcement. The structural developmental approach focuses on how the ability to reason morally develops as a person grows and matures cognitively. The individual's capacity for moral reasoning develops as more mature cognitive reasoning structures form; for example, as one's ability to understand abstractions and the "bigger picture" develops. These two approaches are not contradictory since social learning can occur at each development stage identified by the structure developmental approach.

STAGE THEORY

A widely accepted approach to moral reasoning holds that such reasoning develops in successive – and increasingly sophisticated – stages. Children advance through these stages in a predictable order, albeit at different speeds, depending upon both the rate of maturation in their thinking and how often they have been exposed to situations requiring moral decisions. Theories differ on the types and number of stages, but basically these are the six stages —grouped into three phases:[7]

Phase I: Premoral Reasoning. In this stage the perception of external power ensures a behavior. Removal of the external power source often results in the behavior reverting to the behavior that existed before the power was exerted.

1. **Obedience to Authority.** "I must play fairly or I'll be kicked out of the game." "As long as the ref does not catch me, it's O.K."

2. **Bartering.** "If you play fair, I'll play fair; but if you cheat, so will I." "An eye for an eye."

Phase II: Conformity. Behavior is based on identification and depends on the attractiveness of the model. Removal of the model or the introduction of a more attractive model can result in behavior change.

3. **Attraction.** "I'll play fair even if the others players don't. Isn't that right, Coach?" "I want to be like my hero, LeBron James."

4. **Group Identification.** "I'll play fair even if the others cheat and even if no one else is around to give me credit because that's the way my teammates play!" "I represent my team."

Phase III: Internalization. Behavior is based on the credibility of the idea or reasoning behind the behavior. Such behavior is relatively independent of outside influences because it is based on an internalized attitude or belief that the behavior is right or appropriate. (Figure 6.4.)

5. **Internalized Agreement with Rules.** "If players were to cheat whenever they felt like it, we wouldn't have a very good world." "I don't like the rule, but it was what we agreed upon."

6. **Internalized Personal Code of Justice/Fairness.** "Unless I play fairly, there is no true accomplishment in winning." "I'll never know just how good I am at this sport, unless I play by the rules."

FIGURE 6.4
Sportsmanship may be displayed from elementary levels of moral reasoning (no dissent) to higher levels of reasoning (thanking an official despite having just lost a competition)

LOGIC OF THE STAGES

The Development of Moral Reasoning Is Predictable. Developmental theories emphasize that increasingly sophisticated moral reasoning occurs in a predictable order. The child whose sportsmanship behaviors are different from her teammates is simply functioning at an earlier or later developmental stage. Your encouragement of sportsmanship reasoning should focus on the next stage in the sequence. Youngsters move to higher levels of moral reasoning if they are exposed frequently to the next level and if they are given concrete examples in which the moral reasoning is explicitly outlined for them.

Moral reasoning that is more than one level above the stage at which the youngster is currently functioning is likely to be too abstract and, thus, unlikely to have any effect on moral reasoning. For example, a young athlete who plays fairly for fear of punishment is more likely to be influenced by teammates and coaches who encourage sportsmanship "for the team and your school" than by complex reasoning such as "play fairly so that you can truly test yourself against your opponent's best and know who is truly the best athlete." Similarly, the youngster who learns to cheat because that is how "smart" players earn the respect of their peers can be exposed to the logic that "pleasing yourself" can take precedence over "impressing others."

Moral Reasoning Is Not Equal to Behavior. The Stage Theory separates thinking from behavior. That is, identical behavior can occur at different stages of moral development, but the reasoning behind that behavior may be markedly different. For example, the young athlete must decide whether he should fight or not fight during a confrontation at a junior hockey game. His actual behavior and his reasoning behind that behavior depend on his stage of moral development. Table 6.1 illustrates how the same behavior (fighting) can be motivated by different reasoning at different developmental stages, and how different behaviors (fighting vs. not fighting) can be motivated by similar thinking.

Behavior is not the sole determinant of sportsmanship. Take, for example, a situation in which a tennis umpire incorrectly calls a ball out and a player stands to gain from the incorrect call. The player purposely double faults and the score reverts to a tie where neither player has an advantage. Such behavior may be interpreted as sportsmanship if the intent was to ensure fairness. However, exactly the same behavior might be interpreted as unsportsmanlike conduct if the purpose was to embarrass the umpire or to intimidate him for an advantage on later calls.

TABLE 6.1 Moral Reasoning and Sportsmanship

Stage	Behavior	Reasoning Cause
Phase I: Premoral Reasoning		
Obedience to Authority	Fight	For fear teammates won't talk to me.
	Not Fight	My coach will bench me.
Bartering	Fight	If I protect you, you'll protect me.
	Not Fight	I'll play fair if you play fair
Phase II: Conformity		
Attraction	Fight	My coach will respect and admire me as someone who can "dish it out as well as take it."
	Not Fight	My coach will respect and admire me because I'm a clean player.
Group Identification	Fight	Others will admire me because I'm a tough player.
	Not Fight	Fighting is against the rules and we live by the rules.
Phase III: Internalization		
Internalized Agreement with Rules	Fight	Fighting is accepted as part of the game by all "real" players.
	Not Fight	When I chose to play the game, I agreed to play by the rules and the rules forbid fighting.
Internalized Personal Code of Justice/ Fairness	Fight	Everyone must be willing to stand up and fight for what they believe in.
	Not Fight	Fighting means I've lost my self-control and dignity as a person.

This table draws loosely from multiple theories of moral development (Kohlberg[8]; Gilligan[9]; Weinberg & Gould[10]; Weiss & Bredimeier[11])

Further, the action itself could be classified as at different stages of "good-ness" depending upon whether the player intentionally double faulted to win the approval/respect of her opponent and the fans or whether she was motivated by a desire to see that fairness was maintained. A player functioning at this more advanced stage of morality might double fault in a subtle fashion to avoid embarrassing the referee, while she might blatant-ly double fault if she wished her behavior to win approval from others.

Teaching Sportsmanship Should Focus on Thinking Skills Not Just Behaviors. While at first this approach might seem indirect since sports-manship is evidenced by behavior, it is essential for two reasons. First, there is not a simple list of "good" behaviors that can be contrasted with an equally simple list of "bad" behaviors. Behavior that is considered sportsmanship varies from culture to culture, sport to sport, and skill level to skill level, to mention only a few complicating variables. Second, as the athlete's thinking is influenced, the sportsmanship behavior be-comes internalized and independent of external controls.

The focus on the reasoning process allows teachers of sportsman-ship to focus both on (a) modifying the poor behavior and (b) enhanc-ing the developmental process. For example, consider a sport such as basketball in which "running up the score" is often considered poor sportsmanship. For athletes functioning at the bartering stage of think-ing, the coach can emphasize that running up the score should be avoid-ed so that opponents will be less likely to run up the score on them at some later date. The coach is using an already attained, albeit primitive, level of reasoning to reverse the tendency to run up the score. That same coach can then also emphasize reasoning one stage above the athletes' current level of sophistication not only to modify the behavior but also to promote the development of more sophisticated moral reasoning. For example, he can emphasize that he (as a significant other) and other respected coaches do not believe in humiliating opponents by scoring more points than is necessary to ensure a comfortable win.

Strategies for Developing Sportsmanship

Adults who wish to enhance moral development by teaching sportsman-ship are confronted with a curious dilemma. On the one hand, moral development is a way of thinking, not a specific behavior. On the other hand, sportsmanship is the display of behaviors that reflect an athlete's concern for fairness. Without such positive behaviors, knowing how to be a good sport is of little consequence. Further, since sporting attitudes and behaviors develop at relatively early ages, the use of concrete behaviors is a necessary tool for introducing children to the abstract concepts of sportsmanship. Furthermore, behaviors that merely reflect etiquette and civility can be clearly distinguished from behaviors that reflect an understanding of justice and fair play. However, for coaches, these distinctions are often inconsequential during the initial stages of teaching sportsmanship.

There are two types of skills – and therefore two types of teaching strategies – for developing sportsmanship in young athletes.

STRESS MANAGEMENT TECHNIQUES

These skills involve emotional self control techniques that, while simple, are crucial in controlling anger and frustration. Such techniques are often learned at an early age and involve techniques such as "Take a deep breath," "Count to ten," or "Think before you react."

MORAL REASONING

These skills are more abstract and involve thinking about what's right and why. I behave the way I do because "I treat others the way I want to be treated," or because "I represent my team." This reasoning involves understanding abstract concepts such as "Winning within the rules makes the win worthier."

The importance of this distinction is that it emphasizes that different teaching strategies are involved in developing each type of skill. Both types of skills should be taught but the success at teaching self-control techniques is easier to assess because such behavior is often overt whereas the moral reasoning underlying good sportsmanship behaviors is more abstract.

THE ROLE OF THE COACH

While sportsmanship values may be incorporated within the overall sports program in terms of rules, policies, clinics, and public information, the coach must do the individual teaching of the youngsters. Thus, coaches must value and understand sportsmanship behaviors. As obvious as such a statement is, relatively few sports programs systematically teach the values of sportsmanship to adult coaches. Administrators either assume that such values cannot be taught to adults or that adults already know what values and behaviors constitute sportsmanship. A brief observation of numerous coaches' behavior at practices and competitions suggests that such an assumption may not always be the case.

A variety of strategies and techniques exist for developing sportsmanship. For these strategies to be effective, teachers and coaches must be capable of using these methods during their everyday interactions with the young athletes.

ASSESS READINESS FOR SPORTSMANSHIP INSTRUCTION

Just as coaches assess readiness for learning physical skills, coaches should attempt to assess the level of maturity and the sophistication of their athletes' thinking about sportsmanship issues before attempting to teach moral values through sport. Questions addressed to the young players such as "Why is sportsmanship important?" and "Who controls our behavior?" and "What should you do if an opponent or an opposing team behaves poorly?" can all provide some insight concerning the level of thinking of the young athletes. Determining the level of cognitive development of an entire team of athletes is likely to be challenging for the following reasons:

- While behavior is quite observable, identifying the thinking and moral reasoning that underlies a specific behavior is often difficult.
- Athletes in the same age group on the same team are likely to be at different stages of cognitive development.
- The same athlete may exhibit different levels of moral reasoning in different situations while experimenting with thinking at progressively more sophisticated levels.
- Coaches may see their athletes only on the sports field or only for a season as opposed to a wider array of situations such as in school or within the family.

As a result, coaches should be prepared to instruct young athletes at virtually all levels of moral reasoning with the hope that their young charges will become increasingly more sophisticated in their thinking.

DEFINE SPORTSMANSHIP IN THE CONTEXT OF YOUR SPORT

Identify the Specific Behaviors Expected. Since sportsmanship is ultimately treating others fairly, the exact nature of such behavior may differ dramatically in different sports, different skill levels, or different cultures. For example, physical contact is virtually unheard of in tennis but is expected in rugby. Before the whistle, a hard hit is admired, whereas the same hit after the whistle or out of bounds is a violation of the spirit of fair play. Telling players to respect their opponents does not tell them what specific behaviors reflect respect. Shaking hands after a contest and eliminating abusive comments are specific examples that are measurable and observable. The more specifically you identify a behavior, the more likely it is that you can teach it, model it, and have your athletes learn it.

Teach the Rules (Both Formal and Informal) of Your Sport. Provide your athletes with both the formal and informal rules to help them understand what behaviors are expected. Ignorance of the rules may result in behavior that is seen as poor sportsmanship but where there was no intent to gain unfair advantage or behave in a deceitful or fraudulent way. Rules should be introduced for both competitive and noncompetitive situations. For example, in addition to learning the formal scoring rules, young tennis players can be taught how to walk onto a tennis court without disturbing other players. Young golfers can not only be taught the formal rules about unplayable lies but also to avoid walking across the line of putt of their teammates and opponents. Young soccer players can be taught both a formal understanding of the off sides rule and the informal custom of kicking the ball out of bounds to stop play if an opposing player appears hurt.

Establish Specific Sportsmanship Goals. Establish specific sportsmanship goals just as you would for the physical sports skills and game strategies you wish to teach. Specific sportsmanship goals can involve such concepts as reducing the number of fouls called against your team, shaking hands with your opponents, getting to know opponents by name, and sharing equipment and facilities equally in pre-game warm-ups.

Establish Global Goals. Global goals are goals valued by the participants over and above the immediate goals of the contest. For example, athletes often feel strongly that they or their teams are members of special groups. Thus, their behavior can be influenced by emphasizing that their individual acts of sportsmanship positively represent their team. Athletes and coaches can be encouraged to show sportsmanlike behavior because they represent their team, their school, their league, their

FIGURE 6.5 Good sportsmanship is not an automatic result of sport participation. It is a set of values and behaviors specifically taught by coaches and parents through the vehicle of sport.

country, whichever is applicable. The positive reputation for their team cannot be achieved unless virtually all members of the team support such a goal.

Broaden the Definition of Success. Establish multiple team and individual goals that include but go beyond the goal of winning without demeaning the importance of winning. Establish performance goals such as playing with sustained effort regardless of the score, improving the number of successful first serves in tennis or increasing the number of shots on goal in sports such as hockey, lacrosse and soccer. Develop specific sportsmanship goals such as reducing the number of fouls while still playing aggressively or keeping one's composure after a disputed official's call. Important goals such as these allow athletes to feel and be successful regardless of the outcome of the contest.

Set Clear, Specific, and Public Behavior Codes. Behavior codes spell out specifically what behaviors we expect and why we expect them (See Appendices 6.1 and 6.2). Both those behaviors and the reasoning behind them must be made clear to the athletes. Behavior codes and their rationales must be highly visible and continually reaffirmed to be effective. Providing the rationale for specific behaviors – as opposed to simply requiring those behaviors – helps young athletes internalize the values behind those behaviors. For example, if shaking hands with your opponent after the game is part of your code, shaking hands should be publicly acknowledged as a sign of respect for opponents, not simply a ritual to be carried out without thought. (Figure 6.5) In fact, if shaking hands is required without such a rationale, that same act can become a test of "grip strength." The code can spell out what not to do as well as what to do. For example, swearing, arguing with officials, rolling your eyes at a "bad" call are all examples of specific "Don'ts." Shaking hands after a match, thanking the officials, sharing with teammates and opponents are "Do's." Regularly remind your athletes of what behaviors are appropriate. Brief, but frequent, reminders are better than long discussions. Specific examples about how to behave are much stronger guides than vague references to being a good sport.

Identify the Norms Controlling Sportsmanship. Both good and poor sportsmanship behaviors are often determined by behavioral norms as opposed to rules and regulations. For example, trash talking is more commonly accepted in basketball than it is in tennis. Acknowledging to your players that, "while it may be an accepted behavior by others, it is not acceptable on our team" provides you with a degree of credibility. Clearly, individual coaches cannot change societal norms, but they can influence the norms within and immediately surrounding their teams by recruiting the assistance of parents, teachers, assistant coaches, and older, more experienced team members. Local norms tend to have a strong influence on younger athletes especially if they are perceived as "our code."

Involve Your Athletes in Establishing the Behavior Codes. While some behavioral codes must necessarily be preset by adults (no fighting; no drugs), guidance can be provided by the coaches without **imposing** codes on the athletes. One of the most straightforward and practical findings of psychologists has been that, when people believe that they have had an important role in deciding codes for themselves and their groups, their personal commitment to achieving those codes increases substantially. Athletes can be actively and meaningfully involved in setting appropriate sportsmanship behavior codes without sacrificing the experience, knowledge and perspective of the coaches.

TEACH SPORTSMANSHIP USING SPECIFIC INSTRUCTIONAL TECHNIQUES

Knowing what constitutes sportsmanship is quite different from knowing how to teach it. Coaches who consistently develop players who display high levels of sportsmanship use a variety of instructional techniques. Below are a number of suggestions.

Establish Specific Progressions for Teaching Sportsmanship. Progressions are just as necessary for developing sportsmanship behaviors as for other sports skills. For example, rules of conduct can be introduced a few at a time during practice sessions rather than overwhelming young players with large numbers of detailed rules or simply assuming that the athletes will pick up the appropriate rules along the way. Teach your athletes to treat teammates fairly during practices and scrimmages before expecting them to act similarly to opponents during intense competitions. Sportsmanship, in effect, begins at home.

Be a Role Model. Coaches must value and practice sportsmanship. Young athletes are much more strongly influenced by what we do than what we say. Coaches who preach good sportsmanship but lose their composure with officials' calls or who teach or tacitly accept techniques that are clearly against the rules (e.g., pulling a jersey of an opposing player to gain advantage) develop athletes who also talk about good sportsmanship but who behave poorly.

Role Play. Much of sportsmanship is based upon being able to see the situation from the other person's perspective. This third-party perspective is essential for making moral decisions. Coaches can teach by asking such questions as: "How would you feel if...?" For example, when teaching your athletes to respect and support officials, you might ask your athletes "What grade would you expect on a test if you got 99 questions right of 100?" If they answer, as they are likely to, "We'd expect an A!" – you can point out that an official often makes hundreds of decisions per game. If two or three of those decisions might not be correct ones, those officials should get an A also, not public criticism nor attempts to embarrass them. A further question that attempts to put young athletes in the role of the officials might be: "How would you feel if you volunteered your time to help by officiating and the people you were helping hassled you or tried to embarrass you if you made a mistake?"

Practice Making Choices. "What would you do if...?" Give youngsters opportunities to practice making decisions about difficult situations before those situations occur along with the emotion and urgency often seen in competition. For example, a soccer coach might ask: "What would you do if your opponent cursed at you or attempted to pull you down by your jersey?" "Would you strike back?" "If you did, who is most likely to be penalized by the referee/umpire? First foul or second foul?"

"Would you play on? While your opponent was holding onto you and not playing the ball, could you pass the ball to an open teammate who had a shot on goal?" Use the teaching technique called "Ask, Suggest, Tell."[12] For example: Start with an open-ended question that requires your athletes to think.

> **Ask** – What would you do if, while on attack in soccer, the opposing defender knocks you down with an illegal slide tackle?

> *If the athletes are uncertain how to respond, switch to:*

> **Suggest** – Should you retaliate by knocking him down or pass the ball to an open teammate?

> *If the athlete is still uncertain, switch to:*

> **Tell** – Passing the ball keeps us on offense, gives us an opportunity to score because they have one fewer defender (he's on the ground after the slide tackle), and avoids your getting a yellow or red card from the referee.

Who Controls My Behavior? The belief that one should behave well only if the opponents do so first is not truly sportsmanship. While no one should allow herself to be taken advantage of by an unsportsmanlike opponent, if you simply retaliate, you have given others the control over your behavior. Explore with your athletes ways to protect one's self without "losing your cool." Indicate that it is easy to be a good sport when everything is going well. It is much more difficult when a close officiating call goes against you or you perceive that others have taken advantage of you. Help your athletes understand that poor sportsmanship often results from self-justifying behavior. Point out that many athletes who behave poorly often do so because they believe that they had been taken advantage of. Ask "Who controls your behavior?" "You – or the opponent who just violated the code of conduct?" This technique is particularly effective with young teenagers (10-14 years of age) because of their developing sense of autonomy.

EMPHASIZE THE CONSEQUENCES OF BEING A GOOD SPORT

Acknowledge Good Sportsmanship. When sportsmanship does occur, it must be recognized and rewarded by coaches. Often, good behavior is taken for granted and only poor behavior draws attention. This process is sometimes quite subtle. The baseball player who strikes out, calmly walks back to the bench, and quietly sits down is often thought to be less motivated than another player who, after striking out, throws his bat and helmet, kicks the ground, and shows obvious emotion. Both may be equally motivated but be adhering to different behavior codes. If the coach gives subtle approval by paying attention to the "more motivated" player even while publicly admonishing him for poor behavior, the concepts of self-control and sportsmanship will be undermined. Adults should praise publicly those athletes who show sportsmanlike behavior. However, coaches must be careful not to embarrass those athletes who behave well. A simple "thumbs up" or pat of the back can acknowledge appropriate behavior without making the athlete feel self-conscious. Be aware of quiet behaviors that reflect good sportsmanship and make every attempt to acknowledge good behavior.

Sportsmanship Awards. Sportsmanship awards can highlight sportsmanship as a valued trait approved by the coach, team, and community. Such awards can effectively promote sportsmanship not only because they increase the visibility of sportsmanship behaviors but also because they require that sportsmanship behaviors actually be measured in order to give awards.

From Chalkboard to Playing Field

Sportsmanship Awards

In one high school league, good sportsmanship was measured by officials and coaches by rating teams on a five-point scale from 0 (low) to 4 (high) on sportsmanship after each game during their competitive seasons. Each coach rated the opposing team while the officials rated both teams. At the end of the season, each team's conference rank was determined by their total accumulated points. The team with the highest sportsmanship rating received a trophy reflecting their accomplishment.

One advantage of such a system is that the coaches were constantly being asked to rate opponents and were rated themselves. Thus, their awareness of sporting behavior was continually heightened throughout the season. A disadvantage of this system is that, if the sportsmanship award were to become too highly valued, the pressure to win the award might become so intense that coaches might distort their ratings of the other teams in order to win the award.

Awards given for sportsmanship should be based on **mastery,** not competition or participation. That is, a given level of performance must be mastered to be considered satisfactory sportsmanship (or outstanding sportsmanship, depending upon the level desired). Every individual or team achieving that level should receive the award. The mastery level should be high enough to reflect a truly significant accomplishment but should still be a realistic goal for most of the participants in the program.

If other awards such as "Most Valuable Player" or "Most Improved Player" are given by the sports program, the sportsmanship award can be a prerequisite for an athlete to be even considered for the other awards. In other words, all other awards of merit are awarded only to those young athletes who have first established themselves as good sports. This is quite a radical suggestion. It requires a coach or organization that espouses sportsmanship as the number one priority to literally act in a manner consistent with their words!

Point Out the Benefits of Good Sportsmanship for the Individual Athlete. A major aspect of sportsmanship involves ensuring that all opponents are treated fairly, an approach that often decreases an individual athlete's chances of winning. Coaches can point out in concrete terms the benefits of playing fairly and what athletes gain by behaving in sporting fashion. As discussed earlier in this chapter, good sportsmanship increases the likelihood of making friends, improves one's level of sports performance, and increases both one's self-respect and the respect they earn from others.[13] Being with friends is a major factor in why 8- to 12-year-old children become involved with sport, as is the pursuit of competence.[14]

Involve the Parents. Communication with parents is essential for a successful youth sports experience. Parents should know what the coach's expectations are. Keeping them informed is important for both practical and ethical reasons. Supportive parents who know their expected

FIGURE 6.6 The phrase, "the officials lost control of the game" becomes irrelevant when coach and athletes believe that all participants are responsible for their own behaviors.

role are much more likely to enhance the coach's attempts to develop sportsmanship behaviors than uninformed parents, and parents have a right – even a mandate – to know what values an adult in any program professes to teach their children. Coaches and parents who together are teaching similar values both at home and on the field of play make a powerful combination when teaching young athletes the principles of moral reasoning.

The cooperative efforts of parents and coaches in youth sport settings are important for another compelling reason. As athletes become older and more experienced and become involved with higher levels and more intense competitions, they often show lower levels of moral reasoning in sport settings. This documented finding is not because the moral reasoning of older athletes is less sophisticated than younger athletes. It most likely happens because of what has been termed "Game Reasoning."[15] In some sports (e.g., contact sports) some athletes learn a different pattern of moral reasoning. They – and some of their coaches – believe the referees and game officials are responsible for fairness. This reasoning is illustrated by the not uncommonly uttered phrase, "The officials lost control of the game!" (Figure 6.6) When coaches and athletes believe each individual is responsible for his or her behavior, such a statement becomes irrelevant. Sportsmanship requires that all participants maintain control over game-related behavior. However, when participants believe that the moral reasoning used in "real life" is "set aside" when they walk onto the playing field, game reasoning might produce different types of behaviors. Faking fouls, "working" the officials (attempting to intimidate them), or bending the rules become predictable and acceptable behaviors. When parents and coaches of young athletes work together to teach sportsmanship both on and off the field, the disconnect between game reasoning and real-life reasoning is likely to disappear.

Hold Individuals Responsible for Good Sportsmanship. Avoid, to the extent that you can, situations where the athletes' poor behaviors are anonymous. The card system used by soccer officials is an excellent example of holding an individual responsible for his/her actions in a public sense. Multiple cards within a game or across a series of competitions leads to additional sanctions. Other athletes become aware of the negative consequences of poor sportsmanship and tend to behave better, particularly when they see that the consequences are regularly and fairly enforced – even if not always perfectly. Similar systems could be developed for practice sessions and for other sports if coaches and administrators agreed on its value for reducing acts of unsportsmanlike conduct.

Factors that Undermine Sportsmanship

TREATING SPORTSMANSHIP AS THE CONSOLATION PRIZE

Complimenting athletes for being good sports only after losses relegates sportsmanship to something done when the team is not good enough to win. Sportsmanship must be emphasized equally – win or lose – for your athletes to see it as a primary value.

EXCEPTIONS FOR BETTER PLAYERS

What do you do, as the coach, if your star player cheats or curses at an official? Do you take him or her out of the big game and risk losing or do you only discipline lesser athletes? If you treat your star players differently, none of your players will see sportsmanship as a primary value. They are also likely to question your credibility.

MODELING OTHERS WHO BEHAVE POORLY

Adolescents learn "acceptable" behaviors by watching professional athletes, parents, and coaches. Modeling is a major form of learning. When adults preach sportsmanship yet berate officials or opponents from the sidelines, kids learn to say what we say ("Play fair"), but do as we do (display poor sportsmanship). Seeing poor behavior displayed by professional athletes and/or opponents does not automatically have a negative influence on young athletes. Such poor behavior can be used as concrete examples of **how not to behave.** Youngsters learn by being exposed to both good and bad examples of behaviors and learning to make appropriate choices between them.

Summary

Sportsmanship is as much a way of thinking as it is a specific set of behaviors. That reasoning process can be taught but also depends upon the youngster's stage of maturity. Such instruction must be explicit and structured just as with other forms of learning. Sportsmanship does not develop just through exposure to sports and physical activities. While sportsmanship and character development have long been touted as a highly desirable outcome of sports participation, the evidence suggests that they are not an inevitable outcome of such involvement. Only when specific, systematic instructional programs are given a high priority within youth sports programs, will sportsmanship be purposively developed by sport.

YOUR TURN
Teaching Sportsmanship

You've just watched your team[1] lose a heartbreaker. After leading the contest going into the last few minutes of the game, your team's defense collapses and the opposing team scores twice during those last few minutes to win the game. Your team's bitter disappointment is contrasted by the excitement and elation of the opponents. Both teams pass each other immediately after the game as they leave the court/field/arena. As the opposing coach walks off with several of his players, you overhear two young teens on your team cursing at the coach and his players and telling them to "Get out of here! You just got lucky! You really stink! You're not welcome here!" The athletes don't realize you have overheard them. You realize that the opposing coach and his athletes probably didn't actually hear the comments as they were quite a distance from your players. You do realize that several other athletes on your team have heard the comments loud and clear. No one outside of your team is likely to be aware of these events. What would you do?

POSSIBLE INTERVENTIONS

- **Ignore the situation.** A relatively common response. There are times to ignore outbursts since everyone should have some latitude about expressing feelings. To the extent that the outburst was private or not directed at others, coaches can choose to ignore such behaviors. However, muttering to yourself under your breath or expressing your frustration to yourself or to others in socially acceptable ways is quite different from losing your composure in public or directing your frustration at others. Since the behavior of these youngsters was seen by their teammates and possibly seen by the visiting team, ignoring it would seem inappropriate.

- **Use the incident as a teaching opportunity.** There are a variety of ways to use this event as an opportunity to teach sportsmanship values. Because it is relatively private, the coach can select an approach within the team setting. You could take the boys aside and discuss how to respond after a bitter disappointment. How do they want to be perceived? Do they want to be seen as someone who "can handle it and come back strong" or as poor sports who "lost their cool"?

- **Punishment or suspension.** A brief suspension might be appropriate at the next game. Such a punishment clearly identifies unacceptable behavior and, for those players who are motivated to play, could clearly control their behavior. Punishment, while effective at changing overt behavior, may be less effective at changing internal attitudes.

- **Public vs. private?** You could talk to the athletes privately about why their behaviors were inappropriate. Alternatively, the incident might be an occasion to discuss good sportsmanship with all members of the team. You could point out that the two teens represent their team, and if the opposing players had heard such comments, the likelihood of forming a negative image about your entire team would be quite high. Ask your athletes how they would have felt if they had heard two players on the other team "badmouthing" your team. Would they have limited their judgments to just those two individuals or would they have been likely to think poorly about the entire opposing team?

- **Require an apology.** The opposing coach might be sent a letter of apology written by the offenders. Such a letter could be sent regardless of whether the opposing coach was originally aware of the misbehavior. Further, the teens could be required to formally apologize to their teammates for poorly representing their team.

- **Involve the parents.** Parental support for such an action would be quite helpful especially if the parents were contacted and were supportive before any sanctions were imposed. Such involvement could be much more than simply informing them of their youngster 's indiscretions. Parents could also help use the incident as a teaching opportunity. If they agree that such behavior was inappropriate, they could provide support by talking with their child about "what are standards of acceptable behavior" and "how athletes must learn to control their frustrations after a tough loss." If the parents are not supportive and see such behavior as "acceptable" or "just kids being kids," the coach's actions might have to be directed at identifying what behaviors are acceptable on the team and why. For example, "How team members behave elsewhere is out of my control; however, on our team, what is accepted and demanded as appropriate behavior is...."

CHAPTER REFERENCES

1. Shields, D. L., & Bredemeier, B. L. (2001), Moral development and behavior in sport. In R. N. Singer, H. A. Hausenblas, & C. M. Janelle (Eds.), *Handbook of Sport Psychology,* (2nd ed., pp. 585–603). New York: Wiley.

2. Bean, C., & Forneris, T. (2016). Examining the importance of internally structuring the youth sport context to facilitate positive youth development. *Journal of Applied Sport Psychology, 28,* 1533-1571. DOI: 10.1080/10413200.2016.1164764.

3. Dawes, R.M. (1980). Social dilemmas. *Annual Review of Psychology.* 1980, 31, 169-193.

4. Murphy, S. M. (1995). *Sport psychology interventions.* Champaign, IL: Human Kinetics.

5. Feigley, D. A. (2018). Perspectives on winning in youth sports. *Coaches Reference Manual, Rutgers SAFETY Clinic* (5th ed.).

6. Feigley, D.A. (1983). Is aggression justifiable? *Journal of Health, Physical Education, Recreation and Dance, 54,* 63-64.

7. Kohlberg, L. (1969). The development of children's orientations toward a moral order. I. Sequence in the development of moral thought. *Vita Humana, 6,* 11-33.

8. Kohlberg, L. (1969). The development of children's orientations toward a moral order. I. Sequence in the development of moral thought. *Vita Humana, 6,* 11-33.

9. Gilligan, C. (1982). *In a Different Voice: Psychological Theory and Women's Development.* Cambridge, Mass: Harvard University Press.

10. Weinberg, R. S., & Gould, D. (2015). *Foundations of Sport and Exercise Psychology (6th ed.). Champaign, IL: Human Kinetics.* 554–555.

11. Weiss, M. R., & Bredemeier, B. J. (1991). Moral development in sport. *Exercise and Sport Science Reviews, 18,* 331–378.

12. Elias, M. J. & Tobias, S. E. (1996). *Social problem solving: Interventions in the schools.* New York: The Guilford Press.

13. *Guide to Teaching Sportsmanship – SPORTSTAR, the USTA Sportsmanship Program* (1985). United State Tennis Association Education and Research Center, 729 Alexander Road, Princeton, NJ 08540.

14. Cope, E. J., Bailey, R., & Pearce, G. (2013). Why do children take part in, and remain involved in sport? A literature review and discussion of implications for sports coaches. *International Journal of Coaching Science, 7,* (1), 55–74.

15. Shields, D. L., & Bredemeier, B. L. (2007), Advances in sport morality research. In G. Tenenbaum & R. C. Eklund (Eds.), *Handbook of Sport Psychology,* (3rd ed., pp. 662–684). Hoboken, NJ: John Wiley & Sons.

Working with Athletes with Disabilities

CHAPTER OUTLINE

- Americans with Disabilities Act
- General Guidelines for Coaching Athletes with Disabilities
- Universal Design/Programming
- Coaching Athletes with Intellectual Disabilities
- Coaching Athletes with Behavioral Disorders
- Coaching Athletes with Neuromuscular Disabilities Such as Cerebral Palsy and Spina Bifida
- Coaching Athletes with Upper Extremity Amputation/Limb Deficiency
- Coaching Athletes with Lower Extremity Amputation/Limb Deficiency
- Coaching Athletes with Visual Impairments
- Coaching Athletes with Hearing Impairments
- Coaching Athletes with Autism
- Coaching Athletes with Attention-Deficit/Hyperactivity Disorder (ADHD)
  SPOTLIGHT ON YOUTH SPORTS: Teaching Sportsmanship to an ADHD Athlete
- The Reluctant Participant
- Direct Threats/Risk
- Case Studies and Best Practices
  SPOTLIGHT ON YOUTH SPORTS: An Inclusion Model
  YOUR TURN: Placing Athletes in the Least Restrictive Environment

Y ou've volunteered to coach your son or daughter's team and when you gather the youngsters around you for the first day's practice, you notice that one youngster is noticeably different from the others. The wheel chair makes it obvious. What should you do?

In recreational community youth sport programs, enrollment is typically open to everyone, regardless of ability or prior experience. The "all play" philosophy of these recreation programs can often create significant challenges for volunteer coaches. In addition to being responsible for coaching young athletes of widely differing skills, knowledge, and experiences, these volunteers are often assigned the responsibility of coaching individuals with disabilities. Under Federal law, athletes with disabilities **must be included** if "reasonable accommodations" to rules, policies, practice sessions, and competitions can be made. Often, that inclusion occurs without a great deal of information provided to the volunteer coach regarding how to most effectively include the individual with a disability in a meaningful way with the non-disabled young athletes.

This chapter provides general guidelines for coaching athletes with disabilities; then discusses specific communication and coaching tips for individuals with specific types of disabilities and provides youth sports coaches and administrators with a model for placing athletes with disabilities into the least restrictive environments while permitting a safe and meaningful sports experience. It concludes with access to a web page highlighting actual case studies which integrate athletes with disabilities into the least restrictive environments and identifies additional sources of information for coaches of athletes with disabilities. For young athletes with disabilities, coaches have to alter their coaching style to ensure clear two-way communication and to provide appropriate skills training. The goal is to maximize the quality of the athletes' experiences in recreational sports regardless of the presence or absence of a disability. Those who believe that sports participation benefits children and youth quickly see that such benefits are often magnified for those youngsters who come to the sports experience despite a disability.[*,1]

American with Disabilities Act

Under federal law, youth sport leagues that are open to all must include individuals with disabilities if the disability:

1. **Does not change the "inherent nature of the activity"** Thus, having wrestlers start the first period while physically touching to accommodate a wrestler who has limited vision would normally be considered to be within the bounds of wrestling especially since the wrestlers begin both the second and third periods with contact prior to wrestling.

2. **Does not create "undue hardship"** Having a parent provide the coaches with sign language instruction might be quite reasonable while providing a professional interpreter for all practices and games for a small town recreation league might be an undue financial hardship for a small, nonprofit sport organization.

3. **Does not pose a "direct threat" and** any threat must be documented based upon objective factual evidence, not opinion or subjective concerns such as an infectious disease that cannot be contained because of the nature of sports (e.g., in swimming or a bloody contact sport).

4. **Can be accommodated by reasonable changes to rules, policies or practices.** Providing an individual with perceptual disabilities with four strikes in baseball as opposed to three.

Prior to the start of the season, coaches should meet with the parent/guardians and the athlete to learn more about the athlete's abilities and any prior inclusion strategies, both successful and unsuccessful. The athlete and/or his/her parents or guardians are responsible for notifying

*Many thanks to Dina Trunzo, CTRS and Javier Robles, J.D. for their invaluable critiques and thoughtful contributions to this chapter. Dina is the Manager of the Therapeutic Recreation Department of the Somerset County Park Commission in Somerville, NJ as well as the 2016-17 President of the New Jersey Recreation and Park Association. Javier is an attorney and adjunct professor in the Kinesiology and Health Department, Rutgers University and President of *Thisabled, LLC,* an organization that provides support to persons with disabilities through self-empowerment and perseverance. He was former Deputy Director of the NJ Division of Disability Services.

the administrator and/or the coach of any specific support services and/or modifications required* (e.g., provision of restroom facilities, access ramps, interpreters, large print instructions, etc.). However, administrators and coaches can encourage the sharing of appropriate information by asking the parents or guardians of all participating athletes before the season begins the question, "Is there anything you can tell us about your child so that we can provide him/her with a successful experience?"

General Guidelines for Coaching Athletes with Disabilities

The 1990 Americans with Disabilities Act (ADA)[2] defines a disability as a physical or mental impairment that substantially limits one or more "major life activities" including walking, seeing, hearing, speaking, thinking and/or interacting with others. (Figure 7.1) An example of impaired interacting with others would be Attention Deficit Hyperactivity Disorder (ADHD) which is characterized by inattentiveness, over-activity, impulsivity or a combination thereof.

INCLUSION

Inclusion, or the integration of people with and without disabilities in youth sport programs, is governed by the ADA. What it means for youth sports coaches is, essentially, providing children with disabilities the same choices and opportunities in sport as every other child. A key com-

FIGURE 7.1 While not mentioning sport directly, the Americans with Disabilities Act of 1990 has had a profound effect on providing access to youth sport programs for individuals with disabilities throughout the United States.

---

*Some parents are reluctant to identify their child's disability for fear that the child will be treated differently or be restricted from the opportunities provided for other children.

ponent of this law addresses the need for individuals with disabilities to receive services in the least restrictive setting or environment. In other words, every effort must be made to include children with physical, sensory, behavioral and intellectual disabilities in their community's youth sport programs.

Most administrators and volunteer coaches readily support inclusion, but they often lack specific information for effectively placing and coaching athletes with disabilities. Inclusion requires a collaborative effort among administrators, coaches, parents, and athletes to help participants – both disabled and nondisabled – to overcome challenges and facilitate strategies for providing optimal experiences for all. It involves an evaluation of the program and the environment in which the activity occurs in addition to an assessment of the needs of the athletes with the disabilities.

BENEFITS OF INCLUSION

Benefits go far beyond merely permitting individuals with disabilities to play sport. All of us, throughout our lives, will encounter individuals with disabilities. Exposing youngsters to diverse populations of all types fosters understanding and a sense of awareness instead of limited stereotypes, especially when such interactions lead to successful life experiences such as being part of a team. Further, when both the disabled and non-disabled are given opportunities to interact with each other, they can develop enhanced peer relationships and friendships that would otherwise be denied. The training, the practices and the skill development opportunities have more impact than the competitions alone.

A remarkable similarity exists between effective strategies for including and coaching both disabled and non-disabled. Differences are more often a matter of degree as opposed to qualitatively different strategies. For example, "assessing an athlete's initial ability" or the approach of "avoid making assumptions about the athlete's skills and needs" are just as applicable for the non-disabled as for the disabled. "Keep it simple!" is just as applicable for t-ball coaches as it is for those who coach older athletes with cognitive disabilities. Expanding these strategies to include athletes with disabilities increases coaches' awareness and ability to apply such strategies more effectively to all populations.

Universal Design/Programming[3]

Since the inception of the ADA, the concept of inclusion has changed from merely modifying activities and environments to permit legally required inclusion to a much broader approach focused on designing activities, environments and communication for all. Initially, Universal Design originated from an architectural design approach to physical products and environmental structures. It is defined as "the design of products or environments to be usable by all people to the greatest extent possible without need for adaptation or specialized design[4]." The seven principles[5] that serve as the core of Universal Design rapidly became recognized as an overall strategy that can benefit virtually all segments of society permitting a more receptive approach to learning as well as accessible environments and usable products. Its impact on inclusion for individuals both those with and without disabilities has been immense. It is not a "one size fits all" approach but rather that a "naturally inclusive environment benefits everyone."

UNIVERSAL PROGRAMMING – THE ENVIRONMENT

Provide clearly defined boundaries for activities and drills. Use cones, tape, signage to indicate safe zones. Assign specific areas for activities that are free from hazards and accessible to all. Ensure that the assigned space is adequate and appropriate for the nature of the activity. Keep sensory distractions to a minimum, especially visual and auditory distractions but keep in mind that for some, touch and smell may also be powerful distractions.

UNIVERSAL PROGRAMMING – THE SCHEDULE

Set up clear, consistent schedules and rotations from station to station. Minimize waiting. Standing in line should be by design, not a result of poor planning (for example, a brief rest after an intense activity, not the result of a lack of sufficient equipment). Moving from station to station should be preceded by **transitional prompts.** ("We'll be moving from the warm-ups to the next drill station by the cones in two minutes. Be ready."). Coaches should have back up plans if the originally designed activity is not working or if another group has already occupied the area. Rules and routines should be consistent – and, thus predictable by the athletes.

Universal Programming – The Skill Development

Identify those skills you wish to develop (physical skills – swinging the bat levelly in baseball batting; cognitive skills – being able to recognize balls and strikes in and out of the strike zone; emotional – maintaining one's composure after striking out). Praise the skills; repeat the skills; build the skills progressively.

Universal Programming – The Coaching Staff

The coach's behavior can increase or decrease the inappropriate behavior of the athletes regardless of ability levels (See Chapter 2 on Effective Coaching Strategies and Chapter 4 on Positive Discipline.) Say "Hello" and "Goodbye." Discuss rules and expectations. Learn and use athletes' names. Consistently communicate with everyone. Anticipate and preempt negative behaviors and promote positive behaviors.

Here are general guidelines for coaching athletes with disabilities. (Figure 7.2)

FIGURE 7.2 Effective coaching requires not only enthusiasm and concern for your athletes but it also requires a willingness to learn both the specifics of your athlete's disability and a knowledge of your sport.

COMMUNICATION TIPS

Be enthusiastic and interested in the progress of each athlete. Know both the activity and how you wish to teach and coach it before you begin. Have equipment ready. Give the activity and the objective specific names: ("We're going to do 'Double Touch Drills.' Dribble the soccer ball by touching it every second step!"). Review rules and expectations regularly but more often with younger and less cognitively able individuals. State boundaries and expectations (Be certain to make at least 10 attempts at shooting the basket before we rotate stations in the next 10 minutes.") Gather the group so that they can hear and see you and are paying attention before you begin the instructions (e.g., facing you with their backs toward the older team on the next court and sitting on their basketballs so they are not bouncing the balls.). Give clear, specific instructions in small sequential steps that are consistent with your rules. Ask the athletes to repeat your directions. Where possible post reminders. Prompt them to give you eye contact. Show them what you want them to do and not to do. ("Pass the ball this way, not that way. Do it this way."). Ask before they move to their drills stations "Any questions?" Modify and adapt drills that are not working. Regularly prompt transitions. Encourage them to try the "new ways" without fear and embarrassment. Praise individuals in front of their peers for the skills of learning to learn ("Way to focus." "Excellent concentration!" "Way to hustle even after a miss!").

Meet with the parents/guardians to discuss the disability. Seek pertinent information concerning the athlete's specific disability, including medications and secondary disabilities. For example, Down Syndrome athletes, in addition to the cognitive disability, typically have very loose muscular/skeletal joints and a severe weakness in the neck area, which places them at risk when pressure is placed on the head and neck in sports such as gymnastics when performing forward and backward rolls.

Avoid singling out the athlete with the disability. Look for opportunities to address all your athletes without stigmatizing any one of them. For example, incorporate auditory, visual and tactile demonstrations for all your athletes when introducing new skills. Make certain all athletes understand before initiating a drill.

COACHING TIPS

Assess the disabled athlete using methods similar to those used with nondisabled athletes. Be certain to provide the athlete with opportunities to demonstrate his skills and abilities. Focus on identifying abilities, not disabilities. For example, when assessing a sport skill such as dribbling a ball in soccer, allow the child with the disability to demonstrate how they dribble.

Modify only those aspects of the activities that need to be modified for a given athlete, while still maintaining the integrity of the game. For example, in tennis, an athlete's participation might be facilitated by allowing her to return the ball after two bounces while other players in the same game must play the ball after only one bounce. Allow 4 or 5 strikes in baseball/softball to increase chances of getting a hit (an outcome that increases fielding opportunities as well!). Use a brightly colored ball when a player has difficulty seeing or tracking the ball. Make modifications only when needed to accommodate the athlete's abilities and to ensure the safety of all participants. (Figure 7.3)

Mark positions on the playing field; for example, by taping X's on the floor in basketball as the starting points for a zone defense. Trace an outline of the proper hand position on the football for throwing a spiral forward pass. Make the equipment smaller, lighter, heavier or bigger (Use a size 3 soccer ball or use a beach ball instead of a volleyball).

Encourage parents of the athletes to watch practice so that they may recognize areas where they can encourage and assist their child with "homework;" that is, practicing skills at home.

FIGURE 7.3
Make the equipment such as the ball smaller or larger, lighter or bigger, or with contrasting colors to aid the athlete in tracking the ball.

Be flexible. Different techniques will work for different types of learners. Remember that asking the disabled athlete for input is often an effective way to obtain important information. For example, an upper extremity amputee may need a modification in throwing and catching a softball. Ask him to demonstrate the method he may have already developed. Just as importantly, requesting such input respects the dignity and competence of the disabled athlete.

Coaching Athletes with Intellectual Disabilities

Do not assume that the presence of an intellectual disability means a lack of physical skills and abilities.

COMMUNICATION TIPS

Keep your directions simple and concrete. Verbal instruction should be brief, simple, and to the point. For example, ask the athlete to "look at third base," or "step toward third base" instead of "rotate to the left."

Check to ensure that directions are adequately understood **before** beginning a new activity or drill. For example, instead of asking "Do you understand?" ask, "What were you just asked to do?" The response to "understanding" is often "Yes," regardless of the athlete's level of comprehension.

COACHING TIPS

Be aware of short attention spans. Provide breaks as necessary and compensate for lower skill levels with additional instruction time and smaller, multiple steps in the teaching progressions. Place the athlete next to a peer who already understands the instructions. Pair the athlete with a buddy and/or provide individualized instruction.

Physically demonstrate skills whenever possible but do not rely on mirroring (i.e., demonstrating while facing the athlete). Demonstrate while facing the same direction as the athletes are facing since they may lack the capacity to distinguish left from right. (Figure 7.4)

When possible, use additional cues to aid athletes in following directions. For example, a red bracelet could be used on the demonstrator's right arm to highlight right from left by prompting red equals right.

FIGURE 7.4
Demonstrations that avoid mirroring are often followed more easily by athletes with cognitive disabilities.

Keep athletes in a well-defined area for instruction with clear boundaries such as the infield in baseball or the 18-yard box in soccer. Assign a player a certain portion of the field where only she is permitted to play the ball.

Provide substantial repetition of previously learned skills. Consider setting aside time before the beginning of regular practice to review previously learned skills before initiating new or more advanced instruction with the disabled athlete(s) and others who might benefit from additional repetitions.

Use concrete cues. For example, when coaching a gymnast to take a longer lunge on a round off (i.e., in the hurdle step), place a carpet square on the floor and ask the gymnast to step across the target rather than merely saying "Make your lunge longer." Also, systematically prompt the athlete to refocus on a task or repeat instructions, especially if the task is complex or has multiple steps or sequential components.

Use "whole-part-whole" learning strategies or backward chaining. **Whole-part-whole** involves first demonstrating or having the athlete perform the entire complex skill followed by step-by-step instruction that breaks down and focuses on each of the required component skills, then putting the components back together as an entire skill. For example, first show the athletes the entire baseball swing. Then break the activity into parts and coach those individual parts such as proper foot stance, arm placement, and stepping into the swing. Then have them execute the entire swing. While this strategy differs little from working with all athletes regardless of disability, disabled athletes may require that the skill be broken down into even smaller steps than for typically developing athletes.

With **backward chaining**, the coach helps the athlete with all stages of a skill sequence except the very last stage which the athlete completes by himself, experiencing instant success. After several such successes, the athlete completes the last two stages in the sequence; then the last three stages; etc. until the entire skill can be completed from beginning to end. For example, have the baseball player throw directly to first base. Then have them face sideways from which they must turn and throw. Then throw the ball gently to one side of the player so that they must retrieve the ball, then turn and then throw. Then throw the ball even further away from the players so that they must step to retrieve the ball, then turn and then throw. Even more simplified steps may need to be developed with athletes of lower cognitive and/or physical skill.

Coaching Athletes with Behavioral Disorders

Prior to the season, meet with the athlete's parents or guardians to determine what behavioral management techniques they use and which are applicable in a sport setting. Faster learning, less confusion, and higher motivational levels will result. **Acting out** (displaying disruptive behavior) may be triggered by excessive waiting time, lack of leadership, unclear expectations, lack of predictable structure, environmental distractions, fear of change, and feelings of powerlessness. Sometimes, all you need to do is to simply ask the athlete why he is acting out and then change the triggering element instead of resorting to disciplinary actions.

Take time at the beginning of the season to establish clear expectations and rules. Specificity, clarity and consistency are particularly important concepts for athletes with behavioral problems. Ask the parents if there are techniques, behavioral plans or charting used in the child's school setting that can be replicated on the playing field or gym. Using similar strategies in both settings provides consistency for the athlete and avoids "re-inventing the wheel." Because of confidentiality laws, only the parent or the guardians can provide you with such direct information about their child.

Try to "catch them being good." Rewarding good behavior is key rather than solely focusing on disciplining poor behavior.

COMMUNICATION TIPS

Have realistic expectations. For example, ask the athlete to "stay focused" for 2 minutes rather than for the entire practice. If the athlete is consistently able to focus for 5 minutes, then extend the request to 8 to 10 minutes. Use progressions in "learning to focus and pay attention" just as you use progressions for learning physical sport skills.

Help the athlete focus on the coach's direction and not on parents and spectators. Such a focus minimizes confusion particularly for athletes who are easily distracted. For example, tell the athlete to make eye contact with you during instruction so that "I can see you listening!" "When you look at me while I'm coaching, I know you are paying attention. If you are looking away, you might be listening but I can't tell."

Athletes with behavioral issues often overreact to extraneous stimuli, such as minor noise, touches, or visual distractions. This over-reactivity can disrupt the learning situation and be extremely frustrating for coaches. To maintain their attention, station them close to you and when providing corrections to sport skills or behaviors that may sound like criticisms, preface your instruction with "I'm not mad at you. Keep your hands quiet."

COACHING TIPS

Keep the practice format structured by doing similar skills and drills in similar sequences so the athletes know what to expect. Rely heavily on transition prompts – warnings about what is to come next. State how long before we rotate stations, when warm-ups will end, when practice is over.

Provide sufficient time and practice for each skill before moving on to the next level. Athletes with behavioral issues may require more time to learn than other athletes. In fact, slower learning may be one of the underlying causes of the behavioral problems themselves. Concepts or skills that other athletes might master in a single practice might take multiple sessions for athletes with behavioral issues.

Respect the athlete's right to personal space during your instruction and while they are interacting with teammates. While physical contact is often unavoidable in team sports, strive to be sensitive to the athlete's preferences. If he prefers not to be touched, use visual and auditory coaching techniques.

Coaching Athletes with Neuromuscular Disabilities Such as Cerebral Palsy and Spina Bifida

Prior to the season, meet with the athletes and their parent/guardians to determine their level of intellectual functioning. Do not assume that an athlete with speech difficulties (common with cerebral palsy) has an intellectual impairment. However, for those athletes who also have intellectual deficits, use one-word cues and/or signals developed jointly with the athlete to promote effective, respectful communication.

Because there are different types of cerebral palsy (CP), obtain information on the characteristics of the athlete's CP to determine the conditions for maximal performance. For example, an athlete with spastic CP (stiff, awkward movements) might perform better after a brief warm-up, whereas an athlete with dyskinetic/athetoid CP (involuntary, uncontrollable movements) might perform better by avoiding any warm-up and performing directly after a brief rest.

COMMUNICATION TIPS

Allow additional time for communicating and exchanging information. Ask the athletes for their preferred means of communicating.

COACHING TIPS

Because physical balance is often a problem for CP athletes, use strategies to broaden their physical base of support such as using a wider stance while attempting to throw or hit a pitched ball.

Match the athletes to playing positions that allow them to use their strengths. For example, if an athlete cannot run well, she might be able to function well as a pitcher or catcher, positions from which she can throw and catch from a standing position. Other adaptations may involve the use of pinch runners and/or allowing a baseball player to hit the ball from a tee.

Provide adaptive equipment or devices for athletes of different skill levels and degrees of disabilities; for example, bowling ramps, balls with handles, devices that permit athletes with disabilities to hold bats, racquets or other specialized equipment.

Coaching Athletes with Upper Extremity Amputation/Limb Deficiency

The extent to which an athlete is limited by an upper extremity limb deficiency depends upon whether the deficiency is above or below the elbow. (Figure 7.5) Assess the athletes' abilities rather than disabilities to determine in which aspects of the activity they can participate. For example, are they capable of controlling a basketball sufficiently to shoot the ball at the basket with one hand while stabilizing the ball with the affected limb?

COMMUNICATION TIPS

Rarely does a physical amputee require special communication techniques. However, provide them with the respect of asking if they need assistance and, if so, how might they prefer to be assisted.

FIGURE 7.5 The impact of an upper limb deficiency depends upon whether the deficiency is above or below the elbow and the specific requirements of the sport.

COACHING TIPS

The athlete may use both arms, combining the use of the affected limb and the unaffected limb to participate. For example, a baseball pitcher with a deficiency below the elbow may hold the mitt under his limb while he is pitching the ball and then transfer the mitt to his unaffected limb in preparation for possibly catching the ball hit by the batter.

Amputees may need more frequent rest periods due to the sensitivity of their amputated limb and the tendency toward increased perspiration, particularly if they have lived a sedentary lifestyle and, at least initially, lack the necessary conditioning for playing sport.

Use balls that are easier to grip (nerf balls, partially inflated balls, balls and mitts with Velcro). Allow any type of throwing (overhead, overhand, underhand). Push balls down ramps when bowling or off stationary surfaces such as T-ball stands, laps, tables, ramps). Expand the definition of success. For example, count attempts to throw the runner out as successful if the ball lands within arm's length of the first baseman before the runner crosses the base.

Coaching Athletes with Lower Extremity Amputation/ Limb Deficiency

The extent to which an athlete is limited by a lower extremity limb deficiency depends upon whether the deficiency is above or below the knee (Figure 7.6) Lower-extremity amputees may choose to participate in one sport using an assistive device (such as a wheelchair for a road race) and other sports without such devices (such as ambulating for volleyball either with or without prosthesis). Alternately, they may use a prosthesis specifically designed to enhance performance in their chosen sport or may require adaptive equipment.

COMMUNICATION TIPS

Again, assess the athletes' abilities rather than disabilities to determine in which aspects of the activity they can participate. For example, if they are able to participate in basketball skills and drills but do not meet the performance standards to play in competition, then every effort should be made to include them in that part of the sport they can do. For example, if they are able to bat in baseball, coaches might be able to provide a pinch runner once they have hit the ball to complete the accommodation.

FIGURE 7.6
The impact of a lower limb deficiency depends upon whether the deficiency is above or below the knee and the specific requirements of the sport.

COACHING TIPS

Amputees may need to widen their stance for support for adequate balance. Just as with upper extremity deficiencies, lower extremity amputees may need more frequent rest periods and tend toward increased perspiration due to lower levels of cardiovascular conditioning.

Use kicking modifications such as different size balls. Use different weight balls when strength is an issue. Use alternative kickers. Permit unlimited tries. Kick stationary rather than moving balls. Permit participants to hit, push or touch the ball instead of kicking.

Familiarize yourself with the athlete's assistive devices such as a wheelchair.* A lightweight chair may need to be supported from underneath during outdoor field activities. Some types of wheelchairs may be more prone to tipping over if an athlete leans forward or sideways to retrieve a ball or other sport-related movements.

Those athletes with upper body involvement in sports such as tennis might need additional modification to participate such as a Velcro strap to hold a racquet.

Coaching Athletes with Visual Impairments

Visual impairments range from total blindness (the inability to tell light from dark) to a reduction in vision so severe that it cannot be corrected

---

*Note: The ADA requires that facilities meet minimum accessibility standards. This approach should include playing fields and facilities, locker rooms, parking lots, spectator areas, and restroom facilities.

with glasses or contact lenses and, as a result, reduces a person's ability to function at tasks requiring the ability to see. A visual impairment may also include a limited visual field where the width of the athlete's visual field is so restricted (no greater than 20 degrees) that they literally have "tunnel vision." This category may also include suffering from double vision or distorted visual images.

COMMUNICATION TIPS

Be sensitive to the type of assistance the athlete prefers. Ask if they need help and, if so, what type of assistance is preferred.

COACHING TIPS

Use bigger softer balls for tracking or balls that beep. Use balls whose colors contrast with the typical background.

Coaching Athletes with Hearing Impairments[6]

Athletes with hearing impairments resemble their nondisabled peers in terms of physical abilities. Therefore, minimal physical modifications should be necessary. The term "deaf" typically refers to individuals whose loss of hearing is so profound that they cannot process speech and hearing even with the aid of hearing devices. Hearing impaired individuals may be "hard of hearing" but are still capable of using their limited hearing when communicating with others. Individuals can have a loss of hearing in one or both ears.

COMMUNICATION TIPS

Do not assume that all hearing impaired athletes use sign language. Many athletes with hearing impairments have some residual hearing. They often use combination techniques including sign language, lip reading, and, when possible, any limited auditory cues still available to them. Ask the athletes for the type of communication they most prefer and face the person directly. (Figure 7.7)

Talk in a normal voice. Shouting may actually be painful and/or distracting to athletes wearing hearing aids. Talk at a normal speed. Do not mouth words or exaggerate lip movements. Use short words and sentences with one- or two-word cues to permit better comprehension.

FIGURE 7.7
While signing is often a useful means of communicating by athletes who are deaf, many athletes with hearing impairments have some residual hearing and use multiple techniques to overcome their hearing loss.

Arrange the physical environment to maximize visual cues during instruction and minimize background noise whenever and wherever possible. For example, avoid standing where your face is hidden in shadows (such as in front of a window, light source, or sun). Whenever possible, position the athletes close to you so that instruction can be more easily seen.

Use visual and tactile cues where possible to gain the athlete's attention (e.g., flip lights on and off; use hand signals; touch the athlete's arm). Use physical demonstrations of the skills or drills.

COACHING TIPS

Sport skill instruction should include visual and tactile examples and reinforcement such as hand clapping or pats on the shoulder. Hand signals can be used to officiate, start races, and give directions.

Where there is body contact, have your athletes remove hearing aids or provide them with protective coverings to minimize the possibility of injury.

Where possible, avoid teaching stations and specific exercises that impede vision. For example, instead of having your athletes stand and bend from the waist to touch their toes, have them sit and execute a pike stretch while you stand in front within their field of vision.

Athletes with hearing impairments sometimes experience balance problems. The problem can be minimized by broadening the athlete's physical base of support. Such a strategy can be used in a baseball defensive stance, throwing a baseball, serving a volleyball, or shooting a basketball foul shot.

Coaching Athletes with Autism

Autism describes a spectrum of traits which affect the athlete's ability to communicate, relate to others, understand language and play. Sometimes the behaviors are called Aspergers Syndrome. Autistic children vary widely in their abilities, intelligence and behaviors. They may have difficulty understanding verbal and nonverbal language as well as figurative language. As a result, they may have difficulty telling others what they want or how they are feeling. They may display unusual or odd speech patterns. They often have difficulty adjusting to changes in their routines, changing surroundings and change in general. Repetitive body movements and behavior patterns are quite common. Many have impaired social skills and have difficulty knowing how to play with others, often avoiding eye contact. They often display abnormal responses to sensory stimuli and can respond negatively, sometimes aggressively, to being touched. They may show a limited range of interests and/or a preoccupation with a narrow range of interests (dinosaurs, trains, bugs, etc.)

COMMUNICATION TIPS

Because of the autistic athlete's difficulty with change, regularly warn of upcoming changes by providing transition prompts whenever possible. Announce upcoming changes in an activity ("We're going to stop stretching and begin batting practice, in 10 minutes"). Remind them of the impending change again at 5 minutes prior to the change, etc., etc. Use visual and verbal cues together. Speak in a firm but calm voice and provide clear expectations of the desired behaviors ("Keep your hands to yourself", "Walk, no running", "Hands down and quiet hands," etc.). Use "First, then" statements ("First, we are going to jog; then we are going to stretch").

COACHING TIPS

Provide as much structure as possible. Be predictable; that is, whenever possible, provide a schedule of events or rotations throughout the practice. Where appropriate and possible, use timers. Make certain that the tasks and drills are specific, clear, consistent and easily accomplished. Present tasks or skills one at a time to make it easier for the autistic athlete to process what is expected. Give immediate and specific, positive feedback. Demonstrate the activity or sports skills whenever possible.

Coaching Athletes with Attention-Deficit/Hyperactivity Disorder (ADHD)

Athletes with ADHD show short attention spans, impulsivity, inability to inhibit behaviors, lack of self-control and hyperactivity. They may experience low self-esteem, display a lack of social skills and have difficulty following rules. They have difficulty working on long-term goals and require constant redirection and need close supervision coupled with verbal and visual cues to enable them to stay on task. They often display volatile emotions and frequently overreact to changes in their environment. They tend to respond best to a structured, predictable environment.

SPOTLIGHT ON YOUTH SPORTS

Teaching Sportsmanship to an ADHD Athlete

The following is a potential script for providing a young ADHD athlete with concrete instructions concerning how to behave in situations requiring good sportsmanship.

"Billie, do your best no matter whether we are ahead or behind. Do not make fun of the losing team … Say 'Good Job' or 'Way to go! It was fun playing against you.' Being a good winner means not bragging if your team wins… say 'nice game' to the players on the other team. Stay cool if you lose and say to yourself, 'Oh well, you win some and lose some.' Show respect toward everyone. And remember, we help those who are less skilled."

COMMUNICATION TIPS

Post daily schedules and assignments when possible. Use transition prompts to call their attention to schedule changes. Set specific times for specific tasks. Provide regularly scheduled and frequent breaks. Whenever possible, supplement verbal instructions with visual instructions and demonstrations. Use timers. Use clear, simple and consistent rules and expectations. State consequences ahead of time for both positive and negative behaviors and then deliver those consequences immediately.

COACHING TIPS

Be simple and clear with concrete examples of what behaviors are expected. For example, when teaching sportsmanship, be as specific as possible and give concrete prompts for the behaviors you expect.

The Reluctant Participant

When an athlete is observed not participating, ask yourself several related questions before attempting to engage them in the activity.

DO THEY UNDERSTAND?

Might they be reluctant to participate because they lack understanding of your instructions? Ask them to repeat the instructions or ask "Do you have any questions?"

DO THEY LACK THE SKILLS?

Have the skills been adequately taught? Are they afraid of making a mistake or lack the strength, flexibility and agility to execute the required skills or the prerequisite skills? An athlete not strong enough to support their body weight might justifiably be reluctant to perform a cartwheel or handstand in gymnastics.

DO THEY HAVE AN INTEREST?

Do they want to do the activity? A lack of interest is likely to be displayed if they are afraid, confused, embarrassed, believe they lack the capacity to do the activity or the activity hurts (for example, a flexibility exercise). Ask if they want to try and, if not, why not. Often a simple modification in the activity can spark an interest.

Direct Threats/Risk

There may be occasions when you or a parent of one of your athletes expresses concern about the possibility that an individual with a disability poses a direct threat to themselves or to the health and safety of others. Such concerns often occur with behavioral disabilities or autism but can be raised about virtually any disability. For such a threat to disqualify a participant with a disability, it must be real and not based upon misconceptions or ignorance concerning the particular disability. Further, the risk needs to be of such character that it cannot be eliminated or reduced to an acceptable level by modifying the program's policies, practices or procedures or by the provision of auxiliary aids or services. The existence of a direct threat must be based upon an individualized assessment (current medical evidence or best available objective evidence) that assesses the:

a. Nature, duration and severity of the risk, as well as how imminent the threat of harm is.

b. Probability that a potential injury will actually occur.

c. And whether reasonable modification will eliminate the risk.

In one case[7], a Karate school was found to have justifiably denied admission of a 12-year-old boy with AIDS to their program. The court held that the boy posed a direct threat to other children in the program because of the high risk of blood-to-blood contact between students in this particularly intense form of karate. Bloody injuries were "extremely likely" to produce unavoidable blood-to-blood contact. The court held that, other than private lessons which the school had offered to the boy, no reasonable modification would eliminate the high risk. The court ruled that requiring the school to teach a less aggressive style would constitute a fundamental change to the nature of the program, and that physical protections such as eye coverings and gloves would be ineffective in this type of Karate.

Case Studies and Best Practices

A much more elaborate discussion of techniques for working effectively with young athletes with disabilities is available on the Rutgers Youth Sport Research Council's web page at http://youthsports.rutgers.edu. It provides numerous case studies of successful integration of athletes with disabilities into programs ranging from total integration into community recreation programs to partial integration or assignment to programs dedicated solely to participants with disabilities.

SPOTLIGHT ON YOUTH SPORTS
An Inclusion Model[8]

Placing athletes with disabilities into an appropriate program in competitive youth sports is primarily the responsibility of the youth sport administrator, but the coach can have a dramatic effect on including that individual in the sports program in meaningful ways. Thus, both administrators and coaches benefit from understanding the process by which athletes with disabilities can be assessed and ultimately placed in the least restrictive and most appropriate program.

The placement of disabled athletes can range from programs with no adaptations to programs designed exclusively for the disabled. In making the assessment, administrators should consider the participant's preference ("I'd rather play with similarly disabled individuals" vs. "I'd rather play with all my friends.") while seeking the least restrictive environment from the following options:

Full inclusion. Sport programs and leagues are open to the general population with no modifications for athletes who are disabled.

Inclusion with Support Services. Transportation, instructional aides, and/or supplemental training that do not alter the athletic program itself are provided. For example, permitting golf carts for golfers with ambulatory disabilities when nondisabled golfers must walk or providing signing for a child with a hearing loss.

Inclusion with Modification. Adaptive or assistive devices are provided, such as modified skis for double leg amputees, that do not alter the fundamental nature of the program but without which the disabled athlete could not participate.

Programs for Disabled and Nondisabled. Peer programs incorporate the buddy system designed to promote peer interaction of disabled and nondisabled athletes who are members of the same team. This can be accomplished both within the community (e.g., Challenger Little League) or may be offered by disability specific organizations (e.g., Special Olympics Unified Sports).

Programs Designed Exclusively for the Disabled. Nondisabled athletes are not permitted to participate. Examples include the National Junior Wheelchair Sports and the Special Olympics. The community may consider starting a disability specific program (e.g., basketball league for intellectually disabled) if there is sufficient need or interest.

YOUR TURN
Placing Athletes in the Least Restrictive Environment

Appendix 7.1 provides you with a decision-making tree to assist you in deciding what is the most appropriate placement for an athlete with a disability to ensure the least restrictive youth sports environment. The goal is to place the athlete in an environment where success is possible and the restrictions are minimal yet capable of providing a safe, challenging sport experience. Select an athlete with a specific disability; answer the sequential questions in the decision-making tree; and determine the least restrictive sports program for your athlete based upon the characteristics of that athlete's disability.

CHAPTER REFERENCES

1. Much of the content for this chapter was developed in a research study originally funded by the NJ Developmental Disabilities Council under the direction of David A. Feigley, Ph.D., Linda M. Sharkey, MS and Joanne Hunt, MA, CTRS, all faculty members of the Department of Exercise Science & Sport Studies at Rutgers University (Now the Department of Kinesiology and Health).

2. Feigley, D.A. & Sharkey, L. (1993, October). **The Americans with Disabilities Act: Implications for inclusion in community youth sports.** (.3 CEU Program), National Congress of the National Recreation and Park Association, San Jose, California.

3. http://universaldesign.ie/What-is-Universal-Design/The 7 Principles/, North Carolina State University, 1997

4. https://www.ncsu.edu/ncsu/design/cud/about_ud/about_ud.htm.

5. http://universaldesign.ie/What-is-Universal-Design/The-7-Principles/

6. https://www.eeoc.gov/eeoc/publications/qa_deafness.cfm

7. Montalvo v. Radcliffe, 167 F.3d 873 (4th Cir. 1999)

8. Feigley, D.A., Sharkey, L. & Hunt, J. (1997). **Inclusion – It's Not as Hard as You Think.** 22nd Annual Conference of the New Jersey Recreation and Park Association. (.2 CEU Program), Atlantic City, NJ.

8

Creating a Positive
Team Culture

CHAPTER OUTLINE

- Types of Team Cohesion
- Developing Team Cohesiveness and a Positive Team Climate
- Stage 1: Relating Positively to One's Coach
  GAME #1: What's in Your Gym Bag?
- Stage 2: Relating to One's Teammates
  GAME #2: Telling Whoppers
- Stage 3: Valuing One's Teammates
  GAME #3: Infinity Volleyball
- Stage 4: Establishing a Sense of Community/Team Culture
  YOUR TURN: Strengthening the Team Bond

A youth sports team often starts out merely as a collection of individuals with little connection except their interest in a specific sport. They may be a group of youngsters who just have been assigned to you, as the coach, after tryouts or registrations have been completed. With your guidance, they can become much more than that. Under your care, they can come together for a common purpose and bond as a team. A major task for youth sport coaches is to develop that team cohesiveness in positive ways* in much the same way that they develop individual sports skills.

Mike Krzyzewski (Coach K), head basketball coach of Duke University and a three-time Olympic gold medal winning basketball coach, notes that teams evolve. He believes team building takes time, common goals, and competition.[1] By time, he means the time to form relationships, the time to establish standards, and the time to develop motivation. By goals, he means having a purpose that unites and prepares. By competition, he means an ongoing self-assessment of how effective your training has been for preparing your athletes to perform under pressure and determining what changes and improvements must be made to continue to improve and reach your common goals.

Coaches have a strong influence on the team environment in which team cohesion develops. They determine and model "the values, attitudes and behaviors that are acceptable and encouraged (e.g., mutual support, hard work, communication) as well as those that are discouraged (e.g., tardiness, selfishness, conflict.)"[2] Coaches must directly, clearly, and consistently communicate the values, attitudes, and behaviors necessary for building a group that sees itself as a unified team.

Types of Team Cohesion

Two classic types of cohesion have been identified: **Task cohesion** where the members of the team are united in their efforts to achieve a common goal and **social cohesion** where the members of the team are attracted to one another as part of a special group. Task cohesion typically develops rapidly and naturally in interactive team sports such as basketball, soccer and football. Task cohesion may need to be nurtured in individual

---

* Bonding can result for negative reasons such as group members facing a common threat. Such an approach in youth sports is undesirable, unethical, and unnecessary.

Forming
a Team

Valuing One's Teammates

Relating to One's Teammates

Relating Positively to One's Coach

FIGURE 8.1
The Team Building Pyramid.
Games are one of many important ways to nurture the development of a strong team culture, especially in youth sport programs.

sports such as track and field, gymnastics, and swimming. Social cohesion depends strongly on a positive team climate, a factor over which the youth sport coach has substantial, although not total, control. While the emphasis on developing each type of cohesion may differ depending upon the level of the competition (e.g., "in town" recreational teams vs. higher skill level traveling squads), both are important in youth sports.

While there is debate over whether team cohesiveness causes team success or results from team success, the existence of a positive team climate for youth sport teams is important either way. Belonging to a team -- being part of a special group -- is an important experience for young boys and girls. As a coach, you can enhance a positive team climate and thus encourage the development of strong team cohesion in a number of ways.[3]

Developing Team Cohesiveness and a Positive Team Climate

The model[4] in Figure 8.1 outlines the stages through which both a positive team climate and team cohesion can be enhanced and systematically developed. A team can be a special community for young athletes, a community in which they feel safe, feel a sense of belonging, and believe they can contribute in meaningful ways to common team goals. Team building is not an accidental result of being thrown together on a specific team but rather occurs over time as team members learn to connect with one another. Coaches can facilitate such bonding by providing time for friendships to form both on the practice field and at social functions outside of practices (e.g., a swim party, a trip to an amusement park, an awards banquet, and attending games of higher level teams such as a local high school, college, or professional match).

Let's examine how we can use games appropriate for children and youth at each of these levels for building a positive team climate and a strong sense of belonging to a special group – our team. The games are only a means to an end. The specific games described in this chapter are examples to illustrate team-building strategies. What is important is not the specific game but rather the purpose of the activity. The type of game used should vary depending upon the age, experience, and maturity of the athletes, the length of time the athletes have been together, and what specific aspect of cohesion the coach wishes to develop.

STAGE 1

Relating Positively to One's Coach

When you first meet with your team, they may or may not know each other and they probably do not know you – at least in your role as coach. You want to develop a positive rapport with your athletes.

BE A POSITIVE AUTHORITY FIGURE

Authority and rapport are not incompatible with each other. In fact, they are often complementary. Rapport is an attitude of trust and confidence between you and the team members. It results from your being in charge, being predictable, and being a source of positive experiences for the team members (Figure 8.2). For example, simply asking them questions such as "What is your favorite playing position?" or "What are your favorite skills to practice?" lets them know that, from the very outset, you are interested in them and their concerns. Play games with them, especially with younger teams, where you as the coach get to provide rewards that are independent of skill level (See Game #1).

FIGURE 8.2
Rapport is the result of being predictable, being in charge and being a source of positive experiences for your team.

Let your players know that you believe in them. With high-level teams that belief can be expressed in terms of your belief that they will be successful in competition. For beginning teams that expression of confidence can be in terms of believing they are capable of learning and improving their team skills.

GAME #1: What's in Your Gym Bag?

"Who has a dirty white sock in your gym bag?" "Who has a combination lock for their locker?' In this very simple game, the first youngster who shows what you asked for each time you ask for a new item gets a modest reward (candy bar, lollipop), and you become the positive center of the game.

MAINTAIN TEAM STABILITY

Teams that stay together and play together over longer periods of time tend to have a stronger sense of unity than teams with considerable personnel turnover. As a coach, you cannot totally prevent turnover especially from season to season. Players change age groups, move out of town, move into town, quit to become involved in other appropriate activities, etc., etc. Some turnover is inevitable at virtually all levels of competitive sport. Encouraging your league to keep players together from season to season may be appropriate in some leagues and inappropriate in others. Players will always be moving on, but the concept of the "our team" and "our place" in the community can be highlighted. At the professional level, teams tend to be a collection of mercenary athletes where recruitment is an accepted way of doing business. The professional leagues have strict guidelines defining legal and illegal forms of recruitment (drafts, free-agent time periods, anti-tampering regulations, etc.). In youth leagues, recruitment is often more subtle but just as devastating to group unity. Rules to prevent recruitment, when and if enacted, are difficult, if not impossible, to enforce. Nonetheless, the adults administrating the youth leagues should identify the problems associated with inappropriate recruitment to the adult volunteers in their leagues and make clear to them the child development benefits of maintaining a reasonable degree of group stability on youth sports teams.

 STAGE 2

Relating to One's Teammates

Activities that permit individual group members to meet and get to know one another are an important component of this stage. On day one, the activity can be as simple as pairing each athlete with a teammate and asking them to interview each other. After a 2-minute conversation, they each get to introduce their partners to the other members of the team by telling two or three items about their partner that they learned in the interview and that would otherwise be unlikely for the others on the team to have known (for example, not that the partner is in fourth grade but that his favorite subject is math). Even if the athletes already know one another from the neighborhood, activities can be developed that help the athletes get to know one another even better. For example, the game "Telling Whoppers!" permits athletes to mention things that they might otherwise be too modest to brag about (See Game #2).

> **GAME #2: Telling Whoppers**
>
> Each member of the team gets to tell 3 or 4 whoppers about themselves. A whopper is something special about them. However, all the whoppers must be true except one. Even the coach should play. In fact, the coach can start the game by illustrating the types of self-statements that could be whoppers. After the speaker has stated

the whoppers, teammates get to indicate whether they believe each whopper is true or false. A set of three whoppers is appropriate for very young children, while four might be more challenging for older athletes. For example, 12-year-old Billie states the following four whoppers:

1. I have four grandmothers.
2. I ate 2 gallons of ice cream at one sitting.
3. I went from a D in reading to an A in one marking period at school.
4. I have a pet rat.

Subsequently, after his teammates have voted as to which is the whopper, they find out that item 2 is the false whopper and the other items are true.

1. His parents divorced and both remarried resulting in four sets of grandparents.
2. He never ate 2 gallons of ice cream despite his best efforts!
3. He's proud of his hard work and improvement in reading in school.
4. He has a white pet rat.

IDENTIFY AND WORK WITH TEAM LEADERS

A key technique for discussing important, sometimes controversial team issues is to identify the leaders on the team and discuss those topics with the leaders before discussing them with the entire team. By doing so, you can gauge whether to expect support on these key issues as you attempt to gain a team consensus on topics critical to overall team success. Those team leaders will recognize that you expect leadership from them, and you will be more likely to secure their support before confronting crucial issues with the entire group. Such an approach is particularly important with older, more sophisticated teams where leaders have already been acknowledged by teammates and have an established role on the team.

Appointing team captains, by itself, does not result in other teammates seeing the captains as legitimate sources of team leadership but the coach can provide the captains with credibility by assigning the captains responsibilities important to the team. For example, occasionally a practice can be made a "captain's practice" where adolescent captains can "run" the practice.* They may introduce skills and drills that they have learned in other circumstances such as drills learned at summer sports camp. The coach, in effect, is acknowledging that veteran players may have something to add such as fun drills learned in other practice situations.

As Coach K notes, "Not all good ideas come from the top."[5] With younger athletes, permit them to select and "run" drills from a variety of drills you have previously taught. With the very young, let them choose from two drills you have predetermined, but they get to select the order. In other words, the level of independence needs to be tailored to the developmental level of the athletes.

STAGE 3

Valuing One's Teammates

In this stage of developing cohesion, the emphasis is on developing an appreciation for the need to work as a team and how each person on the team can make a meaningful and necessary contribution to achieving the goals of the team. Playing with talented teammates becomes an opportunity to be part of a special group rather than being seen as a threat to one's playing time and individual contributions to team success.

Games can be played that emphasize that every player's contribution is important. For example, play a variation of a game called Infinity Volleyball (See Game #3).

Be careful to use a game in which the demands of the game (say, keeping the ball in the air) are not beyond the physical or intellectual

GAME #3: Infinity Volleyball

In groups of four, five, or six, attempt to keep a volleyball (or similar type of ball) in the air for, say 2 minutes or until the ball hits the ground. Players use a volleyball set to pass the ball from teammate to teammate. Two or three groups compete against each other – however, each group's score is the fewest number of touches made by any member of the team. If a group keeps the ball in the air for the entire time period, but one player touched the ball only once, the entire group's score is one!

---

*Obviously, permitting your athletes to run the captain's practice does not relieve the adult coach from the responsibility of supervising the practice session.

skill level of any player. Otherwise, a weaker player may become a scape-goat rather than an important member contributing to the group's score.

ENCOURAGE TEAMMATES TO ENCOURAGE TEAMMATES

Helping each other can be initiated through partner teaching. Rather than simply having partner drills where a teammate is necessary to accomplish the drill (for example, learning to pass and receive a soccer ball), develop the drill so that each member of the pair provides feedback ("I can get to the ball even when you lead me by a further distance than the last time.") Encourage teammates to be aware of the facial expressions and body language of their teammate so they become aware of how their teammates react to their behavior.

Make such suggestions as:

"Work together and support one another especially when your teammate is going through a rough time, whether with learning sport skills or personally."

"When your teammate is struggling, show that you are a real friend rather than blaming that person for a poor performance."

Ask your athletes questions such as:

"Do you remember when someone helped you? How did that make you feel?"

"Remember when someone blamed you when you made an honest mistake? How did that make you feel?"

"What kind of team do you want our team to be?"

Encourage your athletes to ask questions of themselves such as:

"When I invite someone to work out with me, how does that make them feel?"

EXPLAIN HOW EACH INDIVIDUAL ROLE CONTRIBUTES TO TEAM SUCCESS

For example, in soccer, the coach can explain why a goal was given up to the opponents. "Yes, the ball got by the goalie, but our defensive backs permitted a shot on goal and our midfielders did not maintain control of the ball in the middle of the field. After our forwards had a shot on our opponents' goal and the ball was blocked, they did not get back on defense to retrieve the ball." On a more positive note, the coach can say: "When the goalie feeds the defensive backs who, in turn, pass the ball quickly to the midfielders while the forwards are making a run toward open space without the ball so they can receive a pass from the midfielders, we'll have a real chance to make a shot on our opponents' goal!"

With reserves waiting on the bench, the coach can say, "you are not starters yet, but it is important, when it is your turn to play, that you come into the game fully involved and aware of the strengths and weaknesses of the player you are assigned to guard. We need you to be ready at a moment's notice."

TELL PLAYERS: ROOT FOR YOUR TEAMMATES, THEN BEAT THEM AT THEIR BEST

This approach is particularly important in individual sports such as swimming, gymnastics, track and field, wrestling, or tennis where teammates are often in direct competition with each other. Encourage team members to root for their teammates to do well in competition – and then go out and beat them. Such an attitude results in team spirit, a focus on performance, and a healthy emphasis on personal accomplishments without undermining teammates. Emphasize that success is more meaningful if you beat others when they are performing at or near their best. Beating other players who compete poorly or who are injured or ill is a lesser accomplishment than winning when your opponents perform well. Just as importantly, point out that, unless others perform well, it becomes difficult, if not impossible, to determine just how well you, as a competitor, have actually performed. Your rank becomes more meaningful and informative if your rank is among other high-level performers.

> **Make such statements as:**
>
> "You may want to beat your teammates and opponents, but you will have much more to be proud of if you root for them to perform well and then defeat them than if you hope they mess up so you can win. Their high-level performance can be a challenge for you to better your own performance."

AVOID SOCIAL CLIQUES

Cliques often develop when teams are losing, when needs are unmet, or when athletes have a different status on the team such as starters vs. non-starters. Encourage regularly working with different partners and explain why such an approach is important for the team. For example,

FIGURE 8.3
Team meetings can be used to teach teammates to communicate with one another, not just be an opportunity for one-way messaging from the coach.

you can say, "We want to work with a different partner in each different set of drills so we get to know each of our teammates and can play well together regardless of who is in the game."

After the members of the team have had a chance to get to know each other across several practices, initiate a team activity where you tape a blank sheet of paper on each athlete's back and then ask each teammate to write one positive characteristic describing that player on his or her back. After the exercise, each person gets to read his or her list aloud. With 15 soccer players on the team, each athlete will have 14 positive traits recognized by his or her teammates.

ALLOW TIME FOR TEAM MEETINGS

Providing opportunities for team members to talk about their concerns provides the coach with information on issues the coach may not have had the opportunity to observe directly (Figure 8.3). Such team meetings also permit the coach to teach team members to learn to really listen to one another. A simple technique for teaching such communication skills to young athletes is to have a *speaker's key*. The key can be a ball in sports such as baseball, basketball, and soccer, or it can be headgear in wrestling or a handgrip in gymnastics. Whoever holds the speaker's key gets to speak while others are expected to listen. The key gets passed to members throughout the meeting until everyone who wishes to speak has done so. Speaking without the key, interrupting the speaker, and side conversations with other teammates are discouraged. As team members become older or more experienced, the physical key can be phased out as long as the speaker is still getting attention, respect, and courtesy from others on the team.

Meetings do not always need to be formal. Provide time for your athletes, particularly when the team is new, for personal communication. For example, in your initial practices when many players may not even know each other's names, specifically encourage them to learn their partner's name before initiating the drills. Provide time both on and off the field when possible.

STAGE 4

Establishing a Sense of Community/Team Culture

ENCOURAGE A TEAM IDENTITY

Develop distinctive team uniforms and speak about "our team" and "our style" of doing things, i.e., with pride, with flair, with success. "We keep our fields (gyms) clean and neat." "We take care of and respect our equipment." "We're a 'no excuses' team." "We never challenge an official's call. We're too tough for that!"

ESTABLISH A TEAM HISTORY

If the team is a veteran team, discuss the team's past successes. If successes were few, discuss how the team was formed and identify players who participated before (e.g., older brothers and sisters of current team members, special events or competitions that were entered). If you are coaching a new team or you are a new coach, discuss the history of your sport (Figure 8.4.) and the special players who have represented your league, town, state, or nation (depending upon the skill level and commitment you expect from your team).

RESOLVE CONFLICTS EARLIER RATHER THAN LATER

If you have a problem, air it. Don't just complain. Suggest a solution or ask for solutions.

FIGURE 8.4
A sense of history of your organization is often a source of team unity based upon team traditions.

SET CHALLENGING TEAM GOALS

Set goals that require working together but have individual contributions. Set goals that are performance rather than outcome based (see Chapter 5 on goal setting). For example, "no yellow cards specifically for dissent in soccer." Set up a team scoring program above and beyond the scoring in a game. For example, "We earn points for scoring a goal, but we also earn team points for the following: Blocking a shot, a shot on goal, an assist to a goal, no fouls during each game period, etc."

SET TEAM STANDARDS RATHER THAN TEAM RULES

This difference is subtle but important. As Coach K strongly recommends, "Rules don't promote teamwork. Standards do."[6] As important as team rules are, standards are something to be lived up to rather than arbitrary behaviors to be punished if they do not occur.

YOUR TURN
Strengthening the Team Bond

Which of the following team policies do you think are most likely to promote high-level performance and strengthen the relationships between team members? Which is least likely? Why?

a. If anyone is late for practice, the whole team runs a lap for each minute late!

b. Be on time: The starting line-up will come from those who attend practice regularly and are on time for each practice.

c. Everyone is expected to be on time because being on time shows respect for your teammates, respect for your coaches, and respect for your sport.

CHAPTER REFERENCES

1. Krzyzewski, M.(2009). *The gold standard: Building a world-class team.* New York, NY:Hachette Book Group, with Spatola, J. L. (page xvii).

2. Schmidt, U., McGuire, R., Humprey, S., Williams, G., & Grawer, B.(2005). Team Cohesion.In Taylor, J. & Wilson, G. (eds.). *Applying sport psychology: Four perspectives.* Champaign, IL:Human Kinetics (page 180).

3. Weinberg, R.S. & Gould, D. (2015). *Foundations of sport and exercise psychology (6th ed.).* Champaign, IL: Human Kinetics (pp. 190- 194).

4. Thanks to Dean Diane Bonanno, Associate Dean and Director of Recreation for Rutgers University (retired), for creating a conceptual model for developing a sense of community and from which this sport-specific, team-building model has evolved.

5. Krzyzewski, M.(2009). *The gold standard:Building a world-class team.* New York, NY: Hachette Book Group, with Spatola, J. L. (page 68).

6. Krzyzewski, M.(2009). *The gold standard:Building a world-class team.* New York, NY: Hachette Book Group, with Spatola, J. L. (page 67).

9

Motivation

CHAPTER OUTLINE

- Pervasiveness of Motivation
- Characteristics of Motivated Behavior
- Effectively Using Rewards
- A Motivational Program for Young Athletes
- Why Kids Stay and Why Kids Quit
  SPOTLIGHT ON YOUTH SPORTS: What You Can Do to Help
- Lack of Playing Time and Perceived Unfairness
- Psychological Burnout

Billy arrives at practice early and leaves late. He works hard in the presence of the head coach, an individual that he idolizes and wants desperately to please. However, when the coach is not paying direct attention to him, Billy rarely completes any of the drills and wanders from station to station in practice with little sense of purpose or direction. The assistant coach sees Billy as having little motivation since Billy works hard when the head coach is present but not for the assistant coach.

Freddie regularly arrives late for practice, leaves immediately when practice ends and is often distracted when working with the coach. The head coach describes him as lacking motivation. What the head coach is unaware of, however, is that Freddie has to walk to practice because both his parents work and are not available to drive him. He leaves practice immediately because he has to complete the long walk home in time to look after his baby sister while his parents work. He wants to improve his sports skills but when the coach critiques him, Freddie feels embarrassed and appears distracted because he tries to avoid the coach whenever possible. On the other hand, the assistant coach sees Freddie as highly motivated because he knows about Freddie's family situation.

Joey arrives and leaves on time, responds positively regardless of which coach is working directly with him and continues to practice hard even when alone. Joey's prime concern is improving his skills to live up to the expectations of his parents. His hard work continues with or without either coach's attention, both of whom describe Joey as motivated.

Motivation is part of virtually every aspect of Billy's, Joey's and Freddie's choices and behaviors but the two coaches have dramatically different interpretations of the athlete's motivation. Motivation has explained everything and nothing simultaneously! The purpose of this chapter is to help coaches understand and effectively use concepts related to motivation.

Pervasiveness of Motivation

Writing a chapter on motivation is challenging because so many topics are related to motivation. A modest estimate is that virtually 75% of all the literature dealing with sport psychology is linked to motivational concepts. Motivational concepts are embedded in most of the topics covered in this text such as peak performance, goal setting and positive discipline. Nonetheless, a specific separate chapter on motivation is necessary because of motivation's importance in enhancing the youth sport experience.

CIRCULAR DEFINITIONS OF MOTIVATION

A common misuse of the concept of motivation is to use it as an explanatory mechanism for virtually every result. Poor performance is seen as due to a lack of motivation while successful performance is the result of high levels of motivation. Such a perception typically renders motivation useless to explain why success or failure occurs. Motivation simply becomes a description of what has happened. Billie works hard; therefore, he is motivated. Freddie does not work hard; therefore, he is lazy. How do we know Billie is motivated? Answer: He works hard. Why does he work hard? Answer: Because he is motivated. Why does Freddie rarely finish an assignment? Answer: Because he is lazy. How do we know he is lazy? Answer: Because he never completes his assignments.

Such circular definitions of motivation do little to explain the differences between Billie's and Freddie's behaviors. They merely describe the different behaviors of the two young athletes. If we want to more fully understand why one boy works hard and the other does not, we have to dig deeper – we need to look at the circumstances which created and perhaps drive the observed behavior. That is the central theme of this chapter – understanding the antecedent events which influence young athletes' behaviors.

COMMON MYTHS ABOUT MOTIVATION

Motivation is one of the most important concepts in sport – yet it is also one of the most misunderstood. Here are just a few of the common misconceptions concerning motivation.

Myth #1: Arousal = Motivation

Two young football players on the sidelines just prior to a game prepare by vigorously jumping up and down, yelling loudly and pumping their fists. They chest bump each other with enough force that one player falls to the ground. A third player sits on the bench, head down quietly reviewing the plays he expects to carry out in the game. Who is more motivated? The two "pumped up" players or the quiet young athlete? The answer is that all can be equally and highly motivated. Motivation is often very quiet and focused. The energetic behavior of the first two and the focused concentration of the third may be two different expressions of intense motivation. In fact, the chest bumping may simply be mimicking older players' behavior seen in previous games and be less focused on the outcome of the game.

Myth #2: Positive Thinking = Motivation

A positive belief may be an important aspect of motivation, but by itself, it is not sufficient to produce high level performance. For the belief that "I can do anything if I try hard enough!" to be a positive influence, the outcome of the behavior must be effort-contingent. If a young athlete is not strong enough to hit the ball the distance to the outfield fence, he cannot hit a home run. However, if he does his strength drills regularly, he may become strong enough to do so.

Myth #3: Either You Have It or You Don't

At one level, it is reasonable to assume that everybody is motivated. But to assume that they are motivated to do what the coach believes they ought to be doing to be successful is not warranted. An athlete may be motivated to protect her self-esteem, to impress her friends or to avoid pain among many possible choices; therefore, when confronted with a challenge for which success is uncertain, she may avoid such challenges and appear unmotivated.

Myth #4: The Coach's Role Is to Motivate the Athlete

Coaches often believe that their role is to motivate their athletes. However, motivation is an abstract concept, not readily manipulated. Few of us have an on-off button that coaches can push to motivate us. Often it is more fruitful for coaches to start from the assumption that all their athletes are initially motivated but that roadblocks and barriers frequently exist to prevent their athletes from achieving their goals. Such an approach often gives the coach insight into specific events or situations in the athlete's experience with which the coach can help the athlete cope. For example, athletes are often ***de-motivated*** by fear, frustration, lack of understanding, or hopelessness.

Characteristics of Motivated Behavior

Motivated behavior is:

1. Energized
2. Persistent
3. Directed
4. Focused on problem solving
5. High quality (relative to one's skill level)

These characteristics are descriptive not explanatory. They do not explain what prior conditions lead to motivated behavior. As a coach, you must examine what are those prior conditions which enhance motivation. The question is "To what extent can motivation be developed and directed in the young athlete?" Coaches can take concrete steps which, if carried out properly, can significantly increase and guide the motivation of their athletes.

Implicit in all these steps are two underlying principles for developing intrinsic motivation. First, these steps attempt to systematically increase the athlete's perception of competency ("I can do it!"). Second, they promote the perception of self-determination ("I can decide!").

The *perceptions* of competency and control are what foster intrinsic motivation. These perceptions are enhanced when the young athlete actually has competency and control, but it is the athlete's belief that he has competency and control that is crucial. A high level athlete who has low self-esteem and feels controlled by others is likely to display less intrinsic motivation than a lower level athlete who believes he is capable of playing well and feels than he can determine when, if, and how he plays. Thus, even those athletes with physical and intellectual disabilities that place limits on their actual performance and self-determination (for example, Down Syndrome athletes in Special Olympics) can display substantial intrinsically motivated behavior if they see themselves as successfully performing the sports skills and feel that they are largely responsible for determining their skill level. (Figure 9.1.)

FIGURE 9.1
Regardless of youngsters' developmental level of maturity or their physical and intellectual capabilities, young athletes can have high levels of intrinsic motivation if they see themselves as capable.

Effectively Using Rewards

Young athletes choose to participate in activities which earn both tangible and intangible rewards. Coaches who understand the effective use of rewards can substantially increase the likelihood of continued participation by their young athletes. The effective use of rewards requires that coaches recognize that rewards can be provided for different types of behaviors as well as there are different types of rewards.

Rewards occur when the athlete receives something pleasant or when something unpleasant is taken away. The giving of rewards constitutes one of the most effective tools at the coach's disposal. Rewarded behaviors tend to persist whereas unrewarded behaviors tend to be extinguished. Thus, rewarding acceptable behavior is an excellent means of improving the discipline and control. To have the greatest impact, rewards should be meaningful to the athlete and should closely follow the acceptable behavior. While the exact type of reward which serves as the best motivation will vary with the age and interest of the individuals, nonmaterial inducements are generally favored as the athlete matures.

It goes almost without saying that positive reinforcement is the backbone of any successful motivational program. However, effective use of positive reinforcement involves an understanding that positive reinforcement is more than being pleasant, smiling, and offering indiscriminant praise. In fact, we know that excessive praise for non-accomplishments can actually undermine motivation and self-esteem. (See Chapter 2 – Teaching Strategies for Effective Coaching).

TYPES OF REWARDS

If athletes are at different maturity levels, different types of rewards may be necessary. Athletes at early stages of development may require a great deal of reinforcement for participation and effort as opposed to mastery and competitiveness. As they become more experienced, those standards should not remain static but should shift toward mastery and competition rewards. The frustration of near misses or the desire of the coach for the athlete to succeed should not result in a dilution of the standards for reinforcement. Such "good heartedness" undermines the effectiveness of the standards and ultimately results in less progress and less satisfaction on the part of both the coach and the athlete.

Material Rewards

Material rewards are quite effective with young children. Candy, toys, and food treats are frequently used to reward young children who have been "good".

Social Rewards

The vast majority of behavior is rewarded by the behavior of other people in the athlete's environment, especially by people held in high personal regard. Such things as affection, approval, personal praise, leadership, responsibility, and increased opportunities for decision making have often proved to be highly effective. The effect of such nonmaterial rewards, however, depends strongly upon the respect and personal feelings which the athletes have for the coach. Unless athletes like and respect their coach, they are not likely to be favorably affected by an increased show of affection or approval.

Activity Rewards

Preferred activities can reinforce less preferred activities. Participating in a soccer scrimmage (the more preferred activity) can be made contingent upon completing a fixed number of skill drills (the less preferred activity).

Symbolic Rewards

Also known as "backup reinforcers", these symbolic rewards can be accumulated and traded in for other rewards (material, social, or activity).

Money is probably the most common example of such rewards, and while monetary rewards are normally inappropriate within a youth sports setting, points have been frequently used. Decals, patches, or other symbols of achievement which can be worn or seen in a public place, such as on a football helmet, an arm patch or team jacket, are also examples of symbolic rewards which mediate social reinforcement.

Covert Rewards

The thoughts and self-evaluations in which an athlete engages following his/her own behavior may be rewarding. Encourage them. Positive or negative evaluations (pride or shame) can produce the same effects as external rewards although clearly the induction of such thoughts is less under the control of the coach than are the external rewards.

TYPES OF BEHAVIORS

Rewards can be provided based upon different types of behaviors. The four dimensions appropriate for young athletes are:

Rewards for Participation

Rewards for simply getting involved; for being there; for taking part.

Rewards for Effort

Rewards for trying hard; for hustling; for doing one's best.

Rewards for Mastery

Rewards for learning the skills; for improving one's performance; for improving one's consistency.

Rewards for Competition

Rewards for being the best; for performing better than others; for winning.

Rewards – Bribes or Prizes

Be careful! Sometimes the same rewards may be seen as a bribe, not a prize. What's the difference? An athlete's reaction to a reward is often due to how the reward is perceived. If it is seen as earned, it is a reflection of the athlete's competency and typically enhances their motivation to continue the rewarded behavior in an effort to earn more. If it is perceived as an attempt to manipulate their behavior, it is typically seen as a bribe attempting to control the behavior and may undermine motivation, actually decreasing the frequency, intensity and/or duration of the rewarded behavior, especially when the reward is discontinued.

THE COACH'S ROLE

As a general rule, coaches should gradually shift their emphasis from participation to effort to mastery and finally to competition as the athlete becomes more skilled, more mature, more self-confident, more aware, and more experienced. These categories are not mutually exclusive nor should the emphasis be all-or-none. Even a mature, skilled, experienced athlete should be rewarded for effort and participating but some praise can also be withheld until performance reflects mastery (successfully completing a skill) or a competitive achievement (placing first, second or third in a race against others). Coaches who confuse the positive reinforcement with the indiscriminant use of praise often become frustrated that their young athletes make little progress in skill learning. (Figure 9.2) An athlete who can earn sufficient praise simply by being there (participatory rewards) may not exert the energy necessary (effort rewards) to learn the skill (mastery rewards) or to rank high (competitive rewards). Her behavior may very well be arrested at a point far below her capabilities simply because the coach, in an effort to be positive, is giving rewards for behaviors which require little or no effort on the part of the athlete.

FIGURE 9.2 Coaches who confuse the indiscriminant use of praise with positive reinforcement often become frustrated when their young athletes make little progress in the learning of sport skills and self-discipline.

REWARDS V. PUNISHMENTS

A second major point of confusion is that positive motivational programs do not eliminate the use of all punishments. As discussed in Chapter 5 (Goal Setting), rewards and punishments are intimately related and are often merely different sides to the same coin, i.e., reinforcement contingencies. A contingency is an "if..., then..." relationship. If the gymnast can support her weight in a handstand, then she can attempt to do a back handspring in tumbling. While this contingency is stated in positive terms, it is exactly the same contingency as the statement, if the gymnast cannot successfully support her weight in a handstand, then she is not ready to perform a back handspring. If a coach has the power to give an athlete something positive (a reward), then that coach must also, by definition, have the power to withhold that reward (a punishment). If a coach can remove an aversive event (a reward), then he can also choose not to remove it (a punishment). Both reward and punishment are essential ingredients in a positive motivational program. Said differently, every reward contingency has both positive and negative interpretations. Whether a motivational program is a positive or negative one is often based more on the attitudes and phrasing of the contingencies than by whether punishment has been eliminated. Strictness is determined by how closely a coach maintains the standards of the contingencies rather than by how harshly the contingencies are stated. Coaches often confuse positive coaching with leniency in their contingencies. Such "positiveness" leads to confusion on the part of the athlete and a lack of progress in motivation and skill development. On the other hand, positively stated contingencies which are strictly enforced result in clear directions and expectations as well as substantial, recognizable progress in both motivation and skill development. In addition, appropriately designed progressions (i.e., those with steps that the young athlete can master) increase the likelihood that the athlete can be successful, and the coach can give earned praise whenever the athlete successfully masters another step. (See Chapter 4 on Positive Discipline for an additional examination of this important concept.)

A Motivational Program for Young Athletes

While the following program may at first seem quite formal, its actual application can be very personable and flexible. Coaches often spend a great deal of their time simply trying to get their athletes to pay attention to the tasks. Often, they find themselves hassling athletes who are not paying attention. A primary benefit of a well-constructed motivational program is that it produces a great deal of positive focus on the task at hand. Both the coach and the athlete find that the situation becomes predictable and understandable. Predictability is an essential first step in the development of a trusting atmosphere. When athletes perceive that good things (i.e., rewards) consistently happen as a result of their efforts, trust develops. The rapport which a coach develops with his or her athletes is a direct result of being consistent. Novice coaches often believe that they must first develop rapport with their athletes and then they can begin teaching. In fact, the coaches who begin with consistent teaching and predictable standards quickly develop the rapport that makes their teaching even more effective.

COMMUNICATION

The first step in developing motivation is to become familiar with your athletes. Often their perceptions are quite different from the coach's perceptions. Sometimes the athletes' motivation is low because goals are imposed upon them by the coach without regard for the athletes' desires. Personal fears, a lack of understanding of the progressions, the desire to remain with friends, the misperception of one's ability may all prevent the athlete from behaving in a manner that the coach sees as "motivated."

GOAL SETTING

Setting goals typically enhances motivation. Goals, especially short-term goals, energize behavior. By setting a target, goals give direction and increase persistence by focusing the athlete's attention on the critical elements leading to success. Goal setting prompts problem solving as the athlete analyzes how to achieve the goals. Goals promote high quality performance relative to the athlete's skill level. All these are characteristics typically cited as motivated behavior (see the previous definition of motivation). In addition, setting goals, especially performance goals, has the benefits of lowering anxiety, enhancing self-confidence, and increasing satisfaction.

An important phase in the development of motivation is the active involvement of the athletes in deciding upon both their long- and short-term goals (see Chapter 5 for a more in-depth examination of goal setting techniques and personal styles). Of course, the coach must have a more substantial guidance role with younger athletes but mutual goal setting is workable even with the very young. For example, the coach can provide the athlete with a choice of two skills and ask which the athlete would prefer to learn first. With a shy athlete or one who is reluctant to become involved, mutual goal setting is often remarkably effective. Rather than saying "Do this" or "Would you like to do this?" the coach can say, "Would you like to do 'A' or 'B'?" If both are important skills to be mastered, the question can be "Which would you rather do first? A or B?" Implicit in the coach's direction is the fact that both skills will be ultimately learned. The choice then becomes selecting between one of the two alternatives rather than a choice between participating or not participating.

An athlete who aspires to goals which the coach feels are too difficult can be given the prerequisite skills as stepping stones towards the athlete's goals. If the goals are set too low, the coach can suggest that the easy goals be used as progressions for the more demanding goals. Athletes who perceive their goals as being partially or wholly determined by themselves are more likely to display a stronger commitment to those goals.

The main point is that athletes, even the very young or inexperienced, can be actively and meaningfully involved in goal setting without sacrificing the experience, knowledge and perspective of the coaches. Substantial and meaningful guidance can be given to athletes of all ages, skill levels and intellectual capacity without imposing these goals on the athletes. The result will be a set of high, realistic goals which the athlete is committed to achieving and which the coach believes are worthwhile. When people believe that they have an important role in deciding the goals for themselves and their groups, their personal commitment to achieving those goals increases substantially . Perhaps the key to motivation is that athletes should be able to assume personal responsibility for their behavior by being permitted and encouraged to make significant – albeit age-appropriate – contributions to all decisions concerning them.

IDENTIFY THE TARGET BEHAVIOR(S)

The behaviors which you wish to teach or modify must be defined in observable, measurable terms and specified clearly to the athlete. Performing a fixed number of skill attempts or regular attendance patterns are easily defined types of behaviors. Measuring them is usually very clear cut. Defining concepts such as "trying your best," "intensity," or "Sticking at it" is much more difficult. Often ambiguous, but important, concepts can be clarified to your athletes (and yourself) by listing specific types of behaviors which illustrate the concept. Rather than saying to the athlete, "You must try harder," the coach must state specifically what the athletes must do. For instance, "You must complete two routines before you can rest," or "You must complete all the specified warm-up exercises before we scrimmage."

SET MUTUALLY AGREED UPON GOALS

The coach must provide a level of involvement on the part of the athlete which is appropriate for the athlete's maturity and level of intellectual development. For example, when softball skills are being taught, the coach can ask the athletes if they wish to practice fielding or hitting first. The coach knows that both are going to be practiced but the athletes are given the choice of the order that skills are learned. As the athletes' skill and maturity develop, their involvement in determining their goals can be increased. For example, instead of merely the choice of the order, subsequently they can choose from a list provided by the coach and ultimately the coach can give them the choice of any of previously learned skills. Those skills have already been taught and the athletes are now asked to select from skills that have been mastered.

MONITOR THE BEHAVIOR

You must know what is happening! While you do not need to watch every movement of every athlete in practice, you must have a systematic plan by which you maintain awareness of what and how the athletes are doing. **Keep personal records. The athletes may do so with a personal diary or log.** (Figure 9.3) Record keeping which is simple is preferred to elaborate procedures. Progress can be written in terms of distance, time, repetitions, or percentage of successes during the performance of the designated skill. For any motivational program to achieve maximal effectiveness, both the coach and the athlete must know exactly what progress is being made. Such awareness requires records that are accurate enough to inform the participants what progress is actually being made yet not so cumbersome that the record keeping process interferes with other aspects of the training program. Both the athlete's and the coach's motivation are enhanced when concrete evidence of progress is available.

Often, simply having athletes record their performances leads to improvements. A simplistic explanation of this phenomenon is that re-

FIGURE 9.3 In addition to setting direction, writing down goals often leads to greater commitment and, ultimately, more progress toward obtaining those goals.

cording their performance increases their motivation to perform better. Actually, there are several reasons for this improvement effect. First, writing down your actual performance clarifies exactly what has to be done. If the coach and the athlete write down how many pull-ups the athlete can do in fifteen seconds, the athlete knows clearly what the coach expects. Second, the records provide feedback that is very clear and specific. Believing that "I am working hard" is quite different from knowing that "I did six pull-ups in 15 seconds." Records clarify very quickly to both the coach and the athlete just exactly how much progress has been made and eliminates the problem of "wishful thinking." When a young basketball player is asked how he is doing during foul shooting practice, an answer of "O.K." or "Pretty good" is not sufficient. On the other hand, if he answers that he has made 4 of 10 tries (40% success rate for baskets) and that 5 of the 6 misses hit the rim (83% success rate for young athletes for hitting the target), both he and the coach have information which is much more usable than the statement that things are "O.K." The player can then be praised for having improved over last week's 30% success rate and at the same time can be encouraged to strive for a 50% or 60% success rate for the following week.

USE THE LEAST INTRUSIVE REWARDS

This is vital. The more motivated your athletes are, the less external rewards they will need. Clearly, the type of reward used depends upon the intellectual level of the athlete as well as the amount of experience and self-confidence which the athlete has attained. Nonetheless, rewards which are too great often redirect the athlete's attention away from the task and to the reward itself. While initially the reward itself may be the major motivating influence on the young athlete, the key is to use only the amount of reward necessary to direct the athletes toward the mutually desired rewards. The smaller the external reward, the greater is the likelihood that the rewards of the activity itself will begin to influence the behavior of the athlete.

CLEARLY STATE THE "IF..., THEN..." RELATIONSHIP

If the exercises are successfully completed, then the scrimmage will start. This contingency must be stated clearly in terms that the athlete can understand and be presented far enough in advance that the athlete can actually meet that contingency. If the athlete must "try harder" in practice, then the behaviors needed to show intensity must be clearly stated along with the minimum acceptable standard which must be met.

BE CONSISTENT

Do not reward "near misses" or lower standards. You are not helping an athlete to progress by rewarding them for less than what the standard demands. Inconsistent application of a standard will result in confusion on the part of the athlete concerning what specific behavior was earning the reward. This is not to say that you should not closely re-examine a standard which is not working because it was set too high or was too abstract for the athlete's intellectual level. When the system is not working, it must be modified; but once the coach has decided upon a course of action, the standards must be applied consistently and fairly to all athletes in the program. Consistency not only increases the likelihood that a standard will appear fair in the eyes of the athletes but consistency also develops an appearance of "inevitability." When athletes perceive a standard as inevitable, they are more likely to focus their energies on meeting that standard instead of circumventing it. Athletes who know they must successfully complete a skill in order to obtain a reward are more likely to concentrate on completing that skill rather than imploring the coach for the reward merely because the athletes have "tried hard."

Remember, consistency is not the unyielding application of the same standard or style to every athlete in every situation. Consistency is applying the same standard and coaching style to similar situations regardless of whether that application is convenient or not .

THINK SMALL

This little bit of pragmatic advice is particularly important when you are first attempting to develop a motivational program. Starting with a small system allows the coach to keep the system under control, to see what procedures actually work, and to make modifications as the coach becomes more experienced. The specific details of your program will have a definite effect on its success. While general guidelines are important for understanding the program, specific details (which rewards, which behaviors, how your athletes react, the intellectual level of the athletes) will make the program successful. Do not attempt to build a grandiose program without practical experience with smaller programs which are easier to modify and expand. Perhaps a truism for successful coaching is to "keep it simple but get it done!"

RE-EVALUATION AND MODIFICATION

For a motivational program to be truly individualized and efficient, it must constantly be monitored and re-examined. This aspect of the program cannot be overemphasized. Progressions which do not work must be altered. As the athletes gain success and self-confidence, their goals should be raised or focused in new directions. A static program, particularly if it works, will soon be outgrown. Slight modifications can often change a slow, sluggish program into a quick, efficient one.

Why Kids Stay and Why Kids Quit

Unless kids participate for substantial periods of time, youth sport is unlikely to have much beneficial effect upon their development. If, as adults, we value those potential benefits for our children, then we need to identify those factors which lead youngsters to both participate and to drop out. Numerous studies[1] have determined that the number one reason why kids play sports is to have "fun." However, fun is a word that means different things to different kids. When we dig a little deeper, we find that the two most powerful reasons for kids deciding to enter sports is to a) be with their friends and b) to be good at the sport (to be competent). Both of these factors are powerful contributors to what kids call "fun" – and both can be substantially influenced by the coach.

To do so, we will examine children's motives for participating and those factors which undermine that motivation. Whether children stay in or drop out of organized youth sports programs depends as much upon the ways in which they think as upon external adult pressures. Their stage of mental development and their motives for participating in sports are at least as important, if not more so, than pressure from parents or coaches or the stress of competition. Previously, demanding parents and/or overbearing coaches were thought to be the primary factors forcing kids "into early retirement."[2] Subsequent research, however, has indicated that only about 10 to 15% of children quit sport for such reasons. "Having other things to do" is cited as an indication that discontinuing participation was more often related to changing priorities.[3] Today, we know that the **level of reasoning** that young athletes are capable of displaying strongly influences whether kids continue to play. We will examine the most commonly expressed motivational factor expressed by kids (that is, they play "to have fun") and determine what factors predict fun. Then, we will suggest strategies that effectively encourage children and adolescents to continue their participation so that they can experience the benefits of sports. Finally, we will briefly explore the concept of psychological burnout, a phenomenon that affects a small, but important, group of highly dedicated athletes.

DEFINING "FUN"

Children participate in organized youth sport for different reasons. A study of approximately 8,000 youth[4] found that the number one reason why both boys and girls participate in sport in both school and non-school programs was "to have fun." This descriptive study is important because it identifies the self-identified motives of the youth participants but it fails to identify what makes sport fun. As obvious as that finding is, it does not explain what fun is. That simple word has dramatically different meanings to different children. For some children, the uncertainty of the outcome (whether we win or lose) is exciting. For others that uncertainty is threatening. For some, "hanging out with my friends" is what makes the activity fun. (Figure 9.4) For some it is "thumping" their opponents. For others, fun is improving their skills and being good at the activity. For still others, it is the opportunity to test one's self against a worthy opponent. Because fun has different meanings to different children, they also choose to discontinue their involvement in sport for different reasons.

FIGURE 9.4 Fun means different things to different kids at different stages of their development. Fun for many youth sport athletes is often strongly linked to affiliation – being with a special group of friends (my team).

To understand why children quit, we must first understand why they choose to participate in the first place. Children usually cited multiple reasons for why they participate in sport. The two most prominent reasons why children between the ages of 8 and 12 say they participate are **affiliation**[5] (to be with friends) and **perceived competency**[6] (to excel). A child who has chosen to participate because his friends have joined may quit if his friends quit. A child who wishes to improve her skills but has been taught very little by an inexperienced coach may drop out to pursue another activity at which she can excel. Saying children drop out when sport no longer is fun, by itself, does not provide us with much useful information concerning how to combat drop out.

THE DROP OUT PROBLEM

Estimates suggest that one of every three kids involved in organized sports quits between the ages of 12 to 17 years[7]. This high dropout rate is not due solely to adult pressure. Certainly, adults can and do place pressure on children; however, if pushy parents and pushy coaches were the only problem, kids would drop out uniformly at all ages. In fact, the dropout rate is not uniform across ages; it increases dramatically at about 12 years of age, just as the cognitive ability of children has matured to near adult-like levels. While they lack the experience of adults at that young age, their abilities to think and reason take on the more mature adult characteristics. For example, they can interpret rewards and praise from adults as reflecting either competency ("I'm good and I earned it.") or as controlling ("The coach is bribing me to do what he wants me to do.") The exact same reward may increase or decrease motivation based upon how that reward is interpreted.

WHY KIDS PARTICIPATE

In her early work at Michigan State University, Martha Ewing, a youth sports researcher, identified 3 primary attitudes[8] which children have toward sports. Ability oriented children enjoy competing and want "to be the best." Task oriented children enjoy the activity itself and often focus on self-improvement at the sport. Social approval oriented children work to please others such as coaches, parents and teammates. Thus, what is perceived as "fun" is quite different for each of these types of children.

Many coaches are convinced that the child "who wants to be the best" is more likely to withstand the rigors of intense competition and remain involved longer than kids with different orientations. That may be true if the child is successful and believes that he or she can be the best. However, a young athlete who is intensely motivated to be the best yet who believes that he or she cannot be is quite vulnerable to the drop-out syndrome. The evidence suggests that those who work for social approval persist the longest. Apparently, within the context of youth sports sufficient reinforcement exists to encourage such children to continue despite limited playing status. Even if they are not among the best, they are less likely to quit than the achievement oriented youngster who interprets not playing as "being no good" or as an "unfair" decision on the part of the coach. Ability oriented players who are not experiencing the success they desire have fewer alternatives and ultimately may decide to quit rather than to be embarrassed or ridiculed.

Given this information, why does the high dropout rate occur after 12 years? The answer – at least in part – involves the young athletes' cognitive ability.

COGNITIVE DEVELOPMENT STAGES

As children mature, their ability to think and understand abstract concepts such as competition, ability and success deepens and becomes more sophisticated. While age and developmental stages are related, cognitive development does not occur at the same rate for all children. Therefore, one individual who is chronologically 10-years-old may be only 8 or 9 intellectually while their 10-year-old classmate may have the cognitive ability maturity of a 12-year-old. Therefore, the ages of the stages discussed below are intentionally presented as overlapping.

Six Years and Younger

Very young children cannot distinguish between ability and effort.[9] They believe that if they are trying hard they are automatically good at what they're doing. "I'm trying hard" means "I'm talented" to a six year old. Thus, when adults offer praise for either exhibiting skill or for trying hard, the effect upon the very young is virtually the same. Praise for ability and for effort enhances the youngster's self-esteem. Praise tends to be accepted positively by very young children regardless of whether the task was successfully completed.

Six to Eleven Year Olds

At this age, children develop the ability to differentiate between having talent and trying hard. They compare themselves with their peers and many begin to realize that, no matter how hard they try, they may never be as good as some of their more talented friends. If they try their very best, they risk exposing their true ability. If they are strongly committed but believe they cannot successfully compete with others of their own age, they may cope by clowning around or by dropping out. They find it easier to attribute failure to a deliberate lack of effort, than to admit they lack ability.

Eleven to Twelve Years and Older

By twelve, most children have become skilled at making social comparisons and realize that expending effort no longer guarantees they will succeed. They understand that in competitive sports their efforts may be of no avail if the others are of higher ability. This is the age at which they are the most vulnerable to dropping out.

PERCEIVED COMPETENCY

At virtually all ages, a major reason why children seek out sport is to place themselves in situations in which they can judge their own ability and receive positive feedback about their competence. A high level of perceived self-competency is a powerful reason why kids continue to play sports. Drop outs consistently display low levels of perceived self-competency. Perceived self-competency is a major determinant of three of the most important elements of youth sports participation: First, it predicts enjoyment. "Fun" is often the belief that "I can do it!" Second, it is a major contributor toward what coaches call "mental toughness." If I believe that I am competent, the fact that I can't do it now simply means, "I haven't learned it yet! Wait 'til next week. I'll have it by then!" Third, it predicts continued involvement. Those high in self-competency continue to seek out and participate in activities (i.e., sport) where they can continually test themselves against others.

Arranging skill progressions that facilitate learning regardless of youngsters' initial skill levels dramatically increases personal enjoyment of physical activities. Further, the coach's positive feedback for actual accomplishments – both great and small – can enhance perceived competency, especially in children initially low in self-confidence.

SPOTLIGHT ON YOUTH SPORTS
What You Can Do to Help

There are at least four ways[10] adults can reduce the pressures which cause kids to quit.

ENCOURAGE CONTINUED SELF-IMPROVEMENT

As children begin to believe they can control those factors which lead to self-improvement, their self-confidence will increase. While you cannot (and probably should not) eliminate the social comparisons of ability inherent in competitive sports, the negative effects of such comparisons can be reduced if youngsters have broader definitions of fun and success than merely winning or losing the contest. In events such as a tennis tournament, there will be only one champion (at least for each age group or skill category). If self-confidence was solely dependent of the success of winning, only a very limited few could benefit from sport. When self-improvement becomes an important part of succeeding, many more athletes benefit from sport participation. The most powerful determinant of self-confidence is the belief that "I am in control of those factors that allow me to improve!" "I may not be the best I can be yet – but I'm getting better!"

ENCOURAGE SOCIAL COMPARISONS AS TOOLS FOR SELF-IMPROVEMENT

When youngsters see others performing better, they should be encouraged to ask the question "What are those others doing that allows them to perform better?" Answers such as: "They practice more intensely, they use a more effective strategy, they cooperate as a team better, or they are in better physical condition" all provide information which allows a young athlete to improve. Comparisons which are limited to "they're better" or "I'm worse" serve little purpose other than to undermine self-esteem. Comparisons which ask "why?" provide strategies for self-improvement.

PRAISE MUST BE AN EARNED REWARD

Look for successful performances and let the youngster know that you recognize those accomplishments. While he may not be a great hitter, he runs the bases well. While she may not be a great tumbler, she has improved dramatically as a vaulter. As youngsters mature, they begin to value praise for successful outcomes much more than praise for "trying hard". Often you must look for very specific accomplishments to praise. You can enhance a child's ability to recognize progress, by focusing on very specific performances within the sport.

REMIND CHILDREN THAT ABILITY OFTEN CHANGES AS THEY MATURE

This recommendation is especially important for kids with low self-confidence. Growth spurts frequently produce temporary difficulty with certain sports skills that had previously been mastered. The smaller youngster at 10 years of age may well become a strapping six footer by 16 or 17 years of age. Such reminders literally give kids hope. Children do not quit because they could fail. They quit when they perceive that they cannot succeed. These perceptions are quite different. The first perception is often perceived as a challenge. The second perception involves the absence of hope! (Figure 9.5).

FIGURE 9.5 Children do not quit because they could fail; overcoming a challenge is what often makes sports exciting. They quit when they perceive that they cannot succeed.

Lack of Playing Time and Perceived Unfairness

Perceived unfairness is a major contributor to why kids choose to discontinue their involvement in organized youth sport. Of all the factors that influence perceived unfairness, lack of playing time is by far the most powerful. In recreational leagues, where all children are expected to play an equitable amount of time, the playing time issue can be effectively dealt with by limiting the number of children assigned to each team. Twenty-five kids on a recreational basketball team, where only 5 at a time get to play, is virtually unworkable regardless of the efforts of the coach to provide equitable playing time. The solution of recruiting sufficient volunteer coaches and securing sufficient basketball courts to field teams with reasonable numbers of players is the job of recreation directors and youth sport administrators. When the ratio of athletes to coaches is reasonable, volunteer coaches can easily provide sufficient playing time for each recreational athlete so that those athletes are likely to continue their participation.

Traveling squad and competitive middle and high school teams are quite a different matter. Here the philosophy of many, if not most leagues, is that the better players should get the majority of the playing time. First, "they have earned it." Second, their contributions toward winning each contest are likely to be more substantial. Reserves quickly learn that their role is that of a backup player and that the likelihood of breaking into the starting lineup diminishes as the season progresses.

So how should coaches handle motivating athletes in these reserve roles? (Figure 9.6.) While some athletes will choose to continue to participate because of factors other than skill (e.g., belonging to a special group, parental expectations, don't want to be labeled a "quitter," wanting to be with their friends on the team), these factors may not be sufficient for the highly competitive athlete. When they (or often their parents) ask "What can I do to earn a starting position on the team or at least earn more playing time?," the coach should provide information about factors within the athlete's control to change or improve. Comparisons to others on the team ("She's not as fast as Mary.") or characteristics over which there is little control ("He's not tall enough.") are not particularly useful. Give information on realistic, changeable characteristics. For a child who lacks speed (primarily a genetic trait) suggest she work on "being in the right place at the right time" on defense. For players lacking skills,

FIGURE 9.6 Perceived unfairness – often based on a lack of opportunity to play – is a major reason why kids drop out of organized youth sport.

suggest they work on those specific skills such as controlled dribbling and trapping in soccer or improving their foul shooting percentage in basketball.

Whatever the cause(s) for children quitting, most experts agree that concerned adults must take corrective action long before the youngster makes the final decision to quit. Coaches and parents who are aware of developmental patterns can reduce the number of dropouts. The perception of "what is fair" is complex and perceptions may be more of a reality to the athlete than the objective facts of the situation.

Psychological Burnout

Burnout is not likely to be a factor in youth sport dropouts at the recreational level but the seeds contributing to burnout can be set in traveling squads where the mentality is often of the belief that "more is better!" It is not workload, however, that predicts burnout. It is the feeling of entrapment.[11]

Psychological burnout is stress related. Burnout results in athletes quitting their sport long before they achieve their potential. **Energetic perfectionists** who are strongly influenced by others and who lack **assertive interpersonal skills** are particularly susceptible to burnout. Demotivating factors include the changing nature of feedback (because the athlete is refining skills rather than learning new ones), the increasing need for personal autonomy, and increasing awareness of the physical, competitive, and social consequences of intense participation. The onset of symptoms is gradual but predictable and avoidable if high-risk, personal characteristics and de-motivating factors are identified.

These dropouts are especially unfortunate because psychological burnout does not appear to be inevitable. Outstanding athletes have competed in virtually every sport until their skills have diminished with age, not psychological staleness.

DEFINING BURNOUT

Not everyone retires from a sport because of negative psychological factors. Often athletes move on to other sports and activities because they believe that they can achieve more or enjoy more. Such changes are more appropriately described as growth, not burnout. On the other hand, when athletes are more repelled by their former activities than attracted to new activities, the concept of burnout becomes more applicable, especially when those former activities had been a long-term source of joy, involvement, and personal satisfaction.

The most systematic studies of burnout have come from researchers of job stress. Many of their findings appear to be directly applicable to burnout in young athletes. The circumstances of job stress and athletic stress show remarkable parallels, even when those comparisons involve children as young as ten years of age.[12] Burnout has been characterized as a condition produced by working too hard for too long in a high-pressured situation, and it is accompanied by a progressive loss of idealism, energy, and purpose that is often paralleled by a feeling of being locked into a routine. The individual displays a pattern of physical and emotional exhaustion involving the development of negative self concepts and negative attitudes towards work, life, and other people. Burnout appears to be a progressive disorder, although some latent symptoms may manifest themselves quite suddenly, particularly in the late stages.

Organized youth sports programs have striking similarities to bureaucratic management organizations. One of the highest compliments that a coach can give an athlete is that he or she is a "hard worker." Many of the early studies of burnout in youth sport essentially focused on burnout resulting from stress; however, the source of the stress (whether in business or sport) has been identified as the feeling of having no control over whether or not I can participate rather than workload alone.

WARNING SIGNS OF BURNOUT

In the **early stages**, the symptoms are generalized and often difficult to link to burnout. Individuals experience a growing state of fatigue, increased irritability, and a loss of enthusiasm that is not specific to a workout. They complain of physical distress including minor body aches, stomach upsets, and headaches. They describe growing feelings of incompetence, fragmentation, alienation, and often an unvoiced anger and frustration that things are not the way they should be. By the **intermediate stages**, they become withdrawn and silent even when directly spoken to. Answers, when given, are frequently sullen and angry. Often they belittle the belief that they could be successful. Physical symptoms include prolonged colds, shortness of breath, shallow breathing patterns, severe fatigue, and weight gains or losses produced by excessive eating or not eating. The **advanced stages** of burnout are evidenced by athletes becoming convinced that they are just not good enough. Cynicism, alienation, and withdrawal become so incisive that they often become obnoxious to others, especially teammates. Escapist behavior is common, and they display an almost total lack of energy regarding their training for their sport.

SUSCEPTIBLE PERSONALITIES

Not everyone who works long and hard under pressure experiences burnout. Solutions lie, in part, in early recognition of people who are particularly susceptible. Several predictable characteristics distinguish athletes who are likely to experience burnout.

Perfectionism

The first cluster of traits relates to perfectionism. There are two forms of perfectionism: One healthy and closely related to high levels of achievement and one unhealthy and a source of self-imposed stress.[13] The first involves conscientiousness – a commitment to working hard until the task is well done. The second involves neuroticism and essentially says, "No matter how well it is done, it is never good enough!"

High Energy Levels

Coupled with this perfectionism is a high energy level. The individual is always active, often attacking several tasks at once, rarely setting priorities concerning these tasks and thus lacking a mechanism for allocating their energy among tasks.

Other-Oriented

High-risk individuals tend to be other-oriented. Their perfectionism is based more on how they feel evaluated by others than simply setting high standards for themselves.

Lack of Assertiveness

Finally, susceptible burnout victims lack assertive interpersonal skills. Such individuals often find it difficult to say no or to express negative feelings – especially anger – without experiencing strong feelings of guilt. They may actually be quite articulate but are reluctant to act assertively because they confuse assertiveness with aggressiveness.

Ironically, these quiet, concerned, energetic perfectionists exhibit those very characteristics that coaches often find most desirable. The solution is not to persuade these youngsters to curtail their intense involvement, but rather to incorporate balance and perspective into living. While dedication to a sport is essential for high-level success, if one's focus is too narrow, too intense, or too prolonged at too early an age, the likelihood of burnout increases dramatically.

COMBATING DEMOTIVATORS

Burnout is more than an internal fire that consumes the athlete's motivation. Often burnout can be traced to specific environmental de-motivators that develop as a result of intense participation. Many of these de-motivators occur predictably, and as awareness of these factors grows, practical steps can be taken to sustain and nurture the athlete's motivation. There are several sources of de-motivation relevant to athletics.

Feedback and the Law of Diminishing Returns

Perhaps the most potent source of demotivation is the changed nature of the feedback that more advanced athletes receive about performance. Young, intermediate athletes experience obvious improvements after moderate investments of training time and effort; but at higher skill levels, this feedback changes in both quantity and quality. Learning proceeds in smaller, less obvious steps, often coming only after substantial effort on the part of the experienced athlete. Furthermore, experienced athletes often work at improving consistency and making detailed, fine improvements of previously learned skills rather than learning new skills. Feedback about such gradual improvement is often subtle, providing less excitement and awareness that learning is, in fact, occurring.

These subtle improvements are essential for athletes to compete at high levels. However, if the athlete perceives that little is being learned, boredom and loss of enthusiasm will follow.

How can this inevitable problem of diminishing returns be prevented? One way is to heighten the athlete's awareness of subtle improvements. For example, consistency charts can be used to make certain that the athlete notes that improvements have occurred. Second, the coach can acknowledge that those improvements are important and praiseworthy. The athlete's name can be placed on a record board, or the coach can praise the accomplishment in the same way that the learning of a new skill is praised. Third, and perhaps most important, the coach and the athlete should jointly agree that such detailed improvements are, in fact, clearly stated and mutually accepted goals. To perform an already learned skill in a higher, better, faster, or more consistent manner when such an improvement is a specified, mutually agreed on goal is an extremely effective technique to increase the athlete's awareness of significant progress. Without such mutual planning, the coach may know that performing higher and faster is a major goal, but the athlete may have an entirely different perception. What the coach perceives as progress may be sheer drudgery to the athlete unless those goals have been mutually emphasized and agreed on. This relates closely to the next major area of concern.

Increased Need for Self Determinism

With increased maturity comes the need for increased autonomy. With the teenage years, but by no means restricted to this period, comes the desire to make decisions for one's self. The sensitive coach can gradually help an athlete develop more control by involving him or her in the decision-making process.

The traditional coaching model has the coach as the leader and the athlete as the follower with little or no intermingling of the roles. Today, such a model is no longer desirable, acceptable, or workable. Coaches who systematically develop a sense of independence and responsibility in their athletes are most likely to counteract psychological burnout of both their athletes and themselves. Motivation is highest and sustained the longest when athletes have substantial input and control over determining their goals as well as the procedures for attaining them. This fact does not mean that the coach relinquishes all control. (The coach's motivation must be nurtured also!) Coaches must use their experience, wisdom, and perspectives to help athletes make informed choices that lead to those mutually agreed upon goals.

Recognizing an athlete's need for self determinism is not incompatible with the understanding that athletes often need and even seek out authority figures. Sometimes athletes work through adversity **because of** the demands of a tough, unyielding coach. At times, conflict and confrontation bring out the best in an athlete. However, coaches who adhere inflexibly to harsh techniques should understand that many athletes succeed in spite of such authoritarian approaches, not because of them. Strictness and demandingness are not the defining characteristics of authoritarianism. Inflexibility is what sets authoritarianism apart from authority and discipline. The inflexible use of authoritarian methods is a major contributor to psychological burnout because it undermines the sense of autonomy and increases the sense of entrapment. Successful coaches vary their coaching style depending on the demands of a situation. At times they are strict and directive. At other times they are empathetic and open to listening to the athlete's concerns. Effective coaches are sensitive to the implications of each coaching style for the behaviors and motivations of their athletes and pick and choose specific coaching styles based upon the specific circumstances and/or outcomes they wish to achieve with their athletes.

Increased Awareness of the Physical Consequences of Participation

With increasing years of participation comes an increased awareness of the physical consequences of participation. Older athletes are more likely to have experienced, and therefore be wary of, the consequences of physical injuries. The hours of rehabilitation, the loss of progress because of lost training, the pain of the injury itself, and the anxiety of performing skills associated with previous injuries are only a few of the demotivating aspects of traumatic injuries.

At a subtler level, the constant physical aches and pains endured at higher levels of sport are substantially harsher than those experienced during the first few years of an athlete's career when the skills were easier and the training less demanding. Continued training in the face of pain, especially the pain from overuse syndromes, can do much to demotivate athletes. The joy of sport can be replaced by the daily grind when everything hurts.

The locker room slogan "No pain, no gain" has just enough truth in it to be dangerously misinterpreted by both coaches and athletes. Such an attitude can be used to justify continued training in spite of painful warning signals of impending problems or injuries that need rest for recuperation. Driving oneself through cardiovascular conditioning or strength drills may be beneficial, but working on a partially sprained ankle or ignoring the symptoms of tendinitis is harmful.

Increased Awareness of the Competitive Consequences of Participation

With increasing experience and skill comes an ability to more realistically evaluate the likelihood for success in competition. Since success is relative to one's goals, the coach and the athlete must be aware of the interaction between goal setting and motivation. Establishing clear, focused goals is important for directing and sustaining motivation. However, if those goals are too narrowly defined or too few in number, serious long-term demotivating effects can result.

Most athletes will not make the All-Star team. The youthful, naive enthusiasm to be an All-Star is replaced by a realistic appraisal of who is likely to make the team. If athletes find that they are unlikely to make it, their enthusiasm is likely to wane in direct proportion to the degree to which that goal is their only goal. When goals are extremely high and narrow, motivation will be sustained only if the athlete believes there is a realistic chance to achieve those goals in the foreseeable future. Goals that focus on the participation process can blunt the de-motivating effect of narrow goals. Such goals include enjoying the act of performing, providing a model for younger athletes, creating and designing personal competitive strategies and routines, and developing self-confidence and poise. Coaches often view these latter goals as a means to an end rather than as an end in themselves. If coaches counsel their athletes to perceive the process of sport as part of their personal goals, the athlete's enjoyment of the sport could be decidedly enhanced.

Increased Awareness of the Social Consequences of Participation

With increasing age and maturity, athletes develop an increased awareness of other social activities. Their interests become more complex and diversified; and conflicts may develop between their desire to train and the desire to participate in other activities. The number one reason given for discontinuing sport is "other things to do." Not being able to do these "others things" is a major contributor to feelings of entrapment, the major characteristic of burnout.

There are two aspects – objective and subjective – of the restrictions placed on the social involvements of athletes training in high level programs. For example, the objective restrictions of time limitations and scheduling conflicts are a substantial problem when athletes train multiple hours a day, multiple days per week across multiple seasons each year. Socializing with friends after school may be dramatically reduced by such training regimens. Even athletic friends may be left behind as the more talented athlete progresses through the skill levels at a more rapid rate.

Objective restrictions can be partially dealt with by rearranging training schedules. For example, in one high-level sports program the older athletes train in the early afternoon and the younger children train later on Fridays. This frees Friday evenings for social activities for the older athletes. Since the younger athletes have no school on the next day, the later hours on a Friday are not too demanding. Social occasions can also be given a higher priority during the off season. Both parents and athletes should be alerted to the need for such diversity.

Subjective restrictions are sometimes more difficult to resolve. The perception that one is somehow losing out on what others can have can be quite demotivating. What you cannot have often becomes even more desirable. One approach to this "forbidden fruit" problem is to combat the inaccurate perception that sports participation and an enjoyable social life are mutually exclusive. Although restrictions exist, the choice is rarely all or none. The attitude that success requires dedication to the point of sacrificing everything else is a stereotype. The fact that some athletes perceive involvement in sports as leading to a better social life and more friends attests to the fact that the problem may be more one of attitude than of actual restrictions.

Thus, psychological burnout need not be an inevitable consequence of intense participation. Early diagnosis of the symptoms, accurate identification of susceptible personalities, and increased awareness of demotivating environmental influences can lead to effective prevention and correction of this syndrome.

CHAPTER REFERENCES

1. Kimiecik, J. C., & Harris, A. T. (1996). What is enjoyment? A conceptual/definitional analysis with implications for sport and exercise psychology, *Journal of Sport and Exercise Psychology, 18 (3)*, 247 – 263. https://doi.org/10.1123/jsep.18.3.247.

2. Orlick, T. D. (1974). The athletic dropout: A high price for inefficiency. *Canadian Association for Health, Physical Education and Recreation Journal.* Nov/Dec, 21-27.

3. Gould, D., Feltz, D., Horn, T., & Weiss, M. (1982). Reasons for attrition in competitive youth swimming, *Journal of Sport Behavior, 5,* 155–165.

4. Ewing, M. E., & Seedfeldt, V. (2002). Patterns of participation in American agency-sponsored sports. In F. L. Smoll & R. E. Smith (Eds.), Children and youth in sport: A biopsychosocial perspective (2nd ed.), pp. 39-56. Dubuque, IA: Kendall/Hunt.

5. Weiss, M., & Smith, A. L. (2001). Friendship quality in youth sport: relationship to age, gender, and motivation variables. *Journal of Sport and Exercise Psychology, 23 (4),* 420-437, https://doi.org/10.1123/jsep.23.4.420.

6. Klint, K. A., & Weiss, M. R. (1987). Perceived competence and motives for participating in youth sports: a test of Harter's competence motivation theory, *Journal of Sport and Exercise Psychology, 9 (1),* 55-65. https://doi.org/10.1123/jsp.9.1.55.

7. Gould, D., & Petlichkoff, L. (1988). Participation motivation and attrition in young athletes. In F. Smoll, R. Magill, & M. Ash (Eds.), <u>Children in sport</u> (3rd ed., pp. 161-178). Champaign, IL: Human Kinetics.

8. Ewing, M. (1981). Achievement orientations and sport behaviors of males and females. Unpublished doctoral dissertation, University of Illinois.

9. Nicholls, J. G., & Miller, A. T. (1983). The differentiation of the concepts of difficulty and ability. *Child development, 54,* 951-959. http://dx.doi.org/10.2307/1129899.

10. Roberts, G. C., Treasure, D. C., & Conroy, D. E. (2007). Understanding the dynamics of motivation in sport and physical activity. In G. Tenenbaum & R. C. Eklund (eds.). Handbook of Sport Psychology (3rd ed.). (pp. 3-30). Hoboken, NJ: John Wiley & Sons.

11. Lancellotti, B. (2010). Sport Programming, Self-Perceptions, and Burnout Among Adolescent Female Athletes. Unpublished doctoral dissertation. Fairleigh Dickinson University, Teaneck, NJ.

12. Feigley, D. A. (1984). Psychological burnout in high level athletes. *The Physician and Sportsmedicine, 12,* 108 119. http://dx.doi.org/10.1080/00913847.1984.11701971.

13. Hill, A. P., Witcher, C. S. G., Gotwals, J. K., & Leyland, A. F. (2015). A qualitative study of perfectionism among self-identified perfectionists in sport and the performing arts. *Sport, Exercise and Performance Psychology, 4,* 237 – 253. http://dx.doi.org/10.1037/spy0000041.

10

Working with Parents

CHAPTER OUTLINE

- Developing the Coach-Parent Relationship
- Effective Communication
  FROM CHALKBOARD TO PLAYING FIELD: Protective Communication Techniques
- Setting a Good Example: Parents and Coaches as Role Models
- Guidelines for Supportive Parents
  YOUR TURN: Working with Parents
- Parents' Orientation Program
  SPOTLIGHT ON YOUTH SPORTS: Sample Parents' Meeting Agenda
  SPOTLIGHT ON YOUTH SPORTS: Parents' Manual Info
- Codes of Conduct

Successful youth sports programs could not exist without parental support, yet working with parents is often identified by coaches as one of the most – if not the very most – vexing problems confronting coaches[1] who are, quite often, a volunteer and usually a parent of one of the young athletes on the team. On the other hand, when parents and coaches work together in the spirit of a common understanding to support the young athlete, a "success triangle" develops resulting in effective communication, mutual support, and a common goal of helping young athletes to develop physically, socially and emotionally.

This chapter focuses on establishing positive working relationships with parents. Coaches and parents are part of the same team—aiding the self-development and mastery of sport skills by the young athletes. Positive parental support is essential to provide high-quality organized youth sport experiences. In this chapter we'll discuss getting the coach-parent relationship off on the right foot and keeping it on track.

Developing the Coach-Parent Relationship

Any relationship takes work. This section presents suggestions to help coaches and parents stay on the right track for offering a healthy, organized youth sports program. Coaches who understand the stresses confronting parents and parents who appreciate the stresses that coaches are under are much more likely to work together effectively.

STRESSORS CONFRONTING PARENTS[2]

- Lack of communication between coach and parent when important issues are being decided (practice schedules, school conflicts, who starts, …)
- Finding a healthy coaching situation for the child
- Watching their child playing poorly without success
- Watching their child behaving badly in the field of play
- Seeing their child bullied, being left out by teammates or feeling dejected
- Watching other adults behaving badly

- Splitting time fairly between multiple children in the family often between one child involved in sport vs. another in non-sport activities

- Financial demands which can escalate quickly as their child becomes more involved.

- Concern about the safety of their child

- Logistics (getting to practice during rush hours, traveling to new locations for competitions)

- Balancing school and sport responsibilities

STRESSORS CONFRONTING COACHES

- Communicating with parents especially when either or both are upset.

- Deciding who starts and who are the reserves.

- Demoting a starter in favor of a reserve whose skill level has improved to that of a starter.

- Providing sufficient playing time for all members on the team when only a limited number can play at any one point in time

- Unrealistic expectations of parents concerning their child's skill level

- Dealing with parents, some of whom are overly involved and some of whom are only marginally involved

- Juggling full time jobs, family time and volunteer obligations

- Coaching sports that, while they might have played, they know little about coaching

- Concerns for the safety of the children

- Accusations – implied or direct – of favoritism if their child is playing regularly

These lists are not – nor were they meant to be – exhaustive of all potential stressors. However, being able to understand the youth sport perspective from both the coach's and parents' points of view goes a long way to developing a strong foundation for an effective coach-parent working relationship.

FIGURE 10.1
Effective
communication is
more of an attitude
than a specific
technique.

This foundation includes (1) effective communication; (2) setting good examples for the young athletes; and (3) defining what it means to be a supportive parent[3].

Effective Communication

While specific communication techniques can enhance a person's ability to understand one another, effective communication is more of an **attitude** than it is specific techniques. (Figure 10.1) Communication requires the attitude that *we will continue to communicate until we really understand each other's point(s) of view – even when we might disagree.* The essence of communication is not how skilled or glib you are with communication techniques, but rather, it is a willingness to keep exchanging thoughts until both parties fully understand each other. Just as with the sport skills you teach your young athletes, communication skills get better with practice.

COMMUNICATION STYLES

Keep everyone in the communication loop. Do not send important messages through the child. Talk to parents directly and ask them to respond in kind.

Share your concerns without blame. Your concern is that Frankie is missing practices. Concern with blame: "Frankie's not playing because he's missed so many practices." Concern without blame: "Frankie is struggling because he has missed so many practices. He is more likely to earn more playing time if he can get to more practices."

Be consistent with your verbal and nonverbal communications. Speaking without giving reasonable eye contact sends mixed messages. Expressing empathy verbally while you stand with your arms folded aggressively across your chest is inconsistent. Saying "Everything's fine," while looking downcast or stone-faced is confusing to others. Ask yourself if your words, tone, and body language are consistent with your message.

Listen with empathy. Empathy does not require agreement but implies understanding. There is a tendency to stop communicating as tensions rise. The ultimate resolution of a conflict requires constructive communication. Continue to communicate even if that means you must take a personal risk of being rejected when you are open and supportive. Taking a risk, however, does not mean that you must endure continued abuse. Should the communication from the other person be continually unfair, you can resort to protective techniques described in the Chalkboard box.

Communicate the problem, not the solution. While this recommendation may appear counterintuitive, describing yourself as "solution oriented" may be a sophisticated way of saying "My way is best." Your solution might not be acceptable to the other person. You both have the problem or there would not be any conflict. If others have input into a solution, they are more likely to find it acceptable. Offer your solution only if the other person has no answer to offer. Even then, do so tentatively allowing them to elaborate or expand on the potential solution that you have offered.

Avoid sarcasm, irony and sardonic remarks. Such approaches cut off true communication. Cynicism rarely leads to solutions.

Encourage parents to discuss conflicts with those who can resolve them. Discussing problems with others who are not involved has little impact on the problem except to prolong or escalate it. Parking lot gossip among parents or discussions with other coaches who already agree with you is likely only to harden positions. Furthermore, the person with whom you have the conflict is likely to hear that you have been airing your concerns in public and will often be even more resistant to constructive confrontation. While occasionally discussing a difficult problem with a close friend or fellow coach may help you develop some successful strategies for approaching a difficult person about a difficult conflict, if you find that you are discussing conflicts with a number of others who are not directly involved, the chances are that you are escalating rather than resolving the actual conflict.

EMPATHETIC CONFRONTATIONS[4]

Every long-term, important relationship experiences conflicts. In the youth sports triad of athlete-coach-parent, conflicts are almost inevitable between the three primary roles. Just as parent-child and coach-athlete conflicts occur and must be resolved, so do coach-parent conflicts. Coach-parent conflicts often appear more difficult to resolve because typically there is not as great a power differential between coaches and parents. However, the techniques discussed below are equally as important in resolving conflicts in all three types of relationships.

Confrontations are face-to-face discussions between the principal parties of a conflict. Most people equate confrontations with personal attacks and adversarial relationships. However, hostile confrontations and escalating tensions are more the result of a lack of interpersonal communication skills than the direct result of a confrontation. Rainer Martens, a youth sport advocate, coined the phrase **"empathetic confrontations,"**[5] a term reflecting the concept that you can resolve even major conflicts without treating those people with whom you have a conflict as opponents or enemies. (Figure 10.2)

FIGURE 10.2
Empathetic confrontations involve face-to-face discussions between the principals of a conflict, not hostility and aggression.

Often the major stress in a conflict is the anticipation of a negative encounter. Avoidance of dealing directly with the conflicting parties leads to prolonged stressful anticipation. Coaches are less likely to be stressed if they see their role as one of "winning others over" (that is, convincing a parent that a particular strategy is in the best interest of the child) rather than "winning over others" (I'm the coach – that's why!). Coaches who see confrontations in the light of winning and losing games often win the confrontation at the expense of maintaining positive relations with others.

The essence of empathetic confrontations is to place yourself in the parent's position and, before initiating contact, try to understand the problem from his or her perspective. Understanding another's point of view in the midst of a conflict is often difficult because emotions tend to be high and may distort both your and the parent's perception of what has happened and why. Ask yourself:

Is she attacking you or defending her child?

Is he belittling you unfairly or is he upset and not thinking clearly?

Do the parents disagree with you or is there some other problem they are dealing with that you are not aware of? For example, parents may have a financial difficulty affording the training you've suggested.

Before speaking, ask yourself if what you are about to say is likely to encourage the parents to re-examine their position or are your words likely to place them on the defensive where they have to either give in or fight back. Look for strategies that allow you to achieve your goal without undermining your relationship with the parent. For example, compare the following two approaches for dealing with an overzealous parent:

"When you watch practices constantly and criticize your son, Billy, you place unrealistic pressure on him and make it more difficult for him to succeed."

vs.

"Billy is still learning how to cope with pressure. We're doing what we can to teach him how to handle the competitive pressures. Sometimes he tries too hard to please us. Is there anything you can suggest that might be done both on or off the field that might help reduce the pressure on him?"

The first approach places blame. The second approach shows that you wish to resolve the conflict, but not at the parents' expense. Emphasize that a mutual solution is desired rather than that one of you must win while the other must lose.

Be tentative when posing a solution. At first, such an approach seems counterintuitive. While you may be quite firm in your beliefs, initially confront tentatively and express your concern about determining if your perceptions about the situation and about the other person's actions are correct. A tentative approach avoids putting the other person on the defensive and increases the chances that they will actually hear the content of your message. Accusations may cause others to quickly set up defenses that block their consideration of your point of view. You must find a balance between being so tentative that you appear indecisive and so aggressive that the other person feels attacked. Be firm, but indicate that you wish to examine the problem as you see it. Here are two examples:

> "If I hear you correctly, you're concerned that your son hasn't had a fair opportunity to earn a starting role on the team. Is that what concerns you?"

> "Is your concern that the conditioning is too demanding because of your daughter's previous injury? Have I heard you correctly?"

Stay focused. Deal with one aspect at a time. Often when a confrontation is finally initiated, the dam breaks and a flood of problems pours out. Presenting too many issues at one time, regardless of your style of presentation, is likely to be seen as an attack. Proceed gradually so that you can change tactics if you see that you were mistaken about the other person's actions or motives.

When should you confront a parent? The old adage that "there's no time like the present," is appropriate when deciding when to initiate a confrontation. Earlier is usually better than later. Conflicts that are kept locked up inside you foster resentments and animosity, not to mention the prolonged stress from anticipating an eventual confrontation. Delaying a confrontation is appropriate only when you believe that the other person is not ready to accept a confrontation because of their emotional state or lack of willingness to talk.

From Chalkboard to Playing Field

Protective Communication Techniques

When honest, open communication fails, the following protective techniques may be helpful[6]. If you feel that regardless of the outcome of an empathetic confrontation, you have specific techniques to protect yourself from unfair or insensitive attacks from the other person, you are much more likely to attempt empathetic confrontations in the first place. Self-confidence is enhanced if you know you have a fallback position should your initial attempts prove unsuccessful. Empathetic confrontation may fail when the other person (a) is too upset or insensitive to respond to open communication from you, or (b) has other interests or motives than communicating with you.

- **Shift from content to process.** "Hold on a second. Before we both get too upset, let's list our differences."

- **Momentary delay.** "Let's take a break and then start again."

- **Time-out.** "Let's think about it for a day and meet again tomorrow."

- **Acknowledgment.** Your critic: "You haven't done what you promised." Your response: "Yes, you're right. I haven't yet." (As opposed to making an apologetic excuse. Use with peers, not your superiors.)

- **Selective ignoring.** You remain silent through unfair, emotional interactions while controlling nonverbal as well as verbal cues. Such a technique may help with relatively immature individuals who simply have to get something out of their system before they can begin to listen and communicate.

- **Active listening.** Rephrase or reflect what the other person has said to show that you have heard and understood their feelings. "I can understand why you're so upset. If what you are describing had happened to my son, I'd be upset too." (Such statements reflect your empathy without implying that you agree or will capitulate to their demands. What they are describing might not be what actually happened but merely their interpretation of what transpired.)

- **Clouding.** These techniques are appropriate in response to nonconstructive criticism or unfair accusations.

  Agree in Probability. "That might be that case" or "You could be right."

  Agree in Part. "You never have time to meet with parents."
    Response: "You're right. I haven't had much time lately." (You agree with the time limitations without conceding you have been unwilling to meet with parents.)

  Agree in Principle. Statement: "If you don't spend more time coaching my daughter, she'll do poorly in the play-offs."
    Response: "If athletes aren't coached, they'll have a difficult time in competition."

  Once you have decided to use a protective technique, watch the people you are speaking with carefully for changes in their communication to you. If the unfair accusations stop and if they begin to be responsive, return quickly to direct, open communication with them.

Setting a Good Example: Parents and Coaches as Role Models

Speak to parents about the need to provide good examples in sporting situations, *especially* in situations where there might be perceived unfairness. Since young athletes learn many, if not most, of their values by modeling others (e.g., parents, coaches, other athletes), setting a good example is crucial, especially in situations where other parents, coaches, and athletes might be behaving poorly. Since most parents already believe in providing good role models for their children, you might introduce this topic by asking them several questions to set the stage for "dealing with the obvious." Ask the parents if they have ever observed poor behavior at a youth sport event. (Figure 10.3) Ask them to describe what happened. After a few examples, ask the parents how such situations made them feel. Ask them also how their child reacted. Finally ask them how they addressed the poor behavior with their child. After a few parents have shared such experiences, talk about these four crucial issues related to setting a good example.

FIGURE 10.3
Regardless of what we say about good behavior, children often learn the most from what we actually do.

RECOGNIZE SELF-JUSTIFYING BEHAVIOR

Ask: "What prevents good people from being good role models?" Point out that often the answer is self-justification. The poor sport might say, "I wasn't behaving badly; I was just protecting my child/my child's team." Parents often take the referee's (or coach's) decision personally. "How could you do that to my child?"

BE A ROLE MODEL "WHEN IT COUNTS"

Setting a good example is even more important under adverse circumstances (e.g., a "bad call" by the official) than when "everything is going right!" Children especially look to parents when there is pressure. Thus, maintaining composure when times are tough is critical to effective modeling. Coaches and parents can still respond to unfair situations, but doing so in a fashion that shows a loss of control can have a much greater negative impact on young athletes than all the positive talk about composure and self-control when things are going well! Older children watch as intensely as younger children but are much less likely to let their parents see them watching.

RESPECT AND SUPPORT COACHES AND OFFICIALS

Without the involvement of coaches and officials, youth sports could not exist. If your team is in a beginner or intermediate level of competition, point out that the officials are likely to be at the beginning and intermediate level of officiating also. Point out that without opponents who respect and follow the rules as spelled out by the "spirit of the game," the game of sport cannot exist. *In a very real sense, sports competition represents the highest form of cooperation.*

Guidelines for Supportive Parents

Most parents want to be supportive of their children. They also frequently struggle with finding that appropriate balance between being supportive and being pushy, particularly when their children are involved with competitive activities such as sport. Indicate your empathy and understanding that such decisions on their part are often difficult and typically not always a matter of "either/or." In fact, what one child sees as parental support, another might see as being overly involved and vice-versa[7]. The same behavior ("How did you play today?") might help one child feel supported while another child feels intruded upon.

Here are a few basic suggestions a coach can make to help parents find that necessary balance between helping and pressuring so they can enhance their child's youth sport experience.

KIDS HAVE A RIGHT TO PLAY – AND NOT TO PLAY

This does not mean that children should be permitted to do "nothing." Parents have a right, actually an obligation, to insist that their children participate in constructive, meaningful activities. While parents should provide a menu of such possibilities, kids should still have some say in such matters. Sport is only one option.

OVER-IDENTIFICATION CREATES PRESSURE

Living their life through their children's sports experience is an occupational hazard of many parents. Most parents do it to some extent. However, they can do so unobtrusively. When parents find that watching their child during competition results in extreme agitation or elation or if the child indicates that her parents' behavior is embarrassing, it may be better to watch from a distance.

EMPHASIZE FUN, PARTICIPATION, AND SELF-IMPROVEMENT – AS OPPOSED TO WINNING

Self-improvement is based upon mastery of skills. Such mastery is the foundation for developing what sports psychologists call "perceived self-competence." Perceived self-competence is a key determinant of whether kids have fun, develop mental toughness, and decide to continue to participate in competitive sports.

TEACH KIDS TO HANDLE BOTH WINNING AND LOSING

A major component of good sportsmanship is learning how to win graciously and lose with dignity. Handling defeat is often a crucial stepping stone to earning long-term success in both sport and life.

EXCESSIVE STRESS UNDERMINES ENJOYMENT

If children are to realize the benefits of participating in organized athletics, then the emphasis should be on having fun. Excessive, prolonged stress is a major cause of psychological burnout and dropping out of organized youth sports.

Beyond these basic suggestions, Appendix 10.1 (Guidelines for Supportive Parents) provides specific guidelines that coaches can share with concerned parents as they both strive to be supportive of their young athletes. It is designed to be photocopied and distributed to parents.

YOUR TURN
Working with Parents

Just as parents should not be telling a coach how to coach, coaches should not fall into the trap of telling parents how to parent their child. On the other hand, coaches can make meaningful suggestions to parents about how the parents might best support their child's youth sport experience. The following are just a few possibilities for helping parents to help their young athlete.

PARENT'S TOOLBOX

Coaches can provide ideas to parents new to youth sports with a variety of strategies to cope with predictable sources of parental stress[8] in organized youth sports.

1. For parents who get overly agitated watching the competitions, suggest that they develop an alternative focus during competition such as charting the plays (e.g., shots on goal) or helping with administrative tasks (e.g.,

calling the on-deck swimmers into position just before their heat).

2. Suggest specific coping skills appropriate for parents to teach their children and encourage parents to challenge their children to use those skills on the sports field just as they might in the family. For example, teach maintaining focus on "what to do" as opposed to focusing on "how I feel." In tennis the parent might teach their child to concentrate on executing the skills that the coach has taught, such as the toss on their serve rather than the child's somewhat natural response of nervousness before a big match. "When I feel nervous, I focus on the toss." By teaching children better coping skills, the parents also learn to execute such coping skills. When upset by the linesman's bad call, focus on maintaining a sense of calm. Teaching your children to keep their composure is likely to help parents keep their composure!

3. When discussing how other parents might behave badly on the sidelines by yelling at their child or the officials, the parents can be encouraged to sit away from those parents (a short-term solution) and to develop social networks with more experienced parents who appear to have learned to cope with the stressors faced by parents (long-term solution).

4. Suggest that spouses work as a team sharing responsibilities – often within each particular parent's expertise (e.g., the organized parent manages the schedule, orders the uniforms and sets up the car pool while the energetic parent drives to competitions, helps with the fund raising, and communicates with the coach).

Parents' Orientation Program

Some organized youth sports programs have developed formal parents' orientation programs. Many have not. As an individual coach, that responsibility often falls on your shoulders. Do not ignore the responsibility for hosting a parents' orientation program. An effective program can pre-empt many predictable parent-coach conflicts and can often help you with everything from generalized support for your coaching objectives to specific, time-saving administrative tasks such as registering athletes, ordering uniforms and fundraising.

Parent orientation programs can be provided either by youth sport program administrators for all parents in the program or by individual coaches for the parents of their individual teams. Depending upon the structure of your program, a combination style might be the most appropriate; for example, the youth sports administrator can host a general, mass meeting of all parents in the program followed by brief, but more specific, meetings with the coach or coaches of their child's team. Whether your parents' education/orientation program is part of a formal program offered by your sports organization or is a program you develop individually for your team, it is an essential part of a quality youth sport program[9].

An **effective parents' orientation program can be one of the very first** steps in establishing that support. Such an orientation can:

- help parents understand your program objectives from the very outset

- acquaint parents with you and your coaches

- provide parents with information about the specific sport in which their child is involved and your program's philosophy

- inform parents what is expected from them and their child(ren)

- allow coaches to develop an awareness of parental concerns

- encourage clear lines of communication between coaches and parents

- obtain parental support for the season's activities.

An orientation program that addresses such goals makes parents part of the program and minimizes potential parent-coach controversies. Parents and coaches who understand and can empathize with each other's concerns are more likely to work together for the best interests of the children.

What constitutes an effective parents' orientation program? One goal is the establishment of specific roles for parents and coaches. For example, parents can assist coaches with transportation, distribution of uniforms, fund-raising, and other general organizational matters that often prevent the coach from working directly with the athletes. Coaches can assist parents by emphasizing the importance of youth athletes completing their schoolwork and being organized about blending sport practices with the completion of family responsibilities.

HOSTING A PRE-SEASON PARENTS MEETING

One means of establishing such roles is to host a parents' meeting. At parents' meetings, coaches can establish guidelines for effective working relationships with parents before the season begins. The coach can discuss the potential conflicts and confusion that often result when parents attempt to help by "coaching over the coach's shoulder' at practices and in competition. Parents can also be given information about how they can help the coach deal with the predictable problems athletes may encounter throughout the season. For example, if an athlete feels left out or neglected, a coach can suggest that the parents notify the coach so the coach can be aware of the athlete's feelings and give whatever attention is necessary. The reaction of parents to a complaint of favoritism on the team is likely to be much different if the parents already know that (a) the coach is concerned about such problems and (b) the coach has already suggested a realistic solution for dealing with such problems BEFORE they arise. Parents who are familiar with the motives, concerns, and restrictions with which a coach must work are less likely to react negatively on the basis of a single incident.

Meetings that promote direct interactions between coaches and parents are usually preferable. The early establishment of clear lines of communication directly between coaches and parents is likely to produce many solutions before problems escalate from minor issues to major problems that undermine the youth sport experience.

Parents' meetings take time. You may be uncomfortable, at least initially, conducting such a meeting. Scheduling may be difficult, especially as one sports season blends into another. Nonetheless, such meetings are extremely valuable. Most parents are quite responsive to coaches once they recognize that their concerns are heard, understood, and acted upon. Effective coaches:

- make time for such meetings
- schedule sufficient notification lead time to enable parents to plan to attend

- hold such meetings before the season begins
- schedule them for approximately 1 ½ hours or less
- have an agenda
- keep the meeting moving
- hold the meeting in a facility large enough and comfortable enough to accommodate the size of your group.

SPOTLIGHT ON YOUTH SPORTS

Sample Parents' Meeting Agenda

A parents' meeting of 1 to 1 ½ hours will likely cover the essential general issues for the upcoming season. (Figure 10.4) The following sample agenda shows topics for running such meetings.

FIGURE 10.4
Your agenda should include not only what information you want to provide but also what information you can get from the parents in the program.

Coach's Introduction. Getting to know the coach's general background, qualifications, and motives for coaching tends to humanize the coach and increase the likelihood for effective communication.

Coaching Philosophy. Coaches can explain why they coach and what they believe is the value of a sport's experience for young athletes. They can discuss their teaching methods and inform parents about the degree of intensity to be expected within the program. They can indicate the extent to which mastery of skills and winning are emphasized and their importance in the program. The coaches can outline their expectations of the athletes and parents for the upcoming season.

Demonstration of the Sport. Coaches can demonstrate the specifics of their sports and discuss the role of officials in maintaining fair play and safety for the athletes.

Specifics of the Program. Coaches can specify: the frequency and length of the practice sessions; the length of the season and the schedule of games or meets; the criteria used for selecting who plays, who does not, or the amount of playing time for each player; expenses, if any, and the purpose of those expenses; what equipment is necessary, where it can be obtained, and its approximate cost.

Question and Answer Session with Parents. Typical questions coaches should be prepared to answer in a fashion consistent with the organization's program goals are:

1. Should the athletes have medical exams?
2. How have the athletes been grouped for competition based upon their skill levels?
3. What are the risks involved?
4. What should these athletes be expected to have accomplished by the end of the season?
5. Can and should parents attend the practices?
6. Can and should parents talk with athletes during a game?
7. What should parents provide for pre-event meals?
8. What can or should parents do at home to help prepare the athletes for practice and competitions?
9. How can parents encourage their children in a positive and effective way after a loss?
10. What kind of behavior is expected of the parents as they cheer for the athletes from the sidelines during games? (See the section, Codes of Conduct, at the end of the chapter.)
11. How can parents contact the coach? (telephone number, e-mail, preferred hours or days?)

CREATING A PARENTS' MANUAL

One particularly important component of the parents' orientation is a **parents' manual.** Hopefully, your sports organization has already developed one. If not, strongly encourage the organization to do so. A brief parents' manual developed either by you or the organization has the following **advantages:**

- Ensures that important policies and the policies of your organization are in writing.
- Helps ensure that those policies are consistently presented to parents.
- Clarifies to both you and the parents the policies of your program.
- Disseminates information to parents not able to attend the initial parents' meeting.

Manuals also have potential **disadvantages:** First, an overreliance on the manual may undermine the development of an effective parent-coach working relationship. Second, people are often quite casual about reading distributed material unless they are convinced of its relevance and importance. Thus, a parents' manual should not be viewed as a replacement for an effective parents' meeting.

SPOTLIGHT ON YOUTH SPORTS

Parents' Manual Info

An effective parents' manual must be individually tailored to the needs of your program. Below are a number of useful topics that should be considered for inclusion.

INFORMATION GIVEN TO PARENTS

1. **Being a team parent.** This section typically describes how parents can effectively work within the program. It might briefly outline your program's philosophy and some predictable experiences (both problems and high points) the parents and their youngsters may encounter. For example, you might describe

briefly how parents in the past have successfully dealt with such predictable concerns as fear, favoritism, sport injuries, winning and losing. This section can briefly give some background on your program and its successes and accomplishments.

2. **General information.** This section might outline the types of personal equipment each athlete needs, policies on attendance at practices, required uniforms, policies for dealing with injuries, insurance, information on team doctors, etc.

3. **Safety rules.** A listing of basic, necessary safety rules that all athletes are expected to learn and to follow.

4. **Team goals.** These goals might consist of general goals such as developing confidence, feelings of self-worth, sportsmanship, independence and self-reliance, and having fun. They can also include specific objectives, such as learning specific sports skills, and acquiring basic knowledge of rules and strategies.

5. **Competition organization.** Depending upon the complexity of the sports organization, this can range from a simple listing of the officers of your league to a description of procedures for advancing to state, regional and national competitions.

6. **Calendar of events for the season.** This listing of events could include instructional clinics, game schedules, and exhibitions.

7. **Who's who in your organization.** This can be a simple list of the coaches and league officials, or it can include those members of the parents' organization who have volunteered to handle various activities or committees (e.g., publicity, fund-raising, uniforms, officers of parents' club).

8. **Expenses.** A brief outline of the costs, if any, of participating in your program (league fees, tuition, entry fees, uniform costs, travel costs, clinic fees).

9. **Fund-raising.** After outlining the fund-raising procedures and policies of the organization, this section should also contain a specific statement of the degree to which parents are expected to be involved in such fund-raising (required, voluntary, expected) and a description of the specific fund-raisers available from which

the parents may choose to participate. A general statement of how and by whom the funds are allocated is appropriate in this section.

10. **Current budget.** For those organizations with substantial parental involvement in fund-raising, a public budget of those funds raised by the group is appropriate.

INFORMATION OBTAINED *FROM* PARENTS

Coaches find it extremely useful to obtain certain information from parents. Having a section of tear-out forms the parents can complete and return immediately at the conclusion of your parents' meeting is an efficient means of collecting information.

1. **Talent and skills inventory.** One key to a successful volunteer program is an awareness of the skills and talents of the members of your group. Placing people in jobs or tasks they enjoy and have the skills for is essential for both satisfaction of the individual volunteer and for the effectiveness of the organization.

2. **Publicity form.** For more competitive, intense programs, the inclusion of a simple information sheet to obtain basic information on each athlete puts appropriate background and demographics right at the fingertips of the publicity person.

3. **Medical permission form.** A form authorizing permission for medical treatment in case a parent is not available can be included. It should be voluntary, contain the dates through which that permission is granted, indicate how the parent can be contacted at home and at work, list the name of any insurance carrier retained by the parent and **be notarized.** Such forms should be duplicated and the coach should have access to those forms at all times, especially when the athlete travels for competition.

4. **An acknowledgment of fees.** A form describing the specific fees involved in participating should be outlined in detail and the parent should sign that form indicating that they understand the cost involved and assume the responsibility for those fees should their child participate.

5. **Athlete registration, membership, or insurance forms.** Many sports require an athlete registration fee for participation and accident/medical or liability insurance for sanctioned competitions. Whenever such memberships are appropriate, duplicate the enrollment forms and include them in the parents' manual.

While initial development of a comprehensive parent's manual takes time and effort, a manual may increase your efficiency substantially by providing information to a broad audience in a compact form. A manual need not include all the information suggested in the Spotlight to be useful. In fact, it is often a good idea to start small and include only a few priority items in the initial attempt. Each year, additional topics can be added as you gain a sense of the informational needs of both you and the parents. Information becomes outdated and needs to be updated or deleted entirely. The shorter and more concise the manual is, the more likely its information will be read and absorbed by parents.

Codes of Conduct

Many sport organizations have developed clear, explicit guidelines for spectator behavior at youth sport competitive events. These were discussed in detail in Chapter 6 when considering behavioral models for sportsmanship. Codes of conduct fall into two broad categories or types of codes. The first are enforceable codes with specific sanctions for failure to adhere to these basic codes of conduct. With the focus on enforceability, they tend to be legalistic and written in the negative (i.e., what you cannot do). Appendix 6.1 in the back of the book provides an example from the New Jersey State Attorney General's Office. It has frequently been incorporated into municipal code by local town councils and boroughs to increase its ability to be enforced.

The second category is education models, which emphasize what to do rather than what not to do. (Figure 10.5) Such codes are difficult to enforce but, when lived up to by participants, result in higher levels of spectator behavior than that brought about by the legalistic codes. Appendix 6.2 in the back of the book is a code developed by the Rutgers Youth Sports Research Council. As an educational model, it promotes

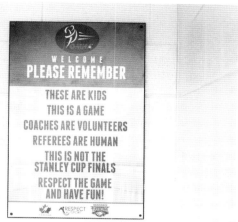

FIGURE 10.5
Codes of conduct for youth sports participants range from educational goals to legally enforceable state and municipal codes of law.

three, increasingly more sophisticated, levels of sportsmanship: Basic Civility, Good Sportsmanship, and Conduct of Distinction.

These codes of conduct have been provided in the appendices each in a form permitting easy photoduplication to be shared with your parents.

CHAPTER REFERENCES

1. Reade, I. L., & Rodgers, W. M. (2009). Common coaching challenges and their association with coach and contextual characteristics. *Journal of Coaching Education, 2(2).* 1-24.

2. Adapted from: Holt, N. L., & Knight, C. J. (2014). Parenting in youth sport: From research to practice. New York: Routledge, pp 90-91; Harwood, C., Drew, A., & Knight, C. J. (2010). Parental stressors in professional youth football academies: A qualitative investigation of specializing stage parents. *Qualitative Research in Sport and Exercise, 2,* 39-55. Doi:10.1016/SI469-0292(02)00040-7.

3. Feigley, D. A., Hunt J. G., & Heinzmann, G. S. (2004). *Rutgers S.P.O.R.T. Program: Supportive Parents on the Right Track.* Rutgers Youth Sports Research Council: New Brunswick, NJ.

4. Feigley, D. A. (1991). "Empathetic Confrontations: Enhancing Coach-Parent Working Relations." *THE REPORTER: The Journal of the New Jersey Association for Health, Physical Education, Recreation and Dance,* 64 (2), 10-12.

5. Adapted from Martens, R. (2012). *Successful coaching.* Champaign, IL: Human Kinetics, pp. 383-385.

6. McKay, M., Davis, M. & Fanning, P. (1995). *Messages: The Communications Skills Book,* 2nd ed. Oakland, CA: New Harbinger Publications.

7. Leff, S. S., & Hoyle, R. H. (1995). Young athletes' perceptions of parental support and pressure. *Journal of Youth and Adolescence. 24* (2), 187-203. doi: 10.1007/BF01537149.

8. Holt, N. L., & Knight, C. J. (2014). Parenting in youth sport: From research to practice. New York: Routledge, pp 92-93.

9. Rutgers Youth Sports Research Council. (2002). A Youth Sports Charter: Guidelines for Recreational Youth Sport Agencies. http://youthsports. rutgers.edu/resources/administrative/a-youth-sports-charter.

11

The Darker Side of Youth Sport

CHAPTER OUTLINE

- Child Abuse
- Drug and Alcohol Use by Young Athletes
- Eating Disorders
- Hazing and Bullying
- Bullying by Coaches

In this chapter we will cover some of the negative aspects found in youth sports, aspects with which volunteer coaches may be confronted, often with little information or resources for dealing with such problems. Topics include abuse, drug and alcohol addictions, eating disorders, hazing and bullying.

No one expects volunteer coaches to be professional counselors responsible for diagnosing and treating certain social disorders such as child abuse, eating disorders and drug or alcohol addiction. However, they will come in contact with such social problems if they coach long enough because such problems are pervasive throughout our society, including youth sports. Volunteers coaches who observe the early warning signs of such problems should recognize their potential severity and, in cooperation with the athlete's parents, seek professional help earlier rather than later. While coaches are not normally in a position to solve these problems directly, their close working relationship with young athletes provides them with unique opportunities to assist that athlete with early detection and referrals for protection and/or treatment.

Child Abuse

As a result of the regular – and often close – contact that coaches have with their young athletes, they are often in a position to see signs of neglect and/or abuse that might not otherwise be observable by the general public. Despite the belief that activities such as youth sports require substantial healthy parental support, sports families are not immune from problems that beset society such as drug addiction, mental illness and crime. Such dysfunctions can lead to inappropriate and often unacceptable behaviors by adults working in programs involving children and youth. Federal law defines child abuse as "Any recent act or failure to act on the part of a parent or caretaker which results in death, serious physical or emotional harm, sexual abuse or exploitation; or an act or failure to act which presents an imminent risk of serious harm."[1] While the laws differ from state to state, most states identify four major elements of child abuse: physical abuse, neglect, sexual abuse and emotional abuse. In addition, some states include abandonment and parental substance abuse as forms of child abuse.

SIGNS OF ABUSE

Signs of abuse may be seen in both the child's behaviors and the behaviors of the adults charged with taking care of the child as well as distortions of the child-adult interactions. Table 11.1 lists warning signs that have been documented by CAPTA.*

The list in Table 11.1 may not be all the signs of abuse or neglect. It is important to pay attention to other behaviors that may seem unusual or disconcerting. In addition to these signs and symptoms, Child Welfare Information Gateway provides information on signs of specific forms of abuse and the risk factors of which the concerned adult should be aware: https://www.childwelfare.gov.

SEXUAL ABUSE

Youth sport programs, unfortunately, provide settings where inappropriate sexual behavior can take place between children and adults. As Willie Sutton said when asked why he robbed banks, "That's where the money is!" Pedophiles are attracted to youth sports because that is where the children and youth are. Screening volunteers for criminal background is an important first step in protecting the young athletes, but such screening is no guarantee that all such predators are identified and precluded from coaching. Some predators have not been caught or have not been convicted despite being charged and as a result have no record accessible via the typical criminal background check.

The word pedophile has a much more restricted meaning in the scientific literature than in the public domain. Pedophilia is defined "as an ongoing sexual attraction toward pre-pubertal children"[3] but in context of youth sports, the term is also used to describe the criminal behavior associated with sexual relations with athletes under the age of adulthood (under 18 years of age). There are two dramatically different types of pedophiles. The first tends to prey on the very young, children younger than those typically involved in youth sports. Such predators tend to be below average in intelligence, inarticulate and treat their victims roughly. As heinous as this category of predator is, the second profile is much more insidious and difficult to identify. They are typically intelligent, articulate and may invest a significant amount of time and effort cultivating

---

*CAPTA stands for Federal Legislation entitled Child Abuse Prevention and Treatment Act.

TABLE 11.1 Observable Signs of Potential Child Abuse[2]

From Observing the Child:

1. Shows sudden changes in behavior or school performance
2. Has not received help for physical or medical problems brought to the parents' attention
3. Has learning problems (or difficulty concentrating) that cannot be attributed to specific physical or psychological causes
4. Is always watchful, as though preparing for something bad to happen
5. Lacks adult supervision
6. Is overly compliant, passive, or withdrawn
7. Comes to school or other activities early, stays late, and does not want to go home
8. Is reluctant to be around a particular person
9. Discloses maltreatment

From Observing the Parent:

1. Denies the existence of—or blames the child for—the child's problems in school or at home
2. Asks teachers or other caregivers to use harsh physical discipline if the child misbehaves
3. Sees the child as entirely bad, worthless, or burdensome
4. Demands a level of physical or academic performance the child cannot achieve
5. Looks primarily to the child for care, attention, and satisfaction of the parent's emotional needs
6. Shows little concern for the child

From Observing the Parent and Child:

1. Rarely touch or look at each other
2. Consider their relationship entirely negative
3. State that they do not like each other

long-term relationships for just a few moments of gratification. They manipulate children until the children become desensitized to inappropriate behavior and may even come to believe that they – i.e., the children – have initiated or are responsible for such inappropriate relationships. In about two out of three cases, pedophiles already know the children or

TABLE 11.2 Guidelines for Parents

1. Criminal Background Checks

Does your organization carry out such background checks?
Where is such information kept and who has access to it?

2. Don't Use Coach as a Babysitter

Don't permit single non-parental adults to drive kids to games and practice alone.
Coaches should avoid being alone with children both for the child's safety and for the coach's reputation.

3. Don't Fall for Flattery

Such techniques are often used to ingratiate the pedophile with caretakers and develop trust.

4. Talk to Your Child & Listen

While care must be taken to avoid unfairly labeling a coach's behavior – the results are devastating – we must watch for warning signs and not simply ignore kid's concerns.

5. Beware the Coach Bearing Gifts

Why would they do so?

6. Stay Informed

Know the details of travel schedules, after-game activities, showering arrangements, etc. Such activities should be appropriate with more than one adult/parent present.

have regular access to them. The perpetrator is often a relative, neighbor, family friend, coach, or clergyman who has an initially appropriate contact with the child. They may volunteer to drive young athletes to games or practices, spend extra time coaching their young protégées with one-on-one coaching; find time to spend with the children on lunch breaks; bring gifts for apparent (birthdays) and non-apparent reasons (just to be nice), and offer to drive to practice and games to give the parents a break from childcare. Table 11.2 provides guidelines for parents and guardians to help detect and avoid situations in which their child may be vulnerable to predatory behavior.

REPORTING CHILD ABUSE

All states and the District of Columbia mandate that professionals working with children must report reasonable suspicions concerning child abuse. Some require that anyone with such suspicions – including volunteers – must report also. The reporting requirements for each state is available at the Child Welfare Information Gateway at www.childwelfare.gov. Most park-and-recreation agencies which provide children and youth programs including sports have procedures for reporting suspected abuse.

Know the agencies in your state that handle reports of child abuse. They typically are Law Enforcement (Police and Detectives) and Child Protective Services (the name may differ in different states). Many states have toll-free lines for reporting suspected child abuse. State by state information for these telephone numbers can be found at www.childwelfare.gov.

Drug and Alcohol Use by Young Athletes

Why should you, as youth sport coach, be concerned about drug and alcohol use in sport? Despite the belief that this is an adult problem, or at worst a problem for high school, collegiate and professional athletes, the reality is that the roots of these problems often lie in the early years of athlete's sports participation. Further, despite the notoriety of performance enhancing drugs, such as steroids and human growth hormone, the two most abused drugs in sport are alcohol and nicotine. Those who start drinking before age 14 years have a greater likelihood of developing lifetime dependence.[4] The startling fact is that the median age of one's first drink of alcohol in the United States for boys is age 11 and girls age 13![5] While no one expects youth sport volunteers to become drug and alcohol counselors, the fact is that youth sport coaches are role models and can have a dramatic influence on the values and attitudes they teach their young athletes.

Kids who are knowledgeable about the dangers of drugs are 50% less likely to use drugs than kids who are naive to the negative effects of drug use.[6] While scare tactics are relatively ineffective, straightforward information in an appropriate context (for example, the impact of substance abuse on sports performance) can help young athletes steer clear of both recreational drugs such as marijuana and cocaine and performance enhancing drugs such as steroids and amphetamines. Discussing the harmful side effects of alcohol and drugs on one's physical and mental capacities – and by direct extension – on one's ability to perform in sports appears to have a greater inhibitory effect than simply warning of the problems of being drunk and/or stoned.[7] Ask your athletes how they feel about professional athletes using illegal drugs. What has drug use done to the reputations and careers of athlete's caught using drugs? Do their performance records, if any, mean the same thing as performance records held by honest, non-drug using athletes?

SYMPTOMS OF DRUG AND/OR ALCOHOL USE

Drug and alcohol use may sometimes be difficult to identify because signs such as mood swings, angry outbursts, changes in social and personal interests are naturally occurring events as youngsters mature and enter puberty. Nonetheless, general signs which parents and youth sport coaches can look for include:

- Mood changes including depression along with withdrawal and/or isolation
- Neglect of personal cleanliness and grooming
- Increased irritability, hostility and rapid moods swings
- Changes in friends and/or increased isolation from current friends and teammates
- Heightened secrecy about activities outside the gym or athletic field
- Use of fragrances previously not used such as mouthwash, deodorants or breath mints to hide the odor of alcohol, cigarettes or other drugs such as marijuana
- Bottled eye drops (for disguising reddened eyes or dilated pupils)
- Secretive conversations which cease or use of coded language when adults are present
- Reports of missing money or attempts to borrow money from friends
- Negative changes in study habits, grades, and school attendance
- Abruptly quitting or missing practices despite supportive parents

NON-CONFRONTATIONAL REFUSAL SCRIPTS TO SUGGEST TO KIDS

Kids rarely get drugs from strangers. They are more likely to be introduced to drugs by friends who they may be unwilling to "rat on" to adults. Having a polite, but clear response declining to use drugs or alcohol can be an essential skill for young athletes to help them to resist the temptation to do drugs or alcohol with friends. In a discussion of drug and alcohol, you can suggest a number of firm but non-confrontational responses young athletes can use to counteract pressure from friends to drink or use.

No thanks, I'm in training for ____(my sport)____.

Thanks, but I'm not into that stuff.

Sorry, but I'm an athlete and that stuff hurts my training.

Thanks, but I promised my team and my coach that I'd stay away from that stuff.

You can also ask members of the team if they ever had to refuse offers to use drugs or alcohol and, if so, how did they say no. You can incorporate useful responses into your discussion with your team.

ADULT ADDICTIONS

It goes beyond the scope of this book to discuss adult addictions in depth. However, since one of eight individuals in the United States suffers from substance abuse at some time in their life, it is clear that they often bring those abuses to their sports participation, including volunteer coaching.[8] In some venues, sports and alcohol are synonymous. Having "a brew" at a ball game is thought by many to be a normal part of an American pastime. Not so with youth sports! One of four individual's lives have been negatively influenced by alcoholism. The stark reality is that alcoholism influences a significant number of adults who volunteer to coach youth sports. Showing up at a practice or competition under the influence of drugs and alcohol, whether addicted or not, is a form of negligence – and a strong argument can be made that it is gross negligence because it places the young athletes at risk and involves a "voluntary" choice to drink or use drugs before coming to the sports venue. The word voluntary has been placed in quotes because, while the actual acts of drinking or using drugs are a choice, the nature of addiction means that many people who have a drinking or drug problem are out of control and as result, their thinking and choices are dictated by their addiction rather than what is in the best interests of themselves and their young athletes.

Eating Disorders

Disordered eating patterns range from mildly distorted restricted eating and short term "crash dieting" to full-fledge clinical disorders such as anorexia and bulimia. Over the years a number of misconceptions[9] have arisen concerning eating disorders. For example, the belief that anorexia and bulimia are restricted to upper middle class white female teenagers is patently false. Eating disorders can affect both boys and girls regardless of economic background and family structure. The belief that dysfunctional family structure, especially the cold "refrigerator mom" who uses withdrawal of love as a primary tool of control is a primary cause of eating disorders is also a myth. In fact, family support and concern is often the very reason why youngsters are initially referred for treatment. We now realize that eating disorders have a substantial genetic component and are much more than simply making bad choices about eating. While a youngster may initially decide to try a fad diet, once the genetic predisposition has been triggered, the compulsive behavior can take on a life of its own and self-determined will power has little impact on overcoming the distorted eating patterns.

Disordered eating can develop over time into serious, potentially deadly afflictions.[10] However, the seeds of such disorders are likely to have been sown early in an athlete's career. For example, in many sports, weight loss may be seen as a positive achievement by both the coach and the athlete, especially if the sport performance is successful. As a result, that weight loss is less likely to be identified as a problem. It may often be reinforced by praise from the coach and parents ("Great! You made weight!"). Therefore, it is crucial that youth sport coaches be informed about the severity of eating disorders so that they can recognize both the early symptoms and the circumstances that might promote the development of disordered eating. They are then more likely to take steps to mitigate such factors and/or encourage the parents of such at risk athletes to seek early treatment.

Of the many types of eating disorders recognized by the medical community, the two that have been examined most often in the context of sport are anorexia and bulimia. Both nervosa anorexia and bulimia are recognized by the American Psychiatric Association as psychiatric disorders. While related and often having similar behaviors, they are viewed as different problems, each with a distinct set of diagnostic criteria. Further, not all disordered eating fits neatly into these two categories. Some disturbed eating patterns do not reach the extreme stages where it fits the formal diagnosis of either disorder. The criteria used to diagnose, and thus to define, anorexia and bulimia are:[11]

ANOREXIA

The clinical name for anorexia is anorexia nervosa. It has been described as "the relentless pursuit of thinness" and has three primary characteristics:

1. Persistent restriction of energy intake (they don't eat).

2. Fear of gaining weight that persists despite a low body weight or persistent behavior that interferes with weight gain (they avoid meals).

3. Disturbed body image (They feel fat despite having normal or below normal weight).

BULIMIA

Outwardly, the symptoms of bulimia are quite different from anorexia. Bulimics typically maintain normal body weights but eat in uncontrolled binges followed by vomiting and/or the misuse of laxatives, diuretics, enemas and exercise to prevent weight gain.[12] Such behavior has been labeled "the binge/purge syndrome." The primary characteristics of bulimia are:

1. Recurrent binge eating coupled with a feeling of a lack of control over what and how much is eaten ("I can't stop.").

2. Recurrent, inappropriate behaviors to prevent weight gain such as:
    • Self-induced vomiting
    • Misuse of laxatives and/or diuretics
    • Strict dieting or fasting
    • Excessive exercising

3. Their self-worth is unduly influenced by their body's shape and weight ("I look worthless!").

Bulimia is classified as a psychiatric disorder when the binging occurs at least once a week for three consecutive months.

IMPLICATIONS FOR ATHLETES

Studies of eating disorders in sport have found few differences between athletes and non-athletes at the youth sport level but distinctly higher rates of occurrence in the adult, elite level sports. These differences are most pronounced in those sports where weight classes (martial arts, wrestling) and physical appearances (gymnastics, ice skating) are part of successful performances.[13] There are at least three possible explanations why the higher rates exist in such sports. First, the higher incidence may exist because weight-class and aesthetic sports attract individuals with eating disorders. Weight loss behaviors common in such sports make it more difficult to identify "at risk" athletes – they can hide. Both their physical look and their unhealthy behaviors are less likely to stand out in sports such as cross-country or gymnastics where slim body types and restricted eating behaviors are common. Second, sport participation may trigger the onset of pre-existing, but latent causal factors thereby increasing the incidence of eating disorders. A third possibility is that sport restrictions such as "making weight" in wrestling – a goal that commonly involves intense, short-term weight losses -- might very well cause eating disorders in individuals normally not prone to disordered eating.

In virtually all intense sport programs, the personal characteristics necessary for competitive success are often very similar to those associated with psychological disorders. Perfectionism and obsessive-compulsiveness (albeit both often described in terms of dedication), high energy levels with little skill at prioritizing needs (the hard worker!), and intense concern about how you are perceived by others (often seen as over compliance to the coach's expectations) have all been found, when carried to extreme, to be at the root of many psychological disorders.[14] The excessive exercise used to control caloric expenditure by the eating disordered individual clearly fits the high achievement orientation profile of a dedicated athlete. Many of the traits coaches wish to see and promote in their athletes are similar to traits found in individuals with eating disorders.[15] Many individuals – and especially athletes – view their eating disorder symptoms as an achievement!

Therefore, the prudent coach will realize that the potential for extremism is always a part of sports programs, even at the youth level, when winning is highly valued and competition is extremely fierce. In sports where pressures exist to "make weight" and where losing weight can often enhance sport performance, athletes may be particularly vulnerable to factors promoting disordered eating. They may also have ample opportunity to learn such behaviors from other athletes, a phenomenon referred to as the Contagion Effect.

Due to the serious nature of eating disorders, coaches and parents should be especially vigilant for the early warning signs of anorexia and bulimia, realizing that these signs are sometimes difficult to identify because they are often confused with traits that are desirable for successful sports performance. Despite coaches' awareness of the serious nature of eating disorders, such syndromes may still be difficult to identify because of the athlete's lack of openness and reluctance to discuss such issues. Further, when athletes fit the sport body profile and have demonstrated successful sport performances, their traits are often interpreted by parents, coaches and athletes alike as positive rather than unhealthy.

Fear of weight gain is a common occurrence in sports such as wrestling with its weight classes or gymnastics where low body weight initially facilitates sport performance and often is reflected in judges' scores. Public weigh-ins or negative comments from coaches may also act as triggers for inappropriate and unhealthy eating behaviors. For example, one technically skilled but inexperienced coach used to say to his young gymnasts, "There are good gymnasts and there are fat gymnasts but there are no good, fat gymnasts!" As he became aware of the negative and potentially deadly impact of such "motivational" comments, he studiously avoided such judgmental remarks. Subtle approval from coaches and judges ("You made weight!" or "You look good!") following rapid weight loss may, despite their positive sounding messages, actually promote those behaviors which initiate eating disorders. Finally, at the highest levels of competitive sport, eating disorders may be fostered by a team culture that places successful sport performance before health. Such programs might very well educate athletes about the risks of eating disorders but place such a strong focus of winning that athletes adopt an attitude that winning is "worth the risk" or feel pressured to make weight in any way that they can rather than follow sound nutritional guidelines.

GENDER ISSUES[16]

While earlier research found the prevalence of eating disorders higher in girls than boys, those differences may have been overestimated because of how researchers looked at the problem. The stereotype of eating disorders as a female illness might result in young boys being reluctant to report that they are suffering from a "girl's disease." Physicians may not ask boys those necessary questions designed to detect disordered eating symptoms because they "know" that disordered eating is found only in girls. For example, the concept of a Female Athletic Triad has long been a well-accepted concept in the medical and coaching communities. The triad consists of osteoporosis (low bone mass; loss of bone mass); lack of or irregularities in menstruation (both in initial onset and irregularity), and energy deficiency (restricted eating). More recently, a Male Athletic Triad has been identified. It also involves osteoporosis and energy deficiencies but instead of a menstrual deficiency specific to females, it postulates reduced testosterone levels. Instead of a primary focus on weight loss, the male triad focuses on a preoccupation with lean muscularity. Such a preoccupation can lead to eating disorders and may be coupled with steroid use at older, more intense competitive levels.

Coaches involved with sports where weight control is crucial for success (e.g., gymnastics, dance, wrestling, skating) are coming to the realization that they must do more than simply counsel their athletes to control weight. A general admonition to avoid crash diets and to lose weight gradually is not sufficient. Not only must coaches give those athletes and their parents safe, nutritionally sound information on "how to" lose, gain or maintain weight, but also they must be reasonably sophisticated in recognizing predictable hazards involved in following such guidelines.

DIAGNOSING EATING DISORDERS: WHAT TO LOOK FOR

One very prominent characteristic of anorexics and bulimics is the hidden nature of their affliction. Most refuse to discuss it with others, often because of a mistaken belief that they are "all alone." With bulimics, the pattern of vomiting after gorging is thought to be so disgusting that bulimics frequently hide the affliction from even those closest to them. Since bulimics rarely experience the dramatic weight losses shown by the anorexics, their problem often goes undetected until the results of their behaviors disturb others around them: e.g., toilets clogged because of the continual vomiting of undigested food; thefts of food for the compulsive binges; or thefts of money to support their costly food bills.

Table 11.3 presents those symptoms most closely linked to serious eating disorders. Obviously, many of these symptoms result from the

TABLE 11.3 Generalized Signs and Symptoms of Eating Disorders[17]

1. Elaborate behavior patterns designed to hide the disordered eating behaviors from others
2. Persistent denial that a problem exists even when confronted with it
3. Withdrawal, isolation and a lack of closeness with others as the problem worsens and concealment becomes more difficult

Specific to Anorexia	Specific to Bulimia
a. Extremely restricted eating	a. Recurrent episodes of eating large amounts of food in short periods of time
b. Extreme thinness and loss of muscle tissue	b. Frequent weight fluctuations of 10 pounds or more due to alternating binges and fasts
c. Dry yellowish skin	
d. With females, an irregularity and ultimate loss of menstrual period	c. Swollen, painful, tender salivary glands
e. Loss of scalp hair	d. Chronic sore throat
f. Continual feelings of being cold	e. Compulsive stealing and hoarding of food and theft of money to obtain food
g. Development of fine, soft hair over the much of the body to help conserve body heat.	f. Sporadic menstrual cycle
h. Dry skin due to reduced fluid intake	g. Decayed, discolored teeth
i. Severe constipation	h. Swelling and puffiness often in the ankles and feet
j. Sodium and potassium deficiencies which cause muscle and heart spasms, cardiac arrest and kidney problems	i. Dry skin
k. Low blood pressure, slow breathing and slow pulse	

starvation and malnutrition caused by the drastically disturbed food intake. The specific cause or causes of eating disorders is not known. They tend to recur in families from one generation to the next, so a genetic predisposition has long been considered a distinct possibility. However, such behaviors can be taught or promoted by inappropriate coaching and parental behaviors. Cultural factors – both sport and non-sport – are almost certainly involved (for example, the belief that "thin" is attractive or necessary to compete well).

EARLY DETECTION AND TREATMENT[18]

Behavioral medicine requires active participation on the part of the patient/athlete. Since the athletes often do not believe they have a problem – a belief labelled denial – the question of active participation is often central to their recovery. Denial is not simply lying such as, "No, I don't have a problem!" It is often a combination of rationalization ("I must do this to be successful!"); justification ("I have to do this to keep up with the competition!") or minimization ("I only do this just before weigh ins!"). Often, overcoming denial is a crucial first step in recovery. Athletes may "role play" that they want to get better simply to minimize the pressure from coaches to change their eating behaviors; but when left on their own they return to the disordered eating in the belief that it is justified and that the problem lies with the unreasonable demands of the medical professionals and the well-meaning, but – in their minds – misguided coaches and parents who won't leave them alone. Effective therapy involves first convincing the athletes that there is a problem, not accusing them of a lack of will power or of making bad decisions.

Combatting the addictive, obsessive compulsive disordered eating behaviors is more than a presentation of a logical argument that disordered eating is unhealthy. Encouragement is often seen as coercion and results in even more resistance to treatment. Athletes should be provided with individualized emotional support such as, "You can do it; we can help!"

While selection of treatment is outside the youth sport coach's prerogative, both coaches and parents should be aware that early detection and referral for professional treatment is a strong predictor of recovery.

Regardless of the treatment chosen or the patient's personal characteristics, two factors are clear: The earlier the treatment begins and the younger the individual is, the better the prognosis is for recovery. Thus, early recognition is a crucial factor over which parents and coaches can have some influence. If they are familiar with the early behavioral signs for detection, they can often thwart what could become a life threatening disorder. Table 11.4 briefly summarizes those signs.

The parent or coach who suspects that their youngster may be exhibiting the early signs of an eating disorder might intervene by sitting down with that youngster and saying something similar to the following: "I know that you are trying to control your weight, but you don't seem to be much happier. Are you aware of the dangers of such behaviors and do you know that there are better ways to control your

TABLE 11.4 Early Detection Behavioral Symptoms of Eating Disorders

a. Eating alone or in secret; refusal to eat with the family

b. Consistently skips meals, often breakfast and lunch

c. Dieting is equated with total fasting

d. An abnormally intense pre-occupation with weight, evidenced by continually stepping on the scale or critically evaluating body proportions before a mirror

e. Substantial weight loss or weight fluctuations

f. Excessive exercising to lose weight above and beyond normal training exercises

g. Secretive or withdrawn behavior in combination with any or all of the above symptoms

weight and your sports performance?" From there, safe, sane weight control procedures can be suggested. For example, specific goals can be set for managing caloric intake based upon the athlete's height, weight, activity level, and percentage body fat. Such procedures allow a return to a normal pattern of eating. However, make no mistake – eating disorders, once developed, are no longer effectively treated with "common sense" cautions. They are a medical problem requiring professional assistance from professionals familiar with eating disorders! Listed below are sources which can assist you if you or a member of your family or team appears to be suffering from anorexia or bulimia.

National Association of Anorexia Nervosa and Associated Disorders
http://www.anad.org
HELPLINE: 630.577.1330
EMAIL: hello@anad.org
PHONE: 630.577.1333
220 N. Green St.
Chicago, IL 60607

National Eating Disorders Association
200 W 41st Street
Suite 1203
New York, NY 10036

HELPLINE: 1-800-931-2237
HELPLINE HOURS: 9:00 AM - 9:00 PM (ET) Mon-Thurs;
    and 9:00 AM to 5:00 PM (ET) Fri.
EMAIL: info@NationalEatingDisorders.org

Hazing and Bullying

Hazing and bullying are closely related issues since both involve the misuse of power to purposely harass, abuse or humiliate another person. A primary distinction that separates these two misuses of power is that with hazing, the victim is typically enduring such abusive action in order to gain access to a special group such as a sports team or, with college students, a fraternity or sorority. In bullying, the individual is often emotionally abused by being intentionally isolated and harassed. Because they both involve intentional abuse, they will be discussed together in the context of organized youth sports.

HAZING

While traditions and ritual initiations may have some benefits in terms of developing a team culture and a sense of unity among team members, sport-related hazing often involves dangerous activities and in many states is illegal whether it occurs within the team setting or outside at, say, a picnic or other informal team gathering. Hazing can be defined as "any activity expected of someone joining a group (or to maintain full status in a group) that humiliates, degrades or risks emotional and/ or physical harm regardless of the person's willingness to participate" (www.StopHazing.org, 2007). This definition points out three crucial dimensions of hazing that can negatively impact young athletes.[19] First, hazing can occur with existing team members as well as newcomers. Second, hazing includes emotional and psychological abuse, both of which can be more devastating and long lasting than physical abuse. Third, while hazing victims often consent to the hazing because of peer pressure, the victim's willingness to participate does not free the coach from the responsibility of adequately supervising the young athletes and preventing hazing from occurring. A coerced choice is no choice at all. While hazing tends to occur more in teams of older athletes (i.e., high school and older), it does occur with younger teams and is often difficult to distinguish from bullying – behaviors which are quite common among school aged children.

BULLYING

Bullying is more than simply being rude or mean. Rudeness might be hurtful but it rarely involves intentional meanness and is unlikely to be systematically inflicted on a single, targeted person. Mean behavior can be quite hurtful and quite intentional but lacks the targeted, systematic imbalance of power that favors the bully over the victim. Bullying involves three primary characteristics: It is systematicaly repeated; it is inflicted intentionally; and it involves aggressive behavior by an individual who is on the strong side of an imbalance of power.[20]

HAZING AND THE LAW[21]

Even recreation coaches have a legal, moral and ethical responsibility to protect their athletes from reasonably foreseeable acts of sport-related hazing. At present, more than 40 states have enacted anti-hazing legislation and, for the most part, treat hazing as a misdemeanor. Substantial differences in how these laws are written exist from state to state. For example, in some states failure to report incidents of hazing is a crime in and of itself. Coaches need to be aware of the laws applicable in their state. Civil liability laws also deal with hazing. The laws typically focus on hazing in public schools and colleges in both sport and fraternal organizations. Nonetheless, the implication for youth sports is clear: Hazing is not a legitimate "rite of passage" and is unacceptable both legally and morally. As a result, a youth sport coach or administrator who fails to provide adequate supervision to stop the occurrence of dangerous hazing activities could be judged as negligent.

Hazing differs from bullying because it is often accepted by the victims as a "necessary evil," i.e., an abuse to be endured in order to be accepted by the group. Hazing involves the power that older members of a group have over younger or aspiring members of the group. This power of seniority can quickly escalate from harmless rituals (i.e., singing a class song) to dangerous activities such as paddling or sexual abuse that can lead to serious injury (both physical and psychological) and even death.[22] For more information on preventing bullying behavior: www. StopHazing.org.

GUIDELINES TO REDUCE OR ELIMINATE HAZING[23]

1. Establish a clear pro-active anti-hazing policy and make certain all members of your team (coaches, assistants, players and parents)

are aware of that policy. If your league or organization does not have such a written policy, strongly encourage the administrators of your organization to develop and publicize that policy.

2. If you believe that "rites of passage" serve a useful purpose of enhancing team cohesion and commitment to the group, develop alternative team building exercises that are safe and distinct from hazing behaviors.

3. If hazing has been ongoing within your team or organization, address the prior incidents directly with your team members stressing emphatically that such behavior is no longer acceptable and encourage your athletes to report incidents of hazing by providing a mechanism for anonymous reporting and by stressing to all concerned that retaliation against the hazing victims will not be tolerated.

4. Involve the parents and other members of the community to develop and implement anti-hazing policies.

5. Develop a culture of respect for others within your team and program by modeling such respectful behavior to your young athletes, fellow coaches, parents, opponents and youth sport administrators.

6. Encourage older and more experienced athletes to mentor younger players to develop positive relationships that can preempt dominating and humiliating based upon power and status within your team.

7. Keep thorough records documenting all reported incidents of hazing.

Bullying by Coaches

Bullying occurs when a more powerful individual abuses that power by systematically intimidating others who are weaker or have less power. Bullying is not just limited to athletes bullying athletes. Coaches can be the bullies under the guise of disciplining or motivating their athletes. When athletes – either individually or as a team – are subjected to demeaning, name-calling and insults, the behavior is unacceptable whether it is athlete-to-athlete or coach-to-athlete where the power imbalance is inherent to the coach-athlete relationship.

Four techniques have been identified by which coaches tend to justify such unjustifiable behavior.[24]

Moral justification is where the bullying is depicted as normal social behavior, i.e., part of the culture in sport. It is the way that sport teaches kids "to be tough."

Backhanded apologies minimize and shift the blame for the reprehensible behavior. "Sorry, I just got a little carried away trying to get the kids to focus and pay attention." The language "a little carried away" minimizes the transgression and the reference to the kids' failure to "pay attention" implies that they are responsible for the bullying behavior.

Advantageous comparisons involve comparing the bullying behavior to something that is worse and never happened. "I never once laid a finger on them!" The physical abuse never occurred but was not the issue in the first place. Verbal intimidation was the concern.

Escalating the consequences is an extension of the bullying behavior. The bullying behavior itself is not what is escalated but rather the consequences for resisting the bullying behavior. When the athlete fights back or identifies the bullying behavior, the coach responds with, "If you don't like it or can't handle it, you can always quit or go to another team."

Ask yourself if you have ever been guilty of such behaviors and/or justifications. A single incident is merely a mistake. A systematic use of such techniques is bullying in every sense of the word and has no place in the world of organized youth sports.

CHAPTER REFERENCES

1. The Federal Child Abuse Prevention and Treatment Act (CAPTA), (42 U.S.C.A.#5106g), as amended and reauthorized by the CAPTA Reauthorization Act of 2010.

2. Child Welfare Information Gateway, www.childwelfare.gov/pubs/factsheets/whatiscan.cfm.

3. Tenbergen, G., Wittfoth, M., Frieling, H., et al. (2015). The neurobiology and psychology of pedophilia: Recent advances and challenges. *Frontiers in Human Neuroscience, 9, 344-376,* doi: 10.3389/fnhum.2015.00344.

4. Hingson, R. W., Heeren, T., & Winter, M. R. (2006). Age of drinking onset and alcohol dependence: Age of onset, duration and severity. Archives of Pediatric and Adolescent Medicine, 160(7), 739-746. doi: 101001/archpedi.160.7.739.

5. 11 facts about teens and alcohol, https://www.dosomething.org/facts/11-facts-about-teens-and-alcohol.

6. Partner Attitude Tracking Study, Teens, 2007, http://Timetotalk.org

7. Buckman, J. (2018). Center of Alcohol Studies, Rutgers University, New Brunswick, NJ (Personal Communication).

8. Grant, B. F., Chou, S. P., Saha, T. D., et al. (2017). Prevalence of 12-Month Alcohol Use, High-Risk Drinking, and DSM-IV Alcohol Use Disorder in the United States, 2001-2002 to 2012-2013. Results From the National Epidemiologic Survey on Alcohol and Related Conditions. JAMA Psychiatry, 74(9), 911-923. Doi:10.1001/jamapsychiatry.2017.2161

9. Bulik, C. (2014). Eating disorders essentials: Replacing myths with realities," NIMH Alliance for Research Progress Winter Meeting, February 7, 2014, Rockville, MD. https://www.nimh.nih.gov/news/science-news/2014/9-eating-disorders-myths-busted.shtml

10. Surgenor, L. J., & Maguire, S. (2013). Assessment of anorexia nervosa: an overview of universal issues and contextual challenges. Journal of Eating Disorders, 1 (29). doi: 10.1186/2050-2974-1-29

11. American Psychiatric Association. (2013). Diagnostic and statistical manual of mental disorders: DSM-V (5th ed.). Washington, DC: American Psychiatric Association.

12. Cogan, K. D. (2004). Eating disorders: When rations become irrational. In: S. Murphy (Ed.), The sport psychology handbook (pp. 237-253). Champaign, IL: Human Kinetics.

13. Sungot-Borgen & Torstveit (2004). Prevalence of eating disorders in elite athletes is higher than in the general population. Clinical Journal of Sports Medicine, 14, 25-32.

14. Feigley, D. A. (1984). Psychological Burnout in High Level Athletes, The Physician and Sportsmedicine, 12, 108 119.

15. Thompson, R. A., & Sherman, R. (1999). "Good Athlete" Traits and Characteristics of Anorexia Nervosa: Are They Similar? Eating Disorders: The Journal of Treatment & Prevention, 7 (3), doi: 10.1080/10640269908249284

16. Thompson, R. A., & Sherman, R. (2014). Reflections on athletes and eating disorders. Psychology of Sport and Exercise, 15, 729-734

17. https://www.nimh.nih.gov/health/topics/eating-disorders

18. Bratland-Sanda, S., & Sudgot-Borgen, J. (2012). Eating disorders in athletes: Overview of prevalence, risk factors and recommendations for prevention and treatment. *European Journal of Sport Science, 13,* 1-10. doi: 10.1080/17461391.2012.740504

19. Carroll, M. S., Cunnaughton, D. P. (2007). Managing risk associated with sport-related hazing. *Safety and Risk Management Council's SAFETY Notebook.* Reston, VA: American Association for Physical Education and Recreation.

20. Whitson, S. (2014). *8 keys to end bullying.* Norton: New York.

21. Staurowsky, E.J. (2017). Hazing. In Cotten, D. J. & Wolohan, J. T. (Eds.), *Law for recreation and sport managers (7th ed.).* (pp. 282-294). Dubuque, Iowa: Kendall/Hunt.

22. Burnett, S. (2012) Hazing At Fraternity: 22 Pi Kappa Alpha Members Charged After Student Dies. Associated Press

23. Sharp, L. A., Moorman, A. M. & Claussen, C. L. (2007). *Sport law: A managerial approach.* Holcomb, Scottsdale AZ: Hathaway Publishers, Inc., (p. 576).

24. Swigonski, N. L., Ennerking, B. A., & Hendrix, K. S. (2014). Bullying behavior by athletic coaches. *Pediatrics,* 133(2), e273-e275; DOI: 10.1542/peds.2013-3146

Training and Conditioning of Youth Athletes

CHAPTER OUTLINE

- Benefits of an Effective Conditioning Program
- Myths About Strength and Conditioning For Children
- General Principles for Effective Conditioning Programs
- The Basics of Strength Training
- Plyometrics for Children and Adolescents
- The Basics of Cardiovascular Conditioning
- The Basics of Flexibility Training
- Use of Professional Trainers

In this chapter, three major topics will be discussed:

- Misconceptions about youth strength training and conditioning
- Basic principles of strength training, cardiovascular conditioning and flexibility in young athletes
- Safety considerations necessary for young athletes

The major focus of this chapter is how to develop and implement a strength and conditioning program for adolescent and pre-adolescent athletes. Proper conditioning and good health are vital to prevent athletic injuries and to enhance sport performance. Moreover, strength and conditioning programs should be concerned about healthy growth and development. As a youth sport coach, you should encourage such programs.

The conditioning drills and activities you use should be consistent with the requirements of your sport and the developmental stages of your athletes. There are three essential components of training and conditioning which are appropriate for young athletes and which can be improved by proper coaching. They are: strength training (strength, power, muscular endurance); cardiovascular conditioning (aerobic, anaerobic); and flexibility (range of motion, ability of muscle to move freely about joints).

Benefits of an Effective Conditioning Program[*]

When you develop a basic, but effective, training and conditioning program for your athletes, you provide them with the following benefits:

- Increased muscular strength and endurance
- Increased cardiovascular fitness
- Decreased risk of injury
- Improved athletic performance
- Ability to compete at higher levels of play and intensity

In addition to these short range benefits, a youth sports fitness and conditioning program can enhance both the knowledge of and the valuing of physical conditioning that can have benefits far beyond the improved fitness during the sports season. Since fitness deteriorates markedly following prolonged periods of inactivity, the adoption of a lifestyle

---

[*]Much of the material and organization of the first portion of this chapter was initially prepared for the Rutgers Youth Sports Research Council by Robb S. Rehberg, Ph.D., William Paterson University.

that includes regular physical activity can actually prolong both life and the quality of that life. Involvement with sports as a youngster does not, by itself predict a longer, higher quality life. However, if young athletes value physical activity and adopt a lifestyle that increases their physical activity to the tune of 2000 Kilocalories per week,* they will live on average two full years longer than their inactive counterparts.[1]

Myths About Strength and Conditioning for Children

There are a number of common misconceptions or myths that you should be aware of as you develop a training and conditioning program for your young athletes:

Misconception #1: Strength training is ineffective in prepubescent children since they lack the testosterone hormone required for strength gain.

> **FACT:** If that were true, women with lower testosterone levels could not experience significant strength gain. Yet, they do. Further, strength gain can develop from a variety of factors. Strength training promotes muscle growth but it also teaches the brain to recruit more neurons to fire simultaneously resulting in more muscle fibers working together at the same time. "Strength gains" also result from athletes learning more biomechanically effective body positions for exerting strength. (Figure 12.1)

FIGURE 12.1 Strength training for prepubescent children involves learning biomechanical effective body positions in addition to recruiting more efficient firing of muscle fibers.

---

*While caloric expenditure is affected by the athlete's weight, fitness level and running speed, 2000 Kilocalories is the equivalent a 135 lb. individual of running about 5 miles 4 times per week or about 3.5 hours of running per week.

Misconception #2: Strength training is unsafe for young athletes.

FACT: When properly performed, strength training is not only safe, but it can aid in decreasing injuries as well. Furthermore, there is no evidence to support the common fear that strength training damages growth plates. With proper instruction and proper supervision, strength training is quite safe, and even recommended, for children and adolescents. Often enhanced strength is necessary for safely performing essential sport skills. A properly supervised strength program using correct strength training techniques does not lead to growth plate injuries.

Misconception #3: Strength training can stunt a child's growth.

FACT: A properly designed and supervised strength training program will not stunt a child's growth; rather, it can help strengthen bones and increase the growth hormone response which helps with physical development.

Misconception #4: Children who lift weights will become muscle-bound and will lose flexibility.

FACT: A properly designed weight training program along with regular stretching exercises will allow children to become stronger without "bulking up" while at the same time maintaining and often even improving flexibility.

General Principles for Effective Conditioning Programs[2]

The following principles are appropriate regardless of whether the primary purpose of your conditioning program focuses on strength, cardiovascular conditioning or flexibility.

WARM-UP/COOL-DOWN BASICS

Warm-ups raise the body temperature by increasing blood flow, while cool-down permits a gradual recovery to pre-exercise heart rate and blood pressure levels. Both minimize muscle soreness following exercise.

Warm-up Length

While conditioning professionals often recommend 15 to 30 minutes of warm-up, such a time period is often seen by youth sport coaches as too

FIGURE 12.2
Transitioning into low intensity sports skills after a short, formal warm up is a partial solution to including an effective warm up of sufficient duration into a typical youth sport training session.

long to comfortably fit into a 1- to 2-hour practice session typically when training young, beginning athletes. A partial solution is to hold a formal warm-up of 5 to 10 minutes followed by a transition into sports skills of low intensity immediately following the warm-up before engaging in more vigorous activities so that the low intensity skills, in fact, become part of the physical warm-up. (Figure 12.2) The short, formal warm-up signals the beginning of the training session, develops the habit of engaging in an initial warm-up before hard training, and becomes part of the "sharp starts" for effective organization of practice sessions. (See Chapter 2, pages 43-45 for organizing effective practices.)

BENEFITS OF A COOL DOWN PERIOD

Cool down consists of engaging in low intensity physical activities following high intensity activities. For example, static stretching at the end of a workout can be used for the dual purpose of cooling down and improving flexibility. The more intense the workout, the more important a formal cool down period becomes. Cooling down reduces the lactate content in fatigued muscles resulting in:

a. reduced fatigue

b. less stiffness

c. faster recovery

SPECIFICITY

You get what you train. Conditioning programs improve specifically what they are designed to improve. If you lift weights quickly, you will improve at lifting weight quickly. If you lift slowly, over a limited range of movement, you will improve at lifting slowly over a limited range.

OVERLOAD

To increase strength, conditioning or flexibility, the training must increase the training load over and above that load the athlete was previously capable of handling. Overload can be accomplished by increasing the weight, the number of repetitions in a set of exercises, the number of sets of the same exercise or by decreasing the rest intervals between sets.

PROGRESSION

Establish a baseline; i.e. Suzy can do 8 sit-ups in 30 seconds. Then gradually and systematically increase the intensity, frequency, and difficulty of the exercises.

VARIATION

The exercise used and the training variables selected should systematically be varied to sustain interest and avoid overuse injuries resulting from repetition.

The Basics of Strength Training

As a volunteer coach, you can help your young athletes develop a safe and effective strength development program by a) setting developmentally appropriate goals, b) designing a program for strength improvement that is consistent with healthy growth and development and c) ensuring that appropriate safety precautions are in place. The American College of sports Medicine (ACSM) asserts that properly designed **and** supervised strength programs are safe and effective for school age children.[3]

SETTING REALISTIC, CHALLENGING GOALS*

Set both performance and process goals related to strength. For example, a **performance goal** would be, "improving my lift strength by 10% within two weeks." This would be a moderately challenging goal for a beginner who lacked much strength to begin with while it might be a quite challenging goal for an athlete who already had developed substantial strength. An example of a **process goal** would be to "train consistently for an hour, three times per week." Goals should be specific and measurable and capable of being realistically accomplished in a reasonable period of time.

PROGRAM DESIGN

Age-Related Factors

The strength training program must be designed for different levels of physical and mental maturity. These levels parallel, but are not completely linked, to age. However, as a general guideline, your strength program should match the following age levels.[4]

a. under 7 years – Use no external weights. Use muscular endurance exercises almost exclusively. Proper weight lifting techniques can be taught without weights on the bar.

b. 8-10 years – Introduce progressive resistance training for those children who are mature enough to regularly accept and follow directions.

c. 11-13 years – Introduce more advanced exercises with the primary emphasis on proper execution rather than the amount of weight lifted.

d. 14-15 years – Begin advanced programs which progressively increase the amount of weight lifted.

e. 16 years and older – Begin entry level adult programs.

*See Chapter 5 for a more in-depth discussion of goal setting.

Brief, focused workouts will be more motivating to young athletes than long, drawn out strength training sessions. Effective work out sessions can be as brief as 20 minutes and should rarely, if ever, exceed 60 minutes with youth athletes. Encourage your athletes to do more sit-ups in 30 seconds rather than simply more sit-ups, but never sacrifice form using this approach. If they break form, stop. Increasing the repetitions within a fixed time interval improves power and muscular endurance without punishing athletes for improving their fitness!

Maximal Lifts and Repetitions

Children under the age of 14 years should not perform maximal lifts (1 RM).* When designing a youth strength training program, use a 10 RM instead of instead of 1 RM. Further, consider the maximum to have occurred when the young athlete loses form during the lift (i.e., the technique becomes sloppy due to fatigue) rather than using complete failure to lift as the definition of "maximum." Try to stop just before the athlete experiences a breakdown in form. At no time should a weight be used that allows less than eight repetitions. While such a design focuses more on muscular endurance training rather than power training, power does develop and damage to growth plates is avoided. Low to moderate intensity plyometrics** can often be used to improve power and are typically incorporated into conditioning drills normally done in practice.

Progressive Resistance Exercise

As strength increases, gradually increase the resistance (i.e., the amount of weight) by the smallest amount of weights possible. These gradual increments should be no more than one to three pounds compared to ten pound increments typical of adult programs. The American College of Sports Medicine guidelines for children recommends an initial weight load that they can lift in one to three sets of 8 to 15 times per set with good form. A set of 8 to 15 reps should stop about one to two reps short of failure. This judgement is typically made based upon evidence that the young athletes are starting to struggle and look as if they are about to break from proper form.

---

*A maximal lift is the maximum amount of weight that can be lifted successfully once. Second attempts at that weight typically fail. 1RM = maximum lift with only 1 repetition. 10 RM = maximum weight that can lifted 10 consecutive times before failure.
**Plyometrics, also known as "jump training," are explosive exercises using jumping, hopping and rebounding where the muscles exert maximum force in short bursts of time to increase power (moving weight rapidly).

FIGURE 12.3
Relying on body weight for resistance training is quite appropriate for youth athletes, especially the very young.

Body Weight vs. External Weights

Relying primarily on body weight for resistance training is an excellent alternative to the use of weights or weight machines, especially with very young children. (Figure 12.3) Not only does it use safe amounts of weight (except possibly with very obese athletes), but also it is typically less expensive and more convenient. Such exercises can be done in the playing area and do not required a specialized weight room or an investment in weight lifting equipment. Table 12.1 lists commonly used strength exercises that rely exclusively on body weight. Even with these basic exercises, make sure proper form is emphasized.

TABLE 12.1 Body Weight Exercise

Pull-ups	Toe Raises
Dips	Crunches (Mini-Sit Ups)
Push-ups	Wall Squats
Lunges	Body Weight Squats

FIGURE 12.4
The three keys to
safe conditioning
programs with
children and youth
are supervision,
supervision,
supervision.

Technique and Safety

Proper lifting technique should always be the primary focus, not the amount of weight to be lifted. When working with young athletes the three most important components of safety are 1) supervision, 2) supervision, and 3) supervision! (Figure 12.4) Always use a spotter when lifting free weights and even with many machines. Caution young athletes not to hold their breath or lock joints when lifting. Use proper warm-up sets and use approximately one to two sets with 50-75% of your normal working weight as their warm up. Wear proper clothing and footwear.

Never allow flip-flops or sandals. Avoid extremely loose fitting clothing which could become entangled in the weights; use non-slippery footwear.

Allow proper rest between sets – for example, 30 to 60 seconds when using light weights for muscular endurance training. With heavier weights use 1 ½ to 2 minutes. Allow proper rest – one day off between sessions (i.e., at least 48 hours) – to avoid overtraining and/or injury. Remember, strength gains result from the rest and recovery period that occur **after** the stress of a resistance training session – ideally 48 hours. In effective strength training programs, young athletes typically train with weights every other day.

Muscular Balance Between Opposing Muscle Groups

Injuries such as pulled muscles and hamstring pulls are more likely when one side of opposing muscle groups becomes stronger and imbalanced than the other side. For example, when the quadriceps muscles that open the knee joint become significantly stronger than the hamstring muscle that closes that same joint, a pulled hamstring is a common injury. Therefore, strengthen hamstring muscles to offset strength gains in quadriceps muscles. Design your program to maintain the normal strength balance and relative strength ratios between opposing muscle groups at all major joints. For example, balance triceps exercises with biceps exercises. Strengthen lower back muscles to balance the strength gains in abdominal muscles.

Plyometrics for Children and Adolescents

According to the American College of Sports Medicine (ASCM), "plyometric training can be a safe, effective and fun activity for children and adolescents provided that the program is properly designed, sensibly progressed and supervised by qualified professionals."[5] It should be part of an overall conditioning program, not a stand alone conditioning element.

WHAT IS PLYOMETRIC TRAINING?

Plyometric exercises exaggerate the muscle's normal cycle of lengthening and shortening in order to increase muscular power. Plyometric exercises are performed quickly and explosively to develop both strength and power. Power is essentially strength executed quickly. It is essential in many sports which rely on explosive muscular contractions. Drills such as hops, jumps and rebounding movements elicit a stretch reflex by stretching the muscle just before it contracts for the jump or hop. The result is the development of greater contracting force. Common plyometric drills include jumping from an elevated surface and rebounding off the floor to another slightly higher surface. Multiple repetitions of such a drill builds power. Jumping rope and hopscotch are essentially plyometric because every time the athletes' rebound from the ground they are performing a plyometric exercise.

Although plyometrics were originally thought to be safe only with fully conditioned adults, the ACSM has judged plyometrics not only as

FIGURE 12.5
Skipping rope is an excellent, safe way to initiate plyometrics with children and adolescents.

safe and appropriate, but when used within a well-designed comprehensive youth conditioning program, plyometrics have proved capable of increasing speed of movement, improving power, strengthening bones, facilitating weight control and reducing the risk of sport-related injuries with children. The program should start with low intensity drills, such as hopping or skipping on a level surface followed by bounding over low objects such as foam blocks before gradually progressing to higher intensity drills such as jumping down from a low, but elevated, surface and then rebounding to a surface of similar height. Once a reasonable level of conditioning has been achieved, the athletes can perform the drills by rebounding to a surface which is even higher than the surface from which they initially jumped. Well-conditioned athletes will benefit from plyometric drills from heights of 6" to 18". However, even highly conditioned athletes typically use heights of no more than 24". When in doubt, lower is better than higher, particularly when initially exposing young athletes to plyometrics. (Figure 12.5)

While plyometric training has typically focused on developing leg strength, certain sports such as gymnastics and wrestling can benefit from upper body plyometric drills such as rebounding from a handstand or from a push-up position. Such drills should only be used after basic handstand skills have been fully mastered and the athletes can maintain a straight spine position and support their body weight on their arms throughout the rebounding handstand drill.

SAFETY GUIDELINES FOR PLYOMETRICS TRAINING WITH YOUNG ATHLETES

a. Plyometrics should begin only after basic conditioning has been achieved and sufficient leg strength has been developed.

b. Warm up thoroughly before initiating plyometrics exercises.

c. Start with low jumps and gradually build to higher jumps.

d. Land on the balls of your feet, not flat footed.

e. Provide substantial rest periods between exercise bouts.

f. Stop, if sharp pains are felt in the joints of the hips, knees and ankles.

g. Athletes should use supportive footwear.

h. While firm landing surfaces such as grass or floating gymnasium floors are necessary to benefit from plyometric drills, avoid landing on rigid surfaces such as concrete or asphalt.

i. Avoid soft surfaces such as spongy mats which negate the positive impact of the plyometric drill.

j. Jump straight to avoid landing with a twisting or sideward motion.

The Basics of Cardiovascular Conditioning

TYPES OF CONDITIONING

There are two basic types of conditioning: Conditioning for activities which actively use oxygen (**aerobic**) and conditioning for activities that because of their intense nature do not actively use oxygen (**anaerobic**). Aerobic exercises would include activities such as jogging and running, bike riding, swimming and other exercises that use sustained, repetitive large muscle movements. Anaerobic exercises would include activities requiring short bursts of energy such as lifting a weight, and brief, intense sprints such as a 40 or 100 yard dash.

PROGRAM DESIGN

For optimal conditioning for young athletes, conditioning sessions should occur three times per week for approximately 30 minutes. Keep the sessions short and focused while improving conditioning as a result of increasing the intensity of the workout session rather than permitting the workouts to become longer and longer. While moderate increases in duration may be necessary for effective training, long, drawn out conditioning sessions tend to undermine the motivation of young athletes.

Use heart rate to determine if intensity level is adequate for improving fitness level. For maximal effect, a heart rate of at least 160 beats per minute for at least 30 minutes should be maintained in children. Teach young athletes to take their pulse by placing their two forefingers on their wrist and, after they successfully find their pulse (over the radial artery), have them count how many beats occur in 10 seconds and multiply by 6. Young children may have difficulty counting fast enough when their pulse is elevated and also with the multiplication but they can achieve reasonable accuracy with practice.

Circuit Training

Circuit training is a popular and effective means of combining strength training and cardiovascular endurance training in a fixed time period. The circuit consists of multiple training stations with a specific exercise set up at each station. Athletes exercise vigorously for a specified time at each station, then rest on a work/rest ratio of approximately 1:1 for aerobic activity (e.g., 2 minutes work; 2 minutes rest) and 1:2 or 3 for anaerobic activity (i.e., 2 minutes work; 4 to 6 minutes rest). Table 12.2 illustrates a nine-station circuit with exercises.

TABLE 12.2 Circuit Training

1. Squats	2. Push-ups	3. Jump Rope
4. Pull-ups	5. Sprints	6. Dips
7. Lunges	8. Crunches	
(the order alternates between upper and lower body drills)		

SAFETY ISSUES

Regardless of the specific cardiovascular drills that you ask your athletes to complete, there are three safety factors which should be considered.

Allow for Adequate Rest Periods

Avoid overtraining by allowing proper rest between conditioning periods. Keep them walking around rather than being completely immobile during the rest periods to help recovery. When having your athletes do conditioning exercises such as sprints, allow approximately two to three times as much rest as the duration of the sprint. For example, if they sprint for 15 seconds, rest for 30 to 45 seconds before repeating the sprint. When training for endurance, your work-to-rest intervals are different than what was just described. If your athletes condition for 3 to 4 minutes, the rest intervals should also be about 3 to 4 minutes.

Heat Illness

Be aware of the temperature, the humidity and the heat index, the latter of which is the combination of heat and humidity. As humidity rises, even moderate temperatures can create dangerous situations. (Figure 12.6) Figure 14.1 in Chapter 14 illustrates the danger zones for various combinations of heat and humidity. See Chapter 14 for more information in avoiding heat illnesses while working out.

FIGURE 12.6
As humidity rises, even moderate temperatures can create dangerous situations.

Running Environment

Since running is perhaps the most common cardiovascular training available, plan your athletes' running carefully. On hot, humid days, run in the early morning or early evening before dark to minimize the effects of heat. Avoid running on roads and/or rough terrain to minimize the likelihood of injury. Running tracks or grass fields are examples of safer, less stressful surfaces.

The Basics of Flexibility Training

Three types of stretching techniques have been studied.[6] The first is called **static stretching** and has been the most traditional technique. It involves holding a stretch position either passively with a partner or actively by one's self for approximately 30 seconds. Static stretching has been found to be less effective at increasing range of motion than the other two commonly used techniques. **Dynamic stretching** involves actively moving the limb through a full range of motion from one end to the other in repetitive movements. It appears to be more effective at increasing range of motion with one very important restriction. If the athlete "bounces" at the end of the full range, the muscle may actually experience a loss of flexibility and be subject to a higher risk of injury. As a result, the bouncing form of dynamic stretching is not recommended. The third form of stretching is **proprioceptive neuromuscular facilitation (PNF)**, sometimes referred to as pre-contraction stretching. It is sometimes called push-pull stretching because it involves pushing by contracting the muscle for 6 to 10 seconds followed by stretching that same muscle for 6 to 10 seconds.

EVALUATE INITIAL FLEXIBILITY

There are two popular methods requiring minimal equipment. A simple sit-and-reach box can be built. The athlete sits with legs straight and the soles of the feet touching the side of the box. The athlete reaches forward with both hand as far as possible. Typically, "zero" is the point at which the athlete's finger would touch his/her toes. Going beyond the toes yield positive scores in inches or centimeters. A reach short of the toes yields negative scores. Alternatively, without a sit-and-reach box, the athletes sit with their legs straddled (like a "V" on the floor) and reach forward with both hands. The maximal reach is measured. The flexibility range should be determined for each individual since the range of motion is jointly determined by hamstring flexibility, lower back flexibility and arm length.

STRETCHING PROGRAMS

Proper stretching should be taught and supervised carefully. Do not assume that young athletes already know proper stretching technique. Despite the conventional practice of stretching before a workout, it is more effective to stretch at the end of the workout. Stretching at the end of the workout avoids a loss of power during the training session and maximizes the improvement in flexibility. Stretching is not warmup.

When using static stretching, hold each stretch steadily for 20 to 30 seconds. Dynamic stretching involves moving the joint through the complete range of motion. Avoid bouncing (ballistic stretching). Bouncing may cause injury and actually reduces flexibility.

SAFETY ISSUES

a. The athlete should feel a tingling sensation or slight discomfort (no pain) in order for the stretch to ultimately lead to improved flexibility; however, sharp pains or the feeling of "needles pricking" should be avoided to prevent a muscle pull.

b. At the very least, never stretch a cold muscle. **Stretching should occur after warm-ups.** Stretching and warm-up are two different components of the training session. (Figure 12.7)

c. Partner stretches can be quite effective but also can be dangerous if done improperly or when one partner is too immature to perform the task properly and fails to be sensitive to the needs of the other partner.

d. Be careful when stretching previously injured muscles. When stretching a muscle that is recovering from injury, follow the guidance of a qualified medical professional such as a physical therapist or an athletic trainer.

FIGURE 12.7
Stretching should occur after warming up. Flexibility training and warming up are not the same.

FIGURE 12.8
PNF Stretching is typically less painful and results in noticeable increments in the range of motion after each cycle of stretching and resistance. However, the stretching partner must be aware that over stretching (the hamstring in this example) can injure the partner being stretched.

PNF STRETCHING

A particularly effective stretching technique involving partners is called *proprioceptive neuromuscular facilitation* stretching or PNF for short. (Figure 12.8) The most common form of PNF stretching alternates between a passive stretch – usually with a partner physically stretching a specific muscle or tendon – and an active muscle contraction by the athlete being stretched. Each phase lasts approximately six to ten seconds. For example, to stretch the hamstring, the athlete lies on his back with one leg extended straight and the other leg lying flat on the floor so that the legs are at right angles to one another. The 'teaching" partner pushes the extended leg into a further split until mild discomfort (a tingling sensation) is felt. The split is held for six to ten seconds. The athlete being stretched then isometrically contracts the hamstring attempting to close the split (i.e., to move the extended leg back down to the floor. The "teaching" partner, however, exerts sufficient resistive force to hold the extended leg in the extended position for, again, approximately six to ten seconds. The stretching athlete is then told to "relax" for a similar period of time; and the "teaching' partner again pushes the extended leg into the maximum range of motion that can be endured with mild discomfort. The stretching athlete will typically experience a noticeable additional range of motion, typically with less pain and discomfort than normally experienced with a passive stretch only. This alternating passive stretch followed by the isometric contraction is typically repeated two to three times on each specific muscle group being stretched.

This type of stretching works more effectively than mere passive stretching because the isometric contraction activates reflexive relaxation which, in turn, protects the muscle from being torn as it is purposely stretched beyond its normal range to increase flexibility.

PNF stretching has two distinct advantages over traditional stretching techniques. First, traditional stretching to improve range of motion occurs relatively slowly. It has been described as "Watching the grass grow." PNF stretching typically results in noticeable improvement in the range of motion following each isometric contraction, sometimes by as much as 10% improvement in the range of motion, especially when the athlete *being stretched* is very strong. Second, the pain is reduced noticeably after each isometric contraction relative to traditional stretching. The major limitations are that 1) the partner must be strong enough to apply sufficient force to prevent the extended joint from closing during the isometric contraction; and 2) the partner must have sufficient maturity to be aware of the athlete being stretched that the extended leg is not over extended during the reflexive relaxation phase. Coaches should emphasize that constant communication is required between partners to ensure effective, but safe pressure by one partner to the other on the muscle groups being stretched. An alternative to partner stretches is to use inexpensive elastic stretch bands as resistance instead of a partner when performing the PNF stretches.

Use of Professional Trainers

In recent years, there has been a dramatic increase in the number of commercial fitness centers offering conditioning programs for young athletes. Parents and coaches who choose to use such services should select individuals who have been certified by reputable national organizations such as the National Strength and Conditioning Association (NSCA), the American College of Sport Medicine, the Society of Health and Physical Educators and/or have a professional background in exercise physiology or kinesiology.

CHAPTER REFERENCES

1. Paffenbarger, Jr., R. S., Hyde, R. T., Wing, A. L., Hsieh, C. (1986). Physical activity, all-cause mortality, and longevity of college alumni. *New England Journal of Medicine. 314*, 605-613.

2. Foundations of Fitness Programming, National Strength and Conditioning Association (2015). DEVELOPMENT TASK FORCE MEMBERS: Clayton, N., Drake, J., Larkin, S, Linkul, R., Martino, M., Nutting, M., & Tumminello, N.

3. Faigenbaum, A., & Micheli, L. J. (2017). Youth strength training. American College of Sports Medicine, Indianapolis, IN.

4. Kraemer, W.J. & Fleck, S.J. (2004). *Strength Training for Young Athletes, (2ⁿᵈ ed.).* Champaign, IL: Human Kinetics Publishers.

5. Faigenbaum, A., & Chu, D. (2017). Plyometric training for children and adolescents. American College of Sport Medicine, Indianapolis, IN (p. 1).

6. Page, P. (2012). Current concepts in muscle stretching for exercise and rehabilitation. *International Journal of Physical Therapy, 7 (1),* 109-119.

13

Care and Management of Sports Injuries

CHAPTER OUTLINE

You've volunteered to coach your son or daughter's team. It's the third day of practice before the first game. Two players running for the ball at full speed collide. One is rolling in the grass crying and clearly in pain. The other lies quietly and motionless on the field. What do you do?

Regardless of how safely a sports program is designed and run, injuries will occur. Chapter 14 (Risk Management) outlines what steps can reasonably be taken to minimize the occurrence of injuries; however, once injuries occur -- and they will -- coaches must be able to recognize the nature of those injuries and be prepared to provide basic first aid and treatment. This chapter provides specific information concerning the care of injuries common in youth sports. That sport injuries will occur is predictable. On the other hand, knowing when, how, to whom and to what extent an injury will happen is usually unpredictable. Nonetheless, injuries, some minor and some major, will occur in virtually all sports programs.

The purpose of this chapter is NOT to serve as a First Aid/CPR Manual, NOR is it meant to be a comprehensive sports medicine text. It will examine representative, concrete examples of possible emergencies involving sports injuries. It is designed to provide volunteers with the knowledge and understanding of their coaching responsibilities. Basic first aid techniques require hands on training by qualified first aid instructors or trained medical personnel such as athletic trainers, EMT staff or doctors. As the coach, you will typically be first on the scene when an athlete is injured. You must have the skills to recognize common sports injuries, assess their severity, provide basic first aid and have pre-planned procedures for obtaining qualified medical aid in the case of serious injury.

The Volunteer Coach's Role in Sport Medicine

As a volunteer, you can have a significant impact on the health and safety of your athletes by knowing and implementing accident and injury prevention policies. Thus, prevention will be emphasized throughout chapters 13 and 14. Nonetheless, in the course of an entire season with multiple athletes involved in vigorous physical activities, accidents and injuries are virtually certain to occur.* Therefore, at least one coach on

---

*Many thanks to Gloria Bachmann, MD, for her thoughtful critique and contributions to this chapter. Dr. Bachmann is Associate Dean of Woman's Health and Director, Women's Health Institute of Rutgers Robert Wood Johnson Medical School and a member of the Rutgers Youth Sport Council's Advisory Board.

site should have the skills taught in a basic First Aid/CPR course. You are strongly encouraged to take such a course including the coverage of the use of Automated External Defibrillators (*AEDs*) and keep your certifications current every season that you coach. As coach, you are responsible for obtaining and maintaining a first aid kit with access to a defibrillator, knowing the contents of such a first aid kit and how to use all its contents as well as the defibrillator. You should have a preplanned Emergency Action Plan (EAP) and have rehearsed it along with all coaches and athletes involved with your team (See Chapter 15 for a more detailed description of the crucial elements of acceptable EAPs).

As the coach, you should teach your athletes that they have an important role in preventing injuries and reporting them if they do occur. Some athletes equate mental toughness with playing in pain and ignoring that pain. Teach your athletes that pain is often a warning sign that action needs to be taken to protect the body and prevent further damage. The old adage "no pain, no gain" is quite appropriate for cardiovascular conditioning and strength training drills, but has no place in reporting injuries that occur in practice or competition. Athletes need to be educated to the fact that pain is an important warning signal that should be reported first to the coach and, when necessary, conveyed to qualified medical professionals and parents.

While pre-participation physical exams are not mandated by most recreational youth sport organizations, coaches should strongly encourage parents to have such exams for their children before participating in your program. Effective coaches collect and keep readily available records of each athlete's medical history provided by the athlete's parents or guardians (asthma; allergies; prior existing conditions, etc.).

The information in this chapter is not intended to replace a diagnosis from a trained medical professional; nor is it meant to train coaches to implement medical treatment without qualified medical advice.

When an Accident Occurs - Assessment

Accidents, by their nature, occur suddenly and, at least in the short run, are unexpected. When confronted with such an event, the coach must be prepared to manage the emergency to eliminate or minimize the danger to all involved by following general procedures such as those outlined below. There are three general phases of which coaches responding to an emergency should be aware.[1]

PHASE I—GENERAL ASSESSMENT OF THE SITUATION

The coach is most likely already at the scene and, thus, is often the first person to attend to an injured athlete. An overall "sizing up" of the situation is essential before rendering aid. Has the competitive play or practice stopped? Are the injured athlete's teammates and opponents being supervised? Are the field conditions, such as slippery or rocky surfaces, of concern when rendering care? Is the general area accessible to emergency medical transportation? Did the injury happen where there is risk from vehicular traffic, for instance with a cross country runner? Do circumstances pose a risk to the coach and others besides the injured athletes— for instance with lightning or severe weather conditions? Is more than one athlete injured and are some injuries more severe than others? All of these can typically be assessed in the few seconds it takes for the coach to approach the scene of the accident.

PHASE II—INITIAL ASSESSMENT OF THE INJURY

Once the scene is judged to be safe, the coach must immediately **determine if the situation is or is not life threatening.** While this judgment may have already been made during the general assessment, it involves three distinct types of questions: a) What is the injury and what signs tell you what is injured? Is there a deformity? Was there a collision? If so, with what? Is the injury **S**imple or **S**erious (SOS)? (Figure 13.1) b) What is the mental status of the injured athlete? Alert and responsive? Slowed or painful responses? Unconscious or unresponsive to basic questions? If the athlete's responses are slow, unresponsive or diminished in any way, anticipate a serious, potentially life-threatening injury. c) Is the athlete's airway open and functioning? Is he breathing? Is there a pulse indicating blood circulation? Check for these ABCs of basic first aid (**A**irways, **B**reathing and **C**irculation). Should any of these be blocked or absent, be prepared to render life sustaining actions such as basic first aid, CPR, or the use of a defibrillator. Initiate the call for professional medical assistance immediately, should it be necessary.

FIGURE 13.1
A crucial decision during the assessment stage is whether an injury is simple – and can be treated by you as the coach – or serious and requires calling for emergency medical professionals.

The term injury is typically used when damage to the athlete results from a sudden or one-time incident while the term illness is generally used to describe damage occurring from longer-term, repeated exposures. If you are ever uncertain about the nature or extent of an injury, you should assume it is serious and treat it as such. Table 13.1 lists common examples of life threatening or life altering injuries and illnesses.

TABLE 13.1 Examples of Serious Life Threatening or Life Altering Injuries or Illnesses

Injuries	Illnesses
Concussion	Hyperthermia (e.g., Heat Stroke; Heat Exhaustion)
Severe Bleeding	Hypothermia (e.g., Frostbite)
Inability to Breath	Reactive Airway Disease (e.g., Asthma; Exercise Induced Asthma)
Shock	Allergic Reactions (e.g., Insect Bites/Stings; Foods)
Eye Injuries	
Spinal Injuries	
Injuries to Internal Organs	
Commotio Cordis	
Fracture with exposed bone	

PHASE III—FOLLOW UP ASSESSMENT OF THE INJURY

Once an assessment has determined that the injury is non-life threatening, the coach can turn to determining what type of treatment is required, keeping in mind that the initial situation may quickly become life-threatening because of shock, excessive bleeding or other delayed reactions to the initial injury such as internal bleeding or severe concussion.

When injuries or illnesses are judged to be non-life threatening, typically the athlete should be immobilized until the coach can check for additional injuries. Continue to monitor the athlete for delayed reactions, especially, but not limited to, potential concussions and/or shock. Such delayed reactions can change the simple injury into a serious one. In ambiguous situations, always choose to treat the injury as severe rather than minor and follow the admonition "When in doubt, sit them out."

TABLE 13.2 Examples of Simple Injuries or Illnesses Requiring Treatment But Unlikely to Be Life Threatening

Injuries	Illnesses
Minor Cuts/Wounds/Abrasions	Respiratory Infections
Puncture Wounds (note: immediate attention is needed if punctured by rusty object – concern about tetanus – or if a piece of glass, wood or other object is embedded under skin)	Skin Disorders
Bruises	Stomach Cramps
Nose Bleeds	
"Wind Knocked-Out"	
Teeth Knocked Out	
Muscle Cramps	
Sprains, Strains and Fractures	

Common Traumatic/Acute Injuries in Sport

What, where, when, to whom or how accidental injuries will occur in sport is, almost by definition, unpredictable. That injuries will happen across a number of players through an entire season for an entire sport is predictable; and, thus, must be prepared for by coaches at all levels, including recreational youth sport coaches. The information that follows is for educational purposes only. Handling injuries requires not only information but also behavioral competencies obtainable primarily through hands on training in first aid and CPR courses available through local chapter of your Red Cross, local hospitals or local EMT training programs. All coaches are strongly urged to take such courses before venturing out on the athletic field with young athletes.

Concussions

Our understanding of concussions has improved dramatically over the past two decades. A concussion is defined as a functional injury and is "the period of neurological impairment " that follows a blow or force to the brain. It is more than a structural injury as had been previously suggested by the outdated description that it was "a bruising of the brain." It is characterized by immediate, but usually temporary, impairment of brain functions, such as thinking, vision, equilibrium, and consciousness. This definition emphasizes that a concussion is a dynamic process that continues long after the traumatic incident itself. While a concussion often results from a blow to the head, even of moderate severity, a concussion can also occur when the brain itself is simply whipped around inside the skull stretching or breaking the tiny cells of the brain. Thus, a concussion can occur even in the absence of a blow to the head. The term concussion also refers to the period during which the brain is attempting to recover from the effects of a blow or force rather than simply the single trauma event caused by that force. It is a cascade of physiological events that occur after a sheering force has been applied to the brain or brain stem. The myelin sheath (the fatty material encasing the nerve axons) can be stretched or even broken resulting in a slowing or complete blockage of nerve impulses. A concussion has been described as a "neurometabolic cascade"*of events that temporarily disrupts brain

* **What is a "Neurometabolic Cascade"?** Within a few minutes after a concussion, a depolarization occurs -- a disruption of the normal electrical charge -- as electrically charged chemicals (ions) begin to leak across the cell membrane upsetting the normal electrical balance of the brain cells. This disruption is accompanied by a decrease in blood flow resulting in a reduction of the brain's primary source of energy – glucose. Following the concussive event, the brain cells immediately attempt to restore their normal electrical balance increasing the brain's demand for energy. Thus, there is an increase in energy demand coupled with a simultaneous decrease in accessible energy resulting in a substantial mismatch between the brain's need for energy and the amount of energy available. The brain literally becomes exhausted. In addition, the myelin sheath, the electrical insulation surrounding the brain cell, may be stretched and/or broken resulting in disruption of the normal electrical messages sent along the cell resulting in diminished cognitive abilities, i.e., the ability to think and process information.

FIGURE 13.2
Concussions are one
of the most serious
injuries in sports but
the signs are often
subtle rather than
obvious. With young
athletes, when in
doubt, sit them out!

function.[3] It is accompanied by decreased blood flow to the brain and thus less energy (glucose) just when the brain is attempting to use more energy to restore normal functioning. The result is a dramatic mismatch between the brain's need for energy and the amount of energy available. In its attempts to recover from the trauma of the concussion event, the brain literally uses up most of the immediately available energy in the cell and has reduced access to additional energy because of the reduced blood flow. Thus, a concussion triggers a prolonged period of energy depletion. The brain literally becomes exhausted for a period of time as it attempts to recover from the traumatic incident, resulting in a 7-to-10-day window of increased susceptibility to further trauma should a second concussive event occur during that period. We now know that the neurological consequences can worsen substantially if sufficient time to heal is not permitted.[4]

Concussions are one of the most serious injuries in sport. They are a silent, almost invisible injury, often displaying subtle rather than obvious symptoms. (Figure 13.2) CT scans and MRIs rarely show any structural damage.* Underreporting occurs because some athletes often chose not to report the symptoms either because they believe they will be re-

---

* MRI = magnetic resonance imaging; CT = computerized tomography

moved from competition or because of the misguided belief that playing through an injury without complaint is a form of mental toughness. In the not too distant past, it was quite common to describe a hard hit resulting in a concussion as having "had your bell rung" with the expectation that a tough athlete should merely shrug it off and play on. Such a culture existed partially because of a lack of awareness that a concussion is **mild traumatic brain injury** requiring immediate and sustained medical treatment.

GREATER SUSCEPTIBILITY/RISK FOR YOUNG ATHLETES

Youth athletes are more susceptible to concussions than adults. The highest incidence occurs in the youth populations. Compared to 20- to 24-year olds (5.2 concussions/1000 patients), the rate of such injuries is tripled for 15- to 19-year-olds (16.5 concussions for every 1000 patients) and doubled for 10- to 14-year-olds (10.5 concussions/1000 patients). The greater susceptibility is even more dramatic when compared to 25- to 29 year olds (2.7/1000). Further, the incidence is on the rise. From 2007 to 2014, diagnosed concussions in the United States have increased by 143% for 10-to-14-year-olds and by 87% for 15- to 19-year-olds.[5] These dramatic increases may be because of greater awareness resulting in increased reporting and increased diagnoses. The increase may also be related to higher participation rates and to a general growth in the overall adolescent population in the United States.

Children and teens tend to have more severe symptoms which often last longer and sometimes even become permanent, ranging from chronic headaches and dizziness to cognitive and intellectual problems such as a lack of focus in the classroom.[6] Concussion rates appear to be higher for girls than boys; and girls tend to take longer to fully recover although the reasons for these differences are not entirely clear.[7] Most adults recover back to how they typically function in 10-14 days; however, the recovery period for children is typically about four weeks.[8] Children and adolescents who suffer a concussion are 4 to 6 times more likely to experience a second concussion. In addition, the younger the athlete, the less developed the brain; thus, an injury at an early age may stunt or distort further brain development producing long-term unpredictable consequences for cognitive development. There is also evidence that the signs and symptoms of concussions are often delayed in children showing up days later than the symptoms reported by adults. The recovery patterns of children also appear to differ from adults with children reporting feeling better rather quickly only to feel worse after several days. Progressively worsening signs and symptoms are important warnings that a concussion may be more serious than initially thought.

SECOND IMPACT SYNDROME (SIS)

Athletes who return to play before complete recovery from an initial concussion are at high risk for a phenomenon known as **second impact syndrome (SIS). SIS** occurs when a second concussion occurs before the athlete has fully recovered from the first concussion. A primary characteristic of SIS is dangerous brain swelling and bleeding that may require surgery and can cause death or permanent disability. SIS can be avoided by removing concussed athletes from practice or play until complete recovery has been determined by a qualified health-care professional who has provided a note indicating that the athlete may return to play. Adolescent athletes seem to be the most at risk to develop second-impact syndrome, partially because their longer, delayed recovery periods increase the time during which they are susceptible to SIS.

DIAGNOSING A CONCUSSION

Even healthcare professionals often have difficulty diagnosing concussion because of its silent nature. It usually goes undetected by MRIs and CT scans. There may or may not be any bruising or swelling. The misdiagnosed and, thus, untreated concussion may have long-term debilitating effects. The best predictor of the athlete's speed of recovery is the severity of the initial symptoms, especially memory loss

SIGNS VS. SYMPTOMS

Concussions are diagnosed using two types of clues: **Signs and Symptoms.** Signs are directly observable events seen by the coach or sport medicine professional. Symptoms are sensations experienced and reported by the athlete. Importantly, symptoms may have a delayed onset with an athlete initially reporting "feeling fine." Thus, if a concussion is suspected, athletes should be monitored for at least a full day, if not more, after an incident and encouraged to see a health care provider

TABLE 13.3 Detecting Concussions[9]

Signs (Observed)	Symptoms (Reported)
Appears dazed, stunned or disoriented	Headache or "pressure" in head that won't go away
Confused about assignment or position	Feels nauseous
Forgets sports plays	Balance problems or dizziness
Unsure of game, score, or opponent	Double or fuzzy/blurry vision
Moves clumsily	Hypersensitivity to light and sound
Can't answer or slow to answer simple questions	Feels sad, depressed or anxious
Loss of consciousness (even briefly)	Feeling sluggish, hazy, foggy, or groggy
Shows behavior or personality changes	Concentration problems or disoriented
Behavior that is out of place	Memory loss
Can't recall events before or after the hit or fall	Confusion
Shows balance or coordination problems	Does not "feel right"
Shows irritability for little or no reason	Low energy level; Fatigue
Increase or decrease in sleep patterns	
Vomiting (early on)	
One pupil (the black part in the middle of the eye) is larger than the other	

knowledgeable in the treatment of concussions. They should never be left alone for prolonged periods of time during that monitoring period.

Self-reports are notoriously unreliable because:

1. Athletes may not recognize their symptoms or their seriousness.
2. Athletes may hide the symptoms to avoid being removed from the game.
3. The symptoms, themselves, may have a delayed onset.

Preseason Baseline Testing

Because a concussion is a functional injury, not a specific event, baseline testing of cognitive function is rapidly becoming the norm for assessing the severity and the recovery from a concussion. However, because of the difficulties of validating the results, especially with group testing, the Berlin Consensus Statement of 2016 concluded that "Baseline testing may be useful, but it is not necessary for interpreting post injury scores."[10] And that baseline testing, while it might be helpful and provide an additional educational opportunity, "...was not felt to be required as a mandatory aspect of every assessment"[11] at the youth sport level.

With the development of computerized tests[12] requiring only 20 to 30 minutes of an athlete's time, it is now possible to test athletes quickly -- often entire teams at one sitting. These tests essentially measure brain functions such as attention, memory, reaction time and concentration. They can be compared to post-concussion test results to determine if and when an athlete has returned to pre-concussion performance levels. Such comparisons help identify subtle losses of brain function and can pinpoint symptoms that the athletes may be reluctant to report – because of fear of lost playing time – or may not recognize – because of lack of awareness.

The primary purpose of such baseline testing is to compare pre- vs. post-test results to determine if and when an athlete has recovered sufficiently to return to play. The results are not to determine how smart an athlete is or to compare scores between different individuals to determine who is "doing better." Athletes must be encouraged to do their best on baseline testing to ensure a valid assessment of any performance loss caused by a concussion. Lack of motivation concerning the importance of the test, intentionally performing poorly to avoid results which might slow return to play, or distractions during group testing may all invalidate the results of any pre- or post-test comparisons and, thus, prevent even qualified medical personnel from making accurate assessments of when an athlete is ready to return to play.[13]

TREATMENT

Regardless of the severity of the suspected concussion, youth sport coaches should treat any instance of suspected concussion seriously enough to seek out qualified medical care.

If you suspect a concussion has occurred, you should:

1. Immediately remove the athlete from play; **"When in doubt, keep them out!"**

2. If a neck or spinal injury is suspected, tell the injured athlete to remain still while emergency medical help is sought. Avoid asking the athlete to move their head from side to side to see if they are OK. If a neck injury has been sustained, such movement could result in permanent paralysis.

3. Send the athlete to a licensed medical professional for assessment EVEN if the symptoms subside quickly or the symptoms do not appear to be severe. Err on the side of caution when attempting to decide whether to seek medical treatment. Coaches should not attempt to judge the seriousness of the injury themselves. Seeking assessment from a qualified medical professional does not mean that an emergency medical squad needs to be called in every case but rather that parents should be informed that a possible concussion should be assessed by a qualified physician and that if suspicion is high, a medical note to return to play should be sought.

4. The primary treatment for concussions, regardless of severity, is rest -- lots of rest. While sitting out can be very frustrating for a young athlete, it is absolutely essential when a concussion has been diagnosed. The rest should be both physical and mental. Without sufficient rest, symptoms may return and further brain injury may occur. Remember, return to practice or competition should never occur without the authorization of a qualified medical professional. Sleep, contrary to conventional wisdom, is advisable.

5. Since athletes are more susceptible to concussions after having had one, careful monitoring of a previously concussed athlete is essential even after they have been cleared to return to play.

6. Collect important information needed by health care professionals for an accurate assessment: What caused the injury? Did the athlete lose consciousness? If so, for how long? Was there any memory loss immediately following the injury? Were there any seizures immediately following the injury? Has the athlete had any prior concussions?

7. Inform the athlete's parents and give them sufficient information about the concussion to ensure that they know the athlete should be examined and monitored by a qualified health care professional.

An athlete should never be permitted to return to play if any symptoms – however mild -- still exist. As simple as this guideline appears, recognizing the presence of such symptoms may be difficult because athletes may minimize symptoms in a misguided attempt to return to play sooner than warranted or because they have not been taught the seriousness of such symptoms and the need to report them. A point that cannot be stressed enough is that following a concussion, athletes should never be permitted to practice or play without clearance by qualified medical personnel.

RETURN TO PLAY (RTP) ISSUES

Allow the athlete to return to play ONLY after being cleared by a health care professional who is knowledgeable in the latest protocols for concussion evaluations.

To compound the problem, the prevailing attitude in sport to "play tough" often results in an early return to play placing the athlete at serious risk of further brain injury, disability or death. A number of organizations[14] have developed return-to-play guidelines for athletes suspected of sustaining or having sustained a concussion. Athletes shall not return to play until they meet all the following criteria:

1. After removal of play, no return to play that day.

2. Medical evaluation to determine the presence or absence of a concussion.

3. If diagnosed with a concussion, the athlete must complete a minimum of one symptom-free week regardless of the number,

type or severity of those symptoms before initiating a graduated return-to-play exercise protocol.

4. The use of tools such as symptom checklists, baseline and balance tests are suggested.

5. A typical protocol for exercise exertion is as follows:

    a. Step 1: No physical or cognitive activity until all symptoms cease. Symptom-free means symptoms are not masked by medications for symptom resolution (e.g., headache free without aspirin, ibuprofen, etc.)

    b. Step 2: Light aerobic activity to increase heart rate but at a level no higher than 70% of the athlete's maximum target heart rate which can be estimated by computing: HRmax = 220 minus the athlete's age. Avoid resistance training.

    c. Step 3: Sport-specific exercises to add movement but avoid head impact activities such as heading a soccer ball or tackling in football.

    d. Step 4: Noncontact training drills including progressive resistance weight training with the objective to increase exercise, coordination and cognitive load.

    e. Step 5: Full-contact practice to restore player's confidence and permit assessment of functional skills by coaches (requires medical clearance from a licensed medical professional)

    f. Step 6: Normal game play; requires medical clearance.

6. If concussion symptoms do recur during any of these steps of the exercise protocol, return the athlete to the previous level of activity where no symptoms were observed, rest for 24 hours before once again attempting the step where symptoms resurfaced.

7. If there is a re-occurrence of any post-concussion symptoms, the athlete should be removed from any physical exertion and returned to a licensed medical professional for re-evaluation.

SPECIAL CONSIDERATIONS

Memory loss for events just prior to or after the concussion appears to be a better predictor of the severity of a concussion than is loss of consciousness. The Center for Disease Control warns that long-term effects from concussions, particularly multiple concussions, can lead to long-term serious disorders such as Alzheimer's disease and Parkinson's disease.

When players and parents perceive removal from play as a severe penalty and they simultaneously underestimate the severity and long-term consequences of a concussion, underreporting of symptoms is a predictable response. Coaches and sport medicine professionals should emphasize that the earlier athletes report a concussion, the sooner they may return to play.

Since the state of Washington passed the first concussion legislation in 2009, every state in the nation has passed legislation concerning concussion safety. A listing of each state and a description of that state's specific legislation is available.[15] Laws which contain the following three principles are generally considered effective:

1. Concussion awareness and educational mandates;

2. Mandatory removal from play following a suspected concussion;

3. Written medical clearance as a prerequisite for return to play.

Minor Bleeding/Cuts/Abrasions

Minor scrapes and abrasions are a part of virtually any sport with vigorous physical activity. Abrasions are often described as brush burns and are caused by friction against a rough surface such as dirt, grass, asphalt, etc. Often the friction results in significant amounts of dirt and debris becoming imbedded in the abrasion. (Figure 13.3)

FIGURE 13.3
Minor scrapes and abrasions often need to be cleansed of the dirt and debris embedded in the wound by the friction which caused the wound. Initial bleeding may actually help cleanse the wound.

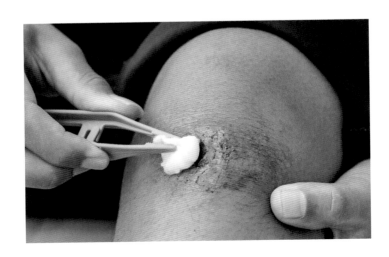

TREATMENT

The initial bleeding may actually be beneficial as it is likely to be helpful as it acts to cleanse the abrasion. Bleeding can be controlled, almost regardless of the severity, by applying direct pressure on the wound itself, preferably with a cold compress or a gauze pad from your first aid kit. If gauze is not available, terrycloth towels work almost as well. Both the applied pressure and the gauze or terrycloth slow blood flow and promote clotting.

After the bleeding has been controlled, cleanse the abrasion with mild soap and water, removing any foreign particles. Tweezers can be used if needed but disinfect them first and avoid digging into the wound, an action that can restart the bleeding and increase the likelihood of bacterial infection. Wear the gloves typically found in a standard first aid kit to avoid coming in contact with the blood. Apply antibiotic ointment and cover with a bandage or gauze to keep the abrasion clean and minimize the likelihood of bacterial infection. If the bleeding does not stop within 10 to 15 minutes or is profuse, seek medical attention.

Most minor cuts, scrapes and abrasions heal within a week. During that time monitor the wound for the development of possible infection. Signs of infection include slow healing of the cut itself, swelling, redness or red streaks surrounding the site of the wound, tenderness and pain to the touch, and oozing or discharge of pus from the site.

Major Cuts/Wounds

If the cut is so deep (1/4 inch or more) that it appears to require stitches or so large that it results in heavy, difficult to stop bleeding or has a foreign object embedded within the wound, seek medical care. Deep puncture wounds or abrasions involving rusty objects should be treated by medical professionals and a tetanus shot should be sought if immunizations shots have not been updated within the last 5 years. Should the wound be the result of a bite by either human or animal, medical assistance is required.

TREATMENT

If the bleeding soaks through the gauze, simply add additional layers of gauze. NEVER remove the initial layers because doing so disrupts the initial clotting and can restart the bleeding.

Tourniquet

The use of a tourniquet is, perhaps the most controversial topic in all of first aid techniques. Tourniquets should be used only as a last resort when the amount of blood loss is life threatening as may occur with a partial or total amputation. They can lead to serious tissue damage, but when loss of blood may result in loss of life, they may be necessary. A tourniquet is a band that can be wrapped tightly around an arm or leg to totally restrict blood flow to a serious wound on a person's limb where the bleeding is so profuse or the damage is so severe that simple pressure is insufficient to control the bleeding. If the wound is below the elbow or the knee, the tourniquet may need to be placed above the joint. If possible, it should be approximately 1 to 2 inches wide. A narrower band will cut into the skin creating additional injury. Unfortunately, the wider the tourniquet, the more tightly it must be wrapped in order to stop the bleeding. Place a strip of cloth between the wound and the rest of the body. The band of cloth should be long enough to be wrapped around the limb twice and to tie a knot with sufficient excess length to tie a stick or other straight, rigid object above the knot to hold it in place. Twist the stick until the tourniquet has been tightened sufficiently to stop the bleeding. Tie the loose ends of the cloth around the stick to hold it in place. Be certain that all bleeding has stopped because if the tourniquet is too loose, arterial bleeding may not stop. Arterial blood flow (coming from the heart) has significantly greater pressure than venous blood (returning to the heart). Insufficient tightening may permit arterial bleeding while stopping only venous bleeding. Never loosen the knot once tied. Leave that task for qualified medical personnel. Make a note of the time that the tourniquet was applied.

NOSE BLEEDS

A nose bleed is a common, but usually minor, injury often caused by a direct blood to the nose or by the strain of overexertion. Have the athlete sit in an erect position with the head turned toward the side of the bleeding thereby confining the blood flow to one nostril and minimizing the likelihood of blood draining backwards into the sinus cavity. DO NOT have the athlete lean backward. Place a cold compress over the nose and have the athlete apply pressure directly to the side of the nose where the bleeding is occurring until the bleeding has stopped. Caution the athlete not to blow the nose for at least two hours after the bleeding has stopped.

BRUISES

Bruises, known as contusions, are indicated by "black and blue" discoloration marks on the skin, often located slightly below the point at which a blow to the area has caused blood cells to leak from broken blood vessels under the skin. In sport, the blow can come from a fall or an external object such as a baseball or lacrosse racquet. Although rare in children, bruises that occur with an external impact can result from a bleeding disorder or because of a medication with a blood thinning effect. Parents of children with such disorders or medication should inform the coach on the child's medical history form. The affected area is often tender to the touch, painful at least at first, and often days after itches as the bruise heals.

Treat with a cold compress that is separated from the skin with a cloth or elastic wrap. The cold tends to reduce swelling, combat pain and facilitate healing by reducing blood flow to the area. With large bruises elevate the body part when possible for the first 24 hours. Over the counter pain medications are appropriate but avoid aspirin because it tends to slow clotting prolonging the initial bleeding. After 48 hours, apply warm compresses for 10 minutes two or three times daily to increase blood flow and healing.

BLOOD BORNE PATHOGENS* /STANDARD PRECAUTIONS[17]

Standard precautions guidelines recommend the use of gloves, masks and protective eyewear and the proper disposal of contaminated waste when an individual risks coming in contact with blood or body secretions containing blood or blood elements to prevent the transmission of disease via blood borne pathogens such as hepatitis** and HIV/AIDS.*** Latex gloves tend to have the best fit but may produce an allergic reaction in some users and, as a result, are not the best choice for a first aid kit accessible to multiple users. Synthetic vinyl gloves are allergy free but typically do not fit as well. Nitrile gloves, while more durable with a lon-

---

*Disease-causing microorganisms present in the human blood.

**Hepatitis is a swelling and/or inflammation of the liver caused by a virus. Hepatitis A is the least serious and mildest form, usually self-correcting. Hepatitis B and C may become chronic conditions resulting in cirrhosis (permanent scarring of the liver). Hepatitis is the leading cause of liver cancer and the most common reason for liver transplants. More than four million Americans have chronic hepatitis, most of whom are unaware of their infection.

***HIV (the human immunodeficiency virus) is the virus that causes AIDS (acquired immunodeficiency syndrome) which is a weakened immune status resulting in a lack of defense against infectious diseases.

ger shelf life are the most expensive. As a result, vinyl gloves are typically the most popular choice for most first aid kits.

The risk of contracting various types of hepatitis HIV/AIDS during sporting events is quite low; nonetheless, procedures for preventing blood-borne infectious diseases should be part of all Emergency Action Plans. Transmission of these infectious agents can be limited by the use of the following procedures:

1. Any athlete who is bleeding, or has blood from himself or others on the person or uniform should be removed from the playing field until the bleeding has stopped and been cleaned from his body and uniform. Extra uniforms should be an item in all emergency kits wherever possible and practical.

2. Gloves (preferably vinyl – see above) should be worn when there is a risk of touching blood or other body fluids, mucous membranes, or open wounds.

3. Hands and other skin surfaces should be washed immediately and thoroughly if contaminated with blood or other body fluids and hands should be washed again immediately after the removal of gloves.

4. All contaminated surfaces and equipment should be cleaned with an appropriate disinfectant before resuming competition. Use gloves while cleaning.

5. All bandages, gauze pads, towels or other first aid equipment that has come in contact with blood or other body fluids should be disposed of properly. Holding small items in the gloved hand and removing the gloves inside out to enclose such items is a convenient and acceptable way of storing the contaminants for a short period until they can be properly discarded.

6. Although saliva is not known to transmit HIV infection, direct mouth-to-mouth resuscitation is no longer recommended for resuscitation.[18]

7. Coaches with open sores, bleeding or oozing skin conditions should refrain from providing direct athletic care until their condition has been resolved.

Shock

Shock occurs when the body's vital functions are threatened by a lack of blood or when major organs fail to receive sufficient oxygen. The main signs of shock are low blood pressure, rapid, shallow breathing; cold, pale skin; rapid, weak pulse; dizziness, fainting, or weakness. The athlete may feel thirsty. Shock is life threatening and requires immediate medical attention to be reversed. Do all you can on site to prevent it from worsening.

TREATMENT

Try to maintain an open airway, control any obvious bleeding and elevate the legs about 12 inches above the heart unless the nature of the injury prevents this. Keep them warm with blankets both over and under the body and avoid giving them anything to eat or drink to minimize the possibility of vomiting.

PREVENTION

Shock often occurs after an injury where blood loss is substantial. Preventing the onset of shock involves the same procedures just listed above used to treat shock.

"Wind Knocked Out" (Solar Plexus Syndrome)

A frequent sport injury is a blow to abdomen or lower back compressing the solar plexus, a network of nerves behind the stomach. It results in a temporary injury known as "having the wind knocked out of you." Its primary characteristic is the inability to take a normal deep breath but is also accompanied by pain, typically at the pit of the stomach, and panic at not being able to take a deep breath. The blow compresses the nerve plexus causing the diaphragm, a large dome-shaped muscle under the lungs, to go into spasms. When operating normally, the diaphragm permits breathing by pulling down under the lungs to facilitate inhaling and then pushes up to facilitate exhaling.

TREATMENT

This disorder is normally self-correcting with the spasms disappearing within a few minutes and breathing returning to normal. To facilitate recovery, have the athlete crouch forward with his/her knees bent while taking slow deep breathes – as opposed to the natural inclination to try to breathe rapidly. Recovery longer than a few minutes suggests that there may be problems other that the "wind being knocked out" such as a broken rib or a collapsed lung. If so, medical assistance should be sought.

Dislodged Tooth

A chipped tooth is not typically considered a medical emergency; however, a partially or totally dislodged tooth requires immediate action. Mouth guards, especially those fitted individually to the young athlete, are quite effective in preventing such injuries.

TREATMENT

A quick response can save a tooth even if it has been totally dislodged. The sooner it is reinserted, the more likely it can be saved. Avoid touching the root of the tooth which most likely will still have live cells attached that are needed to re-affix the root of the tooth back into the gum. Handle the tooth only by the crown (the hard enamel surface seen when the tooth is normally set in the gums). If the tooth is clean, re-insert it immediately, making certain it is positioned normally. If the tooth is dirty, rinse the surface gently (milk or saline is preferred to plain water but speed is of the essence) to cleanse it but do not use a disinfectant or scrub it because doing so may kill or dislodge the fragile cells surrounding the root. Once the tooth is back in its normal position, have the young athlete bite down gently on clean gauze or cloth and maintain the bite to hold the tooth firmly in place until you can get your athlete to a dentist who can secure the tooth to the teeth located on either side of the dislodged tooth. The sooner the dentist can be reached and the sooner the tooth can be re-inserted, the greater the probability that the tooth can be saved.

If the tooth cannot be re-inserted, place the tooth in a cup of milk, or a saline solution or in a commercially available "save a tooth" kit often found in your first kit and transport both the athlete and the tooth immediately to a dentist or the emergency room at a local hospital. Milk or saline are much superior to plain water at preserving the delicate cells attached to the root. They keep the cells moist and alive longer greatly increasing the chance of total recovery of the dislodged tooth.

If the child is 6 or 7 years or younger and the dislodged tooth is clearly a "baby" tooth (i.e., a temporary tooth) do not attempt to re-insert the tooth. The adult tooth will ultimately replace the baby tooth and re-insertion may injure the incoming adult tooth.

Eye Injuries

Eye injuries result from a variety of causes. An eye scratch, termed a corneal abrasion, can occur by literally getting "poked in the eye" or being hit in the eye by a baseball or lacrosse ball but also can occur from rubbing the eye after a foreign object (even a small one) has become lodged on the outer surface of the eye. Scratches of the eye are of concern because they increase the likelihood of an eye infection.

TREATMENT

Treatment of most sport related eye injuries that do not involve a direct hit to the eye with a ball or other hard object such as a hockey puck involve immediate flushing of the eye. This can be done by encouraging blinking to increase natural tears or with water or saline from a first aid kit. Cover the eye with a cool, moist compress but avoid both pressure to the eye itself and rubbing the eye. The athlete should see a doctor or visit an emergency room as soon as possible.

Strains, Sprains and Fractures

A strain is an overstretched or torn muscle or tendon. Tendons are the tissues that connect muscles to bones. A sprain is an overstretched or torn ligament. Ligaments are fibrous tissues that connect bone to bone, stabilizing and supporting the joints in the skeleton. A fracture is a crack, splinter or break in a bone ranging from a minor crack to a complete separation of the bones at the point of the fracture. In both sprains and strains, the symptoms are pain and swelling; however, sprains are more likely to be accompanied by bruising while a strain is more likely to exhibit muscle spasms. While movement of the strained or sprained part of the body is possible, it is typically more painful and the movement is more restricted when the stretch or tear is more severe. Fractures are often accompanied by tenderness at the point of the injury and the symptoms may vary substantially depending on which bones have been fractured and the degree of the fracture (e.g., a crack vs. a total break). A compound fracture involves the broken bone breaking through the skin and will be quite obvious because of the deformity and the pain.

TREATMENT

Because differences between a strain, a sprain and a fracture cannot be fully assessed without X-rays, the initial treatment (**RICE**) is virtually the same. RICE reduces pain and swelling and speeds the healing process. (Figure 13.4)

> **RICE** stands for:
>
> **R**est. Immediately upon recognizing the injury, cease the activity. Immobilize the injured limb or area of the body (e.g., ribs, neck) and avoid the tendency to encourage the athletes to "walk it off." If at all possible, avoid putting weight on the injured area.
>
> **I**ce.   Once life-threatening trauma has been ruled out, apply ice to the injured area. Apply the ice for approximately 20 minutes three to four times daily. Crushed ice in a plastic bag such as a large sandwich bag is ideal because the crushed ice can conform to the shape of the injured body part. First, a single layer of an elastic bandage should be wrapped around the injury where possible. Then place the bag of ice on the injury over top of that single layer. Finally, continue to wrap the elastic bandage around the ice bag to hold it in place. A chemical cold pack or frozen gel pack can be used in place of the bag of ice; however, they lose their cooling effect relatively quickly, are costly, and may leak if they have been stored in a first aid kit for a prolonged period of time.
>
> **C**ompression. Wrap the elastic bandage tightly enough to secure the ice bag and create a reasonable amount of compression on the injured tissue. Such pressure helps to reduce swelling and, if effective, will reduce recovery time of the initial injury. If the athlete complains of pain or numbness, rewrap the elastic bandage a little less tightly.
>
> **E**levation. Whenever possible, elevate the injured portion of the body slightly above the level of the heart. Such elevation helps drain fluids from the injured body part, thereby minimizing any swelling.

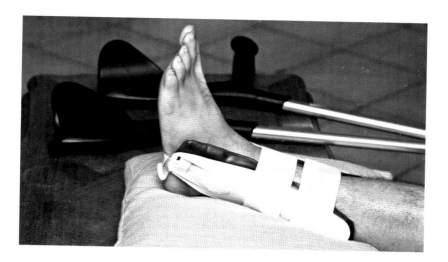

FIGURE 13.4
Regardless of whether the suspected injury is a sprain, strain or fracture, RICE is the recommended treatment.

ICE MASSAGE

Following the initial RICE treatment, an excellent technique for continuing to manage pain and swelling is to massage the injured area with ice. An effective method of doing so is to freeze water in small paper cups. To apply the massage, tear away the upper portion of the cup exposing the ice and, holding the bottom of the remaining portion of the cup, gently massage the injured area for approximately 10 minutes with the exposed surface of the ice. This procedure can be repeated every few hours as needed. It has the advantages of preventing "freezer burn," allows the injured athletes to place the ice on the exact point at which pain is felt and promotes faster vasoconstriction which minimizes swelling. It also gives the injured athlete an active response to treating their own injury.

Referral to a physician for medical assessment that may involve taking an X-ray is strongly recommended following a strain or sprain because the likelihood of a fracture cannot be ruled out by a mere visual evaluation of the injury.

Muscle Cramps

The most common muscle cramps experienced in sport are calf, thigh and hamstring cramps, although cramping can occur in virtually any muscle group such as the fingers or toes. A cramp is an involuntary contraction of the muscle often accompanied by a hard lump at the point of pain. It can result from overstraining the muscle with vigorous physical exertion especially in hot weather where dehydration during prolonged exercise has occurred. Dehydration is often accompanied by a depletion of potassium, calcium and magnesium, minerals which facilitate normal muscle contractions.

TREATMENT

Cramps will almost invariably stop the activity associated with the cramp because of the pain and immobilization of the muscle. Immediately stretch and hold the muscle in a position that stretches the contracted muscle in the opposite direction of the cramp contraction. For example, if the calf muscle has cramped, pull the foot toward your chest with your hands or with a band or strap around the ball of the foot. The athlete can achieve the same stretching position from a standing position by placing his weight on the cramped leg and bending the knee slightly while pressing the heel to the floor. Lightly massage the affected muscle and apply heat with a warm towel, a heating pad or a warm shower with the water directed onto the muscle that is cramped. This is one of the few injuries for which it is appropriate to "walk it off."

The likelihood of cramping can be minimized by staying hydrated, by drinking plenty of water or sport drinks especially in warm weather. Fluids should be replenished regularly throughout the workout and be done more frequently as temperature and humidity increase. Stretching before beginning vigorous activity and light exercise (warm ups) can also help prevent cramping. "Appropriate nutrition and adequate training" are recommended for preventing cramps from "premature fatigue."[19]

Insect Bites or Stings

In outdoor sports, stings from bees, wasps or hornets and bites from flies, spiders or ticks are not uncommon. Most physical reactions to such bites or stings are mild inflammation and swelling, tenderness and itching. (Figure13.5)

TREATMENT

For mild reactions, move to an area free of insects and, if a stinger is present, gently remove it and then wash the site of the sting with soap and water and apply an ice pack or a cold, wet compress for a few minutes to minimize pain swelling. To remove a tick, use tweezers to grasp the tick

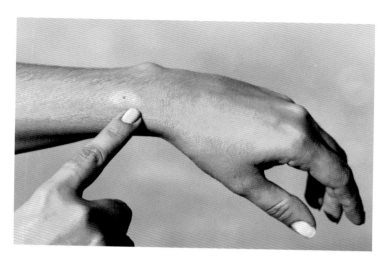

FIGURE 13.5
Most reactions to bee stings and insect bites are mild inflammation, tenderness and itching but allergic reactions can be serious and need immediate attention.

at its head or mouth, as close to the skin as possible. Pull firmly until it is removed. Cleanse the site with alcohol. If the sting or bite is on the athlete's arm or leg, elevate the limb where possible. Then apply a salve containing an analgesic to help control pain. Anti-itch creams such as calamine lotion or baking soda can be applied to minimize any itching that is likely to occur. The itchiness, swelling and pain should subside in a day or so. If not, consult a medical professional.

Watch carefully for an allergic reaction. Such a reaction may be evidenced by "a large area of swelling, abnormal breathing, tightness of the throat or chest, dizziness, nausea or vomiting or fainting, swelling of the lips, eyelids or throat and/or rapid heartbeat.

Call 911 and take these actions immediately even before medical help arrives[20]:

1. Ask if the athlete has an epinephrine auto-injector such as EpiPen or Auvi-Q to treat the allergic attack.

2. If they do and say they need to use an auto-injector, ask whether you should help inject the medication. This is usually done by pressing the auto-injector against their thigh and holding it in place for several seconds.

3. Loosen tight clothing and cover the person with a blanket.

4. Avoid giving them anything to drink.

5. Turn them on a side to prevent choking if they are vomiting or bleeding from the mouth.

6. Begin CPR if no signs of circulation. Signs of circulation include breathing, coughing, movement or a pulse.

Exertional Heat Illness[21]

Heat illnesses range in severity from minor illnesses such as heat rash and cramps to life-threatening disorders such as heatstroke where body temperatures may rise as high as 106°F. Exertional heatstroke (EHS) generally occurs in sport when athletes engage in strenuous physical activity for a prolonged period of time in a hot environment often accompanied with high levels of humidity. High humidity prevents the evaporation of sweat which normally cools the body. Contrary to earlier beliefs, children and youth do not appear to be less effective at tolerating heat than adults.[22]

A number of factors that determine how an athlete reacts to heat are controllable: The amount and intensity of physical exertion, the length of rest and recovery between same-day training sessions, access to water, and the type of clothing, uniforms or protective gear worn which promote or retard heat retention. Every coach should have established procedures to prevent heat disorders by modifying physical activities, minimizing restrictive clothing and providing adequate rehydration when levels of heat and humidity are high and place athletes at risk. With adequate safeguards, many of these heat-related disorders can be prevented (See Chapter 14). Nonetheless, when heat illnesses occur, appropriate treatment initiated quickly by knowledgeable coaches can prevent serious consequences.

TREATMENT

The primary treatment is to cool the athlete's body temperature as quickly as possible. Move the athlete immediately to a cool environment (e.g., to shade, an air conditioned facility indoor or an air conditioned car). Provide water or a sport drink containing carbohydrates and electrolytes such as potassium and sodium if the athlete is conscious. Allow regular access to such drinks during exercise with the frequency being increased as the heat and humidity increase (see chart and guidelines in Chapter 14, pages 360-361). Athletes who experience nausea and/or vomiting should be referred to medical assistance for rapid rehydration intravenously.

PREVENTION

Heat and humidity are the two most important environmental conditions that contribute to deaths from totally preventable exertional heat-induced illnesses. With increasing humidity, the temperatures at which athletes fall victim to heat exhaustion and heat stroke decrease. The intensity of activities lasting 30 minutes or more should be reduced when relative humidity and air temperature are high. Figure 14.10 in the next chapter indicates the combinations of heat and humidity that are potentially dangerous.

When environmental temperatures increase, such as in summertime, both the intensity and duration of exercise should be restrained initially and then gradually increased over a period of 10 to 14 days to permit the athletes to adapt (acclimatize) to the higher temperatures. Clothing should be a single layer of lightweight, absorbent material to permit sweat to evaporate and skin to be exposed to the air as much as possible. Sweat saturated clothing should be replaced with dry clothes as often as possible. Finally, rubberized sweat suits should never be used to promote weight loss.

Effective coaches teach their athletes the safety principles for training in high heat/humidity conditions. For example, teach the warning signs of heat illnesses such as nausea, dizziness, and flushed skin. Athletes should be aware of the risks of exercising in such conditions and the protective steps that they can take, such as acclimatization, proper clothing, and adequate fluid intake. You should provide for unlimited fluid/water intake during physical activity and instruct your athletes about proper hydration.

According to the American Academy of Pediatrics, if appropriate preparation, modifications and monitoring of children's physical activities are implemented, exertional heat illnesses can be prevented. The intensity of activities lasting 30 minutes or more should be reduced when relative humidity and air temperature are high and appropriate fluids should be made available to offset dehydration due to sweating. Encourage hydration **prior** to prolonged bouts of physical exercise and during exercise; 9- to 12-year-old athletes should drink about 100-250 mL of water every 20 minutes (about 3 to 8 ounces) and adolescents should drink 1.0 to 1.5 liters (about 34 to 50 ounces) per hour.[23]

Commotio Cordis*

Commotio Cordis is a "concussion of the heart" that is caused by a blow to the chest by a blunt object such as a baseball or hockey puck. It is extremely rare because the impact must occur precisely at the moment when the heart is "nearly resting" between beats. Despite its rare occurrence, it is mentioned here because most of the reported cases have occurred in sport with young athletes, mainly boys, struck in the left side of the chest over the heart by baseballs, lacrosse balls or hockey pucks.[24] Softer balls and/or chest protectors are recommended as preventative measures although the effectiveness of chest protectors is still in question.

TREATMENT

Commotio Cordis usually results in sudden cardiac death if resuscitation (usually with a defibrillator) is not immediately performed. Survival rates with resuscitation have risen to approximately 35% presumably because of increased public awareness, the increased availability of defibrillators and earlier calls to 911 and more timely initiation of CPR and defibrillation procedures.[25]

Lightning Strikes

Approximately one third of all lightning related incidents occur during outdoor recreational and sporting events;[26] but, contrary to most beliefs, only one of ten lightning strikes results in a fatality although many victims suffer permanent disabilities. Nonetheless, more people are killed by lightning strikes than by tornadoes or hurricanes. (Figure 13.6) This risk is typically underestimated because lightning usually claims only one or two victims at a time and rarely causes mass destruction of property. To protect your athletes, you should realize that:

- All thunderstorms produce lightning
- Strikes may occur up to 10 miles from rainfall

---

*Commotio Cordis is a "concussion of the heart" that is caused by a blow to the chest by a blunt object such as a baseball or hockey puck.

FIGURE 13.6 Where there is thunder, there are lightning strikes. Wait at least 30 minutes after the sound of thunder before resuming your practice or game.

- If you hear thunder, you're in danger
- Many victims are permanently disabled
- Wait 30 minutes after last thunder clap before resuming practice or competition
- See www.lightningsafety.noaa.gov for more information

PREVENTION

There are two common and reasonably accurate methods that volunteer coaches can use for estimating the risk of a lightning strike:[27]

1. Flash-to-Bang Method
   a. An observer begins counting when a lightning flash is heard.
   b. Counting is stopped when the associated bang (thunder) is heard.
   c. Divide this count by 5 to determine the distance to the lightning flash (in miles). For example, a flash-to-bang count of 30 seconds equates to a distance of 6 miles.

2. The "30-30" Rule

   a. Easy to remember and applies to the warning time before the storm and the time that should be waited before resumption of activities.

   b. If the time delay between seeing the flash (lightning) and hearing the bang (thunder) is less than 30 seconds, all individuals should be in or seeking a safer location

TREATMENT

The most immediate concerns following a lightning strike are cardiac arrest and/or cessation of breathing. Brain damage can occur and has long lasting consequences if resuscitation is not initiated immediately. Secondary injuries can occur from a fall following the strike. The following procedures, while they cannot prevent or undo any of the direct injuries sustained by the lightning strike itself, can reduce or avoid further injuries following the strike. Prompt treatment can dramatically increase the likelihood of full recovery regardless of the initial severity of the symptoms.

1. Assess the scene for the likelihood of further lightning strikes, an almost certain risk in an ongoing thunderstorm. Contrary to popular belief, lightning can strike twice.

2. Initiate the Emergency Action Plan (EAP) for obtaining qualified medical assistance.

3. Move the injured athlete to a safer place when necessary, especially away from trees.

4. If there is no pulse and/or the athlete is not breathing, initiate CPR and use an Automated External Defibrillator (AED) unit even if the athlete appears to be dead.

5. Once a pulse and breathing have been reestablished, evaluate and treat for:

   a. Hypothermia and shock

   b. Fractures

   c. Burns

YOUR TURN
Your Knowledge of Lightning Safety Test[28]

TRUE OR FALSE?

1. If caught outside during a thunderstorm, crouching down reduces the risk of being struck..

2. Lightning never strikes the same place twice..

3. If it's not raining or there aren't clouds overhead, you're safe from lightning.

4. Rubber tires on a car protect you from lightning by insulating you from the ground.

5. A lightning victim is electrified. If you touch them, you'll be electrocuted.

6. If outside in a thunderstorm, you should seek shelter under a tree to stay dry.

7. Structures with metal, or metal on the body (jewelry, cell phones, Mp3 players, watches, etc), attract lightning.

8. If trapped outside and lightning is about to strike, I should lie flat on the ground.

(See end of this chapter for the answers.)

Common Overuse Injuries in Youth Sport: Recognition and Prevention

The following information focuses on common overuse injuries that are often preventable through the coach's actions or by modifying the young athletes training regimen. ***It is not intended to replace a diagnosis or trained medical professional; nor is it meant to train coaches to implement medical treatment without qualified medical advice.*** Many of the injuries described below are preventable, if the coach 1) is aware of the causes of such injuries; 2) learns to recognize the early warning signs of injury; and 3) understands that younger athletes are at greater risk for overuse injuries than their older, more physically developed counterparts.

Within the last decade, there has been a significant increase in the incidence of overuse injuries in young athletes, such as stress fractures, tendinitis, chondromalacia, and Osgood-Schlatter disease. Overuse injuries are estimated to represent approximately 50% of all pediatric sport-related injuries and more than half of these injuries are believed to be preventable by effective coaching strategies.[29]

Overuse injuries are not "accidental." They result from continued training in the face of clear warning signs and/or the too rapid escalation of conditioning intensity, duration and repetitions. Coaches who are aware of these risks and are knowledgeable of the early warning signs of overtraining, can moderate the intensity of training to reduce or eliminate overuse injuries in their young athletes.

Although a significant number of sport injuries result from collisions or falling, children's smaller sizes and weaker strength typically makes them **less prone** to such injuries than older, bigger and stronger athletes. However, certain growth factors render children more susceptible to overuse injuries. For example:

1. Rapid growth increases tension on tendons ligaments and muscles.

2. Bones are still soft and growing and are particularly vulnerable in the growth plates situated at the end of each bone.

3. Because of the softness of immature bones, tendons or ligaments can be more easily torn from the surface of the bone at the point of insertion when strong forces are applied, such as lifting heavy weights.

4. Unequal growth is quite common with one leg being slightly longer than the other creating unequal torque when performing sport skills.

Here are some of the more common overuse injuries for which coaches can have a strong preventive influence:

TENDINITIS

Tendinitis is an inflammation or minor tear of the tendon or its sheath (the connective tissue surrounding the tendon). The tendon is the tough, dense banner of connective tissue connecting muscle to bone. The inflammation is caused by repetitive activities such as running and jumping, throwing in baseball, serving in tennis and arm stroking in swimming. It is diagnosed when the athlete reports pain, a pain which typically increases during movement of the affected area. Often there is minor swelling accompanied by a reddening of the area and a feeling of a "hot spot." If a minor tear is involved, a lump may develop externally at the point of the tear. Shoulder tendinitis, Achilles tendinitis, patellar tendinitis (Jumper's Knee), Little League elbow and lateral epicondylitis (Tennis Elbow) are common examples of tendinitis.

Treatment

Acute tendinitis (meaning a case, which comes on a relatively suddenly) usually improves if the affected limbs and joints are given sufficient rest. Conservative treatments include ice massage immediately after exercise, and heat applications several days later. Both aspirin and heat treatment should not be initiated without the advice of a qualified medical professional. Many such professionals are reluctant to use injections or anti-inflammatory drugs such as cortisone with young athletes, especially recreational athletes. Once the acute stage of inflammation has passed, gentle heat and stretching activities before the activity, and the application of ice after the activity, usually allow the athletes to gradually resume the activity. Strength and flexibility exercises are also helpful after specific muscle groups suffering from tendinitis have been accurately identified. Some athletes use external wrappings to hold the tendons of the affected muscles more firmly to the bone to provide additional support.

Prevention

The best prevention for tendinitis is a graduated training program, which avoids increasing workloads too rapidly. Some sports limit the amount of participation for athletes (for example, baseball leagues typically limit the number of innings pitched or the total number of pitches per game a player is permitted to throw). Coaching the correct development of proper mechanics of throwing, running or swinging can also prevent such injuries.

APOPHYSITIS

Apophysitis[30] refers to a family of injuries that are essentially an irritation and inflammation of the points at which tendons are inserted in the bone, often small protrusions that are, in effect, growth plates. These painful overuse injuries occur almost exclusively in young athletes both because their developing bones have not completely ossified (hardened) and because of the repetitive stress applied to the area while playing vigorous sports. Common examples of apophysitis are: Sever's Disease (fragmentation of the large heel bone), Osgood-Schlatter Disease*(inflammation just below the knee), Little League Shoulder, Little

---

*Despite the names, neither Sever's Disease nor Osgood-Schlatter Disease are diseases; they are classified as overuse injuries.

League Elbow, Swimmer's Shoulder and Tennis Elbow to name only a few. Such injuries usually develop following a period of rapid growth in which the length of the bone exceeds the tendon's ability to lengthen. Thus, they are most common among adolescents. They manifest themselves differently in different sports and based upon differences in the physical attributes of the athlete. For example, athletes with very tight hip and thigh muscles are more prone to such injuries in the pelvis area which has numerous points of insertion for tendons. This type of injury almost always involves repetitive motions related to the specific sport. For example, Osgood-Schlatter occurs more often in sports where the stress is on the knee joint such as tumblers in gymnastics or runners in soccer and cross country. Often the name reflects a sport typical of – but not limited to - such injuries.

Treatment

Rest and restriction from the activities which are painful is the most common treatment. However, total elimination of all activity is unrealistic with active teens and preteens. Ice massage and over the counter analgesics are also helpful in relieving acute pain and swelling. Rehabilitation includes physical therapy using exercises specific to the repetitive movements which created the injury.

Prevention

Use sound training principles which carefully regulate the amount of activity young athletes are expected to perform. Once the athletes have matured, the likelihood of such injuries decreases rapidly.

BLISTERS

This injury results from the buildup of fluid between one or more layers of the skin at points where repeated friction occurs. Blisters can be extremely painful and lead to serious infections if not promptly and properly treated.

Treatment

Lance a small hole in the blister with a sterile needle at a point where the fluid can drain from the blister. Compress the outer layers of the skin to force complete drainage through the small hole. Do not remove the skin overlying the blister because the worn skin can protect the tender, underlying tissue and will eventually fall off after the underlying skin has hardened. The area must be washed, kept clean, and treated with an antiseptic to protect against possible infections. Pad the blister to protect the area during subsequent activity. If the blister is large, cut a piece of padded material in the shape of a donut and place around the blistered area before covering with a protective Band-Aid. This prevents direct contact with the raw skin by the Band-Aid while still providing a protective covering. Commercially available bunion pads are an excellent source of such padding.

Prevention

Because blisters are caused by repeated friction, a "hotspot" will occur prior to the formation of a blister. If the athlete is cautioned by the coach to be sensitive to such "hotspots" and to stop the activity when they are felt, blisters can be prevented. Do not return to the activity until the "hotspot" has cooled. This cooling can be accelerated by using ice or cool compresses. Additionally, those points subject to friction can be padded with tape, gloves, hand-grips, or other sports appropriate protective coverings.

SPONDYLOLYSIS

This term refers to a fracture of the vertebrae resulting from continual stress from landings such as dismounts in gymnastics or rebounding in basketball. Tiny cracks develop in the vertebrae and may develop into full-fledged fractures if the source of the stress is not controlled. Often the transverse processes of the vertebrae (the little pieces of bone which extend from the sides of the spine) deteriorate due to repeated impacts. This disorder often occurs in sports where athletes continually land on hard surfaces, especially when the spine is arched such as front hand-springs in gymnastics.

Treatment

Spondylolysis should always be treated by a medical professional. Appropriate treatment includes rest and conditioning to strengthen the muscles supporting the back and spinal alignment. Return to play for the athlete should be by medical clearance.

Prevention

Limit the activities that place stress on the vertebrae and adequately pad landing surfaces where possible, such as during training sessions. Pay careful attention to teaching proper sport-specific techniques which minimize stresses to the back. For example, teach shock-absorbing techniques such as learning to bend the knees on landing and falling correctly (See the illustrations in Chapter 14 on falling techniques).

SPONDYLOLISTHESIS

This injury results from a forward slippage of one or more of the individual vertebrae in the spinal column. It is caused by repeated, excessive bending of the spine. It occurs frequently in gymnasts who land on floor mats with their backs arched and in football players, especially interior linemen as their spine is bent backward during contact with opposing linemen.

Treatment

Treatment depends upon the extent of the slippage and symptoms. This disorder should always be treated by a medical professional. Reduce the stress on the back by either limiting the activity or providing protective braces or back supports via strapping or taping the affected area. Taping is a medical treatment and should only be carried out by a qualified medical professional such as an athletic trainer.

Prevention

A conditioning program which helps strengthen the back muscles can provide additional support for the spine and vertebral alignment. Also, developing increased flexibility and the use of proper mechanics when executing the sports skills can lessen the stress on the lower back.

CHONDROMALACIA

Chondromalacia patella is a general term referring to a variety of problems that create nonspecific pain in the knee joint area. Often it is the softening, irritation and/or wearing away of the cartilage on the underside of the patella (the kneecap) as a result of continual wear and tear. As the knee straightens and flexes, the kneecap tracks along grooves between the bones above and below the joint. When the tracking action fails to follow these grooves precisely, irritation often develops. The label chondromalacia has often been used as a diagnosis by exclusion, meaning that when other specific problems have been ruled out, the painful problem is referred to as chondromalacia. It has been described informally as the "headache of the knee." (Figure 13.7)

FIGURE 13.7
Chondromalacia patella is a quite painful overuse injury where the underside of the kneecap (patella) wears away due to continual wear and tear.

Treatment

Rest when pain is present. Most athletes respond well to a gradual conditioning program that emphasizes flexibility and strengthening of the muscles which flex and extend the hips, the quadriceps and the hamstrings. Short-arc knee extensions (the last 20 degrees of the range of motion) using light weights and a high number of repetitions (20 to 40 reps) are often prescribed by a physician. Often the alignment of the kneecap relative to the other structures of the knee is analyzed. If the knee is misaligned, a correction is attempted using various orthotics such as braces built into the athlete's shoes.

Prevention

Properly fitted shoes or shoes with orthotics recommended by medical professionals to correct the misalignment can minimize the likelihood of developing chondromalacia. Appropriate training schedules involving the gradual build-up of activity and the avoidance of excessive overuse may help.

"SHIN SPLINTS"

A general term referring to pain caused by inflammation of muscles, tendons, bone, and other tissue that surrounds the shin bone between the ankle and knee resulting from repetitive trauma. The injury commonly happens with runners, dancers, and aerobic exercisers where their legs repetitively strike the ground. The pain is usually sharp and throbbing and is perceived as a band of discomfort as opposed to a particular point. The pain may arise from one or more of three categories. First, it may be of bony origin due to an irritation or stress fracture to the bones of the lower limb. Second, it may be of vascular origin such as an interruption of blood flow in the blood vessels of the lower limb due to increased pressure resulting from swelling and inflammation. Third, it may arise from an irritation of the soft tissues such as the muscles or fascia (the smooth, protective covering around muscles and bone). This latter category is what is most typical in young athletes. The interosseous membrane which connects the two long bones of the lower leg becomes inflamed. This membrane has many blood vessels and serves as an attachment for many muscles of the lower leg. The repeated jarring of the leg as a result of running and jumping, particularly on hard surfaces, inflames this membrane creating substantial pain. The cause of shin splints may include excessive training during the early phases of an exercise program, training in poorly fitted shoes, faulty posture, fallen arches, muscle fatigue, weak or inflexible muscles, excessive running on hard surfaces and misalignment syndromes.

Treatment

The usual treatment is ice, compression and rest. Selection of well-fitted, appropriate footwear with excellent shock absorbing qualities can also help. Surgery is rarely necessary Providing additional arch support by taping and/or the insertion of orthotics into the athlete's shoes may help depending upon the medically diagnosed cause of the shin splints. Mild stretching and strength development using manually applied resistance (using rubber surgical tubing or commercially available stretching resistance bands) during active dorsiflexion (upward flexion of the ankle by pointing the toes toward the shin) helps rehabilitate the shin splint problem.

Prevention

Improved conditioning through a gradual build-up of the training intensity is the most effective preventative measure. A mild strength and flexibility program which strengthens the ankle dorsiflexors is helpful. Dorsiflexors are the muscles which allow the foot to flex so that the toes are pointing towards the shins. Shoes with good shock-absorbing qualities and that avoid excessive pronation (a turning out of the feet away from the midline) are highly recommended. Avoid running on hard surfaces whenever possible.

STRESS FRACTURES

Such fractures occur when the bone is subjected to repeated stresses to the extent that the normal process of bone repair and growth is not able to keep pace with the breakdown of bone cells. A stress fracture may become a complete fracture but it differs from an acute fracture in that it is repetitive accumulations of stresses over time rather than a single stress. A stress fracture is typically characterized by pain along the affected bone with a particularly sensitive sore sport at the point of the actual stress fracture. This point of tenderness often results in limping or subtle changes in gait and an over-reliance on the opposite leg. Stress fractures can occur in virtually any bone but are most common in the weight-bearing bones of the lower legs and feet. Stress fractures of the lower arm, wrist and hand frequently occur in athletes who regularly need to support their body weight on their arms (gymnasts and wrestlers).

Treatment

Rehabilitation can be assisted by rest, ice massage and exercise that increase the muscular strength, endurance and flexibility in the ankle's dorsi- and plantar flexors. Occasionally, a cast is prescribed to protect the injured area from further stress and to immobilize the area until sufficient healing has occurred. Referral to a physician is essential if a stress fracture is suspected. Stress fractures may be difficult to diagnose with a traditional X-ray or even a series of X-rays. Sometimes an MRI bone scan is required.

Prevention

A moderate or gradual build-up of the intensity and duration of the training regimen minimizes the likelihood of stress fractures.

Summary As should be abundantly clear from this brief overview, the most common recommendations for prevention and treatment of overuse injuries involve rest, ice and a sensible, well-planned, graduated conditioning program. Both coaches and athletes need to be sensitive to the symptoms of pain and should avoid increasing the training workload so quickly that the body is unable to adapt. While additional therapies and preventative methods are often appropriate (e.g., analgesics medication to control pain and swelling as provided by the athlete's parents), the key is to prevent overuse injuries, a strategy that is well within the coach's ability to control through the use of appropriate conditioning programs.

YOUR TURN
Your Knowledge of Sports Injuries Test

TRUE OR FALSE?

1. If the bleeding from a cut or abrasion bleeds through the bandage, you should remove the bandage and replace it with a fresh bandage

2. The latest guidelines from the Berlin Consensus Statement on Concussions states that baseline testing should be mandatory for all youth sports programs

3. Because of the brain's ability to adapt quickly, once a concussion has occurred, a youth sport athlete is less likely to suffer from a second concussion.

4. Apophysitis, Chondromalacia, "Shin Splints" and Tendinitis are accidental injuries that are difficult to prevent because of their sudden, unexpected onset.

(See last page of this chapter for the answers.)

ANSWERS TO KNOWLEDGE OF LIGHTNING SAFETY TEST

1. **False:** Crouching doesn't make you any safer. Run to a substantial building or hard topped vehicle. If you are too far to run to one of these options, you have no good alternative. You are NOT safe anywhere outdoors.

2. **False:** Lightning often strikes the same place repeatedly, especially if it's a tall, pointy, isolated object. The Empire State Building is hit an average of 23 times a year

3. **False:** Lightning often strikes more than three miles from the center of the thunderstorm, far outside the rain or thunderstorm cloud. "Bolts from the blue" can strike 10-15 miles from the thunderstorm.

4. **False:** Most cars are safe from lightning, but it is the metal roof and metal sides that protect you, NOT the rubber tires. Remember, convertibles, motorcycles, bicycles, open-shelled

outdoor recreational vehicles and cars with fiberglass shells offer no protection from lightning. When lightning strikes a vehicle, it goes through the metal frame into the ground. Don't lean on doors during a thunderstorm.

5. **False:** The human body does not store electricity. It is perfectly safe to touch a lightning victim to give them first aid. Do not be afraid to give CPR!

6. **False:** Being underneath a tree is the second leading cause of lightning casualties. Better to get wet than fried!

7. **False:** Height, pointy shape, and isolation are the dominant factors controlling where a lightning bolt will strike. The presence of metal makes absolutely no difference on where lightning strikes. While metal does not attract lightning, it does conduct it so stay away from metal fences, railing, bleachers, etc.

8. **False:** Lying flat increases your chance of being affected by potentially deadly ground current. If you are caught outside in a thunderstorm, keep moving toward a safe shelter.

ANSWERS TO KNOWLEDGE OF SPORTS INJURIES TEST

1. **False:** If the bleeding soaks through the gauze, simply add additional layers of gauze. NEVER remove the initial layers because doing so disrupts the initial clotting and can restart the bleeding.

2. **False:** Because of the difficulties of validating the results, especially with group testing, the Berlin Consensus Statement of 2016 concluded that "Baseline testing may be useful, but it is not necessary for interpreting post injury scores." Baseline testing, while helpful and an additional educational opportunity, was not required as mandatory.

3. **False:** Athletes who continue to play before complete recovery from an initial concussion are also at high risk for a phenomenon known as **second impact syndrome (SIS). SIS** occurs when a second concussion occurs before the athlete has fully recovered from the first concussion. That risk is especially high during the period of a week to 10 days following the first concussion.

4. **False:** These are all "overuse" injuries caused primarily by repetitious training and can be prevented by good coaching strategies that condition athletes appropriately and limit the amount and intensity of repetitious movements.

CHAPTER REFERENCES

1. Miller, M. G. & Berry, D. C. (2011). *Emergency Response Management for Athletic Trainers.* Lippincott, Williams & Wilkins: Philadelphia, PA.

2. Giza, C. C. & Hovda, D. A. (2001). The neurometabolic cascade of concussion. *Journal of Athletic Training. 36,* 228-235.

3. Echemendia, R. J. (2012). Cerebral concussion in sport: An overview. *Journal of Clinical Sport Psychology. 6,* 207-230.

4. *A Parent's Guide to Concussion,* Brain Injury Alliance of New Jersey, www.bianj.org, 2017.

5. Zhang, A. L., Sing, D. C., Rugg, C. M., Feeley, B. T. & Senter, C. (2016). The rise of concussions in the adolescent population, *Orthopaedic Journal of Sports Medicine, 4 (8),* doi: 10.1177/2325967116662458.

6. Moser, R. S. (2012). *Ahead of the Game: The Parents' Guide to Youth Sports Concussion.* Dartmouth College Press: Hanover, NH.

7. *A Parent's Guide to Concussion,* Brain Injury Alliance of New Jersey, www.bianj.org, 2017.

8. McCrory, P., Meeuwisse, W., Dvorak, J., et al., Consensus statement on concussion in sport – the 5th international conference on concussion in sport, Berlin, Oct. 2016. *British Journal of Sports Medicine, 51,* (p. 842).

9. Adapted from 3 sources:
   a. www.cdc.gov/ConcussionInYouthSports;
   b. www.cdc.gov/Facts about Concussion and Brain Injury, Where to Get Help;
   c. Echemendia, R. J. (2012). Cerebral concussion in sport: An overview. *Journal of Clinical Sport Psychology. 6,* 207-230.

10. McCrory, P., Meeuwisse, W., Dvorak, J., et al., Consensus statement on concussion in sport – the 5th international conference on concussion in sport, Berlin, Oct. 2016. *British Journal of Sports Medicine, 51,* (p. 840).

11. McCrory, P., Meeuwisse, W., Dvorak, J., et al., Consensus statement on concussion in sport – the 5th international conference on concussion in sport, Berlin, Oct. 2016. *British Journal of Sports Medicine, 51,* (p. 841).

12. The four most recognized baseline tests for assessing pre-concussion performance are:
    1. Automated Neuropsychological Assessment Metrics (ANAM)
    2. Axon Sports Computerized Cognitive Assessment Tool (CogSport)

3. Headminder Concussion Resolution Index

4. Immediate Post-Concussion Assessment and Cognitive Test (ImPACT)

13. Moser, R. S. (2012). *Ahead of the Game: The Parents' Guide to Youth Sports Concussion*. Dartmouth College Press: Hanover, NH.

14. Adapted from 3 Sources:

   a. New Jersey State Interscholastic Athletic Association. (2012). Sports-Related Concussion and Head Injury Fact Sheet. http://www.njsiaa.org/NJSIAA/11ConcussionPolicyNJSIAA.pdf.

   b. Wisconsin Interscholastic Athletic Association. (2011). http://www.wiaawi.org/Health/Concussions.aspx

   c. Colorado Department of Education, Concussion Management Guidelines. (2012). http://www.cde.state.co.us/HealthAndWellness/BrainInjury.htm

15. http://www.momsteam.com/print/3015.

16. Moser, R. S. (2012). *Ahead of the Game: The Parents' Guide to Youth Sports Concussion*. Dartmouth College Press: Hanover, NH, p 163.

17. Siegel J. D., Rhinehart, E, Jackson, M & Chiarello, L, and the Healthcare Infection Control Practices Advisory Committee, (2007). Guideline for Isolation Precautions: Preventing Transmission of Infectious Agents in Healthcare Settings. http://www.cdc.gov/ncidod/dhqp/pdf/isolation2007.pdf.

18. Highlights of the 2010 AHA Guidelines for CPR and EC. https://www.heart.org/idc/groups/heart-public/@wcm/@ecc/documents/downloadable/ucm_317350.pdf.

19. Maquirriain, J., & Merello, M. (2007). The athlete with muscle cramps: clinical approach. *Journal of American Academy of Orthopedic Surgery*. 15 (7), 425-431.

20. http://www.mayoclinic.org/first-aid/first-aid-insect-bites/basics/art-20056593.

21. http://www.nata.org/sites/default/files/inter-association-task-force-exertional-heat-illness.pdf.

22. American Academy of Pediatrics. Policy Statement: Climatic Heat Stress and the Exercising Child and Adolescent. *Pediatrics*. (2011). 128(3), e741–e747. Reaffirmed February, 2015.

23. American Academy of Pediatrics. Policy Statement: Climatic Heat Stress and the Exercising Child and Adolescent. *Pediatrics*. (2011). 128(3), e741–e747. Reaffirmed February, 2015.

24. Link, M.S. (2012). Commotio Cordis: Ventricular fibrillation triggered by chest-impact-induced abnormalities in repolarization. *Circulation: Arrhythmia and Electrophysiology, 5*, 425-432

25. Maron, B. J., & Estes, III, N. A. (2010). Medical progress: Commotio Cordis. *New England Journal of Medicine, 362,* 917-927.

26. Zimmermann, C., Cooper, M. A., Holle, R. L. (2002). Lightning safety guidelines. *Annuals of Emergency Medicine, 39 (6),* 660-665.

27. Miller, M. G. & Berry, D. C. (2011). *Emergency Response Management for Athletic Trainers.* Lippincott, Williams & Wilkins: Philadelphia, PA. p. 429

28. http://www.lightningsafety.noaa.gov/myths.shtml, National Oceanic and Atmospheric Administration, 2018.

29. McLeod, T. C. V., Decoster, L. C., Loud, K. J., Micheli, L. J., Parker, J. T. Sandrey, M. A., & White, C. (2011). National Athletic Trainers' Association Position Statement: Prevention of Pediatric Overuse Injuries. *Journal of Athletic Training,* 46 (2), 206-220, doi. org/10.4085/1062-6050-46.2.206

30. Mosby's Medical Dictionary, (9th ed.), 2009, Elsevier.

14

Safety and Risk Management

CHAPTER OUTLINE

- Understanding Risk Management and Negligence
  SPOTLIGHT ON YOUTH SPORTS: Civil Immunity
- The Coach's Responsibility
- Preventing Injuries
  SPOTLIGHT ON YOUTH SPORTS: Legal Details
  FROM CHALKBOARD TO PLAYING FIELD: Examples of Sport-Specific Progression Analyses

  FROM CHALKBOARD TO PLAYING FIELD: Progressions for Falling Safely
- Emergency Action Plan (EAP)
- Insurance for Athletes and for the Program
  YOUR TURN: Three Basic Questions

Volunteer to coach? "Volunteer to coach? O.K., I said 'Yes' but now what? I played a little sport myself but never coached before. Would love to help but how? How old did you say these little kids are? Can I do it? What exactly am I supposed to do? What if I make a mistake? Could I be sued?"

These thoughts and others like them course through the minds of volunteers and potential volunteers throughout the United States every year. This chapter deals with the legal issues of volunteerism and the protections that volunteers have been granted by state legislatures in an effort to protect one of our nation's greatest resources – volunteers. Without volunteer coaches, many opportunities and community services would be unavailable or too expensive for deserving youngsters throughout our nation.

This is a long chapter, and some parts have a bit of legal terminology, but stick with it, and you will find the last section reassuring.

Risk management focuses on protecting your athletes and yourself from harm while simultaneously protecting you, as the coach, and your organization from lawsuits. Preventing harm to your athletes while encouraging them to extend themselves physically while training and competing is not as hard as it might sound. Much of prevention consists of proactive steps, such as ensuring safe facilities, good communication, and planning effective lessons. Your goal, as the coach, is to incorporate both the rules and the attitudes of safety so they are automatic and then to practice these principles of safety without exception.

Understanding Risk Management and Negligence

Risk management refers to a systematic program to eliminate and/or minimize the physical, psychological, and financial risks of participating in an activity offered by an individual or organization. The standard by which the effectiveness of such a program is judged is known as the **standard of care.** This evolving standard is determined by comparing the actions and precautions taken by other similar organizations that are deemed to have acted in a reasonable, prudent manner to protect participants. This standard is generally higher for more experienced and sophisticated individuals and programs. For example, a trained physician would be held to a higher standard of care than a volunteer coach, who in turn might be held to a higher standard than an untrained "Good Samaritan" who offered help in an emergency. When coaches fail to meet an appropriate standard of care, they can be judged as negligent and held responsible for damages. Civil immunity legislation protects coaches despite such judgments.

SPOTLIGHT ON YOUTH SPORTS

Civil Immunity

During the 1980s, state legislatures throughout the United States responded to the legal liability crisis and soaring liability insurance costs by enacting civil immunity laws – laws that protect individuals and agencies from lawsuits. (Figure 14.1.) These laws were often very narrow, targeting specific agencies and activities commonly seen as providing services necessary for the benefit of the community, agencies that used the services of volunteer coaches, general community volunteers, emergency care providers, and people volunteering for policy-making groups such as boards of directors.

FIGURE 14.1 Could I be sued? Yes! But many states have enacted legislation specifically designed to protect volunteer coaches from lawsuits.

On May 12, 1986, New Jersey became the first state in the nation to enact civil immunity legislation[1] protecting volunteer athletic coaches, managers and officials. This legislation, commonly referred to as the "Little League Law," provides partial – but significant – protection from lawsuits to coaches who have attended a "safety orientation and training skills program."

Since that initial passage of civil immunity legislation, approximately 30 states have passed similar legislation. The legislation falls into four basic categories

- Legislation that protects volunteers in general – both sport and non-sport volunteers (e.g., Maryland).

- Legislation that specifically protects volunteer youth sport coaches. Such legislation sometimes provides blanket protection, i.e., protection for all volunteer coaches (e.g., Pennsylvania, Delaware). Sometimes such legislation requires action on the part of the volunteer coach to earn the liability protection; i.e., coaches must first take some type of training (e.g., New Jersey, New Hampshire) or maintain a minimum level of liability insurance (e.g., Maryland).

- Legislation that protects members of policy-making groups such as boards of directors, rules-making committees, etc. (e.g., New Jersey).

- Legislation that protects medical personnel who render medical attention in a volunteer capacity; e.g., physicians who volunteer at games and competitions or rescue squad workers who donate their time at tournaments (e.g., Indiana).

Table 14.1 lists states based upon the level of civil immunity protection provided to volunteers, including but not limited to youth sports coaches.[2] A more detailed discussion of the civil immunity protection provided by individual states is available on the website of the Rutgers University Youth Sports Research Council at http://youthsport.rutgers.edu.

The Youth Sports Research Council of Rutgers University and the New Jersey Recreation and Park Association have combined efforts to jointly provide **The Rutgers SAFETY**tm **Clinic.**[*] These three-

---

[*]SAFETY is an acronym standing for "Sports Awareness for Educating Today's Youth" and is a registered trademark of Rutgers University.

hour clinics – which provide coaches with civil immunity protection in New Jersey only – are taught by instructors trained in **Clinician's Workshops,** which provide those instructors with the information and materials necessary for teaching and implementing **The Rutgers SAFETY**[tm] **Clinic.** The curriculum for both the **SAFETY**[tm] **Clinic** and the **Clinician's Workshops** is based upon the "Minimum Standards for Volunteer Coaches' Safety Orientation and Training Skills Programs"[3] developed by the New Jersey Governor's Council for Physical Fitness and Sport in 1991.

TABLE 14.1 State by State Civil Immunity Protection*

States with No Significant Immunity	States with Simple Negligence Protection	States with Enhanced Negligence Protections
Alaska	Arizona (1993)	Alabama (W, 1991)
California	Arkansas (1987)	Colorado (W, 1992)
Connecticut	Delaware (1989)	District of Columbia (W, 1993)
Florida	Hawaii (1997)	Georgia (W, 1987)
Illinois	Maine (1987)	Idaho (W, 1987)
Indiana	Maryland (1987)	Iowa (I, 1987)
Kentucky	Mississippi (1988)	Kansas (W, 1987)
Louisiana	North Carolina (1987)	Minnesota (R, 1989)
Massachusetts	North Dakota (1987)	Montana (W, 1987)
Michigan	New Hampshire (1988)	Nevada (W, 1987)
Missouri	New Jersey (1986)**	Rhode Island (W, 1984)
Nebraska	Oklahoma (1995)	Texas (R, 1987)
New Mexico	Pennsylvania (1986)**	Utah (W, 1990)
New York	South Carolina (1984)	Wisconsin (W, 1987)
Ohio	South Dakota (1987)	
Oregon	Washington (2001)	
Tennessee	Wyoming (1992)	
Vermont		
Virginia		
West Virginia		

Note: R = shields up to reckless (i.e., gross negligence); W = shields up to willful/ wanton (i.e., gross negligence and recklessness; I = shields up to intentional (i.e., gross negligence, recklessness and willful/wanton)

*Modified from Horwitz & Mead (2009) **Changed from original table

FIGURE 14.2
The Elements of Negligence: A Duty; a Breach (by Omission or Commission); Proximate Cause (Must be Foreseeable); and Damages.

NEGLIGENCE

Negligence occurs when four conditions exist *simultaneously* (Figure 14.2). First, a coach or a sports organization must have a **duty** — i.e., a formal obligation — to provide for the safety and welfare of the injured participant. For example, both a paid professional coach and a volunteer coach have a responsibility to provide adequate first aid and emergency care for any athlete on their team who might sustain an injury. On the other hand, a spectator -- even a spectator trained in first aid and CPR — is not likely to be held responsible for handling emergencies observed on the sports field.

Second, the coach or organization must commit a **breach** by either an act of commission or an act of omission. A commission is an act likely to cause harm, such as teaching a young football player to tackle opponents by "spearing" (using the head as a battering ram). An omission is failing to do something to protect the athlete that any reasonably prudent coach would be expected to do, such as failing to warn the young football players not to use their heads as the first point of contact while tackling. For a breach to occur, the risk and/or the injury must be **foreseeable.** That is, coaches, in the normal function of their duties, must be judged to reasonably have been able to predict or foresee the hazard that caused the injury. For example, no one can foresee that a bolt of lightning from a clear blue sky could strike down a player. On the other hand, a bolt of lightning is a very foreseeable risk when the clouds are dark, thunder is heard, or lightning strikes have just been seen in the vicinity of the field.

Third, the actions or inactions of the coach or organization must be shown to have caused or further aggravated the injury or loss in question – a condition known as **proximate cause.** For example, a coach who issues instructions to run full speed to a wall, touch the wall and then run back to the starting position might well be judged to have issued instructions that "caused" an injury should the athlete not slow up sufficiently and trip, falling into the wall sustaining an injury.

Finally, the victim must have experienced an actual loss or injury. That is, physical, psychological, or financial **damage** must have occurred.

LEVELS OF NEGLIGENCE

Courts distinguish between different levels of negligence and, as a result, laws providing liability protection vary substantially from state to state in the level of civil immunity protections provided (see Table 14.1). State laws typically specify the lowest level of liability for which coaches are protected (e.g., simple negligence) while holding them responsible for all more serious levels of negligence (e.g., gross negligence, wanton & willful negligence and intentional negligence).

Simple Negligence

Simple negligence occurs when the coach has a duty, makes a mistake of omission or commission that contributed to a loss that was foreseeable by a reasonably prudent person. An example might be failing to inspect the playing field for obstacles or holes prior to practices and games or an injury resulting from knowingly permitting an athlete to practice or compete without wearing required safety equipment such as a catcher's face mask in baseball or shin guards in soccer.

Gross Negligence

Gross negligence is a much more serious offense and shows an absence of even a slight amount of diligence or care described often as indifference. An example might be an injury resulting from deliberately punishing with excessive physical drills a player who misbehaved or ignoring a defect in equipment that you were told was defective and that a reasonable person could clearly foresee that failure to correct the defect could lead to serious injury.

Wanton, Willful and Reckless Negligence

Wanton, willful and reckless conduct involves an individual who knowingly disregards an unreasonable degree of risk. An example might be an injury resulting from coaching under the influence of alcohol or drugs.

Intentional Negligence

Intentional negligence involves a purposeful action such as intentionally and roughly grabbing player by the face mask resulting in serious injury or an injury resulting from a coach instructing a player to "take out" an opponent harming either or both athletes.

The Coach's Responsibilities

Even as a volunteer, you assumed certain responsibilities when you stepped forward to coach (or at least failed to step backward fast enough!). Your responsibilities to provide a safe sport experience for your young athletes involve the following (Figure 14.3):

- Preventing Injuries
  1. Communicating the Risks Involved
  2. Adequate Supervision for Safe Participation
  3. Organized and Planned Lessons for Safe Participation
  4. Appropriate Selection and Safe Conduct of the Sports Activity
  5. Proper Instruction in Sport Skills and in Required Safety Behaviors
  6. Provision of Safe Facilities, Equipment, and Environment
- An Emergency Action Plan (EAP)
  1. Actions Prior to the Emergency
  2. Responding Directly to the Emergency
  3. Actions When Professional Assistance Arrives
  4. Follow-up Procedures
- Insurance for the Athletes and the Program
  1. Medical Insurance
  2. Liability Insurance

In the remainder of this chapter, each of these duties will be examined in detail and guidelines for adequately carrying out those duties will be discussed.

Preventing Injuries

The best way to deal with injuries is to prevent them. The coach can do much to protect athletes, with two general strategies: Accident Prevention

FIGURE 14.3
Your duties as a volunteer coach? To ensure a safe environment. To ensure supervision at all times. To select and conduct appropriate activities.

and Injury Prevention. **Preventing accidents** includes strategies such as teaching athletes safety rules and separating drill stations by sufficient distances to prevent accidental contact. **Preventing injury** includes strategies such as teaching athletes falling techniques so that, if they should fall (i.e., experience an accident), they can do so safely. Since certain accidents occur predictably, athletes must be protected from such predictable risks.

"It was just an accident!" The term *accident* often carries the connotation that the injury could not have been prevented. Clearly, some accidents are the result of multiple factors occurring simultaneously, the outcome of which could not have been predicted. However, many accidents are preventable if the coach and athlete are aware of predictable accident patterns.

COMMUNICATING THE RISKS INVOLVED

Your league has the responsibility of properly informing coaching assistants, parent/guardians, and athletes of the inherent risks associated with your sport so that all concerned have the necessary information to make informed decisions about choosing to participate. As part of the process of informing those involved about the risks, your sports organization should require that the parents and guardians have completed and signed all participation agreements, medical histories, medical releases, and medical emergency authorization forms (See Appendices 14.2 and 14.3 for specific examples of such documents).

Informed consent means that they have been provided with the necessary information in a language that they can understand and that they appreciate both the risks and the consequences of taking those risks. Children under the age of consent or adults with cognitive disabilities may not be capable of informed consent. In such cases, the information must be provided to the parents or legal guardians so that they can make such informed decisions.

Sample Safety Rules. An essential part of communication is posting adequate warnings for participation such as safety rules. You must also educate and assess your athletes' and their parents' understanding of these rules. Effective rules are worded in a language that is appropriate for the age and maturity of your athletes and, as a result, are more likely to be understood.

> **Example 1 (for parents):** Practices begin at __ o'clock. Coaches will not be available until __ minutes prior to the start of practice. Please do not drop off athletes or leave them unattended until a coach is present. All athletes must be picked up within ten minutes following the conclusion of each practice or they will be _____ (have an acceptable, previously agreed upon procedure for dealing with safety supervision of athletes not picked up in time).

> **Example 2 (for athletes):** Clothing and Personal Apparel Checklist
> 1. Remove all jewelry, including rings, necklaces and earrings before participating.
> 2. Hair should be groomed or tied back so that it does not block vision or hamper your ability to perform the sport skills.
> 3. Wear appropriate footwear.
> 4. Never have anything in your mouth (food, gum, etc.) while participating except for an appropriately sized safety mouth guard.
> 5. Wear nonrestrictive clothing that allows you to move freely but that is not baggy nor so loose that it might interfere with the safe performance of your sport skills.
> 6. Be certain your clothing is free of protruding, hard objects such as belts, buttons, rivets or zippers.
> 7. If you need eye glasses to participate, wear safety eyeglasses.

SPOTLIGHT ON YOUTH SPORTS
Legal Details

The concept of **assumption of risk** contends that a person who chooses to participate in an activity must assume the inherent risk of accident or injury associated with that activity. However, courts have regularly ruled that this concept has no validity as a separate defense. Legally, no one assumes a risk of which they are not aware. Thus, coaches (and youth sport administrators) are responsible for warning young athletes – and their parents – of the risks involved in ways that are clearly understood by participants. If a person is aware and his/her actions were partially responsible for the injury, there may be grounds in some states for a claim of **comparative fault**, a concept that permits the reduction of the amount of damages that a plaintiff can recover in a law suit based upon the extent to which the plaintiff's own behavior caused the injury.

Permission slips state that the child has parental approval to participate in a specific, designated activity. Parents who send their children to a recreational sports program have certain expectations regarding the type of activities in which their children will participate. Whenever coaches plan activities which are clearly beyond the reasonable limits of these parental expectations or involves transportation away from the program site, they would be wise to obtain a permission slip.

Waivers are signed contracts that attempt to free the coach or the sport organization from liability stemming from an accident or injury associated with the sports program. The protection provided by waivers is limited since the courts traditionally have favored the position that no supervisor or organization can be protected by contract from the consequences of their negligent actions. Further, parents cannot legally waive the rights of their children. Waivers do have value in the sense that they can provide clear evidence that the participants and/or their parents were provided with a clear warning about the nature of the activity and the possibility of accident and injury. Both of these elements are important aspects for defending against lawsuits because "failure to warn" is a common allegation in many lawsuits. While the effectiveness of waivers providing significant defense varies from state to state, the more specifically the waiver is written in terms of the nature of the activity, the more likely it is to be upheld in court.

Coaches are strongly encouraged to develop a "paper trail" in all matters of safety warnings. For example, provide all safety rules in writing to both the athletes and their parents. Document all attempts by coaches to educate themselves and their athletes about safety. Whenever safety matters are discussed in coaches' meetings, parent meetings, or orientation programs, note the date and topic in a log, keep a copy of the agenda and/or minutes and note who was in attendance. Another example might be to assign an assistant coach the responsibility of stocking and providing the first aid kit. Keep a logbook inside the lid of the kit and date it every time the kit is inspected and restocked.

ADEQUATE SUPERVISION FOR SAFE PARTICIPATION

Effective supervision is essential for providing a safe and successful sporting experience and is questioned virtually every time an accident is examined. Two types of supervision must be provided: **General and Specific.**

General supervision is the overall supervision of the team or individual and is required at all times during instruction. General supervision requires that you maintain continual visual contact with the entire team, are immediately accessible to all athletes, systematically monitor the players to ensure that safe procedures are being followed, and be alert for dangers or deviations from normal procedures.

Specific supervision is the direct supervision of one person or a small group. The coach must shift from general to specific supervision when:

Unsafe practices are observed

There is an injury or an emergency occurs

There is a deviation from the norm and corrective action is needed

Coaching younger, less-mature athletes

Coaching novice athletes or those with less skill

Introducing new skills/activities or increased risk.

FIGURE 14.4
The need to provide specific supervision does not reduce the need for continued general supervision of all your athletes.

Thus, the need for specific supervision increases for beginning, immature, and lower ability athletes or when there is an activity involving increased risk for your athletes.

Coaches must be able to shift back and forth between general and specific supervision as circumstances dictate. The need to provide specific supervision to particular players on the team does not reduce the requirement for continued general supervision for all other athletes. Thus, an effective supervising coach would provide individualized feedback to a single athlete while standing in such a position as to be able to continue to monitor the entire group (Figure 14.4). Coaches must establish safe teaching stations, proper placement of safety equipment, appropriately matched athlete grouping, and assess each athlete's ability to work independently. Attention to these factors permits coaches to provide continuous general supervision while still providing specific supervision to those youngsters who need individual instruction.

Generally, athletes need specific supervision until they can (1) understand and appreciate the risks involved in the activity, (2) evaluate their performances, and (3) understand and follow necessary safety practices. In some sport situations young athletes, because of their age and the degree of risk involved in certain activities, should not be allowed to participate without direct, specific supervision.

Never leave athletes unsupervised. Leaving the athletes unattended, however briefly and regardless of the reason, is a potential source of negligence should an accident occur. When facilities are not in use, put all equipment away and secure the area by locking doors and posting notices that the use of the facilities requires supervision.

Effective supervision includes the following specific elements:

1. Equipment should be inaccessible to athletes unless a qualified coach is present. Think of unsupervised equipment as an invitation to participate (an invitation that is legally called an attractive nuisance).

2. Never leave the training or competitive areas unattended while athletes are present.

3. Position yourself so that, with a glance, the entire practice area remains in view at all times. For example, individual instruction should be provided with the coach's back to a wall or empty space so that the entire group and/or practice facility area remains in view.

4. Station yourself in the area you judge to have the greatest need for instruction and/or supervision, for instance when new skills are being introduced or physical assistance is requested by or required for an athlete.

5. Athletes should have direct access to you at all times. Teach them to seek your assistance whenever they are attempting skills of which they are uncertain, such as a new or difficult skill. Teach them to inform you of problems and/or injuries. For example, they should alert you when there is broken equipment, a disturbance, an injury or if someone is breaking a safety rule.

6. Post your rules of conduct and safety conspicuously in the facility or by the field to serve as a constant reminder of the expected behavior. At a minimum, your rules should include the following points regarding supervision:
   a. Without exception, no one is permitted in the training area unless a qualified coach is present.
   b. Practice may not begin without the presence and explicit permission of the coach.

7. Review safety rules with team members on a regular basis to ensure that they know the rules, understand the reasons why the safety rules are required, and appreciate the consequences of violating the safety rules both in terms of potential injury and appropriate sanctions. As a rule, the younger, less experienced and

less mature the athletes, the more frequently the coach needs to provide formal reminders of the rules.

8. All instruction should be provided in language that the young athletes can understand and in a tone which, while nonthreatening, conveys the seriousness of the message.

9. Be certain to know and to follow the policies of your sports organization on facilities security and specific steps for ensuring that an unsupervised facility is never left open to the public. At a minimum, these policies should specify:

   a. Who is responsible for opening and securing the area.
   b. The exact manner in which the area should be opened and secured.
   c. The times and circumstances during which the area is to be opened and secured.
   d. The placement/condition of the equipment when the facility is secured.

ORGANIZED AND PLANNED LESSONS FOR SAFE PARTICIPATION

Lesson plans should be prepared for each instructional period. They should include both the concepts and activities to be taught and the strategies for ensuring safe supervision and the elimination of potential risks. Novice coaches may rely on pre-planned standard workout plans prepared for their league by more experienced coaches. Volunteer coaches often jot down their plans on the back of an envelope just before driving to practice! Regardless of the formal or informal nature of such plans, they should be kept both as documentation and to build on for the next practice. These plans should include, at the very least, the following information:

1. The skill difficulty of the activities matched with the skill level of the athletes. Such a lesson typically provides multiple teaching stations providing for varied levels of direct supervision.

2. Facility layout plans including traffic control patterns and safety zones providing sufficient room for safe drills and skills.

3. The efforts made to ensure your athletes' awareness of the safety rules and the behaviors expected of the athletes.

4. The procedures for securing the facility when the equipment and facilities are not in use by a supervised team.

5. The availability of the coach.

APPROPRIATE SELECTION AND SAFE CONDUCT OF THE SPORTS ACTIVITY

Sports are not unreasonably dangerous activities. The courts rarely judge an activity in and of itself to be unnecessarily dangerous. Rather the safety of the activity is judged by how the skills and drills are selected and how the activity is conducted. The manner in which the sport is conducted can dramatically influence the risk. In general, coaches should teach skills sequentially, progressing from low to high, slow to fast, and part to whole. Regardless of the sport, the selection of the skills and the order in which they will be taught is a crucial aspect of safety. Instruction should be tailored to the needs and preparation level of each student. Novice coaches may have to (1) rely on progressions developed by the league, (2) ask for input from more experienced coaches, or (3) refer to written materials such as books and pamphlets describing such skill progressions.

The conduct of an activity refers to the selection and development of a program of instruction as it relates to the age, ability, maturity, and readiness of the young athlete. The criteria by which the adequacy of an activity's conduct is judged includes the type of instruction offered, the measures enacted to ensure the safety of all, and the warnings provided to ensure the youngsters' understanding of the risks of the skills they are learning. Take care to provide instruction in a language that young athletes fully understand. The tone of instruction should be positive but clearly convey the serious intent of the instruction especially where safety issues are being discussed. The following are important elements related to the conduct of an activity:

Screening. The coach must determine the readiness of each athlete – a highly individual matter. Pre-testing and screening are crucial for assessing appropriate starting levels for conditioning and instruction. Take care to ensure that initial testing situations do not constitute unreasonable danger in and of themselves. Careful record keeping of screening results can document the appropriateness of subsequent activities. Information obtained from "tryouts" usually hosted by the youth sports organization can be used as initial assessments to place young athletes in appropriate skill groups and competitive levels – as opposed to traditional tryouts which are typically used to eliminate less-skilled and less-experienced athletes from participation. Following the initial screening, periodic re-assessments should be made to stay aware of the capacities and limitations of each athlete.

Mismatches. Differences inevitably will exist between participants with regard to size, skill, ability, and maturity. Left uncontrolled, these mismatches place either or both of the athletes at risk of physical injury. As a coach, you have more control when matching athletes in practices than in competitions. Because age is typically used to group young athletes, mismatches in size, experience, and skill are quite likely to occur in competitive situations, especially between the ages of 10 to 14 years when growth spurts often produce athletes of the same age but dramatically different physical sizes. Young athletes are particularly susceptible to injuries during this age period both because of size and strength mismatches between competing athletes and because of the lack of coordination and muscles and ligaments which are "out of sync" with bone growth.

Protective Measures. Require that all your athletes use all necessary protective measures and equipment. If the required protective equipment is not available, then the activity should be modified or participation should be restricted. All recommendations of the governing body should be followed.

Equipment. All protective equipment should be properly fitted to the athlete, regularly inspected by the coach and, to the extent possible, by the athletes themselves. For example, a softball catcher should be taught to make such inspections of all of her equipment habitually before each practice and between innings. Avoid modifying equipment unless absolutely sure that such modifications are safe and necessary. Avoid unsafe uses of otherwise safe equipment.

PROPER INSTRUCTION IN SPORT SKILLS AND REQUIRED SAFETY BEHAVIORS

Teaching specific sport skills requires technical knowledge specific to each sport. A comprehensive coverage of such technical instructional techniques goes far beyond the scope of this book. An excellent source of time-tested, well-respected and sport-specific instructional material is

FIGURE 14.5
Progressions are the backbone of virtually all instruction whether teaching a cartwheel in gymnastics, a bunt in baseball or math in the classroom.

available for more than 20 different sports in a book entitled **Physical Activity & Sport for the Secondary School Student.**[4] It contains illustrations, valuable coaching tips and skill progressions that experienced coaches have accumulated over the many years of teaching specific sports. All effective sport instruction requires a general understanding of proper progressions.

Furthermore, the safe execution of sports skills can be enhanced by teaching your athletes how to fall safely. See the section later in this chapter illustrating safe falling techniques. Falling safely is a set of skills often overlooked despite the inevitability that athletes, regardless of skill level, will fall. That is, in the legal terms presented earlier, falls are foreseeable.

Progressions

Progressions are the backbone of effective instruction in virtually every sport (Figure 14.5). Because of the vast number of different skills taught in a variety of different sports, a list of progressions even in a single sport could literally be endless. Furthermore, more than one set of progressions can be used to safely teach any given specific skill or sequence of skills. Thus, identifying a sole set of approved progressions is not reasonable.

Nonetheless, each set of progressions should include six areas. The following "lesson plan" or skill analysis can be used for skills of virtually any difficulty, from the basic and intermediate skills for recreational athletes to high-level skills used by advanced athletes. This skills analysis allows for a variety of safe and effective progressions to teach virtually every sport skill:

1. What are the **prerequisites** for successfully performing a skill (e.g., the necessary strength, flexibility, body awareness, essential prior skill learning and/or practice).

2. What are effective **progressions** for teaching a skill (i.e., the specific learning steps and/or skill breakdowns).

3. What are effective **teaching cues** for teaching a skill (e.g., verbal commands, feedback signals, what to looks for and/or how it feels).

4. What are **common errors** typically made by athletes during the initial stages of learning; i.e., errors which can be prevented or corrected.

5. What are the **potential risks and/or hazards** (i.e., where is the greatest likelihood of falling; what part of the body must be protected).

6. What are necessary and appropriate **assisting techniques** (i.e., where to stand relative to the apparatus and the athlete; in a sport such as gymnastics, how to spot a skill; what mistakes should be anticipated).

From Chalkboard to Playing Field

Examples of Sport-Specific Progression Analyses

THE CARTWHEEL IN GYMNASTICS

1. **Prerequisites:** Requires the ability to support the entire body on one's hands without collapsing. Assumes the student has the ability to perform a handstand. The ability to perform a Russian Split is helpful but not essential.

2. **Progressions:** Lunge to a side handstand and step down to a stand. Perform a mini-cartwheel where the body weight does not pass directly overhead. Perform the cartwheel on a straight line.

3. **Teaching Cues:** A left leg lunge requires that the left hand is placed down on the floor first. Alternate hand, hand, foot, foot placement with a definite, evenly spaced rhythm or cadence. Place the first hand down as far away from the lunge foot as

possible. The second hand down is placed as far from the first hand as possible, while still comfortably supporting the gymnast's body weight. Look for the floor without raising the head excessively.

4. **Common Errors:** Opposite hand is placed down first. Head is raised excessively causing the back to arch resulting in a loss of strength, balance and direction. Elbows bend causing the sensation of falling and the fear of collapsing. Lunge on a straight leg preventing the student from pushing the body weight over the hands into the cartwheel.

5. **Potential Risks:** Arms collapse causing a fall to the head.

6. **Assisting Techniques:** Stand behind the gymnast so that as the cartwheel is initiated, the gymnast's back is toward the spotter. The spotter's first hand supports the gymnast's hip during the lunge and push-off. Both hands guide and support the gymnast's body during the handstand phase. The spotter's second hand supports the hips during the step-down phase at the completion of the skill. The spotter should anticipate an arch in the student's back and a bending of the leg during the handstand phase of the cartwheel. Such an error increases the possibility that the spotter may be kicked in the face or the chest by the gymnast's feet.

THE SACRIFICE BUNT IN BASEBALL

1. **Prerequisites:** Requires the ability to maintain one's balance while performing multiple skills simultaneously (i.e., rotating the body towards the pitcher while changing hand position on the bat). The batter must also be ready to avoid an errant pitch.

2. **Progressions:** Step sideways to face the pitching mound frontally, but off to the side of base. Pivot on the balls of both feet and rotate the torso towards the pitcher while keeping the knees slightly bent. Slide the right hand (for a right handed batter) approximately halfway down the barrel of the bat. The barrel of the bat should rest on the knuckles of the right index finger and be supported by the thumb.

3. **Teaching Cues:** "Watch the ball hit the bat." "Keep your elbows bent." "Thumbs up as you slide your hand down the bat." "Meet the ball in front of the plate."

4. **Common Errors:** Reaching for the ball with the arms extended rather than waiting for the pitch to reach the hitting zone.

5. **Potential Risks:** A foul tip hitting you in the face. Getting hit by the pitch. Grasping the bat with the finger surrounding the barrel of the bat where the ball can strike the fingers.

6. **Assisting Techniques:** Stand close to the plate and lob the ball softly at first; then gradually increase the velocity and the distance of the pitch. Most children cannot process the multiple tasks required to master this skill until about 11 or 12 years of age; however, regular practice can dramatically improve a child's bunting technique.

Falling Techniques

Falling safely is a skill that can be learned. Safety can be enhanced by teaching your athletes how to fall safely. Falling safely is a set of skills often overlooked despite the inevitability that athletes, regardless of skill level will fall. Falling is a given in most sports. That is, in the legal terms presented earlier, falls are foreseeable. Athletes who master falling techniques are much more likely to avoid injuries in sports such as soccer and football. Falling techniques often allow the athletes to recover more quickly from a fall (e.g., after tripping over the soccer ball or being blocked to the ground in football) and return to their feet to resume the action of the game. A soccer goalie must learn to fall safely after she makes a diving save at the mouth of the goal. The shortstop in baseball who makes a diving catch must fall safely, recover by scrambling to his feet, and make the throw quickly enough to begin the double play.

There are elementary, intermediate, and advanced falls. Learning to fall safely involves using progressions that start with a prepared, low fall involving little energy so that if mistakes are made, there is little risk of injury or pain. The general strategy of safe falling is to spread the force of the landing across the greatest possible distance, time, and area of the body. Short, quick, localized impacts are the most likely to cause injury.

Even novice athletes should be taught to fall forward and backward (Figure 14.6 and 14.7). All falls should start low to the ground to minimize the impact of falling, and further energy should not be added until the falling technique has been mastered safely. Once the techniques of controlled falling have been mastered, the coach should always reinforce proper techniques of falling whenever falls occur. Since falling is usually sudden and unexpected, falling should be as automatic as possible. If athletes perform a fall incorrectly during practice or competition, coaches should remind them immediately of the correct technique.

From Chalkboard to Playing Field

Progressions for Falling Safely

FORWARD FALLING PROGRESSIONS

FIGURE 14.6 Falls are a predictable risk factor in most youth sport programs; and falling safely is a teachable skill that can significantly reduce the likely of injury if and when a fall occurs.

Reprinted with permission from SHAPE America - Society of Health and Physical Educators, 1900 Association Drive, Reston, VA 20191, www.shapeamerica.org.

1. Start in a push-up position on the knees on a soft surface (e.g., a grassy area or an old mattress). Lower the torso to a landing that maintains support initially on the palms of the hands and subsequently on both the palms and the chest. The face should be turned to the side to protect the nose and face.

2. From the push-up position, vigorously push off from the floor and as you fall back to the floor, land with the elbows bent, turning the head to side, landing on the chest while breaking the impact of the fall with the bent arms.

3. Repeat the previous drill from a vertical starting position on your knees. Fall forward and repeat step two.

4. Start from a standing position, drop to the knees and repeat step three. Repeat several times adding force and momentum as the athlete's control increases.

5. After mastery has been demonstrated on the falls with less energy and less impact, repeat Step four with a slight jump before falling to add more energy to the fall.

BACKWARD FALLING PROGRESSIONS

FIGURE 14.7 Backward Falling Progressions

Reprinted with permission from SHAPE America - Society of Health and Physical Educators, 1900 Association Drive, Reston, VA 20191, www.shapeamerica.org.

1. To minimize impact, start from a sitting position on a soft surface and roll backwards with a rounded back and shoulders. Rock backwards and forward to experience maintaining a rounded back while moving. Tighten the neck and shoulder muscles to keep the chin on the chest and avoid the head hitting the ground. Palms and forearms should be placed on the mat to absorb the impact of later, more powerful falls (thumbs in toward the body, fingers pointed toward the toes).

2. Once the backward rocking has been mastered as in Figure 14.7, repeat from a low squat, falling backward onto the buttocks while holding the rounded back as in step one. Hold the chin on the chest as repeated attempts are done with more and more force. Heavier athletes should roll slightly to the side resulting in a shoulder roll where the weight of the body passes to the side of the neck.

3. Finally, from a standing position, drop to a squatting position and fall back immediately to the rounded body position using the arms to absorb the increased impact of falling from a greater height.

PROVISION OF SAFE FACILITIES, EQUIPMENT AND ENVIRONMENT

The environmental conditions in which activities take place and the equipment used must be safe and appropriate. A coach can become aware of potential environmental dangers in two primary ways: **constructive notice** and **actual notice.** Constructive notice results from normal safety inspections such as examining a field before games and practices. Actual notice results when someone points out that a specific hazard exists; e.g., a glass bottle has just been broken in the baseball dugout. In either case, the coach has a clear obligation to correct the condition or stop/curtail the activity until a correction can be made.

Inspection of Facilities and Equipment

Coaches should regularly inspect facilities and equipment (Figure 14.8). If deficiencies are noted, an established procedure should exist for correcting those safety problems. While veteran coaches should have direct input into such safety plans, novice coaches should be knowledgeable enough to inquire about what procedures sports administrators have established to correct safety problems. For example, Little League programs typically have a safety officer and recreation departments have a maintenance department. Coaches (and sport administrators) should be certain that all equipment and facilities meet or exceed applicable safety standards and that all equipment is used for the purposes for which it is intended. Coaches should ensure that all safety equipment is provided for all participants and require that such equipment be used. In baseball, for example, do not permit young baseball players to catch behind the plate without proper catcher's equipment, not even during warm-ups.

FIGURE 14.8 Regular inspection of facilities and equipment is essential. While you may not be able to fix a defect in the equipment or facility, you are responsible for protecting your athletes. For example, you can move to a new location, modify or eliminate the activity or remove the defective equipment so that the situation is safe for all.

Coaches are responsible for ensuring that all equipment and facilities are safe for use – and are safely used. Accidents and injuries can occur when normally safe equipment is misused. A ball bag in baseball is normally used to hold bats, balls and other equipment. However, when used as a makeshift base, it can create a hazard because it is not secured as a base or may have equipment still inside it. Swinging a bat with weights is safe if the bat is held by the handle so the weight cannot fly off but is unsafe if swung by the head of the bat allowing the weights to fly off the thinner handle.

If a piece of equipment is broken or an area of the field or gymnasium is unsafe, the volunteer coach may not be capable of fixing the hazard, but is expected to restrict the activity or move the practice to a safe location. Prior to practice or a game, the prudent coach should carry out a visual inspection of the field or facility. Having the athletes "walk the field" looking for hazards prior to use is also a reasonable procedure. While the ultimate responsibility for safety belongs to the coach, having athletes participate in the pre-use safety inspection serves two purposes. First, it provides extra eyes to identify potential hazards and second, involving the athletes teaches a positive attitude about safety and alerts the young athletes as to what constitutes a hazard. For example, an aluminum soda can that was discarded on the field the day before and has since been run over by a lawn mower may now be "shrapnel" that could easily produce an injury should a player fall or trip on the shredded metal.

Coaches should establish and follow procedures for identifying and correcting unsafe conditions. All fields, facilities, and equipment should be checked for safety before each practice or contest. Your inspections should give special attention to the following:

- **Safe buffer zones.** Is there adequate, unobstructed space around the playing area to provide a buffer space to prevent the possibility of collisions with seated spectators or extra equipment such as balls, bats, helmets? Is there safe walking access and spectator space around and between playing areas? For example, ensure that team benches are located far enough removed from the playing field to eliminate the risk of collisions between athletes actively playing on the field and those sitting on the bench.

- **Fencing, netting and supporting poles.** Are fences free of dangerous protrusions, holes, and other hazards, and are they built high enough to protect the athletes?

- **Presence of dangerous debris.** Is the playing surface clear and safe? (e.g., avoid rock filled fields.)

- **Carelessly placed equipment in playing areas.** Are there hazards on or near the playing surface? (e.g., equipment stored along the wall of a basketball court instead of being removed to a storage closet or an area distant enough to eliminate the possibility of collision; equipment left on the field from a previous activity.)

- **Quality of the playing surface.** Are hazards created by differences in elevation between the playing surface and adjoining areas that can cause athletes to trip? Has there been erosion of base paths or other heavily trafficked areas (e.g., the front of goal cages)? Have gymnasts left chalk on the gym floor creating a hazard for the subsequent basketball practice? Are the field markings adequate to delineate the field of play?

- **Visibility and lighting conditions.** Has dusk set in sufficiently to dangerously limit vision? Do artificial lights shine directly in the eyes of batters or fielders during night baseball?

- **Effects of weather conditions.** Has the field become too wet and slippery for safe play? Have tree branches been blown onto the playing area?

Coaches should be certain that all equipment is appropriate for the skill levels of the participants both for safety purposes and for enhancing skill development. For example, in professional baseball, bases must be firmly anchored in the ground but such equipment poses a significant hazard for novice athletes. A variety of safe bases (e.g., break-away bases, magnetic bases) are available which virtually eliminate foot, ankle, and leg injuries from improper sliding into the base.

When there are hazards that cannot be removed, establish procedures for notifying participants and for marking and avoiding such hazards. For example, stop or modify your practice session or competitive game when unsafe conditions exist. Cones might be placed around obstructions to warn that the area is off limits.

Personal equipment such as safety glasses, mouth guards, helmets, cleated shoes, athletic supporters, tennis racquets and lacrosse sticks should be the appropriate size and fitted to the individual athlete. Require the use of appropriate and adequate safety equipment by all athletes on your team. As the coach, you are responsible for ensuring that protective equipment is in good condition, fits properly, and is worn as prescribed by the manufacturer. Thus, you should know what safety equipment and facilities are needed by athletes and required by rules governing competition in your sport. The athletes and their parents will in all likelihood look to you for assistance in choosing, fitting, and maintaining all equipment -- including safety gear.

Environmental Conditions

Coaches must be aware of environmental conditions that adversely affect both athletic performance and the health of the athletes. The two most profound environmental conditions are heat and humidity. Every year a number of athletes die from totally preventable heat-induced illnesses As humidity rises, the temperatures at which athletes are susceptible to heat exhaustion and heat stroke decreases.

Contrary to earlier beliefs, children and youth do not appear to be less effective at tolerating heat than adults. Furthermore, the factors that determine adverse reactions to heat illness are factors that are controllable: Excessive physical exertion, insufficient rest and recovery between

FIGURE 14.9
Young athletes should be encouraged to drink before prolonged physical exercise to ensure full hydration and have regular access to fluids throughout the exercise sessions.

repeated same-day training sessions, and the wearing of clothing, uniforms or protective gear which promote excessive heat retention.[5] According to the American Academy of Pediatrics, "Most healthy children and adolescents can safely participate in outdoor sports and other physical activities through a wide range of challenging warm to hot climatic conditions. With appropriate preparation, modifications and monitoring, exertional heat illness is usually preventable." In addition, the Academy recommends that the intensity of activities lasting 30 minutes or more be reduced when relative humidity and air temperature are high and that appropriate fluids be available to offset fluid loss due to sweating. Athletes should be encouraged to drink prior to prolonged bouts of physical exercise to ensure full hydration. During exercise, they should drink about 100-250 mL of water every 20 minutes (about 3 to 8 ounces) for 9- to 12-year-olds and 1.0 to 1.5 liters (about 34 to 50 ounces) per hour for adolescents. (Figure 14.9)

When temperatures increase, such as in summertime, both the intensity and duration of exercise should be restrained initially and then gradually increased over a period of 10 to 14 days to permit the athletes to adapt (acclimatize) to the higher temperatures. Clothing should be a single layer of lightweight, absorbent material to permit sweat to evaporate and skin to be exposed to the air as much as possible. Sweat saturated clothing should be replaced with dry clothes as often as possible. Finally, rubberized sweat suits should never be used to promote weight loss. Figure 14.10 shows the heat and humidity combinations that are potentially dangerous.

Effective coaches teach their athletes the safety principles for training in high heat/humidity conditions. Athletes should be aware of the risks of exercising in such conditions and the protective steps that they can take, such as acclimatization, proper clothing, and adequate fluid intake. You should provide for free access to fluids such as water and electrolytic supplemented drinks during physical activity and instruct your athletes about proper hydration and the warning signs of heat illnesses such as nausea, dizziness, and flushed skin.

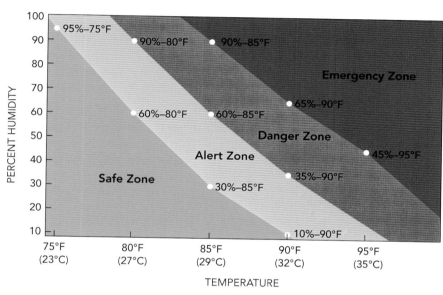

FIGURE 14.10
Guidelines for Avoiding Heat Injuries[6]

Safety zone	What to do
Safe Zone	• Exercise as usual. • Safe to exercise outdoors.
Alert Zone	• Decrease your exercise intensity (slow your walking pace). • Watch for signs (such as shortness of breath, increased tiredness. • No outdoor exercise.
Danger Zone	• Exercise in an air conditioned environment only.
Emergency Zone	• Avoid going outdoors

Copyright © 2014 University Health Network. All rights reserved.

An Emergency Action Plan (EAP)

Responsible coaches have Emergency Action Plans (EAPs) to manage emergencies. While predicting the exact time, place, and type of an emergency is virtually impossible, emergencies are an unavoidable result of sports participation and should be anticipated. The most common emergency is likely to involve sport injuries; however, coaches must also be prepared for illness, allergic reactions, unruly spectators at a game, disruption of an event because of lightning or inclement weather, etc. Share your plans with your assistant coaches, parents, and athletes. The plan should identify what actions can be taken ahead of time in anticipation of an emergency. It should establish rehearsed protocols for obtaining professional help should it be needed (e.g., rescue squad, police or fire); and identify what must be done after the incident to document what happened and record that documentation.

Let's look at the **Emergency Action Plan Time Line,** with its four distinct stages:

1. Actions Necessary Prior to the Emergency
2. Responding Directly to the Emergency
3. Actions Necessary When Professional Assistance Arrives
4. Follow-up Procedures

ACTIONS PRIOR TO THE EMERGENCY

A Rehearsed EAP. A number of actions can and should be performed before an emergency occurs. Have a preplanned procedure that designates ahead of time who has the responsibility to call for professional assistance (e.g., EMS, fire, police) and who will attend directly to the incident (e.g., the injured athletes, the fire, or the altercation). In addition, identify who will be responsible for meeting and providing physical directions to the exact location of the injured athlete or the emergency event. Often sport facilities have multiple fields and the location of the gymnasium in a school may not be immediately apparent to emergency responders. Therefore, a qualified individual should be assigned to meet those providing the professional assistance (EMS, fire, police) at a pre-designated site at the entrance to the fields or facility. Take time to **rehearse** your action plan. In emergencies, what appeared to be simple decisions and simple responses may become quite stressful under pressure to act quickly and decisively in case the injury or incident deteriorates dramatically.

First Aid/CPR/AED Training. Coaches should have the skills and knowledge required to provide first aid and/or CPR as well as to use an Automated External Defibrillator (AED) in a medical emergency or have immediate access to someone who has that capability. First Aid/CPR courses are typically available through local chapters of the Red Cross, through local hospitals and/or rescue squads, or through your community recreation programs. Often these courses are sponsored through your sports league. If not, encourage your youth sport administrators to host such a program.

Properly Equipped First Aid Kit. A properly equipped first aid kit should be available at all times (Figure 14.11). See Appendix 14.1 for a list of recommended contents of an adequately equipped first aid kit for a volunteer youth sport coach.[7]

Ice & Water. Ice and water should be available along with the first aid kit at every practice and competition. These renewable items are perhaps the most beneficial elements in rendering first aid. While chemical ice packs are recommended as part of your first aid kit, ice is preferred but is typically less convenient and requires a separate container or ice chest for transportation and storage.

FIGURE 14.11
Not only should a properly stocked first kit be available, the coach should know a) what's in the kit, b) how to use the contents of the kit and c) what needs to be restocked because it was previously used!

Completed Medical History/Treatment Authorization Forms. In many youth sport programs, these two documents are combined and the medical history is essentially limited to a listing of special medical needs (asthma, hearing loss, epilepsy, allergies). Your youth sport organization should have developed both the forms and the policies for their use. If not, ask that it does so. The treatment authorization should be signed by parents or guardians and should be notarized. These forms should be completed before the season begins and kept where the child's medical personal information is secure, yet in case of an emergency, immediately accessible by those to whom the parents/guardians have granted access. See Appendix 14.3 for an example of such a form. An important note: When a medical history specifies a participant's medical condition (e.g., asthma), the coach has been provided with actual notice of that condition and must take steps to be prepared to deal with it should such a need arise (e.g., an asthma attack).

Injury/Incident Report Forms. Blank injury/incident report forms (See Appendix 14.2 for a sample injury report form) should be available to be filled out after the accident/incident while the details are still fresh in your mind. Keep these forms in a waterproof case along with your first aid kit. In case of a lawsuit, coaches will be asked to recall details of the incident many months or even years after it happened.

Accessible Telephone. You should have access to a telephone at all times. A mobile telephone is increasingly the norm at sports facilities. Landline phones in schools and recreation centers are often locked and inaccessible after hours and on weekends. Telephone numbers for emergency medical services, rescue squads, fire, police, and poison control can be printed in permanent ink on the first aid kit itself and even programmed directly into the mobile phone for "speed dialing." Test the number to ensure it is the correct number to summon the nearest professional assistance to your facility or fields.

RESPONDING DIRECTLY TO THE EMERGENCY

While quick action is important in an emergency, it is also crucial that you take time to accurately assess the overall situation. Your response might involve attending to one or more ill or injured athletes, responding to a fire with a fire extinguisher, or attempting to halt an altercation between spectators and/or athletes. The following procedures minimize the possibility of overlooking crucial aspects of the emergency situation, such as non-obvious injuries or having to choose which of two simultaneously occurring injuries must be treated first.

Attending to the incident. In the case of injury or illness, you should be capable of providing basic first aid and reassuring any and all injured athletes that they are being properly cared for. That reassurance can lower the anxiety experienced by an injured athlete, thus minimizing the likelihood of complications such as the onset of shock.

Note the time. Noting the time takes only a second and may provide EMS, fire, or police personnel valuable information when they first arrive. It also tends to give you a realistic perspective – minutes may seem like hours when waiting for help. The time of the accident/incident is also a detail typically needed for completing a report at a later time.

Assess the nature and severity of the accident/incident. For example, non-emergencies might evolve into emergencies if an injured athlete is moved, goes into shock, or begins bleeding again. A smoldering ember might re-ignite a serious fire. An argument might quickly escalate into a major altercation.

Determine if professional assistance is required. Minor injuries such as scrapes and bruises can normally be dealt with using basic first aid; however, if the injury is serious or if you doubt your ability to provide adequate treatment, initiate your previously planned procedures for summoning medical assistance. Altercations between adults might best be dealt with by police.

Ensure athletes not immediately involved in the emergency are adequately supervised. You should have a plan to continue to provide supervision to all other athletes. This supervision can be as simple as directing those athletes to stay clear of the incident or to sit down until the emergency is resolved or sending them off with an assistant coach to continue practice. Failure to provide such supervision can place those athletes at risk.

Provide appropriate care. This may require the administration of first aid or the use of an AED (defibrillator). You should know and apply standard management procedures designed to minimize exposure to blood-borne pathogens (BBPs); this knowledge should include the specific rules of your sport that limit the exposure of other athletes and officials to the blood or bodily fluids of your injured athlete. For example, athletes are not typically permitted to return to the competition if actively bleeding, no matter how trivial the nosebleed or scrape or cut. Similar precautions should be taken within your practices. Coaches should have a spare uniform available to replace a blood stained uniform and thus permit an athlete to return to competition after minor bleeding has been controlled. Spare clothing for the coach who might be splattered with blood should also be available.

Determine the need for ongoing care. Monitor the incident until professional assistance arrives. In serious injuries, shock may develop and a stabilized, non-threatening situation may become an acute emergency.

FIGURE 14.12
When emergency medical assistance arrives, there are several ways that you, as the coach, can assist the professional help you have called.

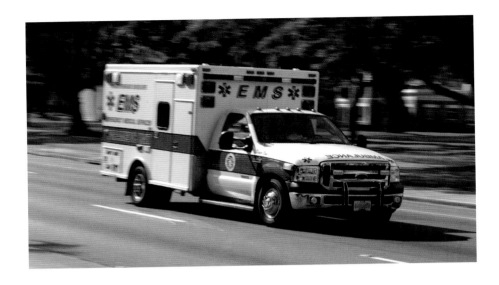

Remain with athletes who may have been injured. Reassurance and periodic, continued monitoring of the injured athlete should be provided as needed.

ACTIONS WHEN PROFESSIONAL ASSISTANCE ARRIVES

When assistance arrives, there are several crucial ways that you, as the coach, can assist the professional help you have summoned. (Figure 14.12)

Intercept and direct the professional helpers to the scene. If you are indoors in a school or recreation center, send someone to the main entrance or parking lot where the police, EMS or fire professionals are most likely to enter so they can be directed immediately to the specific location of the incident. If you are outdoors, particularly if your area contains multiple fields or where several activities are occurring simultaneously, have the contact person ready to direct the professional help when it arrives.

Notify parents/guardians. When appropriate, use the information on the Medical Treatment/Authorization Form (see Appendix 14.3) to contact the parents/guardians.

Explain the incident to the First Responders and describe what actions have already been taken (e.g., first aid). While certain aspects of the emergency may be obvious to the professional helpers, other contributing factors may not. For example, if the athlete is unconscious, the EMS will want to know for how long.

Provide details from the medical history form. This information is especially important in regard to allergies, chronic illnesses, asthma, etc. Also mention if the athlete has experienced this particular injury in the past, for instance, a prior concussion.

Request the hospital destination from the EMS. This information allows you to update the parents/guardians as soon as you contact them. In the event that transport to a hospital is necessary, send a responsible adult know to the injured athlete along with the ambulance for reassurance until the parents arrive at the hospital — often an intimidating place for a youngster alone.

Modify your practice plan accordingly. In the event of a serious emergency, modifying or even canceling the remainder of practice may be appropriate.

FOLLOW-UP PROCEDURES

After the urgency of the immediate accident/incident has passed, a number of administrative and follow up procedures are usually necessary involving proper notification of parents, league officials, and insurance agents and documentation of the injury or incident, especially ones of a serious nature.

Notify league officials and insurance carriers. Some leagues have specific procedures for such notifications; however, many do not. Check with your league administrator or safety officer to determine the exact reporting requirements in the case of an injury. In many cases the responsibility of reporting to the insurance carrier lies with the parents who carry individual medical insurance. Be prepared to provide them with all appropriate information.

Complete the accident/injury report form. Complete this form as soon as possible while the details of the incident are still easily remembered. State only what you saw directly. For example, if Billy reports he saw Freddie trip and fall, report that Billie told you Freddie tripped and fell. Do not indicate that Freddie tripped and fell as if you had seen it directly. Also, do not speculate about what might have caused the accident or how it might have been prevented. That type of information is important but is not appropriate on the accident reporting form, which may ultimately become evidence in the event of litigation.

File the accident/injury report form with the league and keep a copy for your own records. Officials of your sport organization need this information but record keeping in volunteer organizations may be quite informal. Should the need for this information arise for medical and/or legal reasons some time in the future, maintaining your own records of the incident provides you with essential information.

Maintain contact with parents/guardians. A timely phone call to the parents of an injured athlete to keep you informed of their child's status and to demonstrate your genuine concern for the well-being of their son or daughter is an important follow up. Litigation following serious injuries tends to occur more often when medical expenses have not been covered and when parents or guardians perceive that "nobody cared" about their child's well-being both before and after an accident.

Monitor your athlete's rehabilitation. Be certain the athlete has had clearance from qualified medical personnel before returning to practices and competitions. Require a doctor's note for an athlete returning to play after a serious injury or illness. While volunteer coaches are not qualified to design rehabilitation programs for injured athletes, you can help speed recovery by encouraging your athlete to adhere to the rehabilitation plan established by qualified medical personnel and minimizing the sense of isolation that injured athletes often feel when they are prevented by injury from returning immediately to the practices, competitions and interactions with their teammates.

Insurance for the Athletes and the Program

As the coach, you should be aware of the two distinctly different types of insurance required for sports participation: Medical and Liability.

MEDICAL INSURANCE

Medical insurance covers the participants' medical expenses following an injury. Primary insurance covers most legitimate expenses based upon injury or loss. Secondary insurance covers expenses after primary insurance is exhausted or where it fails to cover certain medical expenses. Because participants are often expected to have primary medical coverage from the parents' insurance policy from work or from school policies, leagues quite often require that participants purchase secondary medical insurance because it is less expensive.

LIABILITY INSURANCE

Liability insurance covers the coaches and the organization in the event that the injuries and losses result from their negligence. Even if you reside in a state that provides volunteer coaches with civil immunity (see Table 14.1), such liability insurance is recommended because it typically covers legal expenses that might be incurred to defend yourself from the accusation of negligence even if a lawsuit is eventually dismissed in court.

YOUR TURN
Three Basic Questions

Coaches can easily become overwhelmed with the large number of risk management issues that must be dealt with to run a safe, effective sports program. Fortunately, virtually all these issues can be reduced to three basic questions.[8] If you can answer yes to each of these three questions at each practice or competition, you are most likely running a safe program. (Figure 14.13)

QUESTION 1: Are the athletes properly prepared for participating in their sport?

FIGURE 14.13 Are the athletes prepared?

Have your athletes had a medical exam before participating? Have they been properly conditioned for the rigors of your sport? Have they mastered prerequisite skills before moving on to more advanced skills? Have they been warned and do they understand the risks inherent in their sport? Have they learned and do they understand the basic safety rules and regulations they are expected to follow in order to participate safely?

QUESTION 2: Are you, as the coach, properly prepared to teach the sport skills required and supervise the sports program?

FIGURE 14.14 Are you, as the coach, prepared?

Do you have knowledge to coach the basics of your sport? Are you aware of what additional information you need before coaching? Are you familiar with the level of preparation of each of your athletes and capable of providing individualized instruction suitable for their safe participation? Can you provide skill progression matched to each young athlete's readiness and the difficulty of the sport skill being coached? Are you knowledgeable in first aid/CPR?

QUESTION 3: Is the environment properly prepared for safe performance and participation for your sport?

FIGURE 14.15 Are the facilities prepared?

Is the equipment properly prepared and fitted to the needs of the athletes? Is the weather safe for continued participation or must the activity be curtailed and/or modified? Have the athletes been properly matched for size, skill, and maturity? Is the physical environment adequately prepared and maintained for safe participation? Is there a safe distance between teaching stations to prevent accidents?

Clearly the number of issues related to each of these primary questions has not been exhausted. The exact nature of individual questions in each category will depend on the specific sport you coach and the degree of risk associated with that sport. Satisfactory answers to these three basic questions do, however, provide substantial direction to both beginner and experienced coaches who have volunteered to provide adequate care and supervision for their young athletes.

The seriousness of these three questions is underscored by the fact that they represent the vast majority of questions asked by lawyers at depositions where the factors leading to and causing serious injuries are scrutinized with the advantage of hindsight.

CHAPTER REFERENCES

1. New Jersey legal code: NJ 2A:62A-6.

2. Horwitz, J. R., & Mead, J. (2009). Letting good deeds go unpunished: Volunteer immunity laws and tort deterrence. University of Michigan Law School Scholarship Repository. Journal of Empirical Legal Studies, 6(3), 585-635.

3. New Jersey legal code: N.J.A.C. 5:52.

4. Dougherty, N. E. (Ed.) (2010) **Physical Activity & Sport for the Secondary School Student, (6th ed.)** Reston, VA: National Association for Sport & Physical Education. (also Champaign, IL: Human Kinetics Publishers.

5. American Academy of Pediatrics. Policy Statement: Climatic Heat Stress and the Exercising Child and Adolescent. *Pediatrics*. (2011). 128(3), e741–e747. Reaffirmed February, 2015

6. https://www.healtheuniversity.ca/EN/CardiacCollege/Active/Exercise_And_Hot_Weather/Pages/heat-safety-index-and-air-quality-index.aspx

7. Coaches' Reference Manual (2018). Rutgers SAFETY. Clinic, (5th Ed.), New Brunswick, NJ: Rutgers University.

8. Mitchell, M. F., & Feigley, D. A. (2002). The injury problem. In N.J. Dougherty (Ed.). **Principles of Safety in Physical Education and Sport.** Reston, VA: National Association for Sport & Physical Education. 1-17.

Appendix 1.1
The Role of Winning in Youth Sports

A primary responsibility of every volunteer youth sport coach is to develop a philosophy which reflects the role of winning. Unfortunately, this important topic traditionally has been filled with clichés. At one extreme is the belief that winning is not important in youth sports. At the other is the belief that winning is the only thing. A healthy perspective is probably somewhere between these two beliefs. Clearly, there can be too much emphasis on winning. However, those who suggest that winning is not important fail to recognize that **without an attempt to win, the activity is no longer sport.** The essence of sport is striving to win; without that attempt, the nature of the activity changes. Consider two athletes of dramatically different skill levels playing tennis. Often the superior athlete will begin to teach the less skilled athlete. While admirable, teaching is not sport. Volunteer youth sport coaches should realize that while winning is an essential part of sport, youth sport has many other, complementary goals. A key point is to acknowledge that, while winning is important, it must be kept in perspective with the other valuable aspects of youth sports such as social development, fun and fitness.

CONSIDER THE FOLLOWING STATEMENTS WHEN DEVELOPING YOUR OWN COACHING PHILOSOPHY:

1. Winning Builds Confidence
The old cliché that "Show me a loser and I'll show you a loser" is often cited here. Winning does build confidence, especially when that winning represents a true accomplishment – defeating a worthy opponent. However, winning against teams or individuals of much lower skill levels usually does little to bolster self confidence.

2. Winning Brings Rewards and Special Privileges
Winners and highly skilled athletes often receive more recognition and adulation than less skilled athletes. Denying this does little to keep winning in a healthy perspective. However, youth sports coaches and administrators must guard against denying younger, less skilled athletes opportunities to participate and learn because of the natural attention given outstanding athletes.

3. Winning Increases in Importance as Kids Get Older
Won Loss records prior to the age of puberty have little effect on the respect and regard that kids have for their youth sport coaches. Prior to the age of 12 years, 75% of young athletes would prefer to play for a losing team than sit on the bench of a winning team. As they get older, won loss accomplishments do, in fact, influence the respect which young athletes have for coaches. Because athletes of different ages react differently to winning and losing, coaches of younger athletes should not merely mimic the behavior of successful coaches of older athletes.

4. Winning Builds Team Spirit and Unity
Whether "winning fosters team spirit" or "team spirit fosters winning" is not clear. Intra squad competition often produces better performance but lowered levels of team spirit. That is, winning a spot on the starting line up at the expense of a teammate may create more turmoil within the team if fairness and equal opportunity are not perceived by the majority of team members.

5. Winning Increases Motivation
While this statement may seem self evident, winning can be quite demotivating. For example, when the probability of success (i.e., winning) is very high, the game often lacks excitement and intensity. When the perceived probability of success is approximately 50%, higher levels of sustained involvement and motivation result. Thus, lopsided scores in children's "pick-up" games often cause abrupt changes in who is playing for which team because kids seek the excitement of close contests rather than what adults often perceive as the primary goal – winning.

6. Winning May Be Healthier When More Broadly Defined

In addition to the narrow definition of defeating your opponent, winning can be defined as self improvement and/or as goal attainment. Improving on one's previous performance or attaining previously set goals can be interpreted as success in a sports setting where, by definition, there are only a few first places. To benefit the majority of children, sport must benefit more than just those few who are crowned "champions."

7. Winners Handle Failure Better

Many believe successful athletes were always at the top of their sport. Actually, champions are often those who cope with difficulties, set backs, or losses better than their opponents. A .300 hitter in baseball is out 7 times for every 10 at-bats. The difference between a good .300 hitter and a mediocre .250 hitter is one more hit in every twenty times at bat.

8. Winning Does Not Ensure the Quality of the Performance

An athlete can perform well and still finish second; conversely one can perform poorly yet still win because the opponent was weak or failed to perform well. Mastery programs where the athletes are asked to meet a minimum level of performance often produce higher levels of performance than do competitive programs.

9. Winning in Youth Sports Depends on Who You Play

That is, winning often depends more upon who does the scheduling than the performance level of the athletes. If a team is scheduled only against inferior opponents, the team's won loss record will be good but the accomplishment is clearly devalued. Relative skill level is a crucial factor – especially in youth sport.

10. Winning: "How You Win" Is Often More Important Than "If You Win"

Winning within the boundaries of the rules and ethics of sportsmanship can place a great premium on winning without distorting the basic sporting values that many would like to see our children learn. In fact, true sportsmanship cannot exist unless there is an honest desire to win.

Playing fairly when one has no concern about the outcome of the game is not same level of ethics as playing fairly when one wants strongly to win.

11. Winning Is Primarily Influenced by Physiological Maturity

Physical maturity is the number one predictor of success in youth sport. For example, "clean up batters" in the Little League World Series (i.e., 11- and 12-year-olds) are consistently found to be post pubescent. Coaches are often given credit for an outstanding season when, in fact, they simply have had the more physically gifted or physically mature young athletes.

12. Winning Is Evidenced in Achievement

Successful youth sports coaches reinforce participation, effort, mastery and competitive rank, in that order. As a young athlete's age, maturity and experience develop, successful coaches shift their emphasis from simply encouraging participation to praising putting forth one's best effort. As development continues, the coach's emphasis shifts again toward praising mastering skills and winning contests.

These topics about winning are not meant to be all inclusive and are discussed only briefly. Hopefully, they stimulate discussions of the importance of winning in youth sports that avoid clichés and stereotypes. Clichés such as, "It's all for the kids," while well meaning and socially acceptable, fail to address many of the actual issues in youth sports and, thus, prevent us from designing effective programs. Effective youth sports programs place young athletes' needs first without ignoring the many motivations of parents, coaches, and officials who make these programs possible.

Appendix 1.2

Examples of Developmental Modifications for Youth Sport Programs for Children

Sport	Developmental Modification
Swimming	1. Start the race in the water without a racing dive. 2. Permit swimmer in backstroke events to turn onto their stomachs just prior to touching the wall of the pool at the end of the raceing 3. Have athletes wear a flotation waist belt.
Soccer	1. Smaller sized balls 2. Shorter Fields 3. Second attempt at throw ins if the athlete fouls on the first attempt 4. No offside in smaller fields
Baseball/T-Ball	1. Ball fielded on the third baseline need only be thrown to the pitcher to throw out the runner 2. Six hittable pitches thrown by adults; balls out of strike zone do not count – no walks 3. Fewer innings per game (e.g., 6) and game ends if a team is behind by 10 runs but has played minimum of 4 innings
Football	1. Five downs permitted to make the 10 yards required for a first down 2. No playing starters if ahead by 3 touchdowns 3. Linesmen start from crouch instead of a 3-point stance except the center who is not defended by an opposing player 4. No Tackling (flag football)
Gymnastics	1. Simple compulsory routines for less experienced gymnasts (levels 4, 5, 6). 2. No difficulty bonus for difficult skills; only form and execution count toward score. 3. Awards given for scoring 7's, 8's and 9's (mastery) in addition to finishing 1st, 2nd and 3rd (competitive rank)
Basketball	1. No all court press on defense if ahead by 20 points in second half 2. Lower Baskets 3. Smaller balls
Tennis	1. Larger and lighter "red" tennis balls that move slower and bounce lower 2. Smaller tennis courts (36 feet by 18 feet) with no doubles alleys compared to a full-size court with doubles alleys (78 feet by 36 feet). 3. Shorter tennis rackets (19 – 21 inches) compared to standard size (27 inches)
Wrestling	1. Weight classes determined by computer grouping after weigh-ins have been completed 2. Shorter time periods (say 1 minute vs. older 3-minute periods) with a 15 second break between periods 3. Weight allowance for growth every month (say 2 lbs) during season
Ice Hockey	1. Eliminate icing and offside rules 2. Eliminate goalie position 3. Cross-ice, ½ ice and small area games

Appendix 3.1
Strategies for Combating Choking

Choking Under Pressure

A basketball player throws up a "brick" at the last second of the game when the shot determines who wins or who loses. A tennis player with a commanding lead in the final set falters and allows an inferior player to "steal" the match. An experienced soccer player's penalty shot in a shootout sails many feet over the top of the cross bar. All reflect what is commonly referred to as a "choke" in sport.

Traumatic failure in a high pressure situation can have lasting negative effects on young athletes, just as successful clutch performances can have long lasting positive effects. Exposure to pressure is not the concern. Teaching youngsters to handle such pressure is one of the primary benefits of youth sports. Mental toughness is an important life skill in both sport and non-sport situations. Teaching it requires that we understand what choking is, what causes it and what interventions are effective in helping young athletes to cope.

Choking is not simply losing a winnable game. It is performing *significantly* worse than expected given one's skill level despite one's desire for superior performance in the presence of substantial incentives such as being watched by teammates, fans, coaches and/or opponents. Why such a detailed definition? Because it identifies the four elements defining choking and differentiates choking from other poor performances such as a slump or performing poorly under pressure when executing a partially learned skill. Those four elements are 1) performance is significantly worse than expected; 2) for the skill level already attained; 3) when there is a strong desire to perform well immediately; and 4) there are evaluative consequences.

Striking out in a clutch situation is not, by itself, choking. In baseball, a young player whose overall batting average is .300 and who successfully gets a hit in three of ten clutch situations, is playing at the level for which his skill level has prepared him. In fact, if he gets four or five hits out of ten, he is likely to be labeled a "clutch" hitter because he is performing far above his average.

A slump typically refers to prolonged subpar performance coupled with an inability to pinpoint precisely the cause of the poor performance. It is likely to cut across both clutch and non-clutch situations. Slumps are distinguished from choking because there is no discernable cause of the poor performance.

Choking may result from two totally different, but not mutually exclusive mechanisms. The first is **distraction** – your ability to pay attention to the task at hand is overwhelmed by additional tasks. Thinking of the consequences of your success or failure in addition to thinking of the performance of the task itself becomes a second distracting task that uses up your finite amount of cognitive resources, typically thought to be short-term memory. The second is called **self-focusing** and happens when you begin to explicitly monitor the many components of a well-learned skill. When a skill such as throwing a baseball or kicking a soccer ball is well learned, it is normally performed as a single unit; however, under pressure to perform well, the athlete begins to analyze the component parts of the skill that normally would be performed as a single "chunk." When overanalyzed, the skill now has many parts, each of which can contribute to errors, especially if the athlete attempts to consciously control each part. The distraction mechanism appears to disrupt partially learned skills of novices while the self-focus analysis appears to have greater disruptive effects on the well learned tasks of experienced athletes[1].

Characteristics of Athletes Who Choke

Choking is not totally determined by the external circumstances. Some personal traits appear to contribute to the likelihood of choking.

Paradoxically, a trait such as self-consciousness may increase or decrease the likelihood of choking. Individuals high in self-consciousness would be **less likely** to choke if their extensive experience of self-focusing in pressure-packed situations results in a greater familiarity and comfort with such self-focusing strategies and, thus, they are less likely to experience disruptions when executing well-learned skills under pressure. On the other hand, self-conscious individuals may be **more likely** to choke if they experience even higher levels of self-focus because they are already self-focused, and the extreme levels of self-focus detrimentally affect even well-learned skills. Empirical research has supported both hypotheses leading researchers to believe that self-consciousness most likely interacts with other factors such as task complexity and skill level. The leading expert[2] on this topic concludes that overall, "highly self-conscious people are more prone to choke under pressure" (p. 200).

Athletes high in **trait anxiety** and low in **self-confidence** typically experience high levels of state anxiety when performing in pressure situations. High levels of state anxiety appear to overwhelm short term working memory capacity. Furthermore, individuals high in trait anxiety are prone to using both self-focused monitoring and heightened controlling strategies but are less likely, because of their low self-confidence, to exert strong and sustained effort to overcome these ineffective strategies. Thus, those high in trait anxiety and low in self-confidence are thought to become more likely to choke because of both distraction and self-focus mechanisms.

Skill level produces opposite effects at low and high levels. Novices appear more likely to choke when distracted by additional tasks because they need more of their limited short-term memory capacity to process task relevant information. They have not yet automated the skills. Conversely, self-focus is consistent with the novice's conscious effort to learn and execute the task and, thus, typically results in little or no performance decrement. Skilled athletes, on the other hand, no longer need substantial short-term memory capacity so they appear relatively immune to additional distracting tasks but are prone to disruption if they revert to self-focusing strategies on well-learned skills. However, even veteran athletes require executive decision making when attempting complex skills. Thus, on complex tasks their short-term memory capacity can be insufficient when confronted with distractive tasks because the decision making required by complex tasks is less automatic and, therefore, less protected from the increased demands of the additional distracting tasks.

Effective Interventions to Alleviate Choking

Interventions are of two types: Those that can be learned in practice long before the critical pressure situation occurs and those that can be implemented precisely at the moment when the pressure performance is required. At this phase of our understanding of the phenomenon of choking, some interventions have had empirical support from research studies and some have developed as a result of applied coaching techniques where coaches and athletes have had success overcoming previous choking experiences. The recommendations that follow are a blend of these sources of information.

STRATEGIES FOR THE LEARNING/PRACTICE PHASE

Coaches can provide strategies during the initial learning and practice sessions which reduce the likelihood of athletes choking later during pressure situations.

Implicit Learning Skills learned implicitly appear to be resistant to choking[3]. Coaches refer to such learning as learning "by feel." Because the skill has been learned without explicit steps or specific rules, there is no ability of the athlete to self-focus when confronted with a pressure situation. Therefore, such a process cannot contribute to choking. However, implicit learning has not been enthusiastically adopted by coaches and athletes because implicit learning a) typically takes place more slowly than explicit learning[4] and b) fails to provide coaches and athletes with strategies to learn the skill in the first place. Once a safe level of competency has been reached, providing periods where you let kids simply play without any overt instruction would appear to facilitate implicit learning.

Practice in stressful situations with real negative consequences for failure. Simulations under pressure, even pressure that is mild compared to the actual event, helps inoculate athletes from choking in actual pressure situations. Perform before an audience. Have judges actually score a gymnast's routine in simulated competitions. Shoot a single foul shot after a wind sprint where a successful shot provides you with a rest while a missing shot requires that you – and perhaps your teammates – continue to run through stressful conditioning drills. Attempt "five in a row" where each successful attempt permits you to continue but a single miss ends your opportunity to continue. In soccer, have each athlete "bet" how many conditioning drills they are willing to do if they miss a penalty shot.* Look for and use naturally occurring pressure situations in practice. The more athletes have been successful in actual pressure situations, the more faith they will have in their ability to perform under pressure. It is one thing to believe that you can perform well under pressure because others, such as your coach, tell you "You can do it!" It is quite a different matter to have faith in your performance because, after numerous successful pressure experiences in practice, you can say "I've done it!"

Visual Imagery. Use visual imagery to place the athlete in pressure packed situations that they have yet to experience. To the extent that imagery can anticipate and realistically produce pressure-packed situations, it can be an antidote to choking in rarely experienced or never yet experienced competitive situations. (See Chapter 3 for specific guidelines for developing sport-specific mental imagery exercises.)

Practice with Actual Distracting Events Present. Coaches have long attempted to intervene to prevent choking by practicing under distracting conditions. Play pre-recorded loud crowd noises in spectator sports over a loud speaker when performing a well-learned skill. Shooting foul shots in practice while "opposing fans" heckle the shooter from the bleachers behind the basket in practice is still another. Make the distracting event as specific as possible to events that are likely to happen in actual competition. If the opposing coach in competition is likely to call a time out just before your place kicker attempts a field goal in football, practice calling delays just before the kick – or the foul shot in basketball in scrimmages and practices. You get better at what you practice. Therefore, the more specifically you can anticipate game situations, the more likely that your athletes will thrive rather than falter when they encounter such occurrences.

Practice Focusing on What to Do Rather Than on What Not to Do. "Straighten your knees" on the back handsprings rather than "Don't bend your knees." "Go for it" rather than "Don't miss." Such strategies develop the habit of focusing on what to do rather than on what not to do. Focusing on what to do is a major component of the skill of "staying in the moment."

Re-Interpret Prior Failures as Stepping Stones to Success. John Wooden[5], the legendary basketball coach at UCLA, referred to mistakes as the building blocks for success. Extend that approach to crucial mistakes in pressure situations. Instead of labeling one's self as a choker, try to determine what can be learned from a failure. One characteristic of mental toughness is to recover from a mistake. It appears harder to perform well after an early error than to continue to perform well when you are already in a flow state.

Use Analogy Learning. Analogy learning also helps to prevent choking under pressure. Analogy learning uses biomechanical metaphors to teach complex actions. For example, when teaching a novice to hit a backhand in racquetball, the athlete might be told to swing "as if brushing dust off a long, low bench." Analogy learning differs from implicit learning because in analogy learning the athlete intends to learn the skill while in implicit learning there is no such intent.

Pre-Performance Routines. Develop pre-performance rituals. Such rituals appear to protect the performer from both distractions and self-focusing. For example, a tennis player on her serve may step to the line, bounce the ball three times, toss and serve in the same rhythmic pattern as used for serving in practice, in normal competitive situ-

---

* Too high or too low a wager reveals a lack of confidence that they can, in fact, make the shot.

ations and for the critical serve in the championship match.

Finally, a variety of psychological training techniques have received empirical validation of their positive impact on sport performance (e.g., imagery, overlearning, conditioning, efficient techniques – to mention only a few). Whether these techniques are equally effective with individuals who are prone to choking is yet to be empirically determined. However, such peak performance training strategies discussed throughout Chapter 3 are a logical approach to preventing choking.

STRATEGIES FOR THE CRUCIAL MOMENT PHASE

To successfully combat choking, athletes must have strategies that they can implement precisely at the point of pressure where choking is likely to occur.

Don't slow down. Proceed quickly without rushing just as you would in a less pressured situation. Athletes who choke typically take extra time in preparing for the "big moment" presumably to overthink or overanalyze what should be an automatic, well-rehearsed skill. Step up and "just do it"

Focus on the outcome, not the "how to…". See the ball hitting the back of the net in soccer or hear the golf ball rattle at the bottom of the cup. Feel the back handspring landing securely on the balance beam. See the basketball ripping through the cords of the net. Avoid thinking differently about executing the skills than you normally would in a less pressured situation. Focus on what you want done rather than how to do it. Paradoxically, this approach is in direct contrast to strategies typically used during the learning phase of skill development where the focus is on "How to…".

Used generalized, global key words or sounds that emphasize the entire continuity of the skill. Say "smooth" during a golf stroke. Think "power" during a tumbling run. Say "strong" during a soccer penalty kick. Say "stretch" during the follow through of a basketball foul shot. Such words or thoughts help you to stay focused on the outcome expected of the skill rather than the step-by-step execution of the skill. Such globalized sounding words, termed **"process cues"** have been found to reduce choking. Focusing on cues that promoted a generalized "feel" for the skills appears to result in better performance under pressure than a focus on specific technical steps of executing the skill. The enhanced performance may result because the process cues prevent self-focus[6].

Stay in the moment. Past and future performances are irrelevant. They are internal, distracting events. Think of what you want done, not how you're going to do it – and then do it!

Avoid saying "Don't think about errors." Say "Putt firmly" rather than "don't leave the putt short." Thinking about missing directs one's thoughts to missing.

Use cues consistent with the outcome of highly learned skills. Paradoxically, focusing on outcomes often slows initial learning but facilitates well-learned skills. Outcome cues can actually help performers who have already achieved the level of executing skills automatically even though such distractions typically lower the performances of novices. Use cues which are consistent with the skill yet not overly involved with analysis of the skill components. Focusing on the catcher's mitt (the target) rather than the sequence of movements involved with throwing that ball can actually help a pitcher throw strikes in a pressure situation.

REFERENCES

[1]Hill, D. M, Hanton, S., Matthews, N., & Fleming, S. (2010). Choking in sport: a review, *International Review of Sport and Exercise Psychology, 3: 1,* 24–39. http://dx.doi.org/10.1080/17509840903301199

[2]Beilock, S. L. (2010), Choke: *What the secrets of the brain reveal about getting it right when you have to.* New York: Atria Paperback, Simon & Schuster

[3]Masters, R. S. W. (1992). Knowledge, knerves and know how: The role of explicit versus implicit knowledge in the breakdown of a complex motor skill under pressure. *British Journal of Psychology, 83,* 343—358.

[4]Maxwell, J. P., Masters, R. S. W., & Eves, F. F. (2000). From novice to no know-how: A longitudinal study of implicit motor learning. *Journal of Sports Sciences, 18,* 111—120.

[5]Wooden, J., & Carty, J. (2005). *Coach Wooden's Pyramid of Success: Building Blocks for a Better Life.* Ventura, California: Regal Books.

[6]Jackson, R. C., Ashford, J. J., & Norsworthy, G. (2006). Attentional focus, dispositional reinvestment and skilled performance under pressure. *Journal of Sport and Exercise Psychology, 28,* 49—68.

Appendix 6.1

State of New Jersey
Model Athletic Code of Conduct

The following model athletic code of conduct is promulgated in accordance with the provisions of P.L.2002, Chapter 74.

Preamble:

Interscholastic and youth sports programs play an important role in promoting the physical, social and emotional development of children. It is therefore essential for parents, coaches and officials to encourage youth athletes to embrace the values of good sportsmanship. Moreover, adults involved in youth sports events should be models of good sportsmanship and should lead by example by demonstrating fairness, respect and self-conduct.

I therefore pledge to be responsible for my words and actions while attending, coaching, officiating or participating in a your sports event and shall conform my behavior to the following codes of conduct.

1. I will not engage in unsportsmanlike conduct with any coach, parent, player, participant, official or any other attendee,
2. I will not encourage my child, or any other person, to engage in unsportsmanlike conduct with any coach, parent, player, participant, official or any other attendee.
3. I will not engage in any behavior which would endanger the health, safety or well-being of any coach, parent, player, participant, official or any other attendee.
4. I will not encourage my child, or any other person, to engage in any behavior which would endanger the health, safety or well-being of any coach, parent, participant, official or any other attendee.
5. I will not use drugs or alcohol while at a youth sports event and will not attend, coach, officiate, or participate in a youth sports event while under the influence of drugs or alcohol.
6. I will not permit my child, or encourage any other person, to use drugs or alcohol at a youth sports event and will not permit my child, or encourage any other person, to attend, coach officiate or participate in a youth sports event while under the influence of drugs or alcohol.
7. I will not engage in the use of profanity.
8. I will not encourage my child, or any other person, to engage in the use of profanity.
9. I will treat any coach, parent, player, participant official or anoy other attendee with respect regardless of race, creed, color, national origin, sex, sexual orientation or ability.
10. I will encourage my child to treat any coach, parent, player, participant, official or any other attendee with respect regardless of race, creed, color, national origin, sex, sexual orientation or ability.
11. I will not engage in verbal or physical threats or abuse aimed at any coach, parent, player, participant, official or any other attendee.
12. I will not encourage my child, or any other person, to engage in verbal or physical threats or abuse aimed at any coach, parent, player, participant, official or any other attendee.
13. I will not initiate a fight or scuffle with any coach, parent, player, participant, official or any other attendees.
14. I will not encourage my child, or any other person, to initiate a fight or scuffle with any coach, parent, player, participant, official or any other attendee.

I hereby agree that if I fail to conform my conduct to the foregoing while attending, coaching, officiating or participating in a youth sports event I will be subject to disciplinary action, including but not limited to the following in any order of combination:

1. Verbal warning issued by a league, organization or school official.
2. Written warning issued by a league, organization or school official.
3. Suspension or immediate ejection from a youth sports event issued by a league, organization or school official who is authorized to issue such suspension or ejection by a school board or youth sports organization.
4. Suspension from multiple youth sports events issued by a league, organization or school official who is authorized to issue such suspension by a school board of youth sports organization.
5. Season suspension or multiple season suspension issued buy a school board or youth sports organization.

_____   _____   _____
Name   *Signature*   *Date*

Appendix 6.2
Youth Sports Participants' Code of Conduct

Basic Civility

A. Display appropriate civil behavior at all times by refraining from:

    1. Unsportsmanlike behavior such as verbal abuse, rude gestures, ridicule, obscenities, throwing objects and/or taunting behaviors directed at officials, coaches, players or spectators at any and all sporting events.

    2. Any behaviors by you, your child, or others that might endanger the health and well-being of any official, coach, player or spectator.

    3. Using any controlled substances (alcohol, drugs, tobacco, etc.) before, during, and after contests on or near the site of the sporting event.

B. Avoid coaching your child and/or other players at games or practices unless you are acting in the role of an authorized coach or official.

C. Remain in the appropriate areas designated for spectators throughout the competition.

Good Sportsmanship

A. Rather than emphasizing the outcomes of the competitions, emphasize the developmental aspects of your child's youth sport experience by:

    1. Mastering of skills and game strategies.

    2. Process of enjoyment and having fun.

    3. Process of competing

    4. Striving to reach one's potential

B. Use age appropriate parental guidance to permit your child to choose:

    1. To participate or not to participate in organized youth sport programs.

    2. And, if the child decides to participate, to choose in which specific sport to participate.

C. Provide a positive role model – regardless of the circumstances of the competition.

D. Maintain personal self-control – regardless of the circumstances of the competition.

E. Treat teammates, opposing players, officials, coaches and other spectators with respect and enthusiasm.

F. Learn the rules of the game so that you may comprehend and realize why certain situations occur.

G. Acknowledge outstanding performances by athletes, coaches and officials regardless of team affiliation.

H. Display a genuine concern for the physical and psychological well-being of all participants regardless of team affiliations.

I. Use cheers and positive comments at appropriate times during the contest to recognize positive accomplishments and efforts rather than as attempts to distract opponents and/or to demoralize the opposition.

J. Enjoy winning with humility and accept losing with grace and do both with dignity.

Conduct with Distinction

A. Treat all athletes, coaches, officials and spectators as you would treat an invited guest in your home.

B. Recognize that mistakes made on the playing field by athletes, coaches and officials are learning experiences that are a natural part of sport, not failures to be ridiculed or booed.

C. Behave in a fashion that emphasizes your moral code as your guide rather than merely responding to the behavior of others, be it positive or negative.

D. Respect officials and their judgments regardless of the correctness of their decisions and regardless of the impact of those decisions on the outcome of the competitions, recognizing that without the efforts of those officials, the youth sport experience would not exist.

E. Respect coaches and their judgments regardless of the outcomes of the competitions, recognizing that without the efforts of those coaches, the youth sports experience would not exist.

F. Recognize the public nature of the risks taken by athletes who are displaying their best effort to succeed in sporting contests, the outcomes of which are, by definition, in doubt.

G. Recognize that without a commitment and adherence to the spirit of the game by individuals affiliated with both teams, a true sporting contest – in which contestants test their best efforts against the best efforts of their opponents – cannot exist.

Youth Sports Research Council of Rutgers University, 2018

Appendix 7.1

Sports Inclusion: Guidelines for Placement

Linda Sharkey, M.S.

Identify the prerequisite skills necessary to participate safely: _____

_____

Can the individual participate without any accommodation?

NO

YES → Register and have fun!

In which aspects of the sport can the individual participate?

_____

_____

_____

Can another person help? (i.e., peer, coach)

NO

YES

Who? _____
Type of Help? _____

Can the present instruction be supplemented?

NO

YES → How? _____

Can the individual participate if the equipment is modified?

NO

YES

In which related activities can the individual participate?

_____

_____

Explain: _____

_____

Note: Make sure modifications are based upon individual evaluation and implimented only when absolutely necessary to ensure safe participation.

Appendix 10.1
Guidelines for Supportive Parents
Are You a Supportive Parent?

1. **Supportive parents emphasize improving performance rather than competitive ranking.** Sport mastery focuses on performance that can be controlled by the athlete, while competitive ranking focuses primarily on winning and losing, an outcome frequently outside the athlete's control. An overemphasis on competitive rank and an under emphasis on sport mastery is a primary reason young athletes quit. By emphasizing mastery, parents can help youngsters be the best they can be. Encourage your youngsters to risk giving a 100% effort and not to fear losing.

2. **Supportive parents understand the risks and decrease the pressure to win.** Competitive sport creates its own pressure to succeed. Additional pressure from the parent is likely to be counterproductive, particularly in the long run. Competition places the athlete on center stage. Anytime you attempt to succeed publicly where others can judge you, you risk failing. In the long run, competing is a willingness to chance failure. Striving to win and giving your best are what athletics are all about.

3. **Supportive parents believe that sport's primary value is the opportunity for self-development.** The probability of achieving lasting fame and glory via sport is extremely low. Sport's value is the opportunity it gives participants for self-development. Many outstanding athletes never achieve professional status, but their sports experiences allow them to develop lifelong values and self-respect.

4. **Supportive parents communicate their true concerns directly with the coach.** A positive working relationship is based upon clearly communicated, mutual goals among parents, coaches, and athletes. While parents cannot control the behavior of a coach, you can and should communicate with the coach on a regular basis about your concern for your child's overall development.

5. **Supportive parents understand and respect the differences between parental roles and coaching roles.** Both parents and coaches need to understand their different roles in supporting the young athlete. While parents are ultimately responsible for their child's development, once they have selected a coach, they must leave the coaching to the coach. Even though supportive parents can and should play sports with their child, you should avoid coaching "over the shoulder" of the coach and/or publicly questioning coaching decisions.

6. **Supportive parents control negative emotions and think positively.** Few athletes wish to perform poorly. Negative parental reactions to poor performance only add to an athlete's pressures. Supportive parents realize that even the athlete who "chokes" is trying hard to succeed, sometimes trying too hard. Criticizing such efforts does little to enhance your child's performance.

7. **Supportive parents avoid the use of fear.** Punishment and withdrawal of love can pressure kids to perform better. Unfortunately, such strategies tend to trade short-term performance gains for long-term emotional risks to the youngster's health and well-being. Supportive parents recognize that a love for sport is rarely fostered by fear of the consequences of failure.

8. **Supportive parents avoid criticizing.** Nagging parents often confuse support with constantly reminding the children that they need to practice more, condition more, concentrate more, etc. Overly involved parents frequently lose their objectivity. They are unable to provide the critical emotional support children often need before, during and after highly competitive contests.

9. **Supportive parents understand expressions of insecurity and show empathy.** Youngsters who express high anxiety, more often than not, have parents who are insensitive to their symptoms. When children are nervous, uncertain, or feeling pressured, some parents may trivialize the child's fears or see such concerns as signs of weakness. Realize that such expressions are normal and are usually a call for emotional support. Empathy is not sympathy or agreement but rather is a true understanding that the task is difficult. An ineffective, sympathetic response to the athlete's expression of doubt might be "Perhaps you're right. It might be too difficult. Maybe you shouldn't compete today." Empathy, on the other hand, might be expressed as "Yes, it looks like a tough match today. That's exciting! C'mon, let's get ready."

10. **Supportive parents avoid the use of guilt.** "We've done so much for you," or "The family's sacrificed so much, the least you could do is to …" are typical remarks of unsupportive parents. Guilt is used to manipulate the child to perform the way the parents desire.

*2018 Version

Appendix 14.1

Recommended Contents for Basic First Aid Kits for Youth Sport Coaches

General Supplies:

1. Athletic tape (1½" wide, white adhesive tape) – 2 to 3 rolls
   Adhesive bandages – assorted sizes; Knuckle Bandages; Fingertip Bandages
2. ABD abdominal bandages (absorbent pads)
3. Antiseptic wipes
4. Elastic wrap (Stretchable bandage typically 3" and 4" wide with fasteners) – 1 of each
5. Bandage scissors
6. Disposable vinyl gloves – 3 pairs
7. Sterile gauze pads (small, medium and large sizes)
8. Single Use Instant Chemical Cold Pack (squeezable to activate)
9. Small plastics "sandwich" bags for ice and/or containment and disposal of biohazardous materials (e.g., bloody gauze pads)
10. Saline solution squeeze bottle with saline solution packets
11. Insect sting swab
12. Petroleum jelly – 1 jar
13. Hydrogen peroxide – 1 bottle
14. Triple antibacterial ointment such as Neosporin (bacitracin zinc, neomycin sulfate, polymyxin b sulfate ointment)
15. Antibacterial soap
16. Tweezers
17. Epinephrine auto-injector (e.g., EpiPen or Auvi-Q) for allergic reactions
18. Tongue Depressors (6")
19. Moleskin bandage for prevention of blisters
20. Cotton tip applicators (wooden or plastic)
21. First Aid Booklet describing basic first aid for common injuries
22. Sterile water

ADDITIONAL SUPPLIES

1. Blank injury report forms
2. Writing pen
3. Ice
4. Nail clippers
5. Sunscreen

Appendix 14.2
Sample Accident/Injury Report Form

Date of Injury: _____ Place of Event: _____

Injured Person's Name: _____ Date of Birth: _____ Sex: _____

Address: _____ Phone: (___) _____ - _____

City: _____ State: _____ Zip: _____

Association with Program: _____
(e.g., spectator, coach, athlete)

_____

Description of Injury/Illness: _____

_____

Description of Circumstances: _____

_____

Action Taken: (Check all that apply)

___ a. None required

___ b. Injured refused treatment

___ c. Parent(s) called at _____ AM/PM Caller: _____

___ d. First aid given by: _____

Describe: _____

_____

___ e. Rescue Squad/Ambulance called at: _____ AM/PM Caller: _____

___ f. Injured taken to: _____ By whom: _____
                        (hospital)

Witnesses: (1) _____ Phone: (___) _____ - _____

(2) _____ Phone: (___) _____ - _____

Date of Report: _____ Prepared by: _____
                                        Print name

Signature of Preparer: _____

Retain one copy of this report for your records and submit one copy to league official/insurance company.

Appendix 14.3

Sample Medical History/Treatment-Authorization Form

As a parent and/or a lawful guardian of _____ ,

(Full name of youth sport athlete)

a minor, I hereby authorize the treatment by a qualified and licensed medical doctor in the event of a medical emergency which, in the opinion of the attending physician, may endanger my child's life, cause disfigurement, physical impairment or undue discomfort if delayed. Medical providers are authorized to disclose on a "need to know" basis protected health information to the adult coach in charge, coaching staff and/or youth sport administrators of the program and/or any physician or health-care provider, such as but not limited to EMTs, who are involved in providing medical care to the individual minor named above for the purposes of medical evaluation of the participant, follow-up and communication with the participant's parents or guardians and/or the determination of the youth athlete's ability to continue in the program's activities. This authority is granted only after a reasonable effort has been made to reach me.

Name: _____

(Parent/Guardian with legal custody to be contacted in case of illness or injury)

Address: _____

City: _____ State: _____ Zip: _____

Primary Phone: (___) _____ - _____; email: _____

Secondary Phone: (___) _____ - _____

Family Physician: _____ Phone: (___) _____ - _____

Dates during which this release is granted: From _____ to _____

Indicate medications currently being taken, specific allergies, chronic illnesses, or other medical conditions that coaches and medical personnel should be aware of:

_____

_____

_____

_____

_____

(If additional space is needed, please indicate that information on a separate sheet of paper and attach.)

continued

Other person to contact in case of emergency: _____

Relationship to Child: _____

Primary Phone: (____) _____ - _____ ; email: _____

Secondary Phone: (____) _____ - _____

This release form is completed and signed by my own free will for the sole purpose of authorizing medical treatment under emergency circumstances in my absence.

Signature: _____ Date: _____

Signature: _____ Date: _____
(Second signature if required; for example, the state of California)

NOTARIZED BELOW

Notary Information will differ according to the state in which you reside.

_____

_____

DISCLAIMER FOR MEDICAL AUTHORIZATION SAMPLE FORM

This form is provided as a sample only. Usage of such a form should first be reviewed by the administrators of your youth sport program and their legal advisors.